The NINE DAYS QUEEN

Other Books by Mary Luke

Biography

Catherine, the Queen
A Crown for Elizabeth
Gloriana: The Years of Elizabeth I

Fiction

The Nonsuch Lure

Biographical Novel

The Ivy Crown

The NINE DAYS QUEEN

A PORTRAIT OF LADY JANE GREY

Mary Luke

William Morrow and Company Inc.
New York

Library of Congress Cataloging-in-Publication Data

Luke, Mary M.
The nine days queen.

Bibliography: p.
Includes index.
1. Grey, Jane, Lady, 1537–1554.   2. Great Britain—
History—Edward VI and Mary, 1547–1558.   3. Great
Britain—Kings and rulers—Biography.   4. Tudor, House
of. I. Title.
DA3451.1.C9L84   1986   942.05′3′0924 [B]   85-32040
ISBN 0-688-05771-3

Printed in the United States of America

First Edition

1 2 3 4 5 6 7 8 9 10

BOOK DESIGN BY PATRICE FODERO

For Melinda and Douglas
with love

Grateful acknowledgment is made for permission to use the following photographs:

The National Portrait Gallery Library, Holland's *Herwologia:* Lady Jane Grey

The Bodleian Library, Oxford, England: Bradgate Manor

Guildhall Library, City of London: Chelsea Manor House

Courtesy of the Bedford Estate and the Marquess of Tavistock: Mary Tudor and Charles Brandon

From Anthony van Den Wyngaerde's *Long View of London*, 1544, Ashmolean Museum, Oxford: Suffolk House in Southwark

From the Royal Collection at Windsor Castle. By Gracious Permission of Her Majesty, Elizabeth II: Edward VI; Princess Elizabeth; Thomas Howard

From the Royal Collection at Hampton Court Palace. By Gracious Permission of her Majesty, Elizabeth II: Henry VIII

Kunsthistorischen Museum, Vienna: Jane Seymour

The National Portrait Gallery, London: Queen Katherine Parr; Charles Brandon; John Dudley; Henry Fitzalan; Thomas Cranmer; Sir William Paulet; Thomas Wyatt

From the Knatchbull Family Portrait Collection. Photograph: The Courtauld Institute of Art: Sir Thomas Seymour

By Permission of the Grimsthorpe & Drummond Castle Trustees. Photograph: The Courtauld Institute of Art: Katherine Willoughby Brandon

By Gracious Permission of Her Majesty, Elizabeth II: Henry Brandon and Charles Brandon

The Wallace Collection: Edward Seymour

Isabella Stewart Gardner Museum, Boston: Queen Mary I

Courtesy of the Duke of Northumberland and *Country Life* magazine: Lady Katherine Grey and Her Son

Hardwick Hall Estate: Stephen Gardiner

The Duke of Manchester: Sir William Paget; Sir John Cheke

Greater London Council Publication: The Tower of London

Author's Note

The Life of Lady Jane Grey lasted a few months less than seventeen years. In contemplating an account of those years, I have chosen to mold into the story of this tragic young girl only the people and events that bore directly upon her unfortunate person. Her lineage, the most important factor in her destiny, was immutable. The people who surrounded her are another matter. From her parents, who abused her physically and emotionally, to the political opportunists of the Tudor court who manipulated and used her—all must bear responsibility for setting in sequence the myriad forces that caused her tragic end. They had choices—which Jane did not—and their differing motives are compelling in their raw self-interest. They are the stuff of which a playwright dreams, yet might hesitate to use lest he tax his audience's credulity.

With this in mind, the reader will understand the omission of some well-known events as well as personalities of the Tudor court in the years 1537–1554. Any lengthy account of the many individuals and the roles they played, if not directly affecting Jane Grey, would only burden the reader with extraneous matters and overwhelm what is in essence a simple story of greed, with an innocent, fragile child as its victim. The wars abroad, uprisings at home—such as the religiously motivated and brutal Pilgrimage of Grace—the constantly changing foreign, social and economic policies of the King and his Council, while of great importance to her parents, bore lightly on Jane's shoulders and destiny. This book is a portrait of a girl and an era. It is not a novel, not a fictional biography, not a comprehensive "life." I applaud the words of one noted author who has said, "There is no such thing as a definitive biography," adding that in such scholarly, academic works, "You get just a huge collection of facts, but somehow the personality of the subject seems to slip away."* I hope I've made certain that has not happened here.

Jane Grey was born of Tudor and Plantagenet descent, an illustrious and at the same time dangerous heritage. Fate deemed she be born female instead of the son her parents wanted—for dynastic, not sentimental, reasons. She was born with a sterling intelligence not unusual for women then, though education for females was rarely encouraged or even tolerated until Margaret Beaufort and, later, Katherine of Aragon's time. But Fate had placed her in a family that could—for all the wrong reasons—afford to nurture such intelligence and, unfortunately, use it for their own gain. Jane was endowed with a disposition of unusual sweetness, with a strong desire to please. In an era in which the sanctity of age and acquired wisdom was taken for granted, she was therefore compelled to honor her parents even when—in the face of constant abuse and harassment—she must have accepted that they were not worth it. One cannot help but wonder what Jane Grey might have become if she'd possessed the strong, mercurial and enduring character of that cousin who later became Queen Elizabeth. Or if she'd been born an aggressive and ambitious male.

But Lady Jane was a product of her era, with a prominence she could not help and a future she could not escape. She was surrounded always with "larger than life" personalities, from her great-uncle King Henry VIII to a queen who gave her the happiest years of her short life. And then there were the relatives and friends all destined to play roles—tragic, brave or merely ignoble—during the time she was with them. Diminutive and shy, wise beyond her

*Meryle Secrest, biographer of Bernard Berenson and Lord Kenneth Clark

years and yet emotionally deprived, Jane Grey struggled with what her God had given her, docilely accepting her infamous treatment and shocking fate as His will.

Little is known of Jane Grey's very early years; certainly she lived the life of a privileged young girl of royal blood. Her parents, on the other hand, were very visible at court or in their various homes, accompanying the king and his queens on their royal progresses and serving, in a variety of ways, both the monarch and themselves. These were the years when the major events of Henry VIII's reign—particularly his break with Rome—sent Tudor courtiers scrambling for the Church's loot as they struggled for whatever power they would need after the king was gone. And Jane's parents, Frances Brandon and Henry Grey, were much in the forefront, due in part to their relationship to the king as well as to their desire to lose no chance of personal gain. They all helped set the stage for the drama in the making, in which Lady Jane Grey would play the principal role. In the early part of this story, then, the reader will become acquainted with the major players who participated in the drama that resulted in the tragedy of the *Nine Days Queen*. Once these players are introduced, I have retained and referred to them by their names, not their eventual titles. When one such as Edward Seymour could become, at various times in his life, Lord Hertford, Viscount Beauchamp and, later, the Duke of Somerset, the Protector of England; and John Dudley might be known as Viscount Lisle, the Earl of Warwick and, later, the Duke of Northumberland; to use those proper titles for the brief span in the story their owners bore them invariably confuses the reader.

So, titles aside, the Tudors, Greys, Seymours, Brandons and Dudleys were playing for high stakes—nothing less than the Crown of England. If along the way the life of an innocent child was sullied, then sacrificed, it was all worth the gamble. When the opportunity was there, the reward was simply too high to ignore.

And it almost worked.

MARY LUKE

Ridgefield, Connecticut
1984–1985

Oh, Merciful God, consider my misery, best known unto thee; and be thou unto me a strong tower of defence, I humbly require thee. Suffer me not to be tempted above my power, but either be thou a deliverer unto me out of this great misery, or else give me grace patiently to bear thy heavy hand and sharp correction. . . .

—Written by Lady Jane Grey
in the Tower of London,
February 11, 1554

The
~~~ Players ~~~

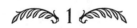 1

In May of 1533 a marriage ceremony held in the Church of St. Saviour, the parish church at Southwark, was notable for many reasons. A king was in attendance; his niece was the bride. The queen was not among the splendid guests clad in their finest damasks, silks and satins. She was pregnant and that day had gone into the Tower of London—as tradition demanded—to await the commencement of her coronation festivities. The mother of the bride, the king's sister, was noticeably ill, with little or no color in the complexion that had earned her the title of the "Tudor Rose." Her rasping cough, heard throughout the ceremony, made many thankful when—after the young couple had exchanged their vows— the choir burst into song.

The bride had complained that the weather, stormy and wet for days, would spoil her elegant gown and ruffle the intricate coiffure with its ribbons and jewels set into her thick chestnut hair. She was well aware she did not have her mother's beauty. The fair complexion, shining red-gold hair and deep-set blue eyes had gone instead to her younger sister, Eleanor. She herself had her father's sturdier frame and the darker coloring which, she'd long ago accepted, did not become her as it did the duke. But she'd learned—the queen now in the Tower had helped by teaching her many tricks—how to draw attention from one's less-than-fine features and emphasize more attractive aspects. Jewels and ribbons, scarves and heavy fringes, ornate embroideries and rich fabrics, she'd found, could hide or accentuate, and she'd become very clever in their use. If true beauty would never be hers, she'd long ago made up her mind that its lack would not prevent her from obtaining whatever she wanted in life.

And now, at this moment of triumph, she was elated at how well everything had worked out. As she walked from the altar with her new husband—not forgetting to curtsey to her parents and her uncle, the king, as she went—her eyes sparkled with an excitement that lent a high color to her normally sallow skin. Even the weather, springlike and dry at last, could not have been better.

As everyone left the church and walked the few steps down the roadway to the duke's great house, where the wedding festivities would soon commence—and go on for the rest of the day and evening if they knew anything of the duke's hospitality!—several commented on the unusual radiance of the bride. It augured well, they said, for she obviously loved her young husband and it was fortunate that of the two she was the stronger.

Not that there was anything seriously wrong with the groom. Young as he was, he'd distinguished himself in the French wars and held his own against the rising "new men" about the king. Upon inheriting his father's title and estates some two years ago, he'd supported the king's new marriage, being among the first to forswear papal supremacy in England—which had come about when the pope had excommunicated the king and present queen for marrying while his former queen was still alive. The groom was handsome, affably impulsive, with an acquisitive yet easygoing nature; his extravagances and the indulgence of his sexual appetites in the "stews" of Bankside, a few steps away from the church, were no stronger than or different from many others of the court. Surely—the more optimistic of the guests thought—his new wife, with her strong and determined nature, would provide a solid foundation for their life together. Already she'd overlooked the fact that her new husband had broken a previous marriage contract with a prospective bride of noble family and great wealth in order to wed *her* instead. The bride had scoffed and laughed along with the rest of her family at the noble's vow to revenge one day the affront to his sister's honor and his family's dignity.

There was little doubt, that fine May morning, in the minds of anyone attending the wedding of the Lady Frances Brandon, daughter of Charles Brandon and Mary Tudor, the Duke and Duchess of Suffolk, to Lord Henry Grey, the Marquis of Dorset, that the new marchioness would be anything but equal to whatever challenges her marriage might bring. Weren't her parents strong characters with formidable wills? Her mother, King Henry VIII's youngest sister, Mary Tudor, had been nineteen—three years older than the bride—when she'd been married against her will to King Louis XII of France. To the intense satisfaction of his wife and his heir, now King François I, Louis had lived only four months longer. King Henry had then consented to the entreaties of his dearest friend and confidant, the Duke of Suffolk, to bring Mary home. In Paris, Brandon found the young Queen of France hysterical. If she returned to England unwed, she told him, she'd never be allowed to marry as she wished, for her brother would only pawn her off on some other monarch. Mary had always fancied the handsome Brandon despite the fact that he'd had two wives and fathered an illegitimate son with another woman. That mattered not, Mary said; she cared more about her future than about his past. Despite his promise to the king that he'd exert no personal pressure on the young girl, Brandon was moved. Mary saw his misgivings and, tearful and pale, said they must be married at once—or never. Within hours a priest was summoned to the Hôtel de Cluny and they were wed. It had been a happy union, producing one boy who'd died very young and two daughters. Now, after nineteen years of marriage, only her ill health—and her disappointment in her brother's new marriage to Anne Boleyn—kept her from the court.

The bride, sixteen-year-old Frances, was the Brandons' elder daughter. She was not as well liked as her sister, Eleanor, for her arrogance and disregard for the feelings of others—family, servants or friends—was too well known. A pessimist by nature, a complainer by habit, the Lady Frances' innate selfishness had been the despair of her more compassionate mother and the cross her younger sister had had to bear. Her father had been heard to say that all that would change once she'd found a man to quell—or beat—her into repressing such unfortunate behavior. If Charles Brandon had any doubts that young Henry Grey was not the man, he'd never said so and had welcomed the Dorset heir as a husband for his daughter.

For the Dorset marquisate was not an empty title. The Greys were wealthy, holding the baronies of Ferrers, Grey, Astley, Boneville and Harrington and owning manors and estates in Leicestershire and other English counties. Indeed, Charles Brandon had insisted that Bradgate Manor, the Grey family seat in Leicestershire, be settled on his daughter as part of her dower. Thomas Grey, the groom's late father, had built Bradgate as a hunting lodge over sixty years ago. *That* Grey, Thomas, the first Marquis of Dorset, had been the last surviving son of Elizabeth Woodville, the queen of Edward IV, by her first marriage to Sir John Grey of Groby. Two half-brothers, those little Plantagenet princes, had disappeared from the Tower of London many years ago and never been heard of since. Elizabeth Woodville, while she lived, had seen to it that her husband, the king, favored her older children, and honors, titles and land had been given to her Grey offspring. Then, after Edward's death, she'd given her daughter, Elizabeth, as wife to Henry Tudor, as a means of uniting the Red Rose of Lancaster and the White Rose of York, even though Henry had taken the crown from her brother-in-law, the last Plantagenet king, Richard III, at Bosworth Field. There were many older nobles at the wedding—the "old aristocracy" as they thought of themselves—who were sad that old Tom Grey, whose mother had been a queen, whose half-sister became a queen and mother of the present king, could not have lived those two more years to see his son wed the daughter of a former queen of France and a niece of the king of England as well.

In the face of such an illustrious union, Henry Grey did not consider the appearance and temperament of his bride of any importance. What did concern him was that if the king never had a son, any issue of his own might be in line for the crown by virtue of his wife's birth. The king had no brothers and there was only one surviving child, the Princess Mary, a year older than her cousin Frances Brandon. But her mother, Katherine of Aragon, had been divorced by the king and lived in exile at Buckden Palace in Huntingdonshire and was separated from Mary, who'd been illegitimized. Certainly, Mary would not inherit and if the present queen never had a son, then *his* wife—and her children—had the best claim.

But on that May day, at Charles Brandon's palatial home in Southwark, with the king and his court in attendance and the happy bridal couple beaming at the splendid company, the future seemed far off. The Great Hall blazed with huge wheels set with hundreds of thick candles which had been lowered from the ceiling. They lit up the long tables where guests sat for dozens of courses of beef and veal cut from the half-sides that had been roasting from late the previous night in the duke's cavernous hearths. Great platters of capon, fish, geese, rabbits and numerous birds accompanied the flagons of Gascon and Rhenish wines from the duke's famed cellar. As the last rays of sunlight streamed through the stained-glass windows with their family crests brilliantly outlined, toasts were made to the family, seated in a row on the dais with the king in the middle. Loud applause greeted each speech as guests pounded on tables and called out their own good wishes. Servants, handsomely dressed in their Suffolk liveries, refilled the rare Venetian goblets and brought in yet more platters of confections of marchpane and spun sugar. Musicians tuned up in the minstrels' gallery at one end of the great room, and with a thumping beat the dancing commenced. Henry beamed, then danced with the bride, her sister and mother—danced as expertly as he rode, hunted, played tennis, shivered a lance in the tiltyard or shot at the butts in "the smooth fields" north of St. Paul's, mostly in the company of Charles Brandon. He greeted the bishops courteously, spoke affably to his former Lord Chancellor, Sir Thomas More, and cheered the loudest as the fireworks, now that darkness had fallen, began. Wildly whirling Catherine wheels and sleek arcs of fire and flame were sent up over the Bishop of Winchester's house next to the Church of St. Saviour, to end in a hissing, smoky death in the Thames.

Everyone attending the wedding of Frances Brandon and Henry Grey could only have thought them extremely fortunate. They were young enough to enjoy good health and in a position to expect many future honors as well as great wealth, not only from their families but from the king. Already it was known that another guest, Thomas Cromwell, the king's Vicar-General, had urged Henry to do something about the deplorable state of the holy houses—the

English monasteries and abbeys—by insisting that the religious orders they housed could not serve two masters, a pope and a king. They must be made to swear an oath of fealty to the true head of the Church, Cronwell said, and since the pope no longer filled that holy office, they must swear fealty to the king, who did. Henry would become the Supreme Head of the Church in England, and the riches and treasures of that Church would become the monarchy's property. And it was not beyond anyone's belief that a good many of those riches might eventually find their way into the royal coffers and the pockets of members of the royal family as well as those of the more prominent loyal courtiers. Certainly the young Greys would be among the first to share in those riches, for the bride was the royal niece and her children would stand in direct line for the throne.

Unless the queen now in the Tower brought forth a son.

In 1533, the year the young Greys were wed, the Tudor dynasty was forty-eight years old. Only two Tudor kings had sat on the throne of England. The first, Henry VII, was the son of Edmund Tudor, the Welsh Earl of Richmond, and the tiny, almost dwarfish fourteen-year-old Margaret Plantagenet, the Countess of Beaufort. Margaret, a great-granddaughter of John of Gaunt by his union with Catherine Swynford, more than compensated for her lack of stature with a formidable will, and pride not only in her own lineage but in her husband's as well.

For it was her husband's grandfather, that tall, lusty Owen ap Meredith ap Twydder, or Tudor, a minor Welsh functionary at the Lancastrian court of Henry V, the victor of Agincourt, who'd so distinguished himself on the field of battle that the king had made him Captain of the King's Guard. Owen was very tall and muscular, with leonine blond locks and a high color, and moved with such "perfect grace" that he was a great favorite with the court ladies. So much so that when Henry V died, his widow, Queen Catherine of Valois, had hurriedly married young Owen, now her Clerk of the Wardrobe, with whom she'd been in love for almost three years. While Catherine and her new husband lived discreetly apart from the court, her nine-month-old son, Henry VI, lived in the care of his uncles until he should attain his majority. When the marriage was ultimately made public, Owen Tudor was imprisoned and the queen banished to Bermondsey Abbey, where she died six months later, leaving her children by Owen Tudor in the abbess's care. When the distraught woman—who needed funds for their sustenance—revealed their existence, there was an even greater furor among the queen's legitimate heirs. Eventually Owen Tudor was released from prison, and for his thirty remaining years he fought for his stepson, Henry VI, in the Lancastrian cause. He was accepted at court, and in 1460 the king made "his well-beloved squire, Owen Tudyer [sic]" keeper of the royal parks in Denbigh, Wales.

Then, at the battle of Mortimer's Cross in February 1461 the old warrior—gray now but with a still magnificent physique and presence—was captured by the Yorkists and, by order of King Edward IV, beheaded in Hereford marketplace. Years later, Englishmen would comment that only the more superstitious of Owen Tudor's Welsh countrymen could ever have envisioned a time when Owen's grandson Henry would wed Edward's eldest daughter and thereby found a new English dynasty. But it had happened.

Henry Tudor, "a man of enormous patience and cunning," was born to Margaret Beaufort on January 28, 1457; his father, Edmund Tudor, Owen's son by the widowed queen, had died three months previously. Margaret was not quite fourteen years old when she entered Pembroke Castle in Wales, the home of Owen's son Jasper Tudor, for her confinement.

Wealthy and widowed, with her own future to determine, the young mother left her son in Wales to marry Henry Stafford, the Duke of Buckingham. While she missed the boy, she knew he'd be safer with his uncle Jasper Tudor as England's nobility—Lancastrian and Yorkist—attempted to decimate each other in the thirty-year Wars of the Roses. For the next fourteen years, seeing her son when she could, Margaret Beaufort, now the Duchess of Buckingham, lived in the midst of the Yorkist court, even though her brother-in-law Jasper had a price on his head for his subversive activities. After the battle of Tewkesbury in May 1471, when the Lancastrian cause and most of the families supporting it—including Margaret Beaufort's—were slaughtered, Jasper Tudor smuggled his young nephew, now the last hope of the Red Rose of Lancaster, abroad to Brittany for safekeeping.

Twelve years passed, during which Margaret, nearing forty and widowed once more, wed Thomas, Lord Stanley. But she never forgot her only son, Henry, who'd lived a poor, humble and joyless existence in a foreign land, waiting only for a chance to claim what he considered his rightful heritage—the Crown of England. Meanwhile, incredibly, his mother had made a place for herself and Lord Stanley at the Yorkist Court and when Edward IV died, it was Lady Stanley who carried the train for the new queen of Richard III at the coronation. Though it was *her* son who claimed the throne, Richard was lenient, merely ordering her husband to prevent any contact with those who might help her communicate with young Henry Tudor.

But Margaret Beaufort, embittered and anxious, never forgot that her son's grandmother had been England's queen and that many considered him the true king. By any means she could find, letters containing money and information about the Yorkist court crossed the Channel to her son and his advisers. If King Richard knew the dangerous game the mother of the Lancastrian claimant was playing, he chose to ignore it, depending upon his faithful Lord Stanley to restrain his wife's activities. However, by August 1485, after one previous abortive effort at Milford Haven, Henry Tudor—now twenty-eight and tired of waiting—landed in South Wales and, with a group of dedicated followers and an army that grew as it progressed, made his way to Bosworth Field to meet the Plantagenet Richard III.

Richard had the larger army, great confidence and a loyal following, with one important exception: Thomas, Lord Stanley. After years of concealing her real feelings, of watching her faithful servants being removed, of having her vast estates and their revenues turned over to her husband so she could not help her son, Margaret Beaufort was ready for revenge. She'd persuaded Lord Stanley to watch the battle closely and see where the best opportunity lay; she knew it was her son's only chance.

At Bosworth, Richard was clearly triumphant. Then—suddenly and treacherously—Lord Stanley gambled, switching his loyalty and his considerable number of followers to young Henry Tudor's cause. In the melee that followed, King Richard was killed and it was Stanley who placed the crown—plucked from a hawthorn bush—on his stepson's head and proclaimed him King of England.

With the shrewdness born of his hazardous upbringing, Henry quickly moved to unite the rival houses of Lancaster and York. A year after Bosworth he married the fallen Richard's niece Elizabeth, daughter of King Edward IV and Elizabeth Woodville, and surprisingly, the cold austere young man found happiness with the radiantly beautiful "White Rose of York." They had a mutual love of music, and what Henry had lacked in his youth—the pageants, fine clothes, the mumming, dancing, hunting and hawking—Elizabeth had enjoyed all her life and she took great pains to introduce her royal husband to their pleasures. They had four children: Prince Arthur, who married the Spanish Princess Katherine of Aragon and died six months later; the second son, Henry, destined for the church, had then become the heir and later married his brother's widow. Princess Margaret, the eldest daughter, was sent to Scotland as a bride for James IV when she was fourteen years old, while Princess Mary, briefly Queen of France, later married Charles Brandon, the Duke of Suffolk. After the death of Arthur, her firstborn, Queen Elizabeth sought to give her husband one more boy. At age thirty-seven, too old for childbearing, it cost her her life.

The grieving husband, whose childhood frugality, conservative common sense and hatred of war had remained even when he became king, never married again. Instead, he concentrated on enriching himself and his kingdom. With the aid of two ambitious lawyers, the notorious Richard Empson and Edmund Dudley, he'd confiscated the property of political offenders and allowed ecclesiastical offices to remain vacant while pocketing their revenues. He cut down on the waste and profligacy of his predecessors, regained many Crown lands, reorganized the governmental offices to reduce pilferage and encouraged trade to increase his tariffs. He levied fines and penalties—which were often nothing but outright extortion—against those who could afford to pay, especially those of the "old nobility" who'd looked askance at the Tudor upstart whose treacherous stepfather had won his battle for him.

But before he died in 1509 at the age of fifty-two Henry VII could look with satisfaction at a realm at peace and richer than ever before, with a treasury of over £1.5 million. And, justifying the pride of his sixty-eight-year-old mother, Margaret Beaufort, who'd lived to see it all, he could point to the illustrious alliances he'd made for her grandchildren with Spain, France and Scotland.

It was a heritage of which the Tudors, the Greys and the Brandons were particularly proud, even as they were conscious that an heir was needed if the new dynasty—and their own good fortunes—were to continue. There were still noble families with Plantagenet blood alive and about the court, and it was only natural they might dream of a chance such as had been given to old Henry VII.

Treachery had paid off once; it might do so again.

2

The manor of Bradgate, the home of the Marquis and Marchioness of Dorset, lay in the Leicestershire hills some five miles from the market town of Leicester. It was surrounded by dense natural forests so thick it was said a man could walk twelve miles and never see the sun. The luxuriant vegetation, clean crystalline streams and the River Soar provided shelter, food and drink for the deer, hare, badgers, squirrels and birds, which were a considerable cause of the family's enthusiasm for Bradgate. The primitive beauty of the slate hills, the great elms and beeches standing mile upon mile through the earth's bracken, fern and heather, often went unnoticed by the Greys, particularly Frances, who was fanatically devoted to the hunt. At Bradgate she could slaughter and maim to her heart's content.

In October 1537 the marchioness had another, more important responsibility, however, and the pleasures of the hunt were temporarily forsaken. In a painful process she'd endured twice previously and as yet with nothing to show for her very real effort, she was in labor with her third child. The first, a boy, had lived only a few days, and a daughter, born less than a year later, had also died. But Frances Grey was grimly determined to give her husband the son he wanted and needed more than anything else in the world. She remembered how much the queen—that queen who'd been so large only five months after her secret wedding that Londoners had laughed aloud and hooted as she'd passed down the Strand toward Whitehall during her coronation festivities—had needed a boy. That queen had complained to the king that no one had doffed his cap or shown her any real respect or affection. And after the birth of a girl, whom her parents named Elizabeth for the king's late mother, the king hadn't shown his queen much respect or affection either and she'd looked for it elsewhere. It had all ended on a May morning just a little over a year ago, when Anne Boleyn laid her head on the block, accused of adultery with a court musician and two of Henry's closest companions, and of incest with her brother, George Boleyn, who'd also been executed.

Henry Grey had waited outside the birth chamber during his wife's labor. He was anxious to be off to the court, where all the nobles would now be in attendance, since the new queen, Jane Seymour—whom Henry had married as soon as Anne was dead—was also about to give birth. As a member of the royal family, he knew he should be at Hampton Court right now. Of course everyone was aware his wife was with child, but still, it appeared unseemly to be absent. When he heard Frances sobbing heartbreakingly, he hardly needed the tired doctor's report that he had a daughter, a healthy and pretty little girl.

Quickly, Henry Grey joined his wife, hoping to console her and hide his own disappointment. The nurse, Mrs. Ellen, had whisked the baby away to clean and put in swaddling clothes. There would be time enough later to see the child; now he must leave. He was grateful that his wife would understand how important it was to be at court when the royal child was born.

Before he left, he and Frances agreed they'd name their daughter for the queen. Neither of them particularly liked Jane Seymour and they disliked her brothers, Edward and Thomas Seymour, even more, considering them parvenus of the worst order, children of minor Somerset gentry whose sister, a former lady-in-waiting to both Queen Katherine of Aragon and Queen Anne Boleyn, had had the good luck to catch the king's eye. At Queen Anne's execution, they'd both believed that while he'd allow Jane to soothe his hurt pride and disappointment, he'd never marry her.

But Jane had proved virtuously elusive, encouraged by her brothers to accept nothing but the marriage which could only prove fortunate for them, since the king was a generous man with honors and titles for his friends and family. Already, Edward—who'd married the proud and ambitious Anne Stanhope—had been made a viscount. Thomas, they knew, was similarly ambitious and openly envious of his brother's good fortune. Edward was serious, competent and trustworthy and had become one of King Henry's most valued councillors. Thomas, however, was neither serious, competent nor to be trusted, looking usually for the best opportunity of the moment. One courtier had described the younger Seymour as "fierce in courage, courtly in fashion, in personage stately, in voice magnificent, but *somewhat empty in matter*"—the last said while tapping his head. While Edward could be inconspicuous in a crowd, Thomas was fine-looking, rakish and brimming with an infectious camaraderie, a favorite with those of similar temperament, who regarded his more austere brother as aloof.

Both Henry and Frances Grey had decided, however, that neither their dislike nor their distrust of the Seymour brothers must color their relationship with them. The Seymours were the king's brothers-in-law and Henry liked them both. He listened to Edward's opinions as eagerly as he roared with laughter at Thomas's latest quips, brought back from his embassies in Brussels or Madrid, or the stories of his sexual exploits in the brothels of Paris. The king had often sent the courtier on official business when he thought Thomas's wit and charm might prove more effective than would his more sober ambassadors.

It was as he arrived in the City, in sight of the Tower, where his barge should be waiting to take him to Hampton Court, that Henry Grey heard the momentous news. A messenger riding up Tower Hill, ready to ride out Aldersgate with the joyous tidings, read him the proclamation and prayer of thanksgiving for "the safe delivery of Our Most High and Mighty Queen Jane who has, the Twelfth Day of October, Twenty-Eighth of Henry VIII, by the Grace of God, presented Us with a beloved son, the Most High and Mighty Prince Edward."

The little prince had been born the same day as Frances Grey's baby daughter. Now there was, at last, a legitimate heir to the English throne. The king's two daughters by two dead queens—

twenty-one-year-old Lady Mary, Katherine of Aragon's daughter, and Lady Elizabeth by Anne Boleyn—had both been bastardized. There was to be no question in anyone's mind of the legitimacy of any son by Jane Seymour. And now he had that heir to carry on the Tudor line.

There was enough English pride in Henry Grey so that he felt some joy in the king's good fortune, even in the face of his own disappointment. But it took almost more self-control than he—not one of even temper or disposition—could muster when he heard that the little prince had been named Edward.

It could be for the child's great-grandfather, that Plantagenet Edward who'd killed the first Tudor, of course. Yet Henry Grey had named his own child for the queen and he thought Jane Seymour had shown a rare lack of tact and propriety in not naming her son for the king. But then, Jane was not as bright, strong and clever as his own wife, Frances. Perhaps the king and queen *had* agreed to name their new son for a royal ancestor. But instinctively, Henry felt it much more likely she'd named him for her own brother, Edward Seymour, now the Viscount Beauchamp.

In 1537, the year Prince Edward and Lady Jane Grey were born, England had about completed the long and tortuous journey—unwittingly commenced by Thomas Wolsey, lamented by Sir Thomas More and zealously completed by Thomas Cromwell—of effecting the schism between the nation and Rome. Henry VIII's love affair with Anne Boleyn and his subsequent abandonment of Katherine of Aragon, who refused to divorce him, had pitted Catholics against one another. For when Pope Clement VII refused Henry's request for a divorce, the king had taken matters into his own hands and wed the pregnant Anne, later ordering his own clergy to declare his first marriage annulled. Following the pope's eventual excommunication of Henry and Anne, England was plunged into civil and religious chaos, for an Englishman was then loyal either to the king or to the pope. In the twenty-eighth year of Henry's reign, he could not be both. The words of the young king, uttered some twenty-one years earlier, were often recalled by veteran courtiers—"I will not allow anyone to have it in their power to govern me, nor will I ever suffer it."

It was not easy even then, as wives, ambassadors and councillors were to find out, to deny the handsomely affable, six-foot-two-inch Henry Tudor—certainly a throwback in size and temperament to his great-grandfather Owen Tudor—anything he desired. Anyone who had lived through the final years of schism—the submission of the English clergy and Henry's assumption as Supreme Head of the Church, the dissolution of the monasteries and abbeys and their eventual destruction or appropriation by the Crown—found it impossible to remain uninvolved, especially if they were of the court. For those of strong belief, like Sir Thomas More and the saintly John Fisher, Bishop of Rochester, who could not accept Henry's supremacy, such disbelief was paid for with their lives. Others, not so prominent or saintly, were burned at the stake, hanged, drawn and quartered or—like More and Fisher—beheaded.

Once he'd taken the step toward schism, Henry Tudor never looked back. It was not, he made plain, that he disagreed with Catholic orthodoxy or ritual. Sixteen years ago, hadn't he written a reply, *Assertio Septem Sacramentorum*, to Martin Luther's attack on the Church and hadn't Leo X, then pope, sent him a golden rose and given him the title *Fidei Defensor*, "Defender of the Faith"? No, said the king; what he disagreed with was the *influence* of the Church in his realm. It was unthinkable that a pope had ignored his need for a new marriage with a woman who might give him a son. It was equally foolish for the pontiff to excommunicate them both after their marriage and expect the English ecclesiastical hierarchy to be loyal to Rome. Step by step, the process of shedding the papal mantle was undertaken. Papal revenues from England and all appeals from English church courts to the Roman curia were cut off; the English elected their own bishops and archbishops and none swore any oath to the Roman pontiff. Catholic creed and ritual remained, and the English Church hierarchy remained, but without its former head. Henry had replaced the pope.

By the time his son and great-niece were born, the king and his Vicar-General, Thomas Cromwell, had ended, on the surface at least, all papal loyalty. The king had his way, saying, "The Kings of England in times past have never had any superior but God only. Wherefore know you well that we will maintain the right of our crown and of our temporal jurisdiction . . . in as ample a wise as any of our progenitors." His archbishops submitted and his nobles bent the knee. But in the smaller country parish churches, especially in the North, which still remained more feudal than the southern counties, the simple, rural people—puzzled and resentful of what many regarded as illegal and irreverent—retained their loyalty to the pope. Wasn't the Lady Mary, the old Spanish queen's daughter, also loyal? they asked each other. Hadn't her father had to exile her, threaten her with abandonment or worse, made her swear her mother's marriage was illegal and that she was a bastard—a process that had taken many months and emotionally exhausted the frail woman—before she submitted to him?

And now the holy houses were all gone. In areas where the local abbey or monastery had played a large part in the life of the community, their loss was mourned. The houses had given spiritual and physical comfort, sustenance, education and help in time of need, whether it was illness or crop failure. Some had hospitals and schools for which there was no other replacement. Now they were destroyed or sold, and thousands of nuns and monks made homeless by the dissolution were vagrants on the roads of England. The pastoral and productive land and the buildings—some of the most noble in the country—had been either destroyed for the value of their materials, given to loyal nobles or sold to those eager buyers who could afford to pay for property of incredible beauty which they'd never dreamt of owning otherwise. And in allowing these church properties to fall into the hands of wealth the king had given the new owners a vested interest in the continuance of the breach with Rome. Who would want to return them?

English Catholics of both kinds—king's or pope's—were facing yet another challenge in the "new religion," which had come years earlier from the Continent and found eager converts in those willing to die for what they considered the true faith of the early Christian fathers. The "protestors" or "new thinkers" had little use for Catholic practices or ritual and regarded the pope and the Vatican hierarchy as one vast cesspool of corruption, privilege and abuse—a feeling as prevalent on the Continent as it was in England.

For it was on the Continent that an Augustininan friar, a professor of philosophy at Wittenberg, had nailed his Ninety-five Theses to the church door. He listed ecclesiastical abuses, the fostering of superstitions, worship of saints and religious pilgrimages among the many ways the Church was deceiving its people. Martin Luther's charges appealed to those in England who'd found many of the lower clergy barely literate and poorly trained, men who'd entered the Church primarily as a means of livelihood, not to serve the religious needs of their parishioners. Absentee bishops and archbishops and those who held duplicate religious offices while actually working in secular administrative posts or in foreign embassies had long angered the genuinely religious and caring.

In 1537, the year Edward Tudor and Jane Grey were born, the religious forces that were to shape their lives had already gathered in combat and, as each day, week and year passed, were to gain in strength and power. In the past these forces had been lacking; strength and power were measured in land, money, jewels, fortified castles and the number of one's followers. Now, for the first time in England's history, the "cause of religion" was to take the place of rival political parties. The truly spiritual-minded, ready to die for their faith, would be matched with the zealous opportunists ready to claim whatever faith or ritual was demanded—if it meant their own cause was better served.

In between, there were bound to be those who would suffer.

Within two weeks of Jane's birth, as she lay in a new oak cradle in the nursery at Bradgate, Queen Jane Seymour died at Hampton Court. The feasts of celebration, the joyous ringing of church bells that had announced the birth of a royal heir, the continuous High Masses of thanksgiving, the glittering receptions for foreign ambassadors and nobles, the street celebrations where the people danced around bonfires and ran to the conduits which spilled wine and ale into their hogsheads, the laughing, shouting, crying and cheering, all came to an end. A stunned nation and its grief-stricken king—who only days before had held his newborn son in his arms, tears pouring down his cheeks—now prepared to bury the slight woman for whom the long ordeal of a grueling childbirth had proven too much.

But Queen Jane, whose motto was "Bound to Obey and Serve," had lived long enough to see the full court—the great lords and ladies, the Privy Councillors, the foreign ambassadors and nobles—crowd into the Hampton Court chapel for her son's christening. The godparents—Charles Brandon, the Duke of Suffolk;

Thomas Howard, the Duke of Norfolk; and Thomas Cranmer, the Archbishop of Canterbury; along with the godmother, the little prince's half-sister the Lady Mary—stood by the font. His other half-sister, the four-year-old Lady Elizabeth, was carried in procession by Edward Seymour; in her hands she proudly held the heavily jeweled chrysom. As the trumpets sounded, Jane Grey's grandmother, Margaret, the Dowager Marchioness of Dorset, and stepgrandmother Katherine Brandon, the young Duchess of Suffolk walked in procession toward the silver-gilt font. There, as the trumpets blared forth again, the little prince was anointed with warmed perfumed water, after which, Garter-King-of-Arms proclaimed, "God of His Almighty and Infinite Grace give and grant good life and long to the right high, right excellent and noble prince, Prince Edward, Duke of Cornwall and Earl of Chester, most dear and most entirely beloved son to our most dread and gracious Lord, King Henry VIII. . . ." Soon, fireworks in the great Base Court turned night into day as the child, carried at the head of the procession by the Duchess of Suffolk, was returned to his own chambers. All over the palace, in London and throughout the nation, the celebrations continued for "the birth of our Prince, whom we hungered for so long."

And then, on the Eve of St. Crispin, October 23, Queen Jane Seymour died. For three weeks she lay in state at Hampton Court so that people might come from long distances to mourn the woman who'd given them a prince—and given her life in the doing. Henry Grey, the Marquis of Dorset, followed by the Lady Mary as Chief Mourner, led the procession from Hampton Court to Windsor Castle. There, after a Requiem Mass was sung, the queen's body was lowered into the crypt in St. George's Chapel. When the long service was complete, the court was free to leave for their own homes and Henry Grey prepared for his return to Bradgate.

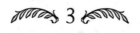

3

The first years of Lady Jane Grey's life were spent in a predictable routine dictated by the fine and varied hunting at Bradgate which so many visitors—unused to the flat low terrain, which might treacherously lead into forest, hillock or age-old dry riverbed—found challenging. Then the family would be off to London for the festivals and holy days at court, as well as the political and social events at which the presence of the Marquis and Marchioness of Dorset was assumed. In either place, Jane Grey was left in the care of a footman, a waiting woman, a maid and her nurse, Mrs. Ellen. After the birth of her sister Katherine in 1540, when Jane was three, the nursery servants were doubled and Mrs. Tylney came to care for the Greys' second daughter.

The nurseries at Bradgate and Dorset Place, the Greys' Westminster home, were similar. Wooden dolls, their painted faces still bright—for Jane was careful of them—lay on chairs and bed. Hobbyhorses, made by the carpenter at Bradgate, were in both nurseries, as were hoops, balls, bells and small toy animals, some with embroidered faces and stuffed limbs. Most were gifts—from the Lady Elizabeth, who was clever with the needle and had little money for expensive gifts, or from the king and his queen, Catherine Howard, or Anne of Cleves, who had been married to him such a short time. Others had been sent by his older daughter, the Lady Mary, who was godmother to countless children and chose her gifts well, saying she wasn't deft with the needle like Elizabeth because of poor eyesight. Jane had heard someone say that while Prince Edward lived in great comfort with a large household, the two former princesses lived very frugally with few attendants, for their father seemed to have little interest in them.

Some of Jane's favorite gifts were small books that Katherine Brandon, the young Duchess of Suffolk, had given her. At fifteen, Katherine Willoughby had married Charles Brandon very soon after his wife, the king's sister, had died in 1533. Jane liked the duchess and looked forward to her visits, for she always spoke kindly and very wittily to everyone. Katherine had given the duke two sons, ten-year-old Henry and eight-year-old Charles. Often, when the duchess visited the Greys—even though she was two years younger, she was the Lady Frances' stepmother—she'd send the boys to the nursery to share Jane's meal and they'd watch solemnly as the little girl lined up her small carved animals, pointing out in her books the pretty pictures of the same beasts.

Arriving in London was always exciting for little Jane. After the journey from Leicestershire and the clean, crisp, biting air—so cold it hurt one's lungs, especially in the early morning—the sight and smell of the City of London was almost overwhelming. First, there was the sound of the City's church bells. Entering Aldersgate, where a Dorset Place steward always awaited them, they were immediately surrounded by the inns and merchants' shops clustered near the Tower. Jostled among the crowds waiting to cross London Bridge to the Southwark side, where Jane's grandfather Charles Brandon lived, they followed the steward as he went on ahead to escort them to their imposing new mansion of red brick dressed with Portland stone a short distance north of Whitehall Palace. "Make way for the Marquis of Dorset! Make way!" the steward would cry and people stepped aside to let the long procession of wagons, carts and handsome litters with the Dorset colors of green, gold and black, lumber by.

After passing Whitehall Palace and the Holbein gate, the steward led the travelers to a small narrow roadway that wound down to the Thames. There, with the Dorset banner already flying from its turrets—informing all London and the court that the Greys were in residence—the grooms and stablehands would come for the horses while the wagons and carts were left to be unloaded by some of the Greys' eighty servants. Dorset Place rose among its humbler neighbors with the grace of the new amid the medieval old. There were some, aristocratic and elderly, whose parents had told them of the Plantagenets and the parsimony of their successor, old Henry VII, and they pointed to Dorset Place as a symbol of the raw newness of Tudor power. Some spat when they said it.

London was a different world from Bradgate. One of Jane Grey's favorite occasions was when she was allowed to join the grown-ups on the terrace parapet, which jutted out over the Thames. It happened rarely, but when it did she sat quietly with Mrs. Ellen, watching the river traffic while her parents and their friends talked and laughed and sipped the wine and ate the small cakes the servants brought. Invariably her mother cautioned her not to sit in the sun because she freckled so easily and ladies were not supposed to have freckles. So Jane stayed out of the sunlight and gazed through the large round circles cut in the terrace's stone wall, to the Thames. Below, at the river's edge, children played in the mud; some of them were very dirty indeed. They waved and shouted to all the rivercraft—the barges, wherries and small boats—and the clear air carried their cries to the little girl on the terrace who wondered at their easy freedom. Downriver, she could see past the great stone palaces that lined the Thames just as it curved on toward the Tower and Greenwich. Once they had all belonged to the Church. Now they were owned by many of the king's and her father's friends. Nearby, the gloomy walls of Baynards Castle rose right out of the river, and behind them, through the green lawns and fields beyond the City walls, were the church spires of Holborn and Clerkenwell.

But it was the river, with "its vast concourse of ships," that held everyone's attention. Swarmed about by swans, the small and large craft—sometimes the royal barge or the Lord Mayor's barge would glide past the terrace—presented a fascinating and enduring panoply of wonder for the adults as well as little Jane Grey. Someone was always arriving or leaving the Dorset Place waterstairs which ran a greater distance out into the Thames than anyone else's, including the king's. And when *he* came to Dorset Place, sometimes he rode his horse down "the streete," as everyone called White-hall, and clattered right into the courtyard just as the family did.

There were other times—especially if the Greys had gone hunting in Hackney, Greenwich or to the king's small palace at Eltham—when Mrs. Ellen and Mrs. Tylney, Katherine's nurse, would take the children abroad on Whitehall. Accompanied by a steward, they'd walk across the road by old Westminster Hall, on through Sanctuary to the old abbey across from Westminster Palace, now almost in ruins after the bad fire a few years ago. There they watched the monks working in the orchards and fields, and Jane listened as the nurses and the steward talked about how nice it was to see the old abbey still being used and not pulled down. Didn't they all remember the time when all those mansions one saw from the Dorset Place terrace had been lived in by the bishops of Durham, Salisbury and Worcester and monks had worked in *those* gardens too? Now most of them belonged to court nobles who'd given the king a lot of money for them.

Leaving the monks at the abbey, the little group might then walk to the Horse Ferry and watch as passengers—some accompanied by their horses—boarded the stout ferries to carry them to the opposite side. One day, Mrs. Ellen, her face flushed with pleasure, held Jane high so she might see the stately procession of the Archbishop of Canterbury as he made ready to cross the Thames on his own barge. Thomas Cranmer, the archbishop, had smiled at the crowd assembled at the landing and, making the sign of the cross, had quickly boarded the heavily carved and gilded episcopal barge and been rowed to the Lambeth Palace waterstairs opposite.

Later, walking back toward Dorset Place, the steward picked Jane up whenever they came to a muddy spot so she would not soil her clothes. Baby Katherine was almost asleep, her head on Mrs. Tylney's ample shoulder, lulled by the woman's rhythmic step. Suddenly a group of knights—the sun gleaming on breastplates and upright swords—rode up "the streete" past Westminster Hall toward the palace a short distance away. In sight of the gates they shouted to the guards, making such a noise that the startled child began screaming, and Jane clutched Mrs. Ellen's hand tightly. She was glad her parents were away with the king and queen. Her mother didn't like any child to cry, and often, if she was around, she'd shake little Katherine to make her stop. Jane could remember her mother shaking *her*, too, and that had been very frightening, for she hadn't even been crying.

If London meant excitement for little Lady Jane—with crowds on the streets and river and a palace nearby giving the king and his court easy access to the chambers and terraces of Dorset Place— Bradgate meant *home*. Jane's earliest recollections were of spacious rooms and familiar servants, of ornate gardens and riding out into the Leicestershire countryside with her sister, steward and groom.

Thomas Grey, the first Marquis of Dorset, Jane's grandfather, had built Bradgate some sixty years before her birth. Thomas, the son of Elizabeth Woodville and Sir John Grey of Groby, was descended from one Rollo, a minor chamberlain to Robert, Duke of Normandy, who gave him the Castle of Croy in Picardy near Montreuil-sur-Mer. A few years later, when Rollo de Croy came to England with William the Conquerer, he'd realized that opportunities to raise his social status and fill his purse existed more plentifully in the newly conquered land than in his own. He soon obtained land in Oxfordshire and anglicized his name to de Grey. For the next four hundred years the Greys of Groby—they'd soon dropped the *de*—had married well, with land, wealth and social prestige major factors in the selection of their brides. By the mid-fifteenth century, when the widow of one of Rollo's descendants, Elizabeth Woodville Grey, married the man who became King Edward IV, their influence and renown had given them great prominence at the Plantagenet court. When Henry Tudor ended that dynasty at Bosworth Field, the Greys switched their loyalty to the young Welsh monarch and his Plantagenet queen; they served Henry VII well. When that monarch died, the Grey loyalty passed to his son. Thomas Grey won the young king's friendship, served on his embassies and fought in his wars. At the end of his life Henry VIII called Thomas "that good and honest man."

When Thomas Grey built Bradgate he built well, setting the house—which was meant to be a hunting lodge—in a "fair park . . . bordered by the forest of Chartley, which was a full twenty-five miles in circumference, watered by the River Soar and teeming with game." The countryside, heavily forested and with hillocks, flat meadows and slate quarries, was left much in its rough and primitive natural state. When Henry Grey inherited Bradgate he built a gatehouse near the long winding approach and replaced the old entry with a massive door, flanked by two tall turreted towers of rosy red brick which led visitors to remark on the resemblance to the king's new palace in St. James's fields in London.

Bradgate was a small community in itself. Some three hundred servants and household officers in smart Dorset livery attended to the needs of the Grey family. There were bakers, brewers, wood-hewers and carters. A miller and a collier worked in back of the stables while joiners, carpenters and turners were kept constantly busy with my Lord Dorset's improvements. Several ladies—wives of the household staff—did little else but card, spin, weave and sew. Stableboys and grooms took care of the fine Dorset stables, and Smythson the falconer watched over Bradgate's mews with its excellent merlins, hawks and falcons.

Henry Grey's improvements had given Bradgate a more formal aspect, with newly glazed windows, both oriel and bay, letting in the clear northern light. In the Great Hall there was a dais at one end for the family members with a musicians' gallery at the opposite end. Every day more than two hundred people—family, guests, travelers who could expect to receive the lord of the manor's hospitality, and servants—all dined in the hall hung with the heads of Lady Frances' unfortunate victims. There was a Long Gallery for exercise on inclement days, chambers for sleeping and rooms for entertainment, one hung with a heavy tapestry with the Dorset motto, *À Ma Puissance*, with two small unicorns crested with ermine adornments. The common rooms were still strewn with the medieval rushes, while floors of newer rooms were covered in the new luxury from Turkey called "carpets."

Outside, the old rustic gardens had given way to acres so embellished with flowers, shrubs and herbs from the Continent that one visitor said they rivaled old Wolsey's gardens at Hampton Court. On the terrace a round fishpond had been dug, and in its murky green depths golden carp swam lazily, brushing against the pale water lilies floating on the surface.

By the time Lady Jane was six the marquis had rebuilt Bradgate and its environs, so that when she rode with her instructor or groom down the long approach lined with Spanish chestnuts and out into the countryside, she was still on cultivated land. Near the river lay an old church and the adjoining Priory of Ulverscroft, famous for its high tower, which years ago had guided strangers out of the dense forest. The Priory was still whole and had even survived the fighting of the Pilgrimage of Grace—that brutal encounter between the king and his Northern subjects who'd wanted to preserve their holy houses from confiscation or destruction. Henry Grey wanted no ruins near his property. Though the Priory had fed six hundred starving peasants the year Jane was born, by the time she was eight it was empty and desolate. Bradgate gardeners kept the lawns and trees neat; otherwise it was unused.

At Bradgate, Jane and Katherine Grey saw even less of their parents than they did in London. The archery contests and hawking, the jousts in the tiltyard and, always, the daily hunt with friends from nearby estates kept everyone busy from very early in the morning until the resplendent and noisy meal in the Great Hall in late afternoon. From their nursery window the little girls might watch as their parents and friends clattered into the courtyard, and a steward flung the bloodied corpses of slain animals to the kitchen scullions, and stableboys came to take the weary mounts away. The guests came from near and far. Often the Lady Mary, the king's daughter, was a guest for several days. Mary and Frances Grey were near the same age and had been students together in the royal classroom. Henry Grey's sister, Lady Audley, or his mother, Margaret, the Dowager Marchioness, Jane's grandmother, often stayed for weeks at a time. Neither the Lady Mary nor the others were as passionate hunters as the Greys and would often come to the nursery, seemingly delighted with the appealing little Jane and Katherine Grey. Jane was diminutive and shy, with the fair skin and reddish hair of her Tudor grandmother and the gray eyes of her Brandon grandfather. Katherine was equally fair, but her hair was more golden and she had, as everyone said, her grandmother Mary Tudor's beautiful blue eyes. Both girls were similarly dressed in long, smocklike gowns that just barely swept the floor. Their hair was drawn back and tucked under a plain little cap that tied under the chin. Whenever they appeared in public with their parents, they were dressed in small versions of the garments their mother wore. Already, Jane and Katherine had little gowns of damask, silk and satin, with furred sleeves; several were set with jewels, as were the little caps they wore.

The guests told the two Grey children of how difficult it was to travel to Bradgate now, what with the dangerous packmen and peddlers, traveling caravans with jugglers and dancing bears and, most of all, the displaced *religieux* who begged what they could and stole when they couldn't. Mounted soldiers and armed men from Leicester patrolled the roads, stopping those itinerants with no honorable reason or business to be in the neighborhood and flogging them when they resisted. It mattered little that they were penniless, ill-clothed and often starving. It mattered only that they be somewhere else.

The responsibilities for their guests, the supervision of Bradgate, and the stately town ceremonies in Leicester—which could never take place without the presence of the Marquis and Marchioness of Dorset—left little time for nursery visits for Jane Grey's parents. But when bad weather and the absence of any social functions kept everyone indoors, Frances Brandon would arrive in the nursery on visits that Mrs. Ellen and Mrs. Tylney had come to dread. It was not because they had anything to hide or be ashamed of; the servants kept the rooms neat and Jane and Katherine were always well cared for. Yet it seemd that the buxom marchioness—pregnant again, and certainly with a son *this* time—came primarily to demean the nurses' work. Jane had spilled a small glass of watered ale she'd been given as a treat by a visitor. Why hadn't the child learned to hold a glass properly? And why had Mrs. Ellen sent her down to the guests in that simple smock which was certainly the wrong color for anyone who was so pale, had such bright-colored hair and got spots on her skin so easily if she was out in the sun. Why hadn't she been dressed in a more becoming color, with the little jeweled cap her grandfather the duke had given her for her seventh birthday?

Long ago the nurses had discovered that it did little good—and only made it worse for both children—if they replied that Jane and Katherine might be frightened in unfamiliar situations. They might drop things or even say things they might not otherwise have done. Mrs. Ellen did not add that if Jane had gone too richly dressed, the marchioness would not have liked that either—especially if she spilled watered ale on her little gown—and that the smock had been clean, in a color that showed Jane's reddish gold hair to best advantage. Above all, they never mentioned the nursery visits of friends and family members who were always very complimentary of the nurses' care of Jane and Katherine Grey.

Standing silently, Mrs. Ellen and Mrs. Tylney merely listened with sober faces to the carping criticism and tried not to notice that Jane's color had grown paler or that Frances Grey's high-pitched voice was so loud it would almost certainly wake Katherine, who, mercifully, was asleep. Whenever the child heard that tone in her mother's voice, she'd cry and hide her head in Mrs. Tylney's full skirts.

Receiving no ready answer or tearful apology to her observations, Frances Grey would heave a loud sigh and, muttering at her fate in having such stupid children and incompetent servants, sweep from the room as everyone curtseyed. There was always one last sharp look from her pale icy-gray eyes at the door.

But now it was becoming worse. Lately, the marchioness had begun to pull Jane forward and roughly shake her, demanding why she'd done or said something that neither nurse could remember and both doubted that Jane did either. That bothered Mrs. Ellen more than anything else. Since discussion with the marchioness was impossible, she felt helpless. Yet it was one thing to feel helpless for oneself; it was another to watch Jane being shaken like one of her stuffed dolls. And it was sadly frustrating to try to think what one might say to the little girl, now rubbing her arm from a vicious pinch, of how one might comfort her when the tears came— after her mother had left.

4

In August 1545, when Jane Grey was eight, her grandfather Charles Brandon, the Duke of Suffolk, died suddenly while visiting his friend Sir William Parr, the brother of Queen Katherine Parr, at Guildford Castle. For several years the duke had suffered from gout, heart trouble and a variety of ailments through which his young wife, the devoted Kate Brandon, had nursed him with a combination of shrewd medication and an abundance of wit and tolerance. Though old enough to be her father, the duke had been the center of the former Katherine Willoughby's life and, with age and a failing body, she'd sought to temper the robust living habits that were partly to blame for his death at fifty-four.

His loss was a great sadness, not only for his family but also for King Henry. In addition to his great prominence at court, Charles Brandon had been a close childhood friend of the king's; they'd competed in all sports, lusted after the same women and finally— with Brandon's marriage to the late Mary Tudor—had become brothers-in-law. The Duke of Suffolk had fought in all the king's battles, from the brutal Pilgrimage of Grace and the Scottish uprisings to the capture of Boulogne, after which he'd brought the king the keys to the French city. It had been a deep, warm and affectionate relationship, remarkable in a court where such intimacy or close familial ties might often end in intrigue, betrayal or worse. It was also a poignant reminder to Henry, who was the same age—and as ill—that mortality awaited all, even those of Divine appointment such as a monarch.

Charles Brandon's death brought together four women, each of whom had close ties with him. First, Katherine, his wife of twelve years and mother of his only sons, of whom Henry, now almost eleven, would inherit the Suffolk dukedom. As a child of eight, the twenty-seven-year-old duchess had gone to live at Westhorpe as the ward of Charles Brandon and his first wife, when her mother, Maria de Salinas, had joined Katherine of Aragon in exile. It had been a happy arrangement; Katherine Willoughby adored the duke and his wife and she knew his children, Frances and Eleanor. After the duchess's early death, the young girl, thinking she might now have to leave the home she loved so much, had counted herself very fortunate when the duke had *married* her instead, though she was not yet fifteen and he over forty. Katherine Brandon loved her country home—its gardens and fountains, the earthy smell of the tall oaks and vast acres of golden wheat, oats and barley—and especially the great black forest that sheltered it all. Now, devastated by her loss, the young duchess readily acquiesced when the king said he would not allow the duke to be buried, as he'd requested, "in the college church in Tattershall . . . without any pomp or outward pride of the world." His best friend must have a funeral befitting his rank, the king insisted, and within a few days a splendid and elaborate service took place in St. George's Chapel at Windsor Castle, with a Requiem Mass for the soul of "the most High and Puissant Prince," while back in London similar obsequies were observed at St. Paul's and in the abbey at Westminster. As the coffin was lowered into a vault to the right of the choir, the sad king noted that the duke had never attempted to hurt an adversary nor had an unkind word for anyone. "Is there any of you, my lords, who can say as much?" he asked those present.

In her grief, Kate Brandon turned to her dearest friend, Katherine Parr, who had married the king two years previously after the execution of his fifth queen, Catherine Howard, for presumed adultery. Katherine Parr had been named for the late Queen

Katherine of Aragon, to whom her mother, Maud, served as confidante as well as a lady-in-waiting. Her father, Sir Thomas Parr, one of the king's boyhood friends, had died when Katherine was about five. Lady Maud never married again, devoting her time instead to seeing that her children had the best home and education her considerable fortune could provide. She vowed she'd have nothing but a peer for her eldest daughter, and Katherine Parr had been wed when she was only thirteen to Lord Borough, an aging Northerner old enough to be her grandfather, becoming stepmother to children many years her senior. Lady Maud Parr had died at twenty-nine, before the widowed Katherine had wed her second husband, another aging noble, Lord Latimer. She'd not lived to see one daughter marry a king; her only son, William Parr, enter into a loveless union with the daughter of the wealthy Earl of Essex; or the middle child, Ann Parr, become a countess. Ann's husband, William Herbert, later the Earl of Pembroke, was a strong advocate of the schism between England and Rome, served on Henry's Privy Council and was a trusted adviser, even though he could neither read nor write.

At thirty-two, Queen Katherine was a striking, auburn-haired woman with an extremely fair complexion, expressive eyes and a soft voice. But it was her kindness—the even temper and sunny disposition—that had long endeared her to the king's children as well as to Jane and Katherine Grey. The elegant and learned Katherine Parr was completely unlike anyone the two little girls had ever known. Her honest interest in them and their welfare, her desire to please and her insistence that they share the company of twelve-year-old Elizabeth and eight-year-old Prince Edward made all their visits to court treasured and talked about for days afterward. Katherine Parr had no children of her own, yet appeared to love everyone else's, including her third set of stepchildren, the motherless Mary, Elizabeth and Edward Tudor.

Shortly after her marriage, the queen had broken with tradition—and the king's own wishes—and asked that they all live together instead of in separate dwellings, as the three royal children had done all their lives. While everyone agreed the queen had done wonders for the king and his children and that the marriage had turned out very well indeed, they also knew there'd been considerable cost to the woman most responsible for its success. For, after her second husband's death, Katherine Parr had fallen deeply in love with Thomas Seymour, Queen Jane's brother, and had been on the point of marrying him when the king had asked her to be his sixth queen.

Undoubtedly wondering at the perverse Fate that cast her as the one to wed old and sick men, even a king, when her heart was with the younger, handsomely virile Thomas Seymour, Katherine accepted—for she had little choice. To refuse the aging monarch was unthinkable. Safe in her own home, Chartreuse near the Charterhouse, or visiting in Kate Brandon's palatial Southwark home, she and Kate had watched the appalling sequence of queens, with one dead, two divorced and two beheaded, and wondered what would become of King Henry. In the past five years he'd gained tremendous weight because of a running sickness in his leg. The sore, open and painful, kept him from hunting, hawking and all the sports in which he and Charles Brandon had reveled for years. The increase in his girth had been accompanied by a lessening of the good humor, tolerance and wit everyone had always taken for granted in the monarch.

After his sixth marriage, Henry had—with just the right amount of tact—dispatched Thomas Seymour abroad as an ambassador to Brussels along with Dr. Wotton, the Dean of Canterbury. It was a coveted assignment and some compensation for the disgruntled Seymour. Only a year ago his older brother Edward had been sent by the king to Scotland to "sack Leith and burn and subvert it . . . putting man, woman and child to fire and sword without exception . . ." That night, Edward Seymour wrote home, "I could not sleep this night for thinking of the king's determination for Leith." He'd carried out the king's bloody order, however, returning home to a hero's welcome and a new title, the Earl of Hertford. His spectacular rise within the Privy Council had dismayed many less competent courtiers, particularly his younger brother. In one year Thomas had lost one of the richest women in England as a bride, and—because it was now diplomatic to absent himself from the court where she was queen—his chances for further advancement or gain by ingratiating himself with king and council were much lessened.

The duchess and the queen were soon joined by Charles Brandon's eldest daughter, Frances Grey, the Marchioness of Dorset, who arrived from childbed at Bradgate Manor. Everyone agreed it would be a kindness not to make too much of the birth, for the child was another girl, named Mary for the king's late sister, Frances' mother. But even more unfortunate was the bizarre prank of nature that had made the child a dwarf. While both Frances and Henry Grey were of normal stature—as their parents on both sides had been—Frances' great-grandmother had been the incredibly tiny Lady Margaret Beaufort, and three generations later the smallness had become freak. Both Jane and Katherine were "neatly made," diminutive and small but not as tiny as the newborn Lady Mary. The child, swaddled and alone at Bradgate with Mrs. Tylney, was best not spoken of. Everyone recognized, too, that the death of Frances Brandon's father emphasized strongly her own lack in providing an heir not only for her husband's title but for the Suffolk dukedom in case anything should happen to the duke's own children. Which was highly unlikely, as he had not just one son but two.

Within a day, Mary Tudor, the king's eldest daughter, arrived from the little manor house at Chelsea which the king had built years ago so his children might have the benefit of fresh river air. It was the first time in several years that the four—the duchess, marchioness, queen and former princess—had all been together at the same time. Had they been asked to speak their closest thoughts, their intimacy might have been strengthened or ended, depending upon the degree of understanding the others revealed. The four were all old friends from their earliest days, when Queen Katherine of Aragon, wanting companionship for her lonely young daughter, Princess Mary, had sought the help of Lady Maud Parr, Katherine's mother. In a move radical for the time, the queen and her lady-in-waiting had started a classroom in old Westminster Palace with the celebrated Juan Luys Vives—highly recommended by Sir Thomas More—as instructor. Until their education ended, the girls—all within three or four years of the same age—were together each day in the classroom as well as in their homes when left with each other for companionship while their parents were away. Each brought to this occasion their own special remembrances.

For Katherine Brandon, now the Dowager Duchess of Suffolk, the reunion was a clear source of comfort; Katherine Parr and Mary

Tudor were her closest and dearest friends. Frances Brandon Grey was another matter. Even in those childhood days at Westhorpe when her mother had been alive, Frances had been a trouble-maker, without the lovable disposition of her sister, the wit and charm of her father or her mother's renowned beauty and kind-ness. In those classroom days which had ended almost twenty years ago, Frances had often exasperated Lady Parr and the tutor. She'd become so adept at conniving, it had horrified the other three, tax-ing Vives's patience to the utmost, for her mischievousness was almost as strong as her complete lack of interest in learning. Prin-cess Mary, Katherine Parr and Katherine Willoughby were all ex-cellent students, which only emphasized the Brandon girl's failing. Everyone agreed there was nothing lacking in her natural intelli-gence; it was simply that she did not choose to use it in study or learning.

For the Lady Mary, the meeting was bittersweet. Walking the palace grounds at Whitehall was a new experience for the former princess. During those classroom years with her friends, Mary had lived at old Westminster Palace—a short distance down "the streete"—with her father and mother. When she was nine, as Princess of Wales and her father's acknowledged heir, she'd been sent with her beloved Countess of Salisbury to live at Ludlow Castle, in the Welsh Marches from which her ancestors had come. Upon her return to London some months later, she'd been dev-astated to find her father involved with Anne Boleyn. For refusing the king the divorce he clearly expected she'd give, Katherine of Aragon was sent into exile and then—when Mary had supported the queen—she, too, was sent away. She'd never seen her adored mother again and most likely, as Tom Cromwell had threatened, would never see her father again either unless she submitted to the king.

Such submission had cost Mary dearly. She'd held out—with as much help as it was possible for Kate Parr, Kate Willoughby and the Countess of Salisbury to give. But ultimately, the exile—a virtual imprisonment, the physical deprivation and verbal abuse of her custodians, even the threat of death—had crushed Mary's staunch spirit. And so the girl who considered the pope God's ap-pointed servant on earth had agreed to her father's supremacy in a Church that was becoming alien to her. She relinquished her ti-

tle, accepted her mother's marriage as illegal and, in so doing, acknowledged that she was a bastard. Until her father's marriage to
Katherine Parr, she'd lived away from the court with a small, devoted group of attendants, many of whom had served her mother,
aware of her father's diffident interest, and at twenty-nine and still
unwed, realizing that life was slipping by. Her solace was her religion and the fact that she could now live with her father and half-
brother and half-sister in the home that her friend Kate Parr had
wrought for them. But it took considerable self-control when she—
a princess by birth, granddaughter of Isabella and Ferdinand of
Spain—was still only "the Lady Mary, the most unhappy woman
in Christendom," while her three friends, born of England's
proudest families, but with no titles, were now a queen, a marchioness and a duchess.

Along with her friends, Mary was aware of Frances Grey's severe attitude toward her children, particularly Jane. Having none
of her own, she considered her cousin blessed with three daughters and if one of them was abnormally small, it was God's Will
and He must have some plan for little Mary Grey. It was right
and proper that parents should be strict with their children, for
how else would they learn? Children must obey at all times, remain silent unless spoken to, never disagree with their parents and
never whine, cry, complain or speak loudly in company. They must
show their elders infinite respect while deferring reverently to their
opinions, and above all they must act as adult as possible. What
bothered Mary Tudor and her friends was that Jane and Katherine Grey were and did all those things. And still it didn't seem
enough for their parents, although five-year-old Katherine appeared not to irk Frances Grey as much as Jane did. Everyone who'd
observed the marchioness's harshness wondered what it was about
her elder daughter that upset her so strongly.

But Mary said nothing to Frances, nor did the others. Mary had
spent too many years uncertain and afraid of her own father, while
desolate at the brutal treatment he was inflicting upon her mother.
She knew from bitter experience that parents often felt little consideration for a child when their own will or desire was brooked.
Now her father had his son, and her own future was certainly
predictable. Unless he chose a husband for her, she'd live and die

"the Lady Mary." For what Catholic prince would accept a bastard wife from a country whose monarch had been excommunicated by the pope?

Her sister, Elizabeth, and brother, Prince Edward, and certainly her little cousin Jane Grey would probably all fare better, for they were of that first English generation to grow up unable to recall a time when the pope had been venerated in their country. Mary did not know whether they were lucky or not. She could not accept, as they had, the teachings of the "new religion," those reformed doctrines that had resulted in the dissolution or destruction of such ancient shrines as Our Lady of Walsingham and Becket's tomb at Canterbury, had tampered with Catholic ritual and belief so that people whose hearts could not accept the new dogma must suffer horribly at the stake or on the scaffold in defense of the old faith, which man had believed in since Christ walked the earth. It didn't help that her two dearest friends, Queen Katherine and Kate Brandon, were students of the reforming movement. The queen particularly was adept and convincing in any theological disputation and presided over weekly afternoon meetings in the palace. There, she and her sister, Ann, the Countess of Pembroke; and close friends Ladies Denny and Fitzwilliam; her stepdaughter, Lady Tyrwhitt; and Jane Dudley, the wife of John Dudley, Lord Lisle, all listened to such reforming zealots as Miles Coverdale or Hugh Latimer. Mary had long ago refused the queen's invitation to participate and Katherine, amiably tactful, had not pressed the matter.

As for Frances Grey and her husband, it appeared to make little difference to them what the king and his bishops said they must believe. All the religious teachings of their childhood had apparently meant little. Frances often attended Queen Katherine's meetings to discuss religion, even though everyone knew her presence was prompted more by a desire to be part of the exclusive and socially fashionable group than because of any strong theological belief. Mary might have envied Frances Grey. How much easier her own life would have been—and her dead mother's as well!— if they'd both been able to renounce their papal loyalty. If they'd both been able to swim with the tide amongst those—many as sincerely Catholic as she—who counted their earthly existence and possessions as more important than the preservation of those religious doctrines that had ensured the destiny of mortal souls for more than fifteen hundred years.

As Mary listened to the funeral services for Charles Brandon and watched the intent expression on the faces of young Lady Elizabeth and Lady Jane, it came as something of a shock that the two—along with the queen, her friends and the rest of the family—all seemed comforted by the services now given in English instead of the ritualistic Latin. Mary missed the rhythmic chanting of the priests, the musky smell of the censer, the bells, the mystical benevolence of the saints' statues, their hands outstretched in blessing. Now all were gone and the niches in which they'd stood were as barren as the plain altar stripped of the rich hangings and jeweled crosses of her childhood.

But Jane and Elizabeth seemed not to notice. Prayer book in hand, both were attentive, quietly wiping their eyes for the lost grandfather and uncle, as mighty and majestic now in their memory as the king himself.

Mary Tudor gave no indication that the service might be painful for her. If she was a product of a careful and loving upbringing which had ended some eighteen years ago, the Lady Elizabeth and Lady Jane were equally the results of *their* backgrounds. Elizabeth had had no real mothering or attention until Queen Katherine had taken her into the royal household. If she knew that her father had had her mother's head cut off, she gave no hint. No stepmother before Katherine Parr, except old Anne of Cleves, had paid her much attention or given her any affection.

But Elizabeth and Prince Edward had enjoyed one superb advantage upon which their father had insisted. Remembering the gifted tutors of his own youth, the best old Henry VII could find, the king and his first queen had found the finest teachers for their daughter, and other children of the royal circle—the Parrs, Brandons and Willoughbys—had profited as well. The result was evident in two learned royal daughters, an exceptionally well educated queen and monarch, all of whom could converse in several languages, knew their history and science, could hold their own in any philosophic or theological disputes and were gifted musicians as well.

Whatever the royal family did, the nobles were certain to emulate. While neither Frances nor Henry Grey was a natural intellectual, with little love of learning, they were determined that their oldest daughter be educated as befitted one of her rank, or even higher. If they were never to have a son, then Jane must be prepared for the illustrious marriage she would surely make. If there was to be no ducal title—and with Frances' two half-brothers, the chances of the title coming to Henry Grey through his wife were remote—then Jane must make up such a loss with one of her own. If there was to be no heir to the Dorset marquisate, then upon the little girl's shoulders fell the responsibility of marrying well and providing sons for it.

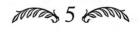

5

In the early 1540s, over a decade after Henry VIII's excommunication, religious politics in the English court had almost replaced
religion itself. In the days of Henry VII, and even in the earlier
years of his son's reign, obedience to the Holy Father was unquestioned. Thus, Henry VIII had been pleased with his golden
rose from the pope and the "Defender of the Faith" title; he would
serve religion and he would serve it well. But after the years of
struggle with Rome and the king's subsequent excommunication,
with so many changes in ritual, custom, elimination of saints' and
other holy days, the dissolution or destruction of the monasteries
and abbeys, the simple Englishman knew not what to believe of
the king's actions. The serving of religious belief had become second; expediency, first.

The "New Learning," that provocative and contentious philosophic gift from the Continent, had helped sweep away the last
lingering traces of medieval thought in education, the arts and sci-
ences—and religion. Parliaments had cringed before the king's authority, and under the "new religion," as defined in various stages
over the years by Henry and his Privy Council, a new breed of
statesman had emerged. The one who was on the strong, winning

side in the "cause of religion" was the one with the most to gain. A few years after the birth of Jane Grey and her cousin Prince Edward, sides had formed, with religious choices the dominating factor in their makeup.

The largest and most powerful was the king's party; its members, along with the king himself, were Catholic in everything but obedience to the pope. The minority party was made up of the staunch papists, diminishing in number as each year passed but still an important force in the more distant counties and country parishes of England, away from the hotbed of dissension that was London and the court. The third party, composed mainly of adherents of the "New Learning," were the "protestors," who would later be called Protestants. Each party was suspicious of the others and regarded the opposing beliefs as heretical and criminal.

In addition to being one of the "protestors," Jane's father, Henry Grey, the Marquis of Dorset, was also of the class that considered itself the "old nobility." He'd favored the king's break with Rome and—along with Sir William Parr, brother of Queen Katherine and recently made Earl of Essex; Stephen Gardiner, the Bishop of Winchester; and the queen's brother-in-law Will Herbert, the Earl of Pembroke—the marquis looked disdainfully on anyone the king favored, while regarding their religious beliefs as suspiciously as he did their political practices.

The objects of their suspicions were primarily the "new men" about the king, such as Thomas Cranmer, the Archbishop of Canterbury, as well as Edward Seymour, the Earl of Hertford, who was the late Queen Jane's brother and one of Henry's most trusted advisers. Edward, married to the proud and ambitious Anne Stanhope, had far exceeded her hopes for his success and she'd repaid him with a clutch of sons and daughters for whom impressive marital alliances were already being considered.

Another family risen to a prominence regarded by the "old nobility" as disastrously unfortunate was that of John Dudley, Lord Lisle. Dudley's wife was Jane Guildford, the daughter of Sir Richard Guildford. With his marriage—a true love match—John Dudley had taken the beginning step toward restoring his family's lost honor, for it was his father, the notorious Edmund Dudley, whom Henry VIII had hanged for corrupt tax collection practices at the beginning of his reign. Over the years, John Dudley had served his king well. But among the "new men" such as Cranmer or Lord Chancellor Wriothesley (as conservatively Catholic as Cranmer was not), he was still regarded with misgiving. A man of superb self-confidence and sophisticated demeanor, he was favored by the king, and several influential councillors, such as Will Paget and Fitzalan, the Earl of Arundel, had followed the king's lead. Dudley, too, had an impressive family, a fact that did not endear him to Henry Grey, for the children were all sons. John Edward, Ambrose, Robert and the youngest, Guildford.

In old Henry's time, such personal distrust or envy would have centered on the size of a courtier's estate, the grandeur of his castle, the number of his retainers, the eligibility of marriageable children and, above all, his influence with the monarch. Now it centered on theological strife, on the "cause of religion"; therefore the personal religious beliefs of those close to the king were of prime importance. Jesus Christ, His mission on earth, the love, dedication of belief and sincerity of the majority of the English people were not considered important by these men, whose lavish estates and full purses were either gifts or purchases from the king or the result of their pillage of Church property. They were eager and determined to stay on the "right side" of religion, not because of any innate philosophical belief but because such a position guaranteed the continuation of their influence and prominence.

And it followed that their families—above all, their younger children—would be steeped in that religious dogma responsible for their success at court as well as the illustrious titles, land and wealth that would have awed their more simple ancestors.

Lady Jane Grey and Prince Edward were two such children. In their grandfathers' youth, learning for itself had been disdained, the last trace of medieval concept being that "to a great gentleman it is a notable reproach to be learned." One could always hire a scribe, a mathematician, a laborer or craftsman. It was more appropriate that the noble be all things—as well as a good example— to those faceless masses who had no time, nor presumably the desire, to become expert swordsmen, dancers, riders, hunters, hawkers, fighters, drinkers or wastrels. Old Henry VII had been discerning enough, as was his formidable mother, Margaret Beaufort, to see the winds of change caused by the "New Learning," and young Henry Tudor had had a superb education. Since what was proper or fashionable at court was relentlessly copied by others over the years, education—even for women—was now taken for granted in those circles that could afford it. The farmer's lass and the merchant's wife, however, still depended upon their husbands, who might or might not be able to read or write.

But at Bradgate or at Dorset Place, Jane Grey's homes, the emphasis on education was not for the joy of learning, the encouragement of a child's superior intelligence or the resulting gratification for both Jane and her instructor. Spurred on by the interest Queen Katherine Parr was showing in her stepchildren's education—and remembering her own failure in the royal classroom—Frances Grey had committed herself very early to her elder daughter's learning. It must be the best available—as good as that afforded the prince or his sister Elizabeth—and it must embrace the concept of the "new religion." With that in mind, she instructed her husband to find someone who would devote himself entirely to the training and instruction of the daughter from whom they expected so much.

Henry Grey had long accepted that it was best to satisfy his wife's determined wishes promptly. He spoke to those at court who were interested in the "New Learning" and especially the reformed faith. None thought it odd that the marquis wished to commence his daughter's education. It was never too early to train a young mind, to equip it with the proper degree of receptivity so that learning became a disciplined habit—not even if the student was a shy child still in the care of her nurse.

Henry Grey, perhaps more so than his wife, "was a Protestant from sincere religious fervor and conviction," and his daughter's tutor must be one also. Along with the thoroughly classical education to be expected for one in Jane Grey's position—the early exposure to Latin, Greek and French, the later study of rhetoric, grammar, philosophy and, even later, to science and mathematics—one must also have an instructor learned and sympathetic in the teaching of Scripture. Henry Grey found all he was looking for in the sober person of John Aylmer, who came to Bradgate when he was twenty years old.

John Aylmer, or Alemer, of Norfolk descent, had been sent to Queen's College, Cambridge, by Henry Grey, for many nobles sponsored the education of worthy young boys who might otherwise have remained relatively untutored, especially since the monasteries' schools no longer existed. Aylmer must have felt some apprehension at the appointment, for to fail his sponsor might endanger his own future prospects. Nevertheless, he arrived at Bradgate to a warm welcome from the marquis and instructions to start Lady Jane's lessons as soon as possible.

At Bradgate a classroom had been set aside for the tutor's use. Each day Mrs. Ellen brought a fresh-faced Jane in her clean morning smock to the room and, ignoring the look of silent distress in the child's eyes, soon bustled off. It did not take John Aylmer long to realize that before any teaching—however simple—could commence, he must deal with Jane's anxiety. After several meetings with the marchioness, of observing her attitude and treatment of Lady Jane, he understood that the child's shy and withdrawn attitude hid a basic distrust and fear of all adults, excepting those who served in the nursery. Jane appeared almost mute in her parents' company, cautiously silent in the presence of other family members or guests, seemingly unable to accept their suggestions for play or even their compliments on her pretty clothes. Instead, she stood wherever the nurse left her, her fingers lost in the folds of her long skirt, her wide eyes on her mother and father as if she might somehow divine what they expected of her. Aylmer soon realized his pupil was an apprehensive little girl, uncomfortable and fearful, who must learn to trust before she could be taught. The child needed some release from constant intimidation, and unless he could reassure her, both of them would fail.

His first step proved the best. When Jane came to the classroom, instead of sitting quietly in his chair, the tutor quickly swooped her up in his arms, amazed at the tiny, almost weightless body. Before she could react, they were walking down the hall and out onto the terrace where, Aylmer knew, he must keep her out of the sun. He told the surprised Jane, whose round gray eyes held an unrestrained amazement, that he was going to speak some phrases in another language and she was to repeat them after him. It was a game, he said.

Relaxing, Jane nodded soberly, her fingers twisting in her skirt less frequently. As the moment, and then the half-hour passed, the tutor spoke to her in Latin and sometimes in Greek, giving her a word, telling her what it meant and asking her to repeat it.

Whenever she succeeded he praised her generously, and after several words were put together to make a phrase—and she repeated it in English—he was rewarded with the child's first smile. When he asked if she'd enjoyed the game, Jane nodded vigorously, the red-gold curls beneath her cap flying about her face.

From then on, their lessons were easier. Gradually Jane's apprehension disappeared, and soon she smiled at him as easily as she did at Mrs. Ellen.

In a few months Jane could pronounce many Latin and Greek words and phrases and she knew what they meant. "Master Elmer," as she called the young tutor, thought her very quick. Within a year, hornbook in hand, Jane was forming neat letters of the alphabet and proudly putting them together to make words. The tutor had nothing but praise for the child's natural intelligence and before long the two had developed a warm relationship. For Jane, classroom time was an extension of the respite she enjoyed in the nursery. Her parents were disappointed in her because she'd shown no liking for horses and little talent for riding, nor had she taken any satisfaction in hawking, which most children enjoyed. By the time Jane was eight she was no longer invited or even considered for their brief rides or forays about Bradgate. She did not, as other children in her position might have done, join her family as they visited the mews where the prized Dorset falcons were kept, nor did she engage in the easy banter of the stables, where the head groom saw to it that milords' children were always cosseted with a ride on the smallest pony or gentlest mare. Aylmer realized— and he suspected that Mrs. Ellen, now her governess, did also— that Jane might not honestly dislike the outdoor activities her parents lived for. But being apart from them, even if it meant solitude or a lack of proper exercise, also meant a blessed absence of carping criticism or sniping remarks about her lack of facility in almost every activity. Aylmer did not think Jane clumsy, stupid, too slow or too quick; she was not undisciplined, arrogant, too meek or too forward. Yet her parents addressed her often in coarse and biting tones, sometimes discussing her between themselves as if she were not in the room, disparaging her lack of understanding of whatever they were trying to teach her, be it manners, horsemanship or even, as her mother pointed out once, being able *to talk* so that she and her guests might not be bored to death. When Jane, with head bent, did not reply or cry, ask for help or understanding, did not promise to do better or ask her parents' forgiveness, she was fortunate to be let go with only one blow, slap or hard twisting pinch.

Aylmer, a university product, had seen boys flogged, beaten, slapped, bruised and often maltreated with malicious sniping or misguided humor. It was part of childhood both in school and at home, where parental discipline was equally firm and any infraction of expected behavior would bring swift retaliation. Everyone—children and parents—understood the rules. In many homes obvious affection between parent and child prohibited physical punishment, which was resorted to only under extreme conditions. Children knew what was expected of them and they complied; good manners and obedience to one's parents were the firm foundations of family harmony.

But such harmony did not exist at Bradgate. John Aylmer—or Mrs. Ellen—would have thought it highly improper to point out to Frances and Henry Grey that their daughter was an extremely engaging child, that the hours spent with her studies stimulated and satisfied her bright mind in much the same way the rigors of the hunt satisfied her parents, who rarely opened a book. He could not say that a child uncomfortable with either mother or father would be ill at ease in the immense Bradgate dining hall. There, from eleven until three and from five until eight o'clock at night— longer on an inclement day—at least two hundred people sat at table waiting to be served in different "messes." Waiters swarmed about bringing innumerable courses of soups and stews made from pheasant or swan, of baked fish, stuffed peacocks, sides of beef or lamb, or wildfowl in various forms, followed by fruits, jellies and "subtleties"—sweets in the form of elaborate marchpane concoctions of dragons, horses, fairy castles, even a huge replica of Bradgate itself.

The few occasions when Queen Katherine Parr, the Lady Mary or Kate Brandon came to visit and asked that, as a treat, the children dine with them were usually easier for Jane. But even then she was constantly admonished to answer the guests' questions, not to sit with arms on the table, not to cross her feet, not to eat too much—or too little—until the child, nervous and pale, was at last handed over to Mrs. Ellen. She was never invited to stay for at least a few moments of the dancing or mumming which followed, although her favorite pastime was music and she devoted as much practice each day to her lute, harp and cithern as she did to her studies.

There were respites from the loneliness of Bradgate, from the studies of languages, grammar and Scripture, from the music lessons or the occasions when her dancing master led Jane in a courtly *pavane* or the more sprightly *galliard* down the hall between the nursery room and her parents' quarters, to music played on the virginals by her music teacher. Whenever Parliament was sitting, when some powerful noble married, or died, when a foreign ambassador arrived in England and royalty must show its respect with great and lavish fetes and other entertainment—then the Marquis and Marchioness of Dorset knew they must return to court. Soon, the great wagon cavalcade would lumber once more down Bradgate's long approach of Spanish chestnuts, past the old priory, where a number of destitute monks had lately taken shelter, onto the road south toward London. Jane would travel on her pony or in the litter with Katherine and baby Mary and their nurses. She knew the continuous pleasant days of study with "Master Elmer" would now be interrupted, even though he traveled with the family and was expected—as were Mrs. Ellen and Mrs. Tylney—to keep Jane busy and occupied. But when her presence was needed, she had to be available.

First, she must go to court to see the king and queen. Jane liked her great-uncle Henry and great-aunt Katherine very much; they spoke kindly to her, and often the queen—so fond of children and yet with none of her own, although she'd been married twice before—had a treat planned just for the younger guests. Then there was her grandfather's widow, Kate Brandon, the Duchess of Suffolk, a tall red-headed lady who made such bright remarks that everyone—even Frances Grey—laughed and called her clever. The Lady Mary and the king's other children, Edward and Elizabeth, were often present and those were the best times. For then, when they were excused they could all go to the prince's quarters, and there were toys or card games or someone might play music and they would practice their dance steps, all under the watchful eyes of the nursery attendants. Sometimes even the Lady Mary came too; she seemed more at ease in the nursery quarters than in the family rooms downstairs. All the children understood—from bits of information they'd picked up from their parents and the servants—that Mary's religion was somewhat different from theirs. All three were devout, attended prayers twice daily and listened to the priest's sermon on Sundays. Elizabeth, Edward and Jane all thought alike; they could not understand how Mary, so sensible and loyal otherwise, could think differently, especially after the pope had treated her father so poorly.

London was full of the unexpected. One day, as Jane sat with her sister Katherine and Mrs. Tylney on the terrace at Dorset Place, shaded by the large plane tree at one end, clouds of smoke to the northeast caused a stir. As the smoke increased and wafted farther eastward, Frances Grey sent a servant to inquire of the palace watch if the fire was dangerous. In a moment the man returned, accompanied by Henry Grey, who hurried to allay his wife's fears. There was a fire, he said, but private property was not endangered. It was a priest who was burning.

Unaware that his young daughters were listening, Grey identified the victim as Father John Forrest, a member of the Order of Observant Friars and a former confessor of Katherine of Aragon's. Forrest had been imprisoned for refusing to acknowledge the king's supremacy. That day he had been drawn from Newgate Prison to Smithfield where a large number of people had assembled before Hugh Latimer, formerly one of the king's chaplains, to witness either Forrest's recanting or his death.

When the bishop asked the friar for his opinions, the priest "obstinately standing still and stiff in his opinions . . . openly declared in a loud voice to the bishop . . . that if an angel should come down from Heaven and show him any other thing than that he had believed all his lifetime past, he would not believe him, and that if his body should be cut joint after joint . . . or burned, hanged or what pain soever might be done to him, he would never turn from his old sect of this Bishop of Rome."

To make things worse, Grey said, the priest had taunted Latimer, saying, "Seven years ago you durst not have made such a sermon for your life!"—referring to the bishop's words before Forrest spoke. After that, the crowd getting restless, the friar was "hanged about the middle in chains of iron on a pair of gallows alive, a great fire made under him and about him . . . and so he was burned for heresy and treason." The burning had been watched not only by Grey but by the Duke of Norfolk, several earls, the Bishop of London and many of the king's Privy Councillors. When the priest was finally dead, an ancient wooden figure dragged from the mountains of Wales, along with several roods from county abbeys as well as the rood wrested from St. Margaret Pattens on Tower Street were all broken and thrown onto the fire as the crowd cheered and Latimer denounced the worship of idols and images as a "great blasphemy against God."

It was not the first time Jane Grey had heard of people being hanged, drawn, quartered, beheaded or burned because they did not believe her great-uncle was the head of the Church. Jane was very devout and she knew her Scripture and nowhere in its pages had she seen anything about loyalty to the Bishop of Rome. She knew she was supposed to love and honor God and that she did each day when she assembled with her family at morning and evening prayers and on those special days like Sunday when they heard Mass. Scripture was one of the things Jane liked to study best and she found it difficult to understand why a priest would be willing to burn because of a bishop her uncle had replaced.

That same bishop was part of a water pageant when, several days later, the king and queen, the Greys and their family and the king's children all assembled for a "triumph" on the Thames. From the palace terrace they watched two boats—one representing the pope and his forces, the other representing the king and his subjects. In the papal barge, soldiers dressed as the pope and his cardinals pulled away from the waterstairs to do battle with those defending the king's church. At Westminster Palace everyone watched as great rounds of "ordinance of warr" were shot off. Inevitably, Majesty triumphed over the Papacy and the "Roman bishop's" boat was overturned, throwing everyone into the Thames.

The triumph of king over pope was loudly cheered by people lining the riverbank as well as the palace terrace, which was "covered with canvas and set with green bows and roses . . ." Jane and Katherine were awed at the sight of so many swimming in the water; their mother did not approve of the sport. But the music of the "sackbuts and waytes" was hearty and the king roundly pleased with the show. He motioned everyone inside, where a feast awaited and where he would meet the dripping participants once they were dry.

If anyone noticed there was one less member of the royal family present, they said nothing. The Lady Mary, who had been on the terrace at the pageant's beginning, was nowhere to be seen.

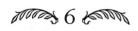

6

In the years following Charles Brandon's death, Jane and her parents spent more time in London. Her father, whose extravagances in rebuilding Bradgate, compounded by an unfortunate tendency to gamble wildly beyond his ability to win, or pay, now felt the necessity of staying close to court. The king was ailing and irascible a good part of the time due to the appalling leg condition which often made his features black with pain. King Henry was unpredictable, and Henry Grey, my Lord Dorset, whose financial affairs were such that he'd recently tried to gain control of part of his aged mother's lands, felt it wiser to be close to the source of his influence: the king, his court and Privy Council. The Dowager Marchioness, enraged by her son's activities, wrote the Lord Chancellor asking his protection for a "poor widow, so unkindly and extremely escheated by my son."

Henry Grey still regarded those "new men" on the Privy Council as an affront to the dignity of the older nobles of ancient family and degree and resented the attention and preference the king gave them. Particularly he lamented the rise of such as Edward Seymour, the Earl of Hertford, and John Dudley, Lord Lisle, whom he considered the gravest examples of the king's misplaced trust.

Their competency, which King Henry had recognized long ago, went unnoticed by my Lord Dorset.

As relatives of the king by marriage and by blood, Henry Grey and his wife were always welcomed at court with the great honor due their rank. But the affairs of state—and Church—were in the hands of others, which caused the Greys resentment and disappointment.

Frances Grey, Jane's mother, also bore a heavy burden. Duke of Suffolk, her late father's title, now graced the handsome person of her half-brother, eleven-year-old Henry Brandon. The next heir was his brother, Charles, only a few months older than Jane. Had there been no sons of that second marriage, the title would have come to Henry Grey. And with it the vast fortune in lands, the palatial London home, Suffolk Place, where his wife and her step-mother had grown up, as well as Westhorpe, their estate in Suffolk. Other county properties throughout England were possessions of the Suffolk dukedom which, since Charles Brandon's death, were now being enjoyed, used, appreciated and held in conveyance for her two Brandon sons until they attained their majority by that classmate of Frances Brandon's schoolroom days, Katherine Willoughby Brandon. The duchess and her boys were all that stood between the Greys and the wealth and prestige of the Suffolk title.

In 1546, Henry Grey, desperate for money, lamenting his limited influence at court and with the king—especially in matters of religion—and irked by the patronization of such as Edward Seymour and John Dudley, decided to be more aggressive about his future prospects. Two results of this decision were soon clear. The family would spend more time at Dorset Place, their London residence, and their eldest daughter, Jane, would become a member of the royal household.

If the king and his councillors guessed the reason for the Greys' move, they paid little attention. My Lord Dorset was charming, affable, a good host and pleasant guest; he was also weak, vacillating and more completely controlled by his wife than most men. But what the king and his advisers did not understand was that along with the ambivalence and charm went a certain determined ambition, fed constantly by Frances Grey. Perhaps judicious attendance at court, a propitious timing in the correct circumstances, might be just what a failing fortune and a certain ennui with their current life needed. And any detractions, such as greed, a noticeable lack of moral obligation or thought for anyone other than themselves, appeared of little concern to Henry and Frances Grey.

Jane Grey's departure from Dorset Place down "the streete" to become a member of the royal household, was an example of an old English custom of "boarding out" one's children—sending them off to another household, usually one more prestigious than their own, where they might learn another degree of good manners, conduct, awareness of customs in differing circumstances, and be in a position—boy or girl—to effect a good marriage. With my Lord Dorset, supposedly one of the wealthiest nobles in the kingdom, with blood ties to the royal family, there was no place eminent or exalted enough for Jane Grey to go but to the king's household. After the matter was discussed with Queen Katherine, it was decided when Jane was ten that she would live with the sovereigns and her cousins Prince Edward, the Lady Elizabeth and the Lady Mary at Whitehall Palace.

With her went Mrs. Ellen and a number of attendants to see to her needs. Most would be housed in the palace servants' quarters, while Mrs. Ellen would be in a room near Jane's. For a child used to the bustle of the nursery quarters with two sisters, familiar attendants and servants, it was a traumatic move, made more so by the fact that her parents had decided that John Aylmer would take a leave of absence and Jane's studies could be continued with the Lady Elizabeth's tutor, William Grindal. No one asked her preference and it certainly never occurred to Jane to protest the dismissal of her beloved "Master Elmer." No one, probably not even Jane herself, realized the importance he'd assumed in her life since, to a child barely out of babyhood, he'd been the focus of her day, the one she wanted most to please—for she'd long ago accepted that pleasing her parents was impossible—the one from whom she expected warmth, encouraging support, even an affection not unlike that which Mrs. Ellen gave so freely. John Aylmer had given Jane a rare attitude toward study and been rewarded with a blossoming of the girl's intelligence that awed him.

And, combined with her acuity for learning, her natural inquisitive scholarliness, was a devout appreciation not only for the "New

Learning," of which John Aylmer was a stout proponent, but for the "new religion" as well. Jane had her own Prayer Book in English and knew it by heart. She'd read the Scriptures in English and in Greek. She'd listened to her parents' discussions of the changes in church ritual which always seemed to be accompanied by bloodshed, torture or murder. Being unfamiliar with the customs and rituals of the Church before her great-uncle had become its head, she realized people were dying because of the only doctrine *she'd* ever known and it was dear to her. God was comforting to experience and offered hope, not only for this life but for the one to come. What Jane would not have understood—and certainly no one ever pointed it out to her—was that the "cause of religion" which consumed so much of her time and thoughts was really just another form of escape from intolerable home conditions. Many devotees of the "new religion" were as serious as Jane in pursuing that deep degree of involvement which, aside from her other studies, was all Jane had. Perhaps the only one who would have understood Jane's devoutness was Mary Tudor, the king's elder daughter, as intense in her loyalty to the old faith as Jane was to the new.

Though her apartments in the palace were only steps away from Dorset Place, Jane now lived in an environment unlike anything she'd ever known. Bradgate and her London home were luxuriously impressive, but nothing could have prepared her for the magnificence of the royal homes, each uniquely different yet all alike in their sumptuous appointments, which were maintained solely for the monarch's comfort and convenience. Whether it was Whitehall in London, Greenwich Palace downriver or Richmond Palace upriver, the awesome castle at Windsor or the grandeur of Hampton Court, there were miles of corridors she must walk in procession past sentries holding arms, hundreds of windows out of which she might look over dozens of gardens stretching for acres along riverbank or touching a distant meadow. Statues of Roman emperors or those of the "King's Beasts," or of saintly figures killing dragons adorned garden and pathways; leering or stern gargoyles watched from every building. Everywhere there were costly tapestries from Flanders or Italy, glass from Venice, supple leathers from Spain. In the King's Guard chamber at Hampton Court, a vivid tapestry with threads of gold and silver told "The Story of

Abraham." In the Audience Chamber at Whitehall, another tapestry depicted the "Acts of the Apostles." No one told Jane it had
been a gift from Pope Leo X when the king's golden rose and "Defender of the Faith" title were conferred. Everywhere rooms were
hung "with cloth of gold, blue cloth of gold, crimson velvet, tawny
velvet, green velvet. . . ." In these rooms were "bedsteads, card
or playing tables, chairs, couches and footstools of carved ebony,
cedar-wood, walnut or oak, inlaid with mother-of-pearl, ivory, or
rich metal wirework and upholstered in silk, satin, velvet or Flor-
ence brocade, fringed with gold, and even with strings of seed
pearls." Persian or "Turkey" carpets covered walls or floors in corridor, gallery, hall and bedchamber. Cupboards held the loot of
the Church—gold and silver plate, bejeweled goblets, bronze, gold
and silver candlesticks and sconces—many studded with Italian
jewels.

And everywhere there were paintings. One day, when the king
and his companions had gone hunting at Eltham, Queen Katherine took an awed Jane into the Privy Council Room in Whitehall
Palace to see the great fresco which the king's sergeant-painter, Hans
Holbein, had painted of the king, his father and mother and the
late Queen Jane. Holding tightly to Katherine Parr's hand, Jane
gazed at the woman for whom she'd been named, Prince Edward's
mother, while the queen told her the sad story of Master Holbein,
who'd died in the plague nearly three years before.

Jane had always been surrounded by servants and she was comfortable with them. But the limited confines of Bradgate and Dorset Place faded with the myriad secretaries; ushers; cupbearers;
carvers; servers; singers or madrigalists, some English, some Italian or French; the dozens of musicians with their flutes, lutes, re-
becks, sackbuts; even Irish harpers, who followed the court to the
smaller royal residences of Eltham or Oatlands or even gaudy
Nonsuch Palace, which the king was building in Surrey for a
hunting lodge. All of these bewilderingly endless abodes of luxury
were cared for by armies of servants in woodyards, bakehouses,
pantries, butteries and kitchens, while dozens of chamberlains,
stewards and other officials—whom the king and queen seemed to
know by name—watched over the king's wardrobe, armories, stables, chariots, his mews and even his trumpeters.

It was a whole new world for Jane Grey, and for one as shy,

used to long periods of solitude after equally long hours of study, it would have been even more taxing but for the kindly interest of Katherine Parr. If Mrs. Ellen was Jane's source of affectionate caring in her private chambers, the queen was her staunch ally when she left them. Katherine Parr had known the child since birth. Along with Kate Brandon and Mary Tudor, she'd lamented the little girl's treatment by her mother and was pleased when the Greys decided to place Jane in her care. There was plenty of room, there were two other royal children in residence, and Mary—who now lived in her Newhall home—visited frequently. On occasion, the offspring of the queen's friends—the Dudleys, Seymours and even Kate Brandon—were left with the servants while their mothers attended the queen's afternoon sessions to discuss religion, to listen to such as Hugh Latimer or Anne Askew, a noted "reformer," define Scripture before the talk evolved to court gossip.

Once Jane had joined the royal household, Queen Katherine wisely left her alone. She knew solitude had been part of Jane's life at Bradgate and she knew the reason why. She did not want the little girl to feel any undue pressure; it would take time for her to find her way. Jane was told that any reasonable request to see the queen would be granted. She was expected, therefore, to conform to the court ceremonies so seriously observed by everyone else—as much for convenience as for show. Ceremony was part of the day's routine and all were aware of their places in it. Conformation was not only expected, it was taken for granted. There was Mass in the morning for those who did not attend the early prayer sessions in their nearby homes or in their palace suites. Then hunting for the king and his companions. The queen did not care for hunting, wishing rather to give her time to her friends, her studies, her ladies-in-waiting and her stepchildren. Katherine Parr was now firmly committed to the "new religion" and she and Kate Brandon spent hours together reading and discussing the latest books, tracts or pamphlets from the Swiss reformers on the Continent. Enthusiastically they'd urged the king to have Bibles in English placed in churches where they might be used by those who could read. Presumably those who could not listened to the interpretation of those who did and this had resulted in so many differing theories of the true meanings of Scripture as to cause King

Henry to harangue at his last Parliament, saying, "I am very sorry to know and to hear how unreverently that most precious jewel, the Word of God, is disputed, rhymed, sung and jangled in every alehouse and tavern."

While the king was hunting—or later attending meetings of the Privy Council—and the queen was educating herself and her ladies in religious liberalism, the royal children spent most of their day in studying with the Lady Elizabeth, the acknowledged scholar, now fourteen. The queen often conversed with her tutors about the girl's proficiency in French, Italian, Spanish and Flemish. Elizabeth had absorbed more geography, mathematics, astronomy, science and rhetoric than many of her elders, and—a tribute to William Grindal, her Cambridge tutor—was flawless in Greek and Latin. Jane Grey, four years younger, commenced on the same path as the king's second daughter and, as a result of John Aylmer's early thoroughness, found no difficulty in her studies in the palace.

One result of her move to the king's household was that Jane now saw more of Edward Tudor, the little Prince of Wales, exactly the same age and not dissimilar in temperament or disposition. While Jane had become almost withdrawn, using her natural intelligence for study, religious or otherwise, as a shield against the unhappiness of her family life, for Edward Tudor there'd been little family life at all. Until Queen Katherine Parr had taken him under her wing, he'd lived—those first six years of his life—with a full complement of servants and attendants sworn to adhere to a book of rules written by the king at the little prince's birth. These governed Edward's daily schedule, the hygiene to be observed about him, as well as his diet, studies and opportunities for sports or play. When "the women were taken from him"—presumably those female attendants who'd cared for him from birth and were responsible for the only affection he'd ever known—it had been traumatic enough for Edward to note it in his *Journal*, commenced when he could write, although his penmanship never equaled that of his sisters or Jane. His education had started almost as early as Jane's, and his tutor, Dr. Richard Cox, found the boy "of such towardness in learning, godliness, gentleness and all honest qualities . . . an imp worthy of his father . . ." Amiably stern and with a genuine interest in the child, Cox had given him a good foundation, although it was clear Edward would never be as gifted as Mary, Elizabeth or Jane.

When the prince was seven, Queen Katherine—whose mind was as nimble, clever and scholarly as any tutor's—had advised another teacher, and the learned John Cheke, a Fellow of St. John's College, Cambridge, was brought to court on the advice of the king's trusted physician, Dr. Butts. Cheke supervised those instructors who taught Edward his German and French, who gave him dancing and fencing lessons and instructed him in "manners and deportment." Remembering the wisdom of Katherine of Aragon and her own mother in allowing children of noble families to study with the royal offspring, Queen Katherine Parr suggested Edward have companions in the classroom as well as on those all too few occasions when he went outside for exercise, sports and games.

The result of so much attention and care was, at eleven, a fair-haired, pale boy who resembled his mother, Jane Seymour, in features and physique. Slight, somewhat diffident, one shoulder a bit higher than the other, a natural intelligence made almost precocious by constant and unrelenting instruction, lonely as only one aware of the vast difference between him and his companions can be, Edward Tudor had much in common with Jane Grey. Although the schedule of their days was rigidly dictated, there were still those moments with the king and queen—or often with only the queen, when she arrived in either Jane's or the prince's quarters, bringing the other child, aware they had something to give each other, if only for a short time. It might be playing with the enormous number of toys or choosing from many card games and puzzles. They might walk in the gardens outside, watch the river traffic from the palace terrace, or ride with the king's falconer in the woods outside Whitehall which extended westward from the abbey at Westminster all the way to the king's little manor house on the river at Chelsea. They might even ride on the river in the royal barge, exclaiming at the unfamiliar aspects of the buildings they knew so well but which looked so different from the water.

Those were the times Jane liked best—when some of the king's children visited her royal great-uncle and great-aunt. Then there was the stimulation of being *together*, a strange excitement rarely experienced. Such as when the Lady Mary came from her country home. Mary always had a surprise for the younger children: a toy, a book or a puzzle. On one occasion she even gave the astonished Jane a small gold necklace set with seed pearls.

Jane often met the same people she'd seen in her parents' homes and others she didn't know as well, such as Thomas Seymour, the brother of the late queen and of Edward Seymour, the Earl of Hertford. As uncles of Prince Edward, the two Seymour brothers occasionally paid visits to Edward's apartments. Jane preferred the witty Thomas to the brusque Edward. The earl, solemn and proper, might bow deferentially to both the prince and Jane, but his mind was clearly on other things. Mrs. Ellen told her he was a great help to the king, industrious and trusted, and had little time for children though he had a large family of his own. The unmarried Thomas, however, always had time for both Edward and Jane. Though he paid Edward the deference due his position and bowed deeply to Jane, there was little condescension in his manner. He might tell a witty story; sometimes he brought them the gift of an unusual book or toy, a pair of gloves of Spanish leather heavily embroidered in gold thread. It was impossible not to like Thomas Seymour and some of the merriest times of all were when Mary and Elizabeth joined them. Then Mary—an excellent musician, with her father's love of music—played the virginals. They all danced together—Thomas and Elizabeth, Jane and Edward—while Mary, smiling broadly, kept the music's beat thumping until Thomas called for mercy.

While it was the sort of family life Jane had never known before, she did not become part of it overnight. The queen did not press; she knew the child must learn to trust, must increase her confidence by small degrees. As each week passed and she saw the little girl, accompanied by the faithful Mrs. Ellen, in the other children's apartments, as she noted the increasing ease with which Jane spoke or responded to further gestures of friendliness, she was gladdened by her obvious happiness.

By the time Jane had been in the royal household for a year, she was less shy with people and more at ease in large social gatherings. She had gained confidence in dealing with sudden changes, whether it was the disruption of a familiar daily routine due perhaps to the hurried departure of the queen and children to Greenwich because the king wished everyone present *that* day, or merely time lost in the classroom because of a tutor's illness. Heretofore, Jane's security had been in an ordered, sheltered, almost solitary life in which the classroom, chapel and nursery were oases of safety where she might escape any participation in family affairs. Now when she must do as others did, no one paid her any attention; it had become her greatest joy and relief.

And then one day in mid-January, 1547, with no explanation, Jane was hustled down "the streete" to her Dorset Place home. In other parts of the palace Edward and Elizabeth were also being sent off, and when Jane asked to say good-bye, Mrs. Ellen just shook her head. The children were to go away as quickly as possible, the nurse said—Edward to Ashridge in Herefordshire and Elizabeth to the Palace of Eltham outside London. The queen was in her chamber weeping and so distraught no one was to disturb her. On their way through the corridor leading to the courtyard, a frightened Jane clung to Mrs. Ellen's hand while the king's councillors hurried by on their way to the Privy Council Room.

The mystery continued for days. Jane's parents acknowledged her return mostly by conferring with Mrs. Ellen. Her sisters, however, were delighted that Jane had come back to the familiar rooms which now looked quite plain after the magnificent luxury in which she'd lived for over a year. At last Mrs. Ellen revealed that the king was sore sick and his ministers thought it best the children stay in other residences until he recovered. Even the queen and her ladies had gone to the little manor house on the river at Chelsea.

Jane was pensive at remembrance of the happy times she'd shared with Queen Katherine and the king's children at Chelsea and told her delighted wide-eyed sisters of many adventures there. She was sad that the great-uncle who'd been so kind to her was ill, and longed to ask her parents about him but lacked the courage. Young as she was, Jane had somehow come to know the monarch was considered inviolate, even immortal, and to talk of death was almost treason. And she was truly confident that such dangerous sicknesses as afflicted the ordinary human body and soul could never affect anyone as awesome as the king. Just to be sure, however, she knelt at the small nursery altar and sent her prayer winging to heaven, completely confident her God was listening—that the friendly ailing giant she'd come to love would rise in the morning, strong and once more in good health.

But even then, just steps away from Dorset Place, a life was departing from the royal bedchamber. King Henry died and the foundation upon which Jane Grey's new life had commenced was gone. Just as she'd settled warily—and then happily—into a palace life where, for the first time ever, a genuine interest had been shown in *her*, by the queen and her other relatives, now all would be changed. Katherine Parr was now the Queen Dowager, and young Edward would be king. Jane wondered if there would be a place for her in that life which the queen and her stepchildren must now lead. It was depressing to think of living at Dorset Place until she was married. Since she was only ten, that would be at least another three years. And the good times with Edward and her other royal cousins would probably be fewer, for her family would undoubtedly now spend more time at Bradgate, since the king was gone. After the comfortable security of life within the royal circle, Jane was desolate at what she'd lost. Never again, she felt, would her life be the same.

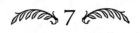

7

During Henry's last illness, while his children and Jane Grey were absent from the palace, courtiers had clustered in groups, speaking in somber tones in nearby hallways. Within the Privy Council Chamber, councillors argued over the awesome heritage that faced the royal children and the responsibility that the council, the king's trusted advisers, must bear to help the ten-year-old King Edward, who had yet to be told his father was mortally sick. Mary and Elizabeth were also ignorant of the seriousness of the king's illness. Henry had been unwell for most of the past year and had rallied before; they had little reason to believe he would not do so again.

The last Privy Council of Henry VIII was comprised of an impressive group of nobles, diplomats, courtiers and churchmen. A balanced mixture of conservatives and liberals, some were close to the king by long association or marriage, such as his brother-in-law Edward Seymour, the Earl of Hertford, and Will Herbert, who'd married Ann Parr, the queen's sister. Others, such as Henry Fitzalan, the Earl of Arundel; Lords Montague, St. John and Russell; and Thomas Radcliffe, the Earl of Sussex, were representative of those courtiers of the "old nobility," of which Jane's father,

Henry Grey, was a part by birth if not by influence. The religious were represented by the queen's cousin Cuthbert Tunstall, the Bishop of Durham, and, more prominent, Thomas Cranmer, the Archbishop of Canterbury, in whom Henry had extraordinary faith, based upon the prelate's genuine devoutness as well as his complicity and support in both of the king's divorces. A speechless Henry had died clutching Cranmer's hand.

There were also those "new men" represented by John Dudley and the king's venerables, "My Wills"—Paget, Paulet and Petre— all as resented by Henry Grey and his friends for the trust the king had shown in them as for their competence. Grey and others were determined that, since their benefactor was now gone, their influence would end. Yet when Henry drew his last breath at two o'clock on that murky Friday morning, January 28, 1547, no one knew how that would be effected.

But others did. The king's earlier illness had predicted a mortality that—though he chose to ignore the possibility—would act as a catalyst by which the country's future as well as the monarchy itself would be set at stake. There were no serious contenders for the throne. The last of the Plantagenets, old Margaret Pole, the Countess of Salisbury, Mary Tudor's beloved governess, had had her head hacked from her body some six years earlier for dubious participation in a plot involving her sons, one of whom was a cardinal in Rome. But the problem presented by Edward's extreme youth made every councillor vitally aware that not only must they aid and support the boy-king, but they must also hoard and use at the right time every talent and diplomatic cleverness—honed to a sharp alertness over the years by Henry VIII's whims and moods—to maintain their standing and influence within the Privy Council which the king had named to guide his son until Edward attained his majority at sixteen.

That had been Henry Tudor's last wish. In his will, his sixteen "entirely beloved councillors" were urged to govern and advise Edward, and he in turn was urged never to "change, molest, trouble nor disquiet" those his father had chosen to guide him. Similarly, Henry had ordered that the Privy Council must agree in all decisions. In this manner, the king presumably had sought to eliminate the possibility of any one strong faction—religious, political or social—becoming too influential. There were many on that council whose fathers had told them of Edward IV's heirs, those little princes in the Tower, undoubtedly done away with by the usurper Richard III, whose own life had been taken by Edward's grandfather Henry VII at Bosworth Field. "Woe to the land where the king is a child" was not an idle adage in 1547. Strength and unity were essential, for the political and religious challenges of Spain, France and Germany were constant and England's interests could best be served by those experienced advisers—a good many of them still young—whom the king had chosen.

That most certainly was Henry VIII's intention until death caught him unawares and forever changed his children's and Jane Grey's lives. In his will, Henry left "the imperial crown and realm of England and Ireland, our title to France, with all dignities, honors, preminences, prerogatives, authorities, jurisdictions, lands and possessions" to his son, Edward, and then to Mary and Elizabeth. Should any of these three not inherit—and the thought was so unlikely as to be almost implausible, for surely Edward would marry and beget his own heirs or else his sisters would—then the crown would go to the family of the king's sister Mary Tudor, the first Duchess of Suffolk, by her marriage to Charles Brandon. These were Lady Jane Grey and her sisters Katherine and the dwarfish Mary. Jane was a reversionary heiress, hardly likely to succeed, since at least one of the king's children would certainly have a male heir. If not, her own mother might yet have a son. Omitted from the will was any mention of the offspring of Henry's sister Margaret, the Queen of Scotland, whose granddaughter, little Mary Stuart, was now the Queen of Scots. It was known the king had hoped to effect a future marriage between Mary and Edward Tudor. But religious differences, the constant Border raids and Henry's brutal Scottish wars in the past years had dampened that hope, with the Scots proclaiming they "dinna like the manner of the wooing."

Henry had died on a Friday, yet the news remained secret until the following Monday, January 31, when—in the Parliament Chamber at Westminster—the speaker, Thomas Wriothesley, was "unspeakably sad and sorrowful . . . and being almost disabled by tears from uttering the words" that announced the king's death. Soon, messengers sent to the Guildhall, St. Magnus' Church, Leadenhall, to the Standard in Cheapside and the conduit in Fleet

Street, read aloud the dire news to the weeping crowds.

Only hours before, messengers had finally left for Beaulieu in Essex to tell Mary of her father's death, to the manor house at Chelsea to inform the queen and to Enfield, where Elizabeth awaited the arrival of Edward. Once told their father was gone, the two children, shocked and saddened, clung to each other, causing one witness to write, "Never was sorrow more sweetly set forth, their faces seeming to beautify their sorrow. The most iron eyes . . . were drawn thereby into the society of their tears."

By the time the royal children heard the news, Jane Grey had also been told and, gazing from her Dorset Place windows, could see the people of London walking in long sad groups to the palace gates or to the old abbey at Westminster, to St. Paul's or crowding into the many City churches where masses were being said for the dead king's soul. In his will, Henry had ordered an altar to be made "for the saying of daily masses while the world shall endure." Great buntings of black cloth were hung outside Jane's home, where family members wore mourning clothing as well as serious and sad expressions, where any hunting expeditions or other sports were now forbidden. At mealtime, only the Irish harpers played long doleful dirges as the family ate in silence. For Jane, the solemnity was not unusual; her home had never been the convivial, comfortable refuge she'd found with Queen Katherine.

Then, on February 14, over two weeks after the king's body had lain in state, Henry was "solemnly, with great honor conveyed in a chariot with his image lying on it toward Windsor," and there, on the sixteenth, the huge coffin was lowered into the floor "midway between the stalls and the high altar" of St. George's Chapel, to join Jane Seymour, his nobles breaking their white wands of office "with much solemnity and . . . hurtling them into the grave." In accordance with tradition no women were present, but they attended services in London at the abbey, St. Paul's or in their own private chapels.

On the following day, within the Tower of London where young Edward awaited his coronation, Henry's Privy Council—now a Council of Regency for the young king—disregarded his will which they'd "reverently and diligently . . . resolved and agreed with one voice . . . to maintain . . . to the uttermost of our power, wits and cunnings" and, a few paragraphs later, agreed that because of his "tenderness and proximity of blood" to the young king, "and of the great experience which he hath in all affairs of the realm," to name Edward Seymour, the Earl of Hertford, Protector of England. This accomplished, the nobles later knelt before the young boy-king while Edward Seymour was invested with his new title and Edward "put on the mantle, girded on the sword, placed the coronet on his uncle's head and delivered him his rod of gold." The new sovereign, a mere child, was docile, obedient and respectful of his uncle Seymour. Hadn't his council told him the welfare of the realm demanded one strong head? Who better than the king's uncle?

Edward Seymour was not only named Protector but also received the dukedom of Somerset and the eminent titles of Lord Treasurer and Lord Marshall of England, an office once held by Jane Grey's grandfather Charles Brandon.

Since such bountiful largesse for even one man demanded payment in kind for the consent of the others, the spoils were shared. Thus, John Dudley, Lord Lisle, became the Earl of Warwick, and Chancellor Wriothesley—who did not vote for the Protectorship—became the Earl of Southampton.

Edward Seymour did not forget his brother Thomas. The younger Seymour was made a member of the Privy Council—an honor Henry VIII had never thought fit to bestow. And in addition to his new responsibilities, Thomas was created Baron Sudeley, with extensive lands in Gloucestershire, and was named Lord Admiral of the Navy, a post previously held by the now exalted John Dudley.

In none of the honors given that day after the king's burial was the name of Henry Grey, Marquis of Dorset, mentioned. He was present with his wife's young half-brother, the Duke of Suffolk, at the investitures. After the arrangements for the coronation became the first order of business for the new Protector and his council, it was agreed that because of his rank and his nearness to the royal family, the Marquis of Dorset would carry the Sceptre in the coronation procession of the Protector's nephew, the new king-to-be Edward VI. After which the new Duke of Somerset, Earl of Warwick and Baron Sudeley rode to Baynards Castle to celebrate at the home of Katherine Parr's brother-in-law Will Herbert. And the little king who had bestowed the honors went gratefully to his bed, to rest alone and silent in the unfamiliar and forbidding Tower.

The Seymour brothers, Edward and Thomas, had come into prominence when their sister Jane married Henry VIII. Neither ever made any secret of their good fortune or their ambition, and over the years, Henry had so rewarded and honored Edward— one of his most valued councillors, advisers and friends—that at forty-seven, the new Protector was wealthy and powerful.

The Protector was a tall man with hollowed cheeks, a long flowing beard, full sensual lips and a discerning and aloof gaze which might discomfit, anger or puzzle the one upon whom it rested. With his dictatorial nature, Edward Seymour had long recognized that he did not have the jocularly easy mien of his younger brother Thomas and, over the years, had sensibly chosen to compensate with a high degree of intelligence, integrity and strength. A curious mixture of idealism and ruthlessness, of ambition and tolerance, he was an excellent soldier and had acquitted himself with distinction in the king's service; many of his honors had come after hazardous expeditions. Seymour's elevation to the Protectorship and his other honors were regarded by the court and the common people, who for the most part admired him, as just reward for long and faithful service.

But not by his brother. For years Thomas Seymour had been one of the most visible—and least rewarded, in his opinion—of King Henry's courtiers. Like his brother he was tall and carried himself with the confidence of one who knows his looks and manner set him apart. As his brother was quiet, unobtrusive and even colorless, Thomas was handsome, arrogant, and garrulously witty, comfortably at home in the company of those who loved the gaming table, abundant drink and the ladies, with whom he was a great favorite. His talent for colorfully unusual and bizarre blasphemy was regarded with great respect by everyone from the lowliest stableboy to the loftiest ambassador. While Edward Seymour's restraint was well known and even admired, Thomas's lack of self-discipline—whether it concerned money, drink or the opposite sex— had long been accepted and had contributed to his failure to rise in court circles. Reckless and shallow, his disposition and temper—so unlike his brother's—had made him many enemies at court.

What he considered years of deprivation and lack of recognition had left the younger Seymour with a biting envy he took little care to hide. He now regarded his appointment to the Privy Council and the Lord Admiralship as long-overdue recognition.

The Privy Council, on the other hand, accepted Seymour's appointment more as a mark of respect for the Protector than of any admiration for his younger brother. Thomas cared nothing for their opinion and made little effort to win their approval by a more sober demeanor or even dependable attendance at the council table. It was the beginning of a rift between the Lord Admiral and the councillors; more important, the continuing of a rift between the brothers.

On the twentieth of February, more than three weeks after his father's death, young Edward Tudor was "crowned King of this realm of England, France and Ireland, within the Church of Westminster, with great honor and solemnity, and a great feast kept that day in Westminster Hall which was richly hanged." It was a lavish proceeding at which Henry Grey carried the Sceptre; the new Protector, the Crown; the young Suffolk, the Orb; and John Dudley, the new Earl of Warwick, carried Edward's train. At the jousts that followed the banquet, the bold Thomas Seymour held his royal nephew's attention by distinguishing himself among all the other participants.

While she was not present at the tournament where Thomas Seymour performed so outstandingly, in the following days Jane Grey often saw the new Lord Admiral at her Dorset Place home. In her year at court she'd seen the younger Seymour brother when he'd returned from various foreign embassies for the king; they were not strangers. But Jane was too young to recognize the incongruity of the presence at Dorset Place of one of the "new men"—that group her father so vociferously disliked—though it caused a stir in court circles. She did not know, though others guessed, that my Lord Dorset and the Lord Admiral shared more than an abiding jealously and resentment of those courtiers who'd reaped such large rewards at the old king's death. Anyone who knew Thomas Seymour well knew him dissatisfied with the honors his loyal brother had given. And the more often they were together, the more the marquis realized they shared a mutual feeling of rejection—which inevitably pointed out to both that they had something in common despite the differences in birth, upbringing and wealth.

In the weeks following Edward's coronation, Thomas Seymour came more often to Dorset Place. More frequently than usual, Mrs. Ellen was ordered to bring Jane to the Great Hall when the family sat for dinner. There the Lord Admiral was particularly attentive to Jane, named for his dead sister, genuinely charmed by the diminutive little figure with the delicate coloring of her cousin Elizabeth. Both children had reddish-auburn hair and the pale skin which, despite all the precautions of nurses and governesses, had freckled. Only Elizabeth's dark eyes bespoke her Boleyn mother.

It was soon apparent to Thomas Seymour that the air of fragility, even delicacy, which charmed so many in Jane, only irritated her mother and father. Seymour realized that part of the disappointment was that Jane should have been a sturdy son and heir instead of the nondescript, silent child her parents saw, useless in most respects, except that her tutors did admit she was almost precociously bright. But since intelligence had never rated strongly with the Greys—or even with Thomas Seymour—it was not highly regarded. Of what use was intelligence in a girl?

However, if they wondered what Seymour saw in their ten-year-old daughter, they were willing to humor the man who was the Protector's brother. Since Jane's return home, the Greys *had* noted she appeared more certain of herself than before she'd been sent away. Jane was now willing to speak up occasionally, respond to a question or statement or even have an opinion, where heretofore she'd been almost silently dumb. If such social graces had come from her year at court, Frances and Henry Grey were grateful. However, whenever they suspected such responses came from an inner desire of the child to assert herself, her statements met with curt dismissal or ridicule—or with the familiar slaps and punches her year away had caused her almost to forget.

While her parents appeared not to notice, it was obvious to Mrs. Ellen that Jane missed the queen, her cousins and that life which seemingly had disappeared with the king's death. Jane heard that the Protector would not permit young Edward to see his stepmother as frequently as he had in the past and she knew how much that would mean to him. It would also be sad for Katherine, who'd adored the little boy and given him the only real home he'd ever known. Edward wasn't as complacent as his sister Mary, who appeared to want only to be left in peace, either at court or in her own home. But neither was he as assertive as his sister Elizabeth, who could be demanding—letting everyone know just what she wanted—and who might sulk or carry on when she was rebuffed. One of Jane Grey's greatest surprises in her year at court was the awareness that it *was* permissible to be different, to be heard and to expect someone to listen. She'd never had the opportunity to test that newfound knowledge; she'd never had to, for the queen had anticipated most of her needs. But her cousins' differing personalities had been an exciting discovery for Jane. Now, just when she'd about gained the courage to try emulating them in some manner—perhaps Mary's generosity and soft kindness and her skillful musical talents, or Elizabeth's deft turn of phrase, that bold approach to her studies where nothing seemed impossible—it was discouraging to be back at Dorset Place, lonely except for Mrs. Ellen and the two sisters with whom she had so little in common.

And then, to her great delight, Jane was told that she might return to Katherine Parr. Only now it would be to the home of the Dowager Queen and the Lord Admiral. For the first time, Jane saw her mother speechless when it was announced that—less than four months after Henry VIII's death—Katherine Parr had secretly wed Thomas Seymour and was living with him at the little manor house at Chelsea.

Jane could not understand why there was such a fuss about the marriage, which her mother called a scandal. At court the Protector and Privy Councillors were in an uproar at Seymour's presumption. Again, Jane wondered why. From her parents' remarks she knew that Mary Tudor, one of Katherine's closest childhood friends, was disappointed in the marriage and had written Katherine a reproving letter. Only Elizabeth, four years older than Jane, was excited and happy that her stepmother had married the man she'd planned to wed before the king had made her his sixth queen.

While she said nothing, Jane was secretly pleased. The queen was a kind and lovely woman and the Lord Admiral a handsome and witty man; why shouldn't they marry? But most important of all, because of the marriage—and because the queen could again provide a home for her—they would be the ones to take her away from Dorset Place once more. If for no other reason than that, Jane was grateful Katherine Parr had married Thomas Seymour.

8

Henry and Frances Grey had discovered a way in which their daughter might serve the family fortune, which was—thanks to the marquis's elaborate improvements at Bradgate and an unwarranted optimism at the gaming tables—seriously diminished. About all the Greys had ever expected of Jane was that, at the proper time, she make an illustrious marriage, which unfortunately could cost them a fortune in the dowry they must provide. Already, Lady Frances was thinking of possible suitors for her daughter. If they'd had a son, another family would have paid handsomely for the privilege of allying themselves with the Greys. Both Henry and Frances were also made constantly aware that the Suffolk inheritance—that of her father, Charles Brandon—was being conspicuously enjoyed by Kate Willoughby Brandon and her two sons. While outwardly they were all friends, the difference in their present wealth and future expectations caused a great irritation in Henry Grey which was continually aggravated by his wife's carping attitude.

It had been a great shock to the marquis when Edward Seymour was named Protector. Seymour's further elevation to a dukedom and the gift of two of the choicest government offices—

each carrying with it either land, servants, castles and manors with small fortunes in perquisites, or subsidies—led Jane Grey's father to brood further at the good fortune of the one who'd become the most powerful man in England. It mattered not that the Privy Council had assented. In Grey's eyes they'd all enriched themselves, leaving not even crumbs for the old aristocracy. And his jealousy became even more spiteful when the Protector's brother married the queen; nothing would now contain the Seymour brothers' acquisitiveness!

Henry Grey's attitude was not intractable, however. When, a few weeks after the marriage, Thomas Seymour sent an emissary named William Harrington to Dorset Place, the marquis listened to what the man had to say. Seymour, Harrington told Jane's father, was interested in her future, and it would be ". . . a goodly thing to happen if Lady Jane were in the keeping of the Lord Admiral." Intrigued, Grey asked what Seymour had in mind.

The plan, according to Harrington, was simple. It was Thomas Seymour's opinion that since he was now Lord Admiral and uncle of the king, he was "like to come to great authority and was most desirous of forming a bond of friendship" with Henry Grey. It would be a wise thing, said Harrington, if the Lady Jane might join the household of the Lord Admiral and the Queen Dowager, who had a great fondness for Jane. During the year she'd lived with the royal family, Jane had endeared herself to everyone. Now that Katherine Parr had wed again, with a new home and husband, it was her dearest wish that Jane come to live with her.

When Henry Grey appeared somewhat puzzled, Harrington urged him to accept. He had, he said, heard Seymour say that Jane was "as handsome a lady as any in England, and that, if the King's Majesty when he came to age, would marry within the realm, it was as likely he would be there as in any other place." Were Jane to live in Seymour's house—as so many children of good families lived in other houses where their futures might be bettered—Thomas Seymour would work most diligently to see her placed in an illustrious marriage. Already Jane had lived in a palace. Would not the home of the Queen Dowager and the Lord Admiral of England be suitable for the marquis's daughter?

Henry Grey's curiosity was aroused. "With whom will he match her?" he asked Seymour's emissary.

"I doubt not," Harrington replied, "but you shall see he will marry her to the king; and fear you not but he will bring it to pass . . . "

Henry Grey, "one of the most credulous of mortals," could scarce believe his good fortune and hurried to consult with his wife. It mattered little to either that the source of such beneficence was the scorned Thomas Seymour. Both Greys agreed that Harrington was right. The Lord Admiral *was* in a position to advance Jane, to help *any* Grey. The fact that many at court disliked him, considered him of questionable morals and temperament mattered little, for Katherine Parr was a woman of undisputed virtue and uncommon kindness. Though her marriage to the bold Seymour had caused a scandal at court, everyone agreed that her husband's somewhat tarnished reputation might soon fade in the light of her respectability and rank. The Admiral had sown his wild oats, apparently, and was now ready to settle into a proper marriage.

The result, a few days later, was a meeting in the Seymour Place gardens between the Lord Admiral and the Marquis of Dorset. The queen was anxious, Thomas said, that little Jane rejoin her household. He himself had nothing but admiration for the child and would welcome her presence. But, Thomas told the marquis, he must be patient. Jane must be allowed to remain with the Queen Dowager, who, he assured Grey, was much in favor of the marriage to Edward. As long as Jane remained in his home, Thomas said, he'd be responsible for her maintenance and care—and for her future. And he was in a position now, he emphasized, to bring about that which would be most desirable. Jane Grey was a most unusual child, he told her uncomprehending father, and alluded once more to a marriage with young Edward, who, he said, "when he comes of age, would marry within the realm."

Slowly, the marquis understood and faced a reality stunning in its possiblities. He and his wife had agreed that if any good might come through their older daughter, they'd be foolish not to accept. The child was a silent enigma, showing little spirit. She had too studious a disposition to be attractive and was overly religious. She hated the sporting life, was too reflective and in all ways would be hard to marry off when the time came. With Jane living with the queen and her husband—a brother of the Protector of England!—what rewards might not come their way? If the Lord Admiral could indeed arrange—even suggest—a marriage between Jane and Edward, their daughter would one day be *queen*! It would mean at least three or four more years of Jane's maintenance—and her unattractive presence—before they could possibly peddle her to the highest bidder in a marriage which, considering all her shortcomings, might be difficult to arrange. It would be foolhardy, they agreed, not to accept Seymour's offer.

And, though they did not discuss it openly, both men were well aware that the first step in the downfall of the Protector had just been taken. How it would happen, whom else it might affect—Katherine Parr, Frances Grey, even Jane Grey—was not thought important. The vital thing was that an agreement between one of the "old aristocracy" and the "new men" had been struck, and if the alliance was incongruous, the end justified the means.

The day Jane arrived at Seymour Place was very different from the first time she'd gone to live in a palace. Again, her new home was not far from Dorset Place. Seymour Place was a large and luxurious dwelling on the Strand which had formerly belonged to the Bishop of Bath. Most of the former Church properties were now owned by nobles of the court, and the Protector, anxious to placate a younger brother, had submitted when Thomas insisted he have the house, one of the choicest episcopal river mansions. It was Thomas Seymour's first home; previously he'd lived in rooms at court or in a small suite of rooms in the City. Now with his brother's rise to power, he could boast of beautiful Seymour Place in London, Sudeley Castle in Gloucestershire, as well as all the manors and residences that belonged to Katherine Parr.

To live in such a house meant one must be properly attended, and when Jane Grey arrived at Seymour Place in that early spring after the king's death, she brought with her Mrs. Ellen, four waiting women and a number of male servants. The new Lord Admiral kept proper estate with his own retainers as well as Katherine Parr's large entourage, many held over from her days as queen. The sudden change did not overwhelm Jane; having lived in a palace, she did not find another crowded household strange.

What was strange was the change in the queen. Previously, Jane had always seen Katherine Parr surrounded by the aura of royalty, the pomp of ceremony. Even on the most leisurely days, when no state visits or official functions were planned, Katherine was a part of that large household with her ever-present ladies-in-waiting nearby, with those household officers and lesser servants, each of whom must be given an audience so that palace routine and the king's comfort might not suffer. Each moment of the royal day was so arranged and scheduled, and had proceeded so effortlessly, it seemed, that a simple, spontaneous visit with the queen, unattended, would have been impossible—even strange and possibly uncomfortable had it occurred. Since much of the same formality existed in her own home, Jane had never found it difficult to accept.

But now everything had changed. The ladies-in-waiting and household officers were still there. The luxury and comfort, which everyone took for granted, could still be enjoyed. But the queen was a changed woman; overnight, it appeared, the handsome, disciplined, regal lady with the soft voice and smile, the kindly and understanding disposition, had become a person Jane had never seen before.

Katherine Parr was now thirty-four years old. Her first two marriages had been arranged by her family to much older men. Henry had been a jaded, ill man, difficult to please, a constant drain on her temper and spirit. Now, released from any obligation except to please herself, the prudent Queen Dowager had done just that. She'd fulfilled her duty to the king and, after all those lost four years, had thrown caution and common sense to the winds and gloried in the doing. She'd married the only man she'd ever truly loved and if there were those who thought less of the prudent queen's haste, Katherine shut her eyes and ears to the criticism, vowing she'd make a happy home for the Lord Admiral and any of the king's children the Privy Council allowed her to have, as well as for Lady Jane Grey, now her husband's legal ward. At the small manor of Chelsea or Seymour Place in London, or any of the queen's manors of Hanworth or Wimbledon, Katherine reveled in her first real love. And for the first time, Jane felt that she herself also might share in the affection that Katherine and Thomas showered on her.

Jane Grey was nearly eleven when she returned to the Queen Dowager's household. She was a solemn child who spoke in low tones, her quiet demeanor lending an almost adult air to one who was barely five feet tall, small-boned, with an almost fragile appearance. Overly sensitive and insecure as she was, any humor that Jane might have possessed had been mercilessly exorcised in her upbringing. Now, sober and dignified, the little figure in the ornate and expensive gowns that her parents considered suitable to her rank moved through the rooms of a new home as different as any she'd ever known.

First, there was the Lord Admiral. It was impossible not to like someone who told stories so outrageous everyone laughed, who broke into song at the slightest provocation, urging everyone to join in. Whether it was a naughty tune he'd learned in Brussels or a hymn sung by the king's choristers during Evensong at Windsor, Thomas sang his own special version, which often brought a blush to the queen's cheek though it only puzzled Jane. At table, where the queen saw to it that her husband's favorite foods were served often and abundantly, Thomas would insist that Jane have another portion or chide her if she'd eaten too little. At home, her mother or father might have pinched or slapped while calling for Mrs. Ellen to come and take such an ignorant and ungrateful child away. Now the admiral merely sighed and announced—as the queen smiled—that until the Lady Jane had finished her meal, everyone would simply have to remain in place, even if it took all night. He would then call for the minstrels to play and lead the queen onto the floor. There, smiling broadly, he'd dip his head each time he whirled by Jane, glancing significantly at her plate. By the time the dance was finished, Jane usually was also. Within days she'd learned to take small portions she could consume easily so that no attention might be called to her. Or, once she'd finished her meal, the Lord Admiral might even ask her to dance!

Even away from home, Thomas was unpredictable. While boating on the river, as he flicked little droplets of water at his wife—despite Katherine's protests that her gowns would be spotted—Jane was shocked when the queen responded with a handful of water showered all over her husband's fine cap. At night, lying in bed, she often heard laughter from their bedchamber; once she saw the two standing in their nightrobes on the terrace in the dark, looking out at the river, Katherine's head on her husband's shoulder, his arm closely about her.

Within weeks of Jane's return to Chelsea, the Privy Council granted permission for the Princess Elizabeth—she and Mary had now regained their titles, since they were in line for the succession—to return to Katherine Parr's care, and there was a joyous return the day the princess' barge arrived at Chelsea with her governess, Catherine Ashley. At fourteen, the king's second daughter was a striking-looking young girl whose coloring and features resembled Jane's. But Elizabeth was now inches taller, with small rounded breasts and hips Jane had never noticed before. She had more jewelry than Jane and, on the long slim fingers of which she was quite vain, proudly wore the rings her stepmother and Mary had given her. Those elegant fingers made Jane aware of her own tiny, almost doll-like hands with their nails bitten to the quick.

But Elizabeth was kind and she was fun. Always in awe of her older half-sister, Mary, she sensed ten-year-old Jane's feelings and, not even needing Katherine Parr's urging, often came to the younger girl's chamber to talk or play the virginals while Jane played the flute. Eagerly, Jane looked forward to the visits. But when Elizabeth complimented her on her musical ability, Jane was uncomfortable; she knew not what to say, even though Mrs. Ellen and the Queen Dowager had always been encouraging about her music. But this was from someone near her own age; this was from *Elizabeth*, who did everything so well, and for that reason it meant more.

Before her estrangement from the Princess Mary due to her early remarriage, Katherine Parr had encouraged the girl to undertake a translation of Erasmus's Latin Paraphrases of the Gospel of St. John, a work Mary had enjoyed seeing published. The Queen Dowager had written her own work *Lamentations of a Sinner* and, intellectually gifted, she encouraged Jane and Elizabeth in their studies; both could now speak and read Latin, French, Spanish, Greek and some Italian. Learning—for young girls particularly—was now so fashionable and desirable, it led a Master of Eton, one Nicholas Udall, to remark, "It was a common thing to see young virgins so nouzled and trained in the study of letters that they willingly set all other pastimes at nought for learning's sake." For the first time, Jane had enjoyable companionship in the classroom. She was challenged to match Elizabeth, which she did easily, and both had the rewards of a shared accomplishment. One result of this, which both Mrs. Ellen and Katherine Parr noticed, was a Jane Grey now more certain of herself. The somber solemnity and sedateness had begun to crumble at last in the face of kindness, humor and the peace of Chelsea.

Many of the court now came to visit the Queen Dowager and Lord Admiral, since the Lord Protector had given a reluctant blessing to the union. Among these were Henry and Frances Grey. They ignored the fact that their daughter had blossomed in her new home, that memory of her rough treatment at their hands was fading. While her mother asked Jane a few questions and then spoke for a long time with Mrs. Ellen before going to greet the Queen Dowager, Henry Grey and Thomas Seymour simply disappeared into the garden or onto the terrace, to talk of their own affairs. From what Jane heard, her parents were concerned about the young king. Apparently Edward was rarely allowed to leave his quarters or the company of his tutor, John Cheke. Visitors were discouraged and had to seek the Protector's permission before an audience might be granted. Jane knew this had distressed the queen, who'd always had easy access to the child before his father's death. Now, even Katherine had to seek the Privy Council's permission to visit her stepson and then Cheke or some household officer was always present to hear what was said. Jane had seen the Queen Dowager weep on her return from one such visit when she told her husband that Edward was so straitly kept, with little chance to exercise, with so much emphasis placed on his studies, he was pale, wan and nervous, uncomfortable even with her. Jane could imagine how difficult it would be for the boy who'd had four years of Katherine's loving care to be suddenly deprived of such attention, his exposure to others so tightly controlled. About the only thing everyone agreed with—except the Catholic Princess Mary, of course—was Edward's religious training, which was continuing apace, with the boy "exhorted to see that God was worshipped, idolatry destroyed, the tyranny of the Bishop of Rome banished, and images removed. . . ." The Mass was still a part of daily worship but the Protector was known to be in favor of its abolishment. When the staunch Catholic Wriothesley, the Lord Chancellor and only dissident to Edward Seymour's assumption of the Protectorship, protested some of the new duke's ecclesiastical reforms, he was quickly relieved of his post and placed under house arrest. It was of particular interest to Henry Grey and Thomas Seymour that the Protector intended further spoliation of church property; it was of greater concern to both just who of the court and the Privy Council would benefit the most.

The magic summer with the Queen Dowager and Lord Admiral continued. Jane was as happy as Elizabeth when a penitent Princess Mary arrived to embrace Katherine and return Thomas Seymour's elaborate bow with a smile. And when Katherine Willoughby Brandon, the Duchess of Suffolk, arrived with her two sons, the trio spent hours on the seawall near the manor house terrace, remembering the days when they'd all been classmates in Katherine of Aragon's classroom, with Juan Luys Vives their formidable tutor. The duchess's two boys, Frances Grey's half-brothers, joined Elizabeth and Jane in their games, lost themselves in the maze, or listened to the tales the Lord Admiral spun while his wife and her companions visited.

And then, just as Jane began to take her contentment for granted and not as something to be marveled at each day, it was all over. The troubled time began in the late fall, when preparations were being made to return to Seymour Place in London. For weeks Jane had heard the early-morning sounds of laughter, doors closing, feminine shrieks and loud cursing coming from Elizabeth's quarters at the end of the hall. Once she saw the Lord Admiral himself, clothed in his nightrobe and slippers, leaving Elizabeth's room, as a red-faced Ashley, her governess, remonstrated with him that the lady-princess was not yet awake and it was unseemly that a gentleman so little dressed should enter a maiden's chambers before she was even out of her bed! Ashley's round face was filled with indignation, her voice outraged. Fearful, Jane had closed her door, wondering what had happened, knowing she'd never have the courage to ask.

The Lord Admiral and Elizabeth also puzzled Jane. Irreverent as always, Thomas would interrupt the girls' breakfast, accost them on their way to chapel, making some remark on Elizabeth's clothing or demeanor. The princess would color and appear flustered, a reaction that had surprised Jane, for usually Elizabeth was more than a match for the Lord Admiral and equal to any situation. Thomas would then make remarks to Elizabeth that Jane did not understand; often her very ignorance seemed as humorous to the others as the remarks themselves. But she'd paid little attention, knowing the Lord Admiral to be unique, unpredictable and a law unto himself. Elizabeth, she thought, could take care of herself.

But something obviously had gone wrong. Jane pieced the story together from what a lady-in-waiting's servant told her. Ashley had gone to the Queen Dowager, protesting that no man should enter a young maiden's chambers in a state of undress, before the girl was even out of bed! There'd been too much horseplay, too much early-morning excitement, and Elizabeth, high-strung and nubile, was no match for Thomas Seymour. Katherine Parr had laughed at Ashley, saying she'd only misconstrued innocent fun. But she knew her husband's high spirits and she'd see to it that the visits ceased. And they had. Then, within days, Thomas Seymour had accosted Elizabeth when he found her alone in a private chamber and, thinking they'd not be interrupted, had attempted to kiss her. At which precise moment Katherine Parr had walked in.

Jane never knew what happened afterward; she was heartbroken when Katherine announced that Elizabeth would be leaving shortly to visit the home of Sir Anthony Denny, an old friend of the royal family, in Cheshunt. Elizabeth, with red-rimmed eyes and bowed head, looked so unlike herself, Jane was almost sick with sadness and her own cowardice in not speaking out to her and offering some solace. Only Ashley, her lips pursed with anger, spoke openly that her charge was suffering from another's careless selfishness. The Princess Elizabeth was not to blame for another's indiscretions, she made certain everyone realized, and Jane was relieved to see that Katherine appeared to agree. When Elizabeth left, the Queen Dowager hugged the princess and spoke to her kindly; both were in tears as they said good-bye on the riverbank before Elizabeth boarded the waiting barge.

Within days, as Jane moped about a classroom no longer exciting, Mrs. Ellen said they would soon be leaving Chelsea. Katherine Parr was to have a baby and she wanted it born as far from London as possible. Jane had guessed—and Mrs. Ellen's tone bore out her suspicion—that the Queen Dowager and the Lord Admiral's happiness had been greatly marred by the incident involving the Princess Elizabeth. Katherine Parr also argued with her husband that he should accept that his brother was now the Protector who'd given him generous gifts. One was Sudeley Castle in Gloucestershire, where Katherine Parr said she'd like her baby to be born. There, away from the sight of his brother's affluence and power, Katherine hoped the joys of fatherhood would make her husband relinquish the festering envy of his brother's success.

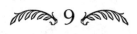

9

The site of Sudeley Castle was ancient. If, on that day the Lord
Admiral brought his family and ward to Sudeley, the castle itself
was only a hundred years old, it looked older. The sun shone on
the warmly mellowed building of Cotswold stone with its battle-
mented ramparts and peaked columns from which the Seymour
colors flew. Sudeley rose from the Gloucestershire countryside with
that timeless essence belonging to a site that had known the Romans. There was even a Roman burial site on the place, Thomas
told an awed Jane; the estate workers often churned up bits of
weapons, household articles or decaying leather sandals. A thousand years later Ethelred the Unready had built a manor house on
the site, and in the middle of the twelfth century a Crusader, Ralph
de Sudeleye, whose family had served King Edward III and the
Black Prince, built his castle on land that the Romans and Saxons
had occupied. Somewhere on the estate, Thomas said, there was
even a huge tithe barn more than six hundred years old that had
once belonged to the abbey in nearby Winchcombe when the little
market town had been the capital of the ancient kingdom of
Mercia.

Even though it was not as grand as Bradgate, upon which her

father had spent so much money, Jane Grey loved Sudeley on sight. And it was obvious the Queen Dowager did also. There were grand views in almost any direction—of great black forests sweeping up against the clear blue sky, or cleared, open land upon which large herds of deer might be seen browsing in the early morning. A small army of gardeners kept the high ornamental yew hedges neatly clipped and the geometrically perfect gardens with their lush foliage—all aided by the milder Gloucestershire climate—in a constant state of perfection. Both Jane Grey and Katherine Parr were Northern-born; after years of bracing Northern air, then the crowded, ofttimes odorous London streets or the thick roiling fog on a Chelsea riverbank, Sudeley appeared as a welcoming and comfortable refuge.

And it was refuge that Katherine Parr sought. Not only for herself and the child she would have—and, of course, for Jane Grey—but mostly for her husband. Only as they'd prepared to leave London had Katherine learned the full extent of Thomas Seymour's poor relationship with his brother and his nephew, little King Edward. It had caused the Queen Dowager much heartbreak and shame that, during the first year of marriage, she'd let herself be so mercilessly duped by the man whom—in spite of his all too apparent shortcomings—she still loved as she'd never loved anyone else in her thirty-five years.

The scene with Elizabeth had been the first instance of reality intruding upon the fantasy Katherine had woven about her marriage. The young princess had gone, heartbroken and ashamed, and the Queen Dowager wrote to her often; she was determined that Elizabeth not feel responsible for what had happened. Elizabeth was profoundly grateful, telling her stepmother she gave thanks "for the manifold kindness received at your Highness' hands at my departure. . . ." Katherine, wise in the ways of the court, knew there might be talk; servants loved to boast of their supposed knowledge of the great they served and she'd warned Elizabeth of that possibility. Again, the practical Elizabeth was touched, telling Katherine she "weighed it more deep when you said you would warn me of all evils that you should hear of me. . . . But what more may I say than 'Thank God for providing such good friends to me . . . !'"

But the situation with the Protector—as well as the Protector's wife, Anne Stanhope, the Duchess of Somerset, and especially Thomas's maneuverings with young Edward—tore at Katherine's heart and conscience.

When Henry VIII had died, he'd left his queen a dower of £7,000 a year, several valuable pieces of property, including the manor house at Chelsea, and all her jewels. In the secrecy prevailing before the king died, Katherine had been sent to Chelsea, leaving her jewels behind at the palace. When, later, she'd requested they be sent to her, the Protector maintained they were Crown property, and within several weeks his wife was seen wearing them.

A heated battle for the jewels followed. Arguments and letters, even meetings with the Protector—nothing resulted in the gems' return. After receiving one letter, an indignant Katherine wrote from Chelsea to her husband still at court. "My lord, your brother," she noted, "hath this afternoon made me a little warm. It was fortunate we were so much distant, for I suppose else I should have bitten him! What cause have they to fear—having such a wife!" To which a vexed and frustrated Thomas replied, "My brother is wondrous hot in helping every man to his right, save me. He maketh a great matter to let me have the queen's jewels. . . ." But, Thomas said, the Protector believed the gems belonged to the Crown, "and all under pretence that he would not the king should lose so much—as if it were a loss to the king to let me have mine own!" But the Protector "had a wife prouder than he was and she ruled him so completely that he did whatever she wished and, finding herself in such great state, became more presumptuous than Lucifer." It was the "unquiet vanity of a mannish or rather a devilish woman . . ." that caused the battle between the two brothers to extend also to their wives. And there were many about the Seymours eager to feed the fire of envy in one while stoking the simmering suspicions of the other. The Queen Dowager and the young king were in the middle.

In addition to a difficult pregnancy, Katherine worried also about her stepson. The boy, whom she'd had difficulty in seeing before she left London for Sudeley, had told Jane Grey's father that "my Uncle of Somerset dealeth very hardly with me, and keepeth me so straight that I cannot have money at my will." The marquis had quickly relayed the information to Thomas Seymour. It was obvious to many that the Protector had, indeed, kept the boy as isolated and restrained as possible. John Cheke, his faithful tutor, was rarely from his side. Edward's only other companion was Barnaby Fitzpatrick, the son of an Irish lord, sent to the English court to be brought up with the king and those sons of the nobility who often attended his classes. When the school day ended, so did the companionship and then Edward must plod through hours of schoolwork and religious study. Any memory of the last four years when he'd enjoyed the loving interest of Katherine Parr and a real home, as well as the company of his half-sisters, began to fade; he was still only eleven years old. While Jane Grey was now sharing in that affectionate and caring home life, Edward's seemed to have disappeared in the welter of opportunists who surrounded him daily—Cheke was the one exception—all looking for whatever it was in his power to give. And all the while he, the king, was deprived of any consultation by the Protector, who rarely came to see him. He was even deprived of the ordinary pocket money that one in his position might expect to have, to jingle in his breeches and give to an itinerant beggar on the street or to the jugglers and mummers who came to the court infrequently to entertain him. Instead, he must watch empty-handed and in hot embarrassment as his almoner gave the group the few coins he wished with all his heart *he* could give. At times, they even looked at him with something like pity.

It was this discontent that Thomas Seymour quickly recognized and seized upon. "Ye are but even a very beggarly king now. Ye have not enough to play dice or to give to your servants . . ." he told the humiliated child. It was easy on subsequent occasions to chide Edward that not only was he a poor king with no coins in his pocket, he was also a very bashful and backward lad who told no one his thoughts, never rendered an opinion and did not, in any way, "bear rule as did other kings." The Lord Admiral let no opportunity slide where he might impress upon Edward that no one—not even the Queen Dowager or his half-sisters, the princesses—could come easily to his presence. And all the while, laws were being made for the realm of which he, the king, knew nothing. Thomas Seymour constantly impressed upon the child the fact that the Protector had taken the reins of power and strength and was ruling in Edward's name while paying little attention to Edward himself.

It had not taken long—steady gifts of money had helped—to win the young king's dependence. The Lord Admiral told Thomas Fowler, for whom he'd secured a place as an attendant in the King's Bedchamber, "If His Highness lacks any money, send to me for it—and nobody else." By assuring Fowler that the same offer also extended to him, he'd found an assured accomplice in his desire to win his nephew's loyalty.

But Edward was never comfortable with Thomas Seymour. If he disliked the aloof and grasping Protector and his overbearing wife, neither was he at ease with the Lord Admiral. Undoubtedly, he feared both. One signed documents in his name and had now left to lead an army into Scotland against the wishes of other Privy Councillors. The other gave him money, telling him that since in only a few years he would be king in fact as well as name, he must "take it upon yourself to rule." But how could he do that, a boy of eleven?

There were others about Edward who took sides as well. Both the Lord Admiral and the Protector had their followers, eager to stir up any resentment or suspicion in the boy—even going so far as to remind him of those two other little princes in the Tower who'd disappeared less than a hundred years ago and all because an uncle, also a *Protector*, had wanted to be king.

One of those firmly committed to undermining Edward Seymour's power—while outwardly compliant with his policies—was Jane Grey's father, the Marquis of Dorset. Henry Grey came to Sudeley while the Protector and the English army were in Scotland to discuss the alliance of his daughter and Edward Tudor. Grey was also eager to discern how he might gain a more personal popularity with those of lower rank who might be dissatisfied with the Protector. Many on the Privy Council were, but what of the common people who appeared to have a genuine admiration for Edward Seymour? How could he and other nobles combat such feeling?

Shrewdly, the Lord Admiral advised the marquis not to "trust too much to the gentlemen, for they have something to lose." Instead, the marquis should do as Seymour did. He was to make friends with the lower classes—yeomen and merchants—because they could "persuade the multitude." Presents of venison and wine would help to win their loyalty and trust, he said. Grey was soothed by the Lord Admiral's confidence, which appeared boundless. He was convinced that if anyone could bring the marriage of his daughter and the boy-king to a successful conclusion—and perhaps oust the Protector at the same time—it was Thomas Seymour. As a member of the Privy Council, which Grey was not, the Lord Admiral would be in a position to promote the marriage when the proper time came.

No one had told Jane, happy with her new life at Sudeley, of the plans in which she figured so prominently. Each day, she awoke to sounds of estate servants and laborers as they worked in gardens, stables and mews, as stewards rushed to greet new arrivals or wished Godspeed to departing guests clattering noisily about the courtyard. Soon, after prayers and the morning meal, which she took in her chamber with Mrs. Ellen and the other attendants, Jane went to the classroom where her tutor waited. She was the only student, but it mattered not. Next to her religious studies, Jane loved the hours spent with the ancient Latin and Greek authors; even the lore of astronomy was tinged with the view of a celestial Heaven, which her religion promised for those of virtuous intent and pure spirit. Whatever knowledge she had of her family was usually brought by visitors from the court. If Jane ever wondered about her sisters, the difference in her life and theirs could only have made her thankful prayers for her deliverance to Sudeley all the more intense.

Engrossed in her studies, Jane often missed the worried expression on the Queen Dowager's face. Katherine was now far advanced in her pregnancy. She missed Thomas, who, once his family was safely ensconced at Sudeley, had returned to London to attend to his admiralty duties. Katherine never told anyone—not even her close friend Kate Brandon, the young Duchess of Suffolk— her fear that Thomas's impulsive and thoughtless behavior might jeopardize his family, and Jane Grey as well. Instead, she attempted to shake off her forebodings and give her young ward the security she'd wish for any child of her own.

It would not have helped Katherine's peace of mind had she known that while riding to the opening of Parliament, Thomas had told Lord Clinton of his dissatisfaction with his brother, who'd refused to return Katherine's jewels or share the great power he'd taken unto himself. "If I be thus used," Thomas told Clinton angrily, "they speak of a black Parliament . . . by God's precious soul, I will make the blackest Parliament that ever was in England!"

Clinton, a friend of Edward Seymour's, warned Thomas, "If you speak such words, you shall lose my lord [the Protector] and undo yourself!" But Thomas would not be brooked and had shouted angrily, "I would you should know, by God's precious soul, I may better live without him than he without me! And whosoever shall go about to speak evil of the Queen, I will take my fist—from the first ears to the last!" The fact that no one had spoken evilly of the Queen Dowager, who was genuinely loved and whose reputation had survived even her early remarriage, was lost on Thomas Seymour, anxious to make issue of anything that might discredit his brother.

But there had been too many such outbursts. Word of such haranguings—as well as the scandalous rompings with the Princess Elizabeth at Chelsea—finally reached Edward Seymour's ears. His wife, Anne Stanhope, pleaded with the Protector to chastise his petulant younger brother, whose one purpose in life seemed to be to undermine the older one's authority. Furious at the rumors flying about London, she cautioned her husband: "I tell you that if your brother does not die, he will be *your* death."

At last, harassed by his wife and encouraged by those councillors who disliked his implacable brother, feared his influence on the young king and the careless, slanderous remarks on the Protector's policies, Edward Seymour ordered Thomas to appear before the Privy Council to answer their charges.

When informed of the situation, Henry Grey, Jane's father, was anxious and fearful, for any action against the Lord Admiral might reflect on *him*. Hadn't he put his eldest daughter in Seymour's home? Weren't he and his wife on good terms with the Lord Admiral? Not for any great liking, to be sure, but because of Thomas's marriage to Katherine Parr and his relationship to the Protector? Hadn't he encouraged Thomas's ambitious plans for Jane's future, and since those plans might include a marriage with the young king, was not such action treasonous, since no alliance for young Edward Tudor could be formed without the entire Privy Council's approval? It was a genuinely alarming moment for the marquis, who wondered if all the plans he and the Lord Admiral had discussed would be his undoing. Even if the Privy Council was lenient, the confrontation might discourage Seymour from pursuing Jane's marriage more aggressively.

But Grey need not have worried. To the disgust of those councillors who genuinely deplored Thomas's behavior and feared his intentions, the mild-tempered Edward Seymour found blood thicker and more meaningful than suspicion. When Thomas, coolly confident, appeared before his fellow councillors, he swore he'd only been misunderstood. There were always those talebearers, envious and cruel, he said, eager to spoil any hope for his future success or happiness. Everything he did was honorable and justifiable and if they, the councillors, had heard anything else, it was nought but gossip. Thomas was magnificent in his insolence as he dared the Protector and Privy Council to name names, dates, and any infraction of behavior that could be considered treasonous. Since they could not—for even they did not know the depth of the Lord Admiral's influence with young Edward, and since their respect for the Queen Dowager's common sense prohibited any belief in Seymour's improper conduct with the Princess Elizabeth—Thomas was dismissed. His great oaths and arrogance had had just the proper effect; now he appealed to his brother's sympathy for his position. He was the Protector's nearest kin, uncle of the king, had married the Queen Dowager, and one of the most noble children in the realm lived in his home under her care. And he was about to become a father. How could he provide an estate proper for one of his rank, who carried his responsibilities? He must have more money and more influence, he told Edward Seymour.

It had all had the proper effect, and when an unchastened and unrepentent Lord Admiral accepted the warm welcome Katherine and Jane gave him upon his return to Sudeley, he could repeat —with much satisfaction—that all his wife's fears had been ungrounded and he had been reconciled with his brother. The Protector had wrung his hand, wished him well and embellished his affection with additional grants of land worth £800 a year. Nothing was said of his conduct with Edward and Elizabeth or his intentions for Lady Jane Grey.

* * *

Thomas returned to Sudeley in time for his daughter's birth on August 30, 1548. At first everything seemed to go well. The baby, whom Katherine named for her dear friend the Princess Mary, was healthy and if her husband was bitterly disappointed at not having a son, little Mary Seymour—the child for which she'd waited so long—made the Queen Dowager radiantly happy.

On the day after the birth, Jane Grey was brought by Mrs. Ellen to Katherine's chamber and, after curtseying solemnly, ran to the pale figure in the bed to receive Katherine's kiss on her forehead. Jane did not linger, for Mrs. Ellen could see that the new mother tired easily. Better to return to her studies and let the Queen Dowager rest, she told a concerned Jane. Already Mary Seymour had been placed in a wet nurse's care, and already Thomas was preparing to return to London, where—remembrance of his fellow councillors' bitter words in his mind—he'd resolved to pay closer attention to his admiralty duties.

Then, between two and three in the morning of September 6, 1548, a day before Princess Elizabeth's fifteenth birthday, all of Thomas Seymour's fine intentions and Jane Grey's innocent assumption that after Katherine's baby was born, her life would resume its pleasant routine, ended. After falling into a light slumber, the thirty-six-year-old Katherine Parr—delirious now and consumed by childbed fever—died, leaving everything she possessed to her husband. Amid the sobbing and laments of the queen's ladies, Jane sat stunned and tearless as Mrs. Ellen gently told her what had happened. Jane had never thought the Queen Dowager might die. The baby had been born rosy and healthy, and everyone had admired her. Jane had watched during the last five days as Lady Tyrwhitt had combed Katherine Parr's long tresses and tidied her chamber. She'd heard the letters of congratulation that couriers brought to Sudeley as soon as Mary Seymour's birth had become known; the Queen Dowager had read them with sparkling eyes, her happiness evident to all. Even one from the Protector—". . . it would have been both to us, and (we suppose) also to you, a more joy and comfort if it had, this the first-born, been a son . . ."—had not diminished Katherine's elation.

Instead, suddenly, Jane was being fitted with somber black clothing. Mrs. Ellen said she was to be Chief Mourner—that person who followed the casket and held the candle aloft in front of her—during the service which would be held in Sudeley Chapel. The thought of walking that long chapel aisle with everyone's eyes upon her, of holding the lighted candle in trembling hands while, as Mrs. Ellen stressed, not letting the wax drip on her black gloves or skirt, terrified young Jane. As Sudeley filled with those close neighbors who'd loved Katherine Parr, a stunned Thomas Seymour—embracing the tradition that nonattendance at a spouse's funeral was not unseemly—rode off to London.

Two days later, a long procession wound through Sudeley Castle's courtyard. "First, two conductors in black, with black staves; then gentlemen and esquires, then knights, then officers of the household, with their white staves; then the gentlemen ushers; then Somerset herald, in the tabard coat; then the corpse, borne by six gentlemen in black gowns, with their hoods on their heads, the eleven staff torches, borne on each side by yeomen around the corpse, and at each corner, a knight for assistance, with their hoods on their heads; then the Lady Jane . . ."

There was, thankfully, no wind, and the candle flame in Jane Grey's hand was steadier than the hand itself. Mrs. Ellen had impressed upon her charge the decorum that was expected; it was to be her last gesture of love and respect for Katherine Parr. Solemnly the little girl had nodded, put on the heavy black clothing which only made her freckled skin more prominent and emphasized the daintily tiny figure. When the candle was placed in her hand she grasped it strongly and, with her eyes on the covered casket immediately ahead, never wavered.

At last the chapel, hung with black cloth, its seats and rails covered in black, was reached and Jane was relieved of her responsibility. "When the corpse was set within the rails, and the mourners placed, the whole choir began and sung certain psalms in English, and read three lessons; and after the third lesson, the mourners, according to their degrees and that which is accustomed, offered into the alms-box. . . ."

Jane sat with Mrs. Ellen, who cried softly as Dr. Coverdale, the Queen Dowager's almoner, began his sermon. As translator of the first Bible to be printed in English and mindful of Katherine Parr's interest—an interest that matched his own—in the new religion,

Miles Coverdale pointedly remarked to the mourners that "they should none there think, say, or spread abroad that the offering which was there done, was done anything to benefit the dead, but for the poor only; and also the lights, which were carried and stood about the corpse, were for the honor of the person, and for none other intent nor purpose. . . ."

As Dr. Coverdale proceeded with the sermon, Jane tried to concentrate. When anyone discussed God or Jesus Christ, the Passion or His teachings, she was usually alert and receptive. But the sunlight streaming through the stained-glass windows, colorfully disfiguring the hard stone floor and anything else it touched, distracted her. Her mind would not quiet itself and she sat, eyes on the casket, the minister's words hovering on her consciousness, aware something precious in her life had ended and that it would never again be the same.

At the sermon's end, the body of the Queen Dowager was lowered into a crypt near the chancel while the choir sang a loud *Te Deum.* As the mourners filed back to the castle to dine before their departure, Jane was happy to take Mrs. Ellen's hand and let herself be led back to her chamber, where the governess helped her remove the heavy, unfamiliar black clothing. She heard Jane's prayers and embraced her tightly before leaving her alone.

And then, silent and hot, the tears came. Jane had held them back as long as possible; she'd honored the truest and kindest friend she'd ever had in the ceremony just ended. Now she cried not for Katherine Parr, safe at last in His care, nor for little Mary Seymour, asleep and unknowing of what her birth had cost. She cried not for the Lord Admiral, who, shaken and distraught as she'd never before seen him, was even now in London receiving the solace of friends and family.

Muffling her sobs, yet relieved at being able to vent the emotion she'd restrained all day, Jane Grey cried for herself—and for the bright, happy future she'd anticipated which might now be lost forever.

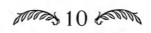

10

While Jane Grey mourned her lost friend and patron, Thomas Seymour remained at the little manor of Hanworth in Middlesex, one of Katherine Parr's legacies from King Henry. In London, the populace had filled the City churches to say prayers for the dead Queen Dowager. In a court chapel, Edward attended services for the stepmother he hadn't seen in almost a year, while in many nobles' private chapels, friends of the Parr family consoled one another on Katherine's loss. At Bradgate, though Frances and Henry Grey wondered what effect her death might have on their daughter's future, they sent no message to solace or comfort Jane.

Once the impact of his wife's death, so shocking after her apparent early recovery from childbirth had subsided, an anxious Thomas Seymour reviewed his position. He was astute enough to realize that with Katherine's death, he'd lost an immeasurable amount of prestige and protection. Katherine had been so revered, with numerous powerful connections at court through her own family as well as the royal stepchildren, that much of that luster had enveloped her husband. Thomas was perceptive enough—when he thought of it at all—to accept that many of his fellow councillors and other court nobles hated him; he'd seen their expressions when, only a few short months ago, he'd confronted them and flung their charges in their faces. Most of them had been his wife's friends and supporters; some were connected with the Parr family through intermarriage. Now that she was gone, they'd never be as tolerant again.

In the few days after Katherine's death, desolate at what he saw as the end of a privileged life and with little real influence of his own, Thomas wrote to Henry Grey advising that someone be sent to Sudeley to return Jane to her parents. It had been a bitter moment, symbolizing the loss of the power and prestige that had come with marrying a queen, the wardship of as noble a girl as Jane Grey and the hopes of her marriage with his nephew the king. While in London, he'd heard startling rumors that his sister-in-law, the Protector's wife, wished her own daughter, Lady Jane Seymour, to marry Edward, while her son, Lord Hertford, would wed Jane Grey. Anne Stanhope's ambitions were as strong as Thomas's, and if only one marriage took place, it spelled the end of his own ambitious schemes.

By the end of that first week after Katherine Parr's funeral, however, Thomas began to feel that something might be retrieved from the tragedy. On September 17 he wrote to Henry Grey:

> My last letters, written at a time when, partly with the queen's highness' death, I was so amazed that I had small regard either to myself or to my doings, and partly then thinking that my great loss must presently have constrained me to have broken up and dissolved my whole house, I offered unto your lordship to send my Lady Jane unto you. . . . Now, I find, indeed, that with God's help, I shall right well be able to continue my household together, without diminishing any great part thereof. . . .

Thomas said he meant to keep not only the gentlewomen and maids that had waited upon Katherine Parr, but also the hundred and twenty "gentlemen and yeomen" that had served the household and the Sudeley estate. And in addition, to act as chaperone for Jane Grey, he meant to send to Wiltshire for "my lady mother [who] shall and will, I doubt not, be as dear unto her [Lady Jane] as though she were her own daughter." Thomas did not think the Greys were any more anxious to have Jane returned to them than he was to lose her. But he underestimated Henry Grey's shrewdness. The marquis knew, as did the admiral, the high stakes for which he was playing.

Despite his rank, Henry Grey had had few opportunities where he alone could control, manipulate or coerce others. His wife managed him, his estates and his life; at court he was tolerated because of his rank. But now he was in a position to display initiative and cunning. He guessed what the collapse of Thomas's plans for Jane Grey meant to the Lord Admiral. Even to maintain Sudeley as before Katherine's death would not be easy. Despite the Queen Dowager's bequests, it would be many months before Thomas would enjoy her estates and money. Having Jane in his control, legally as well as physically, was paramount to his plans, for he alone could—as a Privy Councillor and uncle of the king and brother of the Protector—work at the right time for her marriage with Edward. Therefore, in a delaying gesture meant to discomfit, Grey did not immediately agree with Thomas's request for Jane to remain at Sudeley. He wrote the Lord Admiral:

> My most hearty commendations unto your good lordship. Whereas it hath pleased you, by your most gentle letter, to offer me the abode of my daughter at your lordship's house . . . nevertheless, considering the state of my daughter and her tender years, wherein she shall hardly rule herself (as yet) without a guide, lest she should, for the want of a bridle, take too much to head, and conceive such an opinion of herself that all such good behaviour as she heretofore hath learned by the queen's and your most wholesome instructions, should either altogether be quenched in her, or, at the least, much diminished, I shall . . . require your lordship to commit her to the guidance of her mother, by whom, for the fear and duty she oweth her, she shall be more easily framed and ruled towards virtue. . . .

After reiterating that "the oversight [i.e., superintendence] of my wife shall be in this respect most necessary," Henry Grey then alluded to the marriage with Edward. He did not intend, he wrote, to withdraw from the alliance and he promised Thomas, "God

willing, to use your discreet advice and consent in that behalf. . . ."
The letter continued:

> Only, I seek in these, her young years . . . either to make or
> mar (as the common saying is) the addressing of her mind to
> humility, soberness and obedience. Wherefore, looking on that
> fatherly affection which you bear her, my trust is that (you)
> will be content to charge her mother (the Lady Frances) with
> her, whose waking eye, respecting her demeanour shall be . . .
> as a father would wish. . . .

The letter, discouraging to Thomas, who'd already charged his
household officers to retain as many of Katherine Parr's entourage
as wished to stay and invited his mother to become Jane's companion and chaperone, left him with no recourse other than to
comply. A courier was sent to return the Lady Jane to Bradgate
at once. And with her leaving, the bereaved Lord Admiral saw
the end of his most aspiring dream. Now, most likely, the Protector's daughter would marry Edward, and Jane would become the
bride of the Protector's son. In all the maneuverings, there would
be little thought—or reward—for Thomas Seymour. It was one
more thorny dart in the shield of the Lord Admiral's pride. Even
his famed oaths and black temper held little solace as Thomas saw
the plans he'd had for his nephew and ward wrecked in the aftermath of Queen Katherine's death.

When the London courier brought word to Sudeley that she must
return to her parents' home and care, Jane was not surprised. Why
would the Lord Admiral wish her to remain? He now had his own
child, little Mary Seymour, to think of. And with no wife to su-
pervise his household, it was possible he might even stay in London permanently to be nearer the court, which the Queen Dowager
had always said he preferred. Why would anyone as boisterously
alive and ambitious as Thomas Seymour want to live in the country and why would he want to be bothered with an eleven-year-
old girl?

But memories of Chelsea and Seymour Place and the absence of
the loving companionship of Katherine Parr made leaving difficult
for Jane. She could not have put it into words, but her feeling was

apparent to Mrs. Ellen and the Queen Dowager's attendants. Jane had *really* left home almost two years before when she'd gone to live with the king and queen in a palace. She remembered her joy and relief when at last she'd been sent to live with Katherine and her new husband. She was at an age when youthful memory fades easily—but she'd forgotten nothing of what life was like in the cheerless Grey home. The one bright spot was that her sisters, too, were now older; she'd have to make their acquaintance all over again. Perhaps they might even be good companions, as she and Elizabeth had been before all the trouble occurred and Elizabeth was sent away.

Jane's return to Bradgate, however, was accompanied by little notice from her parents. There were no cries of welcome, no tight hugs and long talks such as she'd had with Katherine Parr when the queen had returned to Chelsea from even a few days at court. There was no Lord Admiral with his loud speech and great oaths, the jokes and games he loved, the singing in the evening after a meal at which everyone talked, even while they ate. There'd been formality in the Queen Dowager's household, but it had been tempered with common sense; ritual was observed because it was right and proper and expected. After that, one enjoyed the moment and each other.

But not at Bradgate. Her parents had stiffly greeted her, and after curtseying briefly to both, Jane was relieved to follow Mrs. Ellen to the old nursery, where her sisters waited. As she embraced each one, calling them by name, they stared at her, eyes bright, and smiling tremulously, but mute. Eight-year-old Katherine was fair-haired and beautiful, with Jane's porcelain skin, though unmarred by freckles. She was obviously as delighted to see Mrs. Ellen as she was to see her older sister. Three-year-old Mary, standing nearby, was dark-skinned, with deep chestnut hair curling about her face. She was very tiny, resembling an ill-formed doll, and now, Jane noticed, there was a pronounced hump on her back. She appeared withdrawn and uncertain until Mrs. Tylney, her governess, pushed her toward Jane, who kissed her on the cheek. Neither little girl spoke easily and both appeared strained; it was a look Jane recognized and remembered.

In the following days Jane saw little of her parents, whose life still revolved about hunting and entertaining their Leicester neighbors or visitors from court. When she did see them—usually at mealtime—they asked questions about her life at Sudeley, about the Queen Dowager's last days, even about Elizabeth. Jane was surprised, for they'd never before shown any interest in her or her opinions. She answered as best she could, often including her own observations and opinions which Katherine Parr and Thomas Seymour had urged her to do. Unconsciously she adopted the same *persona* at Bradgate she'd become accustomed to at Chelsea and Sudeley, never noticing her parents' obvious disapproval. Chattering on one day about a pleasant occasion with the Queen Dowager and Lord Admiral, she was shocked when, suddenly and unexpectedly, her mother silenced her with a swift blow to the side of her head. Tears of outrage as much as pain rose in Jane's eyes as she left the room, not even waiting for her parents' dismissal, something she'd never have done even a year ago. Then she'd have sat mute, holding back the tears, waiting for another blow or pinch and praying she'd be let go.

It had taken only that one occasion to impress upon Jane that she had indeed returned home and this time probably for good. This time there was no kind fairy in the person of a queen to rescue her. She must remember to watch her words and actions, to be alert always for any infraction of her parents' unspoken rules, which must guide her everyday behavior. She was back with her mother, father and sisters, and this time, undoubtedly, she'd stay until she married.

Thomas Seymour, however, had not given up. As the days passed and he dwelt on the enormity of his loss—especially the prestigious influence that had disappeared with Katherine Parr's death—he wrote Henry Grey once more. He insisted Jane be returned to him and hinted that unless he had her in his household, the marriage with Edward might never come to pass. Thomas had returned to London and was determined that his nephew, to whom he still sent pocket money, would agree that the Protector had overstepped the bounds of his authority—wasn't the war in Scotland a good example?—and was unfit to serve. He spent his days talking with courtiers and noblemen and those on the Privy Council whom he knew to be dissatisfied, especially with the war in Scotland. Though the Protector had been victorious, it had cost England an alliance with their northern neighbor through the marriage of Edward and the little Queen of Scots. Thomas enlisted the help of the master of the Royal Mint at Bristol, Sir William Shering-ton, a rank opportunist avid to line his pockets—and those of the Lord Admiral as well—by debasing the coinage. With the elimi-nation of precious metals and the substitution of worthless alloys, within a short time more than £4,000 was accumulated. Even the Royal Navy—of which he was the admiral—fell prey to Sey-mour's greed. When pirates operating in the Channel and along the coast of Devon and Cornwall were apprehended by the navy, their goods were appropriated and the offenders set free to plun-der again. The stolen property was kept in the Scilly Isles, and eventually Sherington amassed arms and ammunition in Holt Cas-tle, a veritable fortress, which the Lord Admiral would use when the time came to wrest the government from Edward Seymour's capable hands.

Many of these schemes had been in progress before Katherine Parr's death; all were unknown to her. Several Privy Councillors had been suspicious when Thomas stood before them; but with no proof—and his older brother's protection—they knew their accu-sations were worthless. In the last several months, however, Thomas had become wealthier than he'd ever dreamed—and he still had Katherine Parr's legacies to enjoy. The one person—the one most important to his scheme—with whom he was less successful was his nephew the king. The second most important was Lady Jane Grey.

If he was to effect a marriage between the two children—and Thomas never doubted but that he would—he must have Jane in his possession. Otherwise, the Greys might accept the Protector's proposal that she marry his fourteen-year-old son, Edward, the Earl of Hertford, or his daughter Jane Seymour might be affianced to King Edward. Haste was imperative and Thomas impressed upon Henry Grey that letters were not enough; they must see each other and soon.

The marquis and his wife soon arrived at their London home and on September 23, a little over two weeks after Katherine Parr's death, Thomas and Henry met in the garden of Dorset Place to talk of Jane's future. Sir William Sherington accompanied Thomas, and there the marquis learned the full extent of the piracy, Edward's reliance on the Lord Admiral, and the successful maneuverings with the coinage of the realm. Such revelations obviously implied Grey might share in future profits. Thomas recounted his conversations with those few nobles who'd ingratiated themselves with him, turning from the Protector's stern policies and his wife, the duchess's arrogant pretensions. He impressed Grey strongly that Jane must be returned to his care. "If I may *once* get the king at liberty," he promised, "I dare warrant you that his majesty shall marry no other but Jane." He neglected to tell the marquis that of late his access to Edward had been hampered, either by Cheke or the boy himself. Thomas, as usual, laid such restrictions to the Protector.

Grey was torn. The riches of the royal treasury, the implied agreement of others at court who might gain the great rewards that, by delaying, he might himself lose—and the fact that his daughter had a good chance of becoming queen—all dazzled him. Thomas Seymour was convincing and firmly committed to the marriage he alone could bring about.

But Henry Grey was, for all his vacillation, a practical man. And he was deeply in debt. Something more definite than a promise should accompany Jane's delivery. A wardship was customary and practicable and when he broached it to Thomas, there was no hesitancy. He named a sum, a generous one, and Thomas accepted, though it was more than most wardships brought. The two men shook hands and on that late fall afternoon of 1548 in the Dorset Place gardens, Lady Jane Grey was sold to Sir Thomas Seymour for the sum of £2,000 with an immediate payment of £500 on account.

Seymour declined any receipt for the money, saying, "The Lady Jane herself is a pledge for it."

A week later, Thomas received a letter from Bradgate:

To the Right Honorable and my singular good lord, the Lord-Admiral, give these.

My duty to your lordship, in most humble wise remembered, with no less thanks for the gentle letters which I received from you. Thinking myself so much bound to your lordship for your great goodness towards me from time to time, that I cannot by any means be able to recompense the least part thereof, I purposed to write a few rude lines unto your lordship, rather as a token to show how much worthier I think your lordship's goodness, than to give worthy thanks for the same; and these my letters shall be to testify unto you that, like as you have become towards me a loving and kind father, so I shall be always most ready to obey your godly monitions and good instructions, as becometh one upon whom you have heaped so many benefits. And thus fearing I should trouble your lordship too much, I most humbly take my leave of your good lordship.

Your humble servant during my life,

Jane Grey

Enclosed with Jane's letter was one from her mother. Lady Frances, overjoyed that at last the marriage between Jane and Edward might come to pass, wrote thanking Thomas for "your approved goodwill, which you bear unto my daughter Jane, for the which I think myself most bounden to you, for that you are so desirous . . . to have her continue with you."

Jane was not told that her wardship had been sold to Sir Thomas Seymour and, had she known, would not have thought it odd. She was relieved and happy at the thought of returning to the Lord Admiral's home. And she knew wardships were bought and sold frequently. Katherine Brandon, the young Duchess of Suffolk, her stepgrandmother, had been Charles Brandon's ward when he married her. It did not mean the end of a family relationship; rather it meant that the person owning the wardship would be in a better position to negotiate for their ward's marriage or the management of their estate than the natural parents, particularly when the ward was orphaned. Wardships for young boys were as common, and if a ward was wealthy, the one successful in securing him in marriage must be prepared to pay a huge fee to the one holding the legal wardship. In the case of Jane, there was no further question of a fee other than the £2,000. Becoming Edward's wife and queen would be sufficient.

But Jane cared little for the circumstances that released her from life at Bradgate. Less than three weeks after her return she happily prepared to join Sir Thomas Seymour, this time in London and at the court, where, she excitedly told Mrs. Ellen, she might even have the chance see Edward, Mary and Elizabeth.

A great welcome awaited Jane's return to Seymour Place. Many of Katherine Parr's maids were still in residence and there was even an affectionate greeting from the Lord Admiral himself. It was the first time the two had seen each other since he'd ridden off from Sudeley and she'd prepared to become Chief Mourner. Within a few days Jane resumed the routine she'd always enjoyed with Katherine. There were prayers in the morning; then Mrs. Ellen left her in the classroom. Later they might meet in the chapel for prayers again, after which there were visits to court or guests to receive. On one memorable day the whole household gathered at Paul's Cross to hear Bishop Ridley and Archbishop Cranmer hold forth on such weighty topics as Transubstantiation, the Intercession of Saints and Worship of the Virgin. When they returned home there were more prayers and then the evening meal with other household members over which the Lord Admiral presided with great estate and style.

But more often than not Thomas was absent. There was pressure upon him from the Greys to bring about that of which he'd boasted—the promised marriage. Soon he was intimating to others that such was *his* responsibility. On one occasion he met William Parr, the Marquis of Northampton, Katherine's brother. "There will be much ado for my Lady Jane," Thomas confided. "My Lord Protector and my Lady Somerset will do what they can to obtain her . . . for my Lord of Hertford. But they shall not prevail there. . . ." When Northampton asked if Henry Grey might not agree with the Protector's plan, Thomas arrogantly told his brother-in-law, "I will not consent thereto . . . !"

Having Jane in his possession had increased Thomas's luster in the eyes of many. He took no pains to conceal that he was now her legal guardian, reveling in the knowledge that such wardship effectively canceled the plans for any marriage between Jane and the Protector's son. Edward Seymour, usually a calm man, was furious when he learned Henry Grey had sold Jane's wardship to his brother. Thomas became even more careless in his speech, defying his brother to prove he'd poisoned the young king's mind against him and demanding easier access to Edward as well as some share in planning the boy's education and daily routine. He still pressed for the return of Katherine Parr's jewels, as well as more influence at the council table. When logic failed him, colorful oaths and a hot temper sufficed.

"I would the king should have the honor of his own things," he told Henry Grey, "for of his years, he is wise and well learned." When Grey urged quick action for the marriage, Thomas replied, "I shall bring it to pass within these three years. . . ." Then, covering himself, he told Grey, "I will not meddle with the doings either of the Protector or the Council till I have seen the King's Majesty a year older, who then, I trust, should be able to rule his own." Impressed, Grey was fervently thankful, telling Seymour that apart from the little king himself, "I will spend my life and blood in your part against all men."

But access to His Majesty was becoming more difficult. Edward, old for his eleven years and wiser than Thomas believed, had begun to tire of his uncle's demands—demands that he ask things of the Protector the boy was afraid to ask, or sign papers containing Edward knew not what. Once, when Edward told John Cheke, his tutor, he'd refused to comply, Cheke had said, "It is best not to sign." After that, Edward was often unavailable when his uncle Thomas called. He'd begun—with a maturity his years of solitude had bestowed—to withdraw from a man he mistrusted and sensed was dangerous. Edward could not have described why he thought so. He rarely saw the Protector, but when he did, their meetings were businesslike and brief. When he saw Thomas, there was always the uncertain chance that he might be asked to do things he did not understand and which he was beginning to believe were wrong. His perception was obvious when he called William Parr, Katherine's brother, "mine *honest* uncle."

Thomas did not recognize the extent of Edward's withdrawal and laid it to the strict routine of his day, the constant study, both religious and academic, that kept the child so confined. Annoyed at being refused admittance to the boy's quarters, he was wont to blame Cheke or the Protector. He was certain if he could only have Edward with him for some length of time—alone and with no interference from tutor or priest—he could convince the child of Edward Seymour's failings. He startled Fowler, the man he'd placed in the king's quarters, by remarking—after he'd been told the king could not see him—that getting in and out of the royal quarters would not be difficult. But even Fowler would have been stunned had he known the Lord Admiral's thoughts.

For Thomas's extravagant self-confidence was proving his undoing. He'd amassed considerable wealth from his criminal acts and was thinking of remarriage. He made no secret of the fact that the Princess Elizabeth was his first choice. Though she blushed when she heard it—and with memory of what her first encounter with Thomas Seymour had cost her—Elizabeth refrained from comment and refused even to write him a letter of condolence on his wife's death. *"He needs it not,"* she told a startled Cat Ashley, her governess. Jokingly, Thomas told Parry, Elizabeth's almoner, that eventually even *he* might wed Lady Jane Grey. Seeing Parry's look of astonishment, he slapped the man on the shoulder and with a loud laugh said, "I tell you this merrily, but merrily."

But an exorbitant pride and resentment of the Protector still remained. Thomas reacted angrily when one courtier jibed, "I fear your lordship's power is much diminished by the queen's death." Bitterly, Thomas cried, "The council never feared me as much as they do now!" When he carelessly asked the Earl of Rutland how he would feel if, sometime in the near future, it was proposed that the young king take rule and the Protectorship be dissolved, Rutland was wise enough not to answer. But he told others. Soon ex-Chancellor Wriothesley, no friend of Edward Seymour, who'd ousted him from his position, warned Thomas on his behavior: "Beware what you are doing," Wriothesley said. "It were better for you if you had never been born, nay that you were burnt quick alive, than that you should attempt it."

Thomas's conversations with Rutland and Wriothesley soon reached others. Two months after Jane had returned to Seymour Place, Lord Russell warned him that such actions were not conducive to a good relationship between the Seymour brothers. Even when one of Thomas's own followers subtly suggested there was nothing commendable about how Seymour was behaving "in this time of the King's Majesty's tender years, when one day's service is worth a whole year's . . ." and suggested that the Lord Admiral be patient, circumspect and "more humble in heart and stomach to the Protector," Seymour would not be deterred.

Some inkling of Seymour's deteriorating sense of reality is evident in his having a stamp made of Edward's signature and, obtaining a set of keys to Edward's chambers—probably from Fowler—having duplicates made. The constant pressure of maintaining his influence and trying to gain more, the demands of those implicated with him in his dealings at the Royal Mint and with the West Country pirates, even the daily effort to keep up appearances at Seymour Place and advance Lady Jane Grey in what he saw as the saving of his nephew the king from the Protector's intent—as well as his daughter—were beginning to take their toll. His eccentric behavior, wild oaths and threats, lacking any shred of common sense or lucidity, at last brought a summons from the Privy Council to answer their charges. The Protector had at last accepted the extent of his brother's aberrations, even if he did not know the details.

The summons brought a clear threat of danger even to Thomas's twisted senses. He felt if he could just *see* Edward, he could influence him as he had in the past and impress upon him the necessity for removing the Protector. And then Edward would "have the honor of his own things"—to rule in his own right. Thomas had little doubt he could then persuade the boy to marry Jane Grey.

It all ended on the night of January 16, 1549, four months after Katherine Parr's death. Entering the palace through the Privy Garden and avoiding the guards, Thomas used his keys to gain admittance to the little king's private chambers. Down at the end of a long corridor, Edward lay asleep. Thomas did not know the boy had his own fears and had bolted the door from the inside. As an extra added precaution, he'd put his little dog outside the door in the hall.

There it lay at the door as the Lord Admiral confidently strode down the hall, convinced of the rightness of his cause and sure of its success. When he attempted to open the door, the small dog barked furiously, and angered, Thomas pulled his pistol and shot it. Soon the corridor was alive with guards, Edward's personal attendants in their nightshirts, and halberdiers with their weapons pointed directly at him. The dog, bloodied and dead, was pushed aside as a Gentleman of the Privy Chamber rushed inside to find

Edward, white-faced and tearful, trembling in his bed. Smoke from the pistol wafted into the room as the little boy was told what had happened to his dog. His uncle had killed it. But everything was all right now, the man said, attempting to comfort the child. The Lord Admiral had been arrested and would bother him no more.

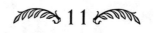

11

Lady Jane Grey had been at Seymour Place with the Lord Admiral for only four months when he was arrested and sent to the Tower. Upon re-joining him, she'd happily assumed she'd remain there until her parents arranged her marriage. The shocking encounter in the palace had ended that possibility; the terrifying events that now unfolded appalled young Jane. Though in later years she would not refer to them, she never forgot the painful days as the sordid charges of wrongdoing were leveled against Thomas Seymour. The accusations confused, puzzled, even outraged the girl who'd had only the best the Lord Admiral could give in physical and emotional care, whatever his motives. The sensitive Jane could only recoil as, one by one, the tragic revelations disclosed a man so insatiably ambitious she could scarce believe he was the one she'd known. Amazement and shock were followed by disbelief. And always the question: *why?* The final stunning shock for Jane was the discovery that *she*, unaware and loyal, had played a large part in the flamboyant Seymour's tragedy.

No one attempted to allay Jane's fears or explain Thomas's erratic behavior. It did not occur to her parents when, within days, they hurriedly appeared at Seymour Place to take her and her at-

tendants to Dorset Place, that their daughter might need an explanation. It was only a short distance down "the streete," but a world
apart in every other way. Even Mrs. Ellen, bewildered and tight-
lipped, was unusually reticent. Jane didn't dare ask her father, for
the normally self-confident marquis looked continually harassed and
worried. As the Privy Councillors arrived to disappear with him
behind closed doors, Henry Grey attempted to explain his part in
Thomas Seymour's plotting, to salvage a tarnished reputation and
prevent confiscation of his estates. Since she couldn't ask her father
what had happened to the Lord Admiral, Jane asked Mrs. Ellen.
The kindly governess's heart ached for the child who constantly
questioned: What had Thomas Seymour done?

Eventually, from bits and pieces Mrs. Ellen heard, from servants' gossip and the Privy Councillors' comments overheard in the
hall when they thought she wasn't listening, Jane discovered most
of what she wanted to know. She found it difficult to believe, and
each day when she rose she hoped to find it was all a mistake—
that Thomas and her own father hadn't conspired against the king,
hadn't connived to overthrow the Protector and marry her to Edward. That was the part that puzzled Jane the most. Suppose Edward didn't want to marry *her*? Could they make a king marry
someone he didn't wish to wed?

Away from Jane's home, at Whitehall, the Privy Council met,
dominated by John Dudley, the Earl of Warwick. Dudley was no
friend of the Seymour family; he was as jealous of the Protector
and as underhanded as Thomas. But, over the last two years, he'd
maintained a surface cordiality with Edward Seymour while losing no chance to disparage Thomas and his activities. Learning that
the Protector would be happy to forget the charges and send his
brother into exile, Dudley firmly protested that Thomas would work
against him from abroad and civil war might result. And what of
the rumors that he'd poisoned Katherine Parr so he might wed the
Princess Elizabeth, whom he'd seduced at Chelsea and who was
now with child? Hadn't he hoped to kidnap young Edward and
marry him to Lady Jane Grey without the council's permission?
Members of Elizabeth's household—her governess, Cat Ashley, and
her almoner, Thomas Parry—had been taken to the Tower and
mercilessly interrogated for days to discern if she was implicated
in Seymour's plotting. When Elizabeth heard the rumors of her

pregnancy, she bravely wrote the Protector from Hatfield, denying the "shameful slanders" and insisting she be brought to the court
"to show myself there as I am."

The Privy Council, at Dudley's suggestion, said that "the case
was so heavy and lamentable to the Lord Protector, they would
proceed without further troubling or molesting either His Highness or the Lord Protector. . . ." In the House of Lords, when
the Bill of Attainder against Thomas was presented, Edward Seymour "for natural pity's sake, desired leave to withdraw . . ."; it
had already been decided the two brothers would not meet. Thus
consideration for the Protector reduced any chances that brotherly
compassion might result in less than the sentence against Thomas
Seymour the majority of them wanted. The Protector said "that
he did yet rather regard his bounden duty to the King's Majesty
and the Crown of England than his own son or brother." Appearing "genuinely sorrowful," he said he could not "refuse justice."

Although Thomas and the Protector asked for an open trial, the
prisoner was given no chance to defend himself. However, as
Sherington, Henry Grey, Fowler and others divulged their activities to the council, it would have been difficult to save the Lord
Admiral. His boasts and threats, the alleged poisoning of a queen,
intimate romps at Chelsea with Elizabeth and an intent to marry
her, as well as the purchase of Lady Jane Grey's wardship—all
serious enough for short imprisonment or a loss of title and estates—faded before the indisputable evidence of a debased coinage, cannon foundries and ammunition dumps in castles and manors
throughout the countryside, and the stolen plunder from wide-
spread piracy which had accumulated in the Scilly Isles in direct
violation of Seymour's trust as Lord Admiral of the Navy. When
the little king was told the full story by the Protector and members of the council, he was advised to agree with them, respond-
ing, "We perceive that you require but justice to be done."

In the Tower, Thomas waited, certain his brother and nephew
would intercede. "They cannot kill me, except they do me wrong,"
he confidently told a guard, "and if they do, I shall die but once
. . . and I have a master that will at once revenge it." Thomas
never accepted that Edward, least of all, would fail him. He'd never
recognized the boy's resentment of his taunts and, later, Edward's
apprehension as his uncle demanded of him more than he, for

prudence's sake, wished to give. Thomas's only support came from relatives—Katherine's brother, William Parr, and William Herbert, her brother-in-law—who derided the rumors of poisoning and Thomas's intentions to marry Elizabeth. But they could hardly explain the other more devastating charges. Their support of Thomas Seymour was as much opposition to John Dudley, whom they knew to be responsible for much of the brothers' discord, as it was any real belief in Seymour's innocence. Dudley had been the Lord Admiral before the Protector had given the office to Thomas and, capable as he was, resented the manner in which Thomas had despoiled it. But even Parr and Herbert must have known their support was meaningless.

At last, as Thomas waited with waning hope in the Tower, the Privy Council acted. On March 17, the execution warrant was signed and the Lord Admiral sentenced to death by beheading. When informed of the verdict, Thomas reacted fiercely with great oaths, cursing each of the councillors. The warrant was then taken to Edward, who, with tears in his eyes and trembling hand, signed the document.

On March 20, 1549, six months after Katherine Parr's death, Thomas was taken to Tower Hill. John Dudley and many Privy Councillors watched as he strode up the hill from the Tower; the Protector and the king did not attend. Thomas had always been popular with the common people. Now they accompanied him on his last walk, tearfully shouting cries of encouragement and reviling his accusers. Thomas was heartened, but knew there was no escape.

At the scaffold he whispered to a servant who'd accompanied him that there were messages for the Princesses Mary and Elizabeth sewn into his shoe. In the letters, Thomas said the Protector was attempting to estrange them from their brother and oust them from the succession. He urged them to vindicate his death by continuing the conspiracy against the Protector. What Thomas, in his last days of incarceration and blasted hopes, thought the two could do—or would even wish to do—only he knew. He never considered that such messages only implicated them in his misfortune.

On the scaffold, facing his ignominious end, the Lord Admiral was overwhelmed by a desire to live. Instead of the traditional

confession and expiation of guilt, of forgiving his accusers and re-
quiring prayers for the heavenly receipt of his soul, he reviled the
minister sent for a last solacing moment, cursing him to be gone.
When an official ordered him to remove his jacket and place his
head upon the block, an enraged Thomas refused, striking at him
blindly. The executioner, standing nearby, axe in hand, was assaulted as Thomas wrestled him to the scaffold floor. But the executioner—strong, as one of his trade had to be—threw the slim
Thomas to the ground and hacked away with great blows at the
head. Within several moments the Lord Admiral was silent and
the head neatly cut away.

Several days later at Paul's Cross, the Sunday sermon of Hugh
Latimer caused much rumbling among the listeners. Bitterly the
minister cried out, "This I say, if they ask me what I think of the
Lord Admiral's death, that he died very dangerously, irksomely
and horribly. God had left him to himself . . . he had clean forsaken him. . . ." As the populace muttered and some even hooted
loudly, Latimer continued, "He shall be to me, Lot's wife as long
as I live. He was a covetous man—I would there were no more in
England. He was an ambitious man—I would there were no more
in England. He was a seditious man—a contemner of the Common Prayer. I would there were no more in England. He is gone.
I would he had left none behind him."

At Dorset Place, a white-faced Jane, hiding her tears, closed the
door of her bedchamber and knelt in prayer for the soul of Thomas
Seymour. At Hatfield, where she'd been constantly questioned by
the Protector's men while her governess and almoner languished
in the Tower, a sober Princess Elizabeth was informed of the Lord
Admiral's death. Aware of eyes intent upon perceiving any emotion in her, she coolly remarked, "This day died a man of much
wit—and very little judgment." If anyone had expected tears from
Anne Boleyn's daughter, they were disappointed.

And from Seymour Place, a steward accompanied by several
servants emerged carrying little Mary Seymour on her way to
Suffolk House in Southwark, the home of Lady Jane's stepgrandmother, the young Duchess of Suffolk, Kate Brandon, one of
Katherine Parr's closest friends. Orphaned by the execution of her
father, Mary Seymour was also penniless, since Thomas's estates

and those her mother had left him were confiscated. By the Protector.

Following Thomas Seymour's execution, the Marquis and Marchioness of Dorset hurriedly left London for their country seat at Bradgate. The Privy Council had been lenient with Henry Grey. He'd committed no crime in selling the wardship of his daughter to the Lord Admiral, whatever the behavior of that unfortunate man had been. In his deposition Grey said the Lord Admiral "was so earnestly in hand with me and my wife, the Lady Frances, that in the end, because he would have no nay, we were content that Jane should return to his house." Grey admitted knowing of Seymour's intention to attempt a marriage of his daughter with Edward; it was not dangerous to do so, for Jane's royal blood made her a proper choice. It was more difficult to prove just how much the marquis had known of Thomas's other, more criminal, activities. In the end, with no sufficient evidence other than poor judgment—and with Grey blaming everyone but himself—he was acquitted. His cohort Sir William Sherington, after a brief stay in the Tower, turned informer and was pardoned. The only one to suffer harshly was the "poor faithful creature," Thomas's servant, who'd taken the message for the princesses from the executed man's shoe. He was hanged as an accomplice.

Thomas Seymour's execution brought to the surface the intriguings and conspiracies within the Privy Council. Several individuals—of whom John Dudley was the most prominent—constantly sought more authority, with scant conscience regarding the methods by which it might be obtained. Prestigious colleagues of little *real* influence—such as Henry Grey—were pushed aside. As many of the older, more statesmanlike advisers of Henry's reign died or withdrew, younger councillors were chosen for their partisanship and malleability. The stalking horse of power and influence was, on the surface, the "cause of religion"; the true desire was nothing less than outright greed, as well as a cutthroat willingness to employ any means toward achieving one's goal.

But some—not of the august Privy Council—felt otherwise. One was young King Edward; another was Lady Jane Grey. Both were firmly committed to the "new religion," to which they'd been exposed since birth. Another, just as strongly opposed to the new beliefs that had taken root during her childhood at the unhappy times of her mother's divorce, was the Princess Mary. The middle child of Henry VIII, Princess Elizabeth, born during the time of her father's assumption of supremacy in the English Church, observed whatever the bishops and Privy Council decided was right and proper—even when what might at one time have been considered heresy later became dogma. Elizabeth's beliefs were known only to Elizabeth.

Theological disputation was fashionable among the sincerely knowledgeable elite. Queen Katherine Parr and her learned ladies were good examples of those who genuinely sought a spiritual peace of mind. Others, while accepting king over pope, were still staunchly Catholic in belief and lamented the changes Archbishop Cranmer and the council had made in the beloved ancient rituals.

Henry VIII had died "a good Catholic," albeit with no loyalty to Rome. Two of the most emotionally charged issues of the old faith were Transubstantiation and the Mass, precious foundation stones of Catholic belief. Even many of the more milder adherents of the "new religion" accepted that, in communion, they were partaking of the Very Presence of Christ's Body and Blood in the Sacrament. However, to the radical and increasing number of opponents, once "Protestors," now "Protestants," the sacrament was a mythical disbelief insulting to intelligence, common sense and faith. Some accepted the Mass in Latin while many deplored it as "too Romish." Others—especially the true seeker—welcomed it in the English he could understand; others thought it an instrument of the Devil. The Act of Uniformity—an attempt to bring all dissenting factors into line—was in reality fought by the bishops, who could not even agree among themselves.

At the time of the Lord Admiral's death Edward Seymour had been the Protector for more than two years. While the London populace generally admired the tall, somber figure, riding a discreet distance in procession behind the king, the Protector's religious policies were another matter—especially in the small parish churches throughout the English countryside. When services contained in the Book of Common Prayer replaced the Mass, it puzzled and confused the average commoners, most of whom could not read. Edward Seymour had returned from a Scottish victory with a "halo of splendor" about his head. The halo had faded somewhat in the aftermath of his brother's execution, with Edward making no strong attempt to save him. But his popularity was more directly challenged by the numerous religious changes coming too soon and too fast. The weighty discourses on—or abolishment of—Transubstantiation, Intercession of Saints, Purgatory, Worship of Mary, even Prayers for the Dead, from which the average Englishman had derived inspiration and comfort for generations, caused dissension and spiritual distress among the English people. The very pro-Catholic Stephen Gardiner, Archbishop of Winchester, begged the Protector to forget his august office and "listen to him as a friend." He implored Seymour "not to trouble the realm with novelties in religion so long as the king is a child." Certainly Henry VIII had introduced reforms, but they'd been cautious ones and had, for the most part, given "quiet and satisfaction," the priest said. Gardiner was so disturbed that he wrote Princess Mary, urging her to speak out against the Protector's reforms. "I see my late sovereign slandered," he wrote, "religion assaulted, the realm troubled, and peaceable men disquieted." But Mary would not be drawn into the controversy; she'd learned her lesson well during the time of her "troubles."

Even Sir William Paget, one of Henry VIII's old war-horses and a Privy Councillor, was disturbed by the tampering with ritual, the destruction of church property—the saintly images, centuries-old paintings and exquisite rood lofts—and the theft of gold and silver plate. "Society in a realm," he wrote the Protector, "doth consist . . . of religion and law and these two or one wanting, farewell all just society, government, justice. I fear at home is neither. The use of the old religion is forbidden, the use of the new is not yet printed in the stomachs of eleven of twelve parts of the realm." Paget's opinion pointed up a condition many councillors overlooked or chose not to recognize—that in the tiny churches of England where generations of families had been baptized, wed and buried, the smashed glass, statues pulled from niches or so mud-bedaubed and vandalized they were useless, with ancient wall paintings whitewashed and bells and roofs stripped for lead—the peasant and squire were shocked and resentful. While some vacillated, others spoke their conscience in outright fashion; the Privy Council had not enlightened or inspired as it had thought. Instead, Catholic malcontents thrived as the Protestant supporters looked to Protector and king for more laws to guard their hard-won spiritual freedom.

At Bradgate there was no vacillation or examination of conscience. To the extent that Henry Grey personally observed religious ritual or studied dogma, his beliefs were strongly in the "new religion"; he was avidly Protestant. Jane, Katherine and Mary Grey's spiritual instructions had never been otherwise. The two younger girls accepted such observances as they accepted any other aspect of their life, as a routine that was part and parcel of their day.

But Jane Grey went further. Religious study and religious observance were deeply ingrained habits of thought and feeling; she would have been bereft without them. Upon her return to Bradgate after the Seymour tragedy, which had touched her as nothing in her twelve years had affected her previously, the solace of her spiritual beliefs became stronger and even more satisfying. The remembered discussion with the strongly Protestant Katherine Parr and her chaplain, Miles Coverdale, the spirited arguments of the queen and her ladies—as well as the daily observance of the religious rituals she'd known from birth—had given Jane a bedrock of spiritual belief. While it was unusual in one so young, it was not unexpected considering her sensitivity and the deprived emotional environment in which she lived, surrounded by others completely lacking in that gift.

Upon her return to Bradgate, in a family shaken but thankfully unscathed by the Lord Admiral's execution, Jane had only her sisters, Mrs. Ellen and Mrs. Tylney for companionship. She understood now the part she'd played in Thomas Seymour's tragedy. She accepted it even as she recalled his kindnesses to her, the months of comfortably happy living such as she'd never known before. If Thomas had used her, she'd been the winner, he the loser. Jane never doubted the sincerity of his feeling toward her, even if the reason for it had been self-serving. In her own mind she remembered Katherine and Thomas with love and mourned them both, knowing she'd never see their like again.

And with a maturity unusual for her twelve years, she accepted also that she was a great disappointment to her parents. Certainly they overlooked no opportunity to point out her many disadvantages. She was too plain and freckled, unmannered and undepend-

IANA GRAYA

*Regia stirps tristi cinxi diademate crines
Regna sed omnipotens hinc meliora dedit*

Lady Jane Grey

Artist Unknown

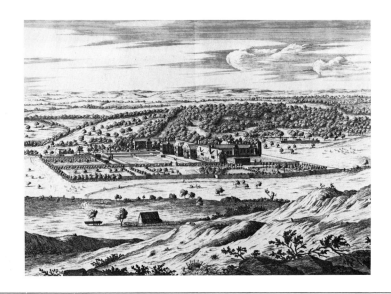

Bradgate Manor

Lady Jane Grey's ancestral home near the City of
Leicester in Leicestershire

Chelsea Manor House

The house built by Henry VIII at Chelsea and later
lived in by his children as well as Anne of Cleves and
Katherine Parr. Jane Grey spent one summer at the
Manor House with Katherine Parr and, several years
later, left it for Syon House, where she learned she
was to be queen.

Mary Tudor and Charles Brandon

"The French Queen," sister of Henry VIII and
the Duke of Suffolk, at the time of their
marriage. The Suffolks were Lady Jane Grey's
grandparents.

Suffolk House in Southwark

The residence of Mary Tudor and
Charles Brandon, the Duke and
Duchess of Suffolk, in Southwark.
The handsome three-turreted
house is located just below the
Church of St. Savior, today's
Southwark Cathedral, where
Frances Brandon and Henry Grey
were married.

Edward VI
Age 10

Artist Unknown

Henry VIII as a young
man

by Joos Van Cleve

Jane Seymour

by Hans Holbein

Queen Katherine Parr

by William Scrots (Stretes)

Sir Thomas Seymour
Lord Sudeley
The Lord High Admiral
Husband of Katherine
Parr

Charles Brandon
The Duke of Suffolk

Artist Unknown

Lady Jane Grey's grandfather

Katherine Willoughby Brandon
The Duchess of Suffolk

Lady Jane Grey's step-grandmother

Henry Brandon   Charles Brandon

The children of Charles Brandon
and Katherine Willoughby Brandon, whose early death brought
the Dukedom of Suffolk to Henry
Grey, the Marquis of Dorset, Jane
Grey's father.

able in conversation, too withdrawn or too forward, possessed no skill in hunting nor any desire to learn the sport. She did, they reluctantly admitted, have an inclination toward learning and if she was to amount to anything—the Greys never disclosed exactly what—she must use that intelligence, which might compensate in some manner for all those other unattractive physical and psychological impediments.

Jane was never consulted about any activity her parents might have in mind, whether it concerned her studies, the planning of her day or her future. If her enthusiasm was less than desired—or if she ventured an opinion or observation at odds with her parents' wishes—she expected and received the blow, slap or pinch that was their way of expressing their displeasure. Jane was relieved such reactions did not extend as frequently to Katherine and Mary, and in a moment of unusual insight, she accepted the cause. *She* was the oldest and she should have been a boy, an heir. *She* was the one from whom her parents had expected so much—and so far had been nothing but trouble, as her mother never left off saying. Their hopes for her had been blighted, a friend had died in the aftermath of that dream, and the fact that she herself had done nothing to cause such disappointment made little difference. And now, after the Lord Admiral's execution and their own disgrace, she was back on their hands. Who else would want her after her association with such a criminal figure, even if he had been the Protector's brother?

But, unknown to Jane, her parents hadn't given up. Relieved as they were to have escaped any punishment in the Seymour tragedy, in the year following they decided the Lord Admiral's original aim had been sound. Why shouldn't Jane Grey—of royal blood, the same age and the same religious beliefs—marry Edward Tudor? Who else could he wed? The Scots had refused little Mary Stuart. What princess of Catholic Europe would come to England to wed a king practicing the "new religion"? Katherine of Aragon had arrived from Spain nearly half a century before and look what *that* had brought about! There were other noble English girls, of course, the foremost being young Jane Seymour, the Protector's child. When Frances and Henry thought of the daughter of one they still considered *arriviste* sitting on the English throne—despite the fact that her aunt had once been queen—they looked at their own Jane with new eyes. If the child was valueless in every way they thought important, if they had wasted over a year on the Lord Admiral's schemes, there was still one way in which she might yet serve the Grey fortunes. She *could* become queen.

The first year of Jane's return home had one rewarding aspect. John Aylmer, her beloved "Mr. Elmer," returned to Bradgate to continue Jane's education. It had been over a year since they'd seen each other and their reunion was a happy one. Other than Mrs. Ellen—and Katherine Parr and the Lord Admiral—the tutor was the only person Jane knew sincerely interested in her, ready to show his affection with grace and wit. Aylmer was not surprised to find an older Jane still interested in her studies and proficient in Latin and Greek, which she spoke as easily as French and her native English. In the old classroom where he also taught the less gifted Katherine while Mary might watch, finger in mouth, from the door, the tutor found himself challenged by the nimble, receptive and seeking intelligence of his star pupil.

He also observed other, less attractive, details of Jane's life. The Greys' savage treatment of their daughter had not lessened; if anything, it had become more severely pitiless—and pointless. While any family might admonish children for lack of obedience, respect or consideration, Aylmer found no cause for Jane's chastisement; she was a model of good deportment with impeccable manners. She exhibited a gracious regard for her parents which bordered on subservience and in a way which often, the tutor knew, was opposite to her own inclination or desire. It deeply angered John Aylmer to see Jane pummeled, pinched, humiliated, castigated or mocked by the two who should have regarded her with an aloof respect if they could not give love.

But what interested him most was that in a subtle manner, delicate and cunning, Jane had begun to fight back. And she was doing it in a way certainly beyond her parents' ability to grasp.

First there was her steely determination to learn. By *not* being as lazy, disobedient or saucy, as completely lacking in grace or consideration of others as her parents constantly complained, she was setting herself as far apart—and above—the two whom God had ordained she must respect. To study, she must have *time*, time that would not have to be explained or excused and would keep her from her parents' presence. Once in the classroom, she was out of their reach. And since her sister Katherine had learned to ride and now spent time in the stables and mews, a good deal of attention had, thankfully, been diverted from Jane.

In another sense, as Aylmer soon realized, Jane's studies were a remarkable and endless source of comfort. For the girl, now thirteen, who had *nothing* else except the love of her governess and the affectionate respect of her tutor, it was challenging and rewarding—even a source of that pride which Scripture said was not to be tolerated—to excel in either academic or religious studies. If the Hebrew language would help her understand Scripture more clearly, then she would learn Hebrew. If Plato's *Phaedo* would bring her closer to that master, then she would read it in his Grecian tongue. To discuss Martial's epigrams and relish the satires of Juvenal, to read Demosthenes and Isocrates—old friends both—were havens of inspiration of which Jane never tired. Incessant reading, music, drawing, anything creative in which her family would not participate, drew Jane like a magnet, allowing her personality and intellect to broaden. In all her endeavors, John Aylmer soon realized, Jane was unconsciously further removing herself from her imperious and brutal mother and the easygoing, thoughtless father, only too eager to follow a stronger wife's example. What Jane saw as defense, however, her family regarded as defiance.

What Aylmer didn't anticipate—and soon realized—was that in Jane's budding maturity, she could show a determination as strong as her mother's.

In that year in the North in which her parents felt it circumspect to remain away from the court until all memory of Henry Grey's malfeasance had faded, Bradgate Hall was the scene of many lively hunting parties. Games, picnics and roisterous music and dancing in the Great Hall, until what Aylmer considered unearthly late hours, helped relieve the Greys' despondency at being away from that center of power, the court. Guests from the neighboring countryside and courtiers from London—at times the Princess Mary or Frances Grey's stepmother, Kate Brandon, the Duchess of Suffolk, and her two sons, even those few Privy Councillors sympathetic to Grey—all arrived to stay at Bradgate for days or weeks. And entertainment had to be provided, for in that respect the marquis and marchioness were superior hosts. Their passion was gambling, about which the otherwise sober Princess Mary was passionately enthusiastic, and it was assumed the guests would all participate, often for high stakes.

Outside of her daily attendance in the classroom, Jane had few diversions. While religious study was one, the second was music. From early childhood she'd had competent musical training and could play the virginals as well as the Princess Mary and better than Elizabeth. On the harp and cithern she was more than competent; on the lute, superior. It was a source of personal pride that she should excel in something she loved, and in the evenings of entertainment for family and guests, Jane was often called upon to perform. This she did happily, flushing with pleasure at the guests' exuberant reception and praise; her parents rarely commented but neither did they criticize, and she was soon dismissed. As Jane returned to her quarters, Mrs. Ellen would compliment her for the performance she'd observed from a doorway or balcony corner. Master Aylmer rarely watched for he disliked the time taken from her studies.

Such performances—and Frances Grey's determination that anything that reflected upon her must be of the best—had resulted in Jane's wardrobe being replenished. Her figure was filling out and too-youthful patterns were no longer becoming, her mother said. A dressmaker was summoned and Jane was measured, fitted and supplied with a wardrobe that she gazed upon with wonder when it was complete. Silks, satins, damasks, skirts with furred hems, jeweled caps and collars, long tight-fitting sleeves embellished with intricate ribbon design or heavy moss-work embroidery in the violets, tawnies, delicate greens and heathers so complimentary to her pale skin and vivid red-gold hair, filled the wardrobe in the chamber she now had all to herself. Jane had always had rich clothing; a daughter of the house of Dorset could hardly be garbed otherwise. But her new garments were so much more extravagant and rich, so *adult*—and there were so many of them! Jane overlooked her tutor's sniff of disapproval as she remarked on their beauty. She knew he disliked the time she'd taken for fittings as much as he disliked the time she gave to her music, reminding her there was less opportunity for studying. Jane agreed, yet wondered aloud if such distraction—flighty, to be sure—wasn't a means of resting her brain so that on the morrow she'd absorb that much more? Surely, an hour or two on the lute would only make her more receptive to the delights of Scripture or the *Aeneid*? In the end Aylmer found himself agreeing, when in point of fact he did not agree at all. It was one more example, he realized, of Jane Grey's growing up.

One of the visitors to Bradgate that first summer after Jane returned was Roger Ascham, a former tutor of Princess Elizabeth whom Jane had shared at Whitehall and Chelsea in those days when she'd lived with the queen. Lady Jane was fond of Master Ascham and he of her, and passing through the countryside outside Leicester, he saw the Marquis and Marchioness of Dorset and their guests hunting. Greeting them, he noted Jane's absence and inquired for her, being told she was at her studies at home. Master Ascham rode to Bradgate and, coming upon Jane in her classroom, "found her reading the *Phaedo* of Plato in Greek, with as much delight as gentlemen read a merry tale in Boccaccio."

Why, asked Ascham after Jane had greeted him with pleasure and surprise, wasn't she out in the air and enjoying "such pastime as was then going on in the park?" It was then that Jane Grey for the first and last time revealed to her old tutor—whose gentleness was in such contrast to what she normally expected—what the circumstances of her everyday life were.

"I wis [think] all their sport in the park is but a shadow to that pleasure I find in Plato!" Jane told her visitor with a smile. "Alas! good folk, they never felt what true pleasure means." When Ascham asked why she sought such knowledge, "seeing that few women and no many men have arrived at it," Jane did not spare her old friend.

"I will tell you," she said plainly, "and tell you a truth which, perchance, you will marvel at. One of the greatest benefits that God gave me is that He sent me, with sharp, severe parents, so gentle a schoolmaster. When I am in the presence of either father or mother, whether I speak, keep silence, sit, stand or go, eat, drink, be merry or sad, be sewing, playing, dancing or doing anything else, I must do it, as it were, in such weight, measure and number, even as perfectly as God made the world, or else I am so sharply taunted, so cruelly threatened, yea, presented sometimes with pinches, nips and bobs, and other ways (which I will not name for the honor I bear them) so without measure misordered, that I think myself in Hell, 'til the time comes when I must go to Mr. Elmer, who teacheth me so gently, so pleasantly, with such fair allurements to learning, that I think all the time nothing while I am with him. And when I am called from him, I fall on weeping, because whatever I do else but learning is full of great trouble, fear, and whole misliking unto me. And thus my book hath been so much my pleasure, and bringeth daily to me more pleasure and more, that in respect of it, all other pleasures in very deed, be but trifles and troubles to me."

A sobered and saddened Master Ascham spoke a bit longer with Jane and then left to continue his journey. As he left, she returned to her book, but the celebrated tutor never forgot his visit with her "because it was the last . . . he ever beheld that sweet and noble lady."

Another guest at Bradgate in the year following the Lord Admiral's execution was John Ulmis, a penniless Swiss Calvinist. For several months, in the tradition of the time, Henry Grey had sponsored young Ulmis's studies and livelihood at Oxford. The cost was trifling compared with the marquis's more impressive gambling debts or the Bradgate or Dorset Place maintenance, and Ulmis was pleased to have Henry Grey, whom many considered—along with John Dudley, the Earl of Warwick—"as a shining light of the Church," as his patron. Ulmis, fervently Protestant, was but a few years older than the thirteen-year-old Jane and the two saw much of each other during the student's visit. Ulmis was devoted to John Aylmer and concerned that Henry Grey might relinquish his Oxford sponsorship. He courted Frances Grey, complimenting her on her home, her splendid self, her lovely daughters—especially the learned Jane—her impressive abilities during the hunt or nightly dancing. Ulmis did not mention the marquis's disastrous performance at the gaming tables, for he, along with Aylmer and James Haddon, the Bradgate chaplain, still protested the gaming sessions, which both considered an assault on the spiritual integrity of the household.

It was Aylmer's suggestion that a tangible way of Ulmis's ensuring Henry Grey's continued patronage might be a contact with a noted member of the Swiss Reformers, the celebrated Heinrich Bullinger at Zurich. Knowing Bullinger to be writing a religious thesis, Ulmis urged the reformer to dedicate the book to the Marquis of Dorset, whom he described as "the thunderbolt and terror of the Papists, that is, a fierce and terrible adversary. The marquis has a daughter, about fourteen years of age, pious and accomplished beyond what can be expressed, to whom I hope shortly to present your *The Holy Marriage of Christians*." When Bullinger replied he would do as Ulmis requested, the student presented the letter to Henry Grey. Impressed, the marquis promised to write Bullinger, and Ulmis forwarded his intention to Zurich. Then, realizing there was yet one more way of impressing both Bullinger and Grey, he suggested the reformer also write Lady Jane Grey, promising he would then "soon receive from her a most learned and courteous letter in Greek."

When Bullinger's letter arrived at Bradgate, Jane was entranced. It was contact with the larger world of which she knew so little, and with one whom she regarded with awe. Much to Aylmer's satisfaction, she could hardly wait to reply. Expressing herself came easily and what could be more exciting—as lonely and housebound as she was—than to correspond with such a prominent member of the noted Swiss Reformers from whom she might learn so much? Bullinger was, in Jane's view, as much a "thunderbolt of the Papists" as Ulmis thought her father.

Urged on by Aylmer, Haddon and Ulmis, Jane wrote, thanking Bullinger for his little book of "pure and unsophisticated religion," which she was reading. Her father, she said, had many "weighty engagements" but was determined to read it. Jane was also obviously delighted with the subtle flattery contained in his letter. She wrote:

> I now come to that part of your letter which contains a commendation of myself, which, as I cannot claim, so also I ought not to allow; but whatever the divine Goodness may have bestowed on me, I ascribe wholly to Himself, as the chief and sole Author of anything in me that bears any semblance to what is good, and to whom I entreat you, most accomplished sir, to offer your constant prayers in my behalf, that He may so direct me and all my actions that I may not be found unworthy of His great goodness. . . .

Farewell, brightest ornament and support of the whole

Church of Christ and may Almighty God long preserve you to us and to His Church!

Your most devoted,
Jana Graia

Ulmis was pleased with Jane's letter and knew Bullinger would be also. Any contact with a house as prominent as My Lord Dorset's, with ties to the royal family, were welcome to obscure penniless students and religious reformers. Patrons and sponsors might give so little of their time or money, but to the recipient it meant much; not the least being their support of the Protestant church. Immediately, Ulmis wrote Bullinger, stressing Jane's "veneration and esteem" of him. "For my own part," he said, "I do not think there ever lived anyone more deserving of respect than this young lady, if you regard her family; or more learned, if you consider her age. . . . A report has prevailed, and has begun to be talked of by persons of consequence, that this most noble virgin is to be betrothed and given in marriage to the king's majesty. Oh! if that event should take place, how happy would be the union, and how beneficial to the Church!"

Both John Aylmer and the chaplain Haddon, impressed with Bullinger's response, encouraged the correspondence between him and their pupil. Jane was soon absorbed in Bullinger's letters, which were written as to an adult; they were enlightening and comforting, for his religious beliefs were also hers. She felt the challenge in replying. The letters took hours to write, for she must think, draw upon her deepest convictions, word her letters as gracefully and as scholarly as possible in whatever language she was using. And always remember to remain true to the ideal, the perfect, that John Aylmer and others had set for her. To do better than her *best*.

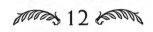

12

As life continued for the Greys at Bradgate, the political scene at court was changing with a rapidity reminiscent of those few weeks after the death of Henry VIII. Again it involved the same councillors, nobles and courtiers who'd disregarded the king's will by forming a Protectorship with Edward Seymour at its head. In the following months—as the doctrinal reforms and liturgical changes that the Protector insisted upon split council and clergy—a political scheming of which he was often ignorant reached its height. And as church and government officials fought among themselves, they incurred the Protector's wrath more often than his cooperation.

Much of it was Seymour's own fault. Many thought "he had sealed his doom the day on which he signed the warrant for the execution of his brother." Thomas's death pointed up flaws in Edward's character—while similar flaws in his colleagues and churchmen were often overlooked. The Protector had exercised poor judgment in the Scottish wars, losing England its possible alliance through the marriage of the little Queen of Scots to Edward Tudor. Reeking corpses of men and women, even children, left in the path of English troops in the Border lands, had made "his very name stink of blood." At home, the coinage, debased by Thomas Seymour and Sherington, had given the royal exchequer a tinge of bankruptcy; English coin was not respected or welcomed in the marketplaces of Europe. The navy had been corrupted by its Lord Admiral and his pirates; the army enfeebled, its soliders muttering at their poor provisioning and lack of pay. But it was over the "cause of religion" and the agrarian policies of the Privy Council that the Protector and his advisers quarreled most bitterly and most frequently.

When Henry VIII died, Sir William Paget and Edward Seymour had suggested a Protectorship and obtained the Privy Council's support by agreeing that he would not "do any act but with the advice and consent of the rest of the executors, in such manner, order, and form as in the will of our late sovereign lord is appointed and prescribed, which the said Earl [Edward Seymour] hath promised to perform accordingly." After two years in the august position as "Protector of all the realms and dominions of the king's majesty, and governor of his most royal person," Seymour had progressed along the path of pride and arrogance; in this he was not unlike Thomas. But the influence and power that Thomas sought and never acquired, Edward had, and it was his special tragedy that he never learned how to use it. There was none of the carelessness, bluster or incompetency that had marred the younger brother's personality and performance. Edward was soft-spoken, capable and determined. But—not unlike Thomas—he bore a natural contempt for tradition and found it difficult to share authority or power. He was intolerant of opinions that were not his, and most of all, he was impatient.

The Protector had tried—honestly and with more regard for the poor than his colleagues ever exhibited—to attempt agrarian reform by issuing a proclamation against continued enclosure of the open lands held for common use by small farmers and tenant-holders. As a generous example, which he hoped his wealthy councillors and friends would follow, he even gave away to farmers and small tenant-holders many of his own lands that surrounded Hampton Court.

But such example was lost on the gentry or nobility—already enriched with plundered church loot—who wished to enclose even more property with hedges and fencing for sheep raising. New owners of abbeys and other ecclesiastical property had also enclosed land that for generations had sheltered and fed thousands. The high price that wool commanded in the European market and the cheapness of such farming encouraged landlords to turn plowland to grassland. When, consequently, hundreds of small farmers were turned off lands to be devoted to pasture instead of tillage, there was little they could do but starve. They joined the miserable hordes of half-naked, emaciated men and women—even whole families—who'd become vagrants after being evicted from lands, either private or church-owned, which had been their only subsistence. They lived a wretched existence on the roads of England, driven from one place to another, seeking nonexistent employment and then, giving up, resorting to vagabondage, thievery and murder in order to live. The noted Hugh Latimer preached violently upon "the new order of things." His father, he said, had been a "yeoman who lived comfortably, educated his children, served the king and gave to the poor, on a farm the rent of which has been increased four-fold. . . ." He accused the nobility, "I fully certify you as extortioners, violent oppressors, engrossers of tenements and lands, through whose covetousness villages decay and fall down."

One councillor owning former church property in Norfolk was John Dudley, the Earl of Warwick, who'd purchased Wymondham Abbey and its lands from a wealthy tanner, Robert Ket of Norfolk. Ket was angered by the changes in religious doctrine and the Privy Council's harsh agrarian policies. While he could blame the Protector for the former, it was known Seymour did not always agree with his advisers on the use of land and the prerogatives of those who owned it. Matters came to a head when Ket heard that Dudley was anticipating tearing down the Wymondham Abbey, "which was most dear to the people's affection," in order to enclose the land, which had been open since time immemorial. When rebellious peasants needed a leader, he joined them as they vented their anger by pulling down fences and palings, uprooting hedges and killing deer and sheep.

In London, Seymour lectured the Privy Council, saying he "liked well the doings of the people . . . the covetousness of gentlemen gave them occasion to rise." He then pardoned the offenders on condition they return to their homes. When they did not—and with the council plainly showing its contempt for such tolerance—Seymour was forced to order troops to bring the rebels under control. Many Englishmen, their hearts with the peasants, refused to fight and foreign mercenaries had to be called in. The startled rebels, who thought they were fighting to uphold a cause in which Seymour believed, soon had their ranks increased as Norfolkmen and Suffolkmen joined in the common cause. Though informed they were now considered rebels against King Edward, they continued the fight until John Dudley, with twelve thousand men, was sent to quell the uprising. When the rebels refused the pardon, soldiers stormed the ancient city of Norwich, where, by the day's end, three thousand English lay dead. And within days, Robert Ket was hanged from Norwich Castle while his brother William, a monk of the Hospitallers of St. John's, dangled from the tower of Wymondham Abbey—the very one the Ket brothers had hoped to save from Dudley's destruction.

The Protector's action in finally sending in soldiers stunned the rebels. His consideration for the commoner had won Edward Seymour an affectionate regard from the ordinary Englishman. The Privy Council, however, did not share this regard for the "Good Duke," as he was called. They considered him too lenient and vacillating, too strange a mixture of compassion, indulgence and ruthlessness. Again, William Paget warned him. He accosted Seymour one day after a bitter argument within the council, warning him that the "king's subjects [are] all out of discipline, out of obedience, caring neither for Protector nor for king. What is the matter? Marry, sir, that which I said to your Grace in the gallery. Liberty! Liberty! And your Grace's too much gentleness, your softness, your opinion to be good to the poor—the opinion of such as saith to your Grace, 'Oh, sir, there was never man that had the hearts of the poor as you have!' " The sagacious advice was overlooked. Paget, one of Seymour's closest friends and an able councillor, was now plainly at odds with the Protector over his agrarian policies. The only other area where they differed more strongly was in the matter of religious reform.

When the Mass and other simple Catholic practices that Henry VIII himself had observed—the Creeping to the Cross on Good Friday, the touch of forehead ashes on Ash Wednesday, candles at Candlemas, the palm-carrying on Palm Sunday—were abolished, Seymour lost much of the Privy Council's support. Henry VIII had introduced great reform, starting with his own supremacy in the English Church; regarding ritual and doctrine, he'd been cautious and conservative. But those strongly Protestant now urged Edward Seymour not only to further spoliation of church property but to radical changes in doctrine as well. Paget's opinion that "to alter the state of the realm would ask ten years' deliberation" was ignored. When some councillors insisted upon moderation, Seymour would not be brooked. He incurred the displeasure of that part of the clergy who'd hoped to retain a few remnants of a thousand-year-old faith they'd been allowed to practice until as little as two years previously. When Seymour insisted upon strong changes, it was typical of his inconstancy that he then allowed the Catholic Princess Mary to be exempt from the new laws. When Mary was asked to receive the new Book of Common Prayer, she refused, writing the Protector: "Although the council had forgotten the king, her father, and their oaths to observe his will, yet for herself she would observe his laws as he left them," until her brother had attained his majority and ruled in his own right. It was then the Protector allowed Mary to celebrate the Mass and other forbidden rituals in her own home.

But for the ordinary Englishman there was no exemption, or even education in the "new religion." There was now only the constant sermonizing of an often incompetent minister, a Book of Homilies supposed to serve as a guide to what was considered proper, to instruct the often resistant and combative clergy. There was a Prayer Book they might use—if they could read—in churches bereft of color, statues, incense, mysticism or any familiar and beloved relics of their faith.

While the Protector convinced himself such measures were for the spiritual good of the English populace, he lost much of their support by overlooking the fact that what might be acceptable to courtier, councillor and sophisticated Londoner—either prelate or commoner—might not be acceptable to the average country Englishman. "Our curate is naught," said one resentful parishioner, "as ass-head, a dodipot, a lack-Latin and can-do-nothing! Shall I pay him tithe that does no good, nor none will do?" As many country churches disregarded the new reform, the Protector found he might order, but was not always obeyed. "We'll have none of the new fashion—we will have the old religion of our fathers!" one citizen shouted, reminding the minister that Henry VIII himself had observed the Mass. At which a "joyful" priest put on his forbidden vestments and celebrated the Mass in the forbidden Latin while "the common people from all the country around clapped their hands for joy."

Within six months of Thomas's death, the strain on the Protector had begun to show. His short-tempered duchess, Anne Stanhope, had made many enemies with her arrogance and ambition. Seymour, who'd divorced his first wife to marry Anne, was no match for his peppery spouse, of whom one councillor said "he'd gotten rid of a dove to saddle himself with a scorpion." Discord in the home was reflected in the Privy Council and again Sir William Paget sought to remonstrate with Seymour. When the Protector irked a fellow councillor strongly, the distraught fellow burst into tears and left the council room. Later, Paget implored Seymour to use restraint, telling him he'd become so emotionally violent, his colleagues no longer spoke their minds because they might be "whipped with sharp words." He warned Seymour such behavior would not long be tolerated. "How it cometh to pass I cannot tell," he wrote to the Protector, "but of late your Grace is grown into great choleric fashion, whensoever you are contraried in that which you have conceived in your head. A king which shall give men occasion of discourage to say their opinions frankly, receiveth thereby great hurt and peril to his realm. But a subject in great authority as your Grace, in using such fashion, is like to fall into great danger and peril of his own person, besides that to the commonwealth. For the love I bear to your Grace, I beseech you to consider and weigh it well."

But the Protector seemed beyond reasoning. Despite his ownership of more than two hundred manors and a comfortable London home, he proceeded with plans to build Somerset House, a hugely ornate new dwelling place in the Strand. Losing the touch that had won him support and endeared him to many after the old king's death, Seymour ordered the destruction of his old house and several adjoining buildings for material for the new home where he, his family and more than two hundred servants would lodge in great comfort and splendor. Though destruction of church property was not uncommon, there was much muttering within the council and among the people when the Church of St. John at Clerkenwell was blown up for its stone. Next, the northern cloisters of St. Paul's, its charnel house and an ancient burial site was opened and the contents carted away to be buried in the fields of Finsbury. Bridges, tenements and two former episcopal residences on the river were leveled for their materials. When Seymour cast covetous eyes upon little St. Margaret's Church next to the old abbey at Westminster, a horde of citizens showed more courage than their bishop and met the workers consigned to its destruction with pickaxes. It was saved and the Protector withdrew.

Edward Seymour had obviously begun to believe in his own inviolability. With more than a touch of his brother Thomas's rashness, he again ignored Paget's plea that he had "too many irons in the fire" and that he would accept no advice, "which promise I wish your Grace had kept, for then I am sure things had not gone altogether as they go now. . . ." When John Dudley—his reputation greatly enhanced by his skill and courage in quelling the rebel uprising—returned to London, accompanied by his own troops and the foreign mercenaries, he asked to reward them beyond their due. When the Protector refused to pay anything other than ordinary wages, Dudley was indignant and singled out Seymour's profligacy in building Somerset House as one reason why there were no funds for those who had done him service. The two parted in great anger. It was the beginning of the end for Edward Seymour.

Though the Greys remained at Bradgate as the Protector's tragedy unfolded, they were aware of what was going on at court. Couriers often passed between Frances Grey's stepmother—Kate Brandon, the Duchess of Suffolk—and the Greys and the Princess Mary. The marquis had his own contacts and the marchioness, a willing and gifted hostess, kept Bradgate filled with those who brought gossip of London and the court, so that they were as informed as those who attended the little king, the Protector or his Privy Councillors.

Regarding the old king's children, Mary, Elizabeth and Edward, Seymour had not allowed that closeness of relationship, which Queen Katherine Parr had encouraged, to continue. The Greys' guests admitted it was difficult for the three orphaned children, who had no one to whom they could appeal but the Protector. Mary was now thirty-four, often ill with toothaches and poor eyesight, constantly worried that she might be called to account for her religious deviations. She was equally concerned that her brother's own religious beliefs were being corrupted. Mary knew that Edward, not the pope, was supreme in the English Church, as their father had been. But she was angrily disillusioned at the haste and ferocity with which the young king's council had disregarded her father's will, tampered with the religious ritual he'd left, and then demanded the malleable boy accept what they had wrought.

Elizabeth was seventeen years old and lived with her own household at either Hatfield, Ashridge, Hunsdon or any dwelling suitable for royalty to which the council sent her. She showed no anger or disappointment with the religious changes made by the Protector and, as each became law, ordered her chaplain to conform. She kept in touch with Mary and Edward with frequent letters, and gifts on birthdays and holidays. Elizabeth was supremely aware of how closely the Thomas Seymour scandal had touched her; the swift retribution had stunned her. She'd done *nothing*, yet her attendants, Ashley and Parry, had spent weeks in the Tower and she'd been a virtual prisoner in her own home, under constant interrogation, her reputation in shreds in London and at court. The experience had honed a certain innate caution in Elizabeth, aware that yet another such experience might be disastrous. Determined to recoup her apparently lost honor, she dressed simply and wore no jewels; the exuberant manner of the old Chelsea days simply disappeared. Prudence was Elizabeth's byword. She found respite from such constant discretion in her studies, and of all the king's children, she learned her academic lessons the quickest—as quickly as she'd absorbed the experience life had just taught.

In the years since his coronation, Edward had remained at Whitehall, leaving with the court for holidays to Greenwich, Richmond, Hampton Court or on short progresses to nearby countries. He was the same age as Lady Jane Grey and, though her studies gave her a comfort and inspiration he did not share, as lonely as she. Edward was a competent student. He possessed a good brain, was blessed with an excellent tutor, plenty of time, and there was a constant encouragement to *learn*. But he had little of Mary's intuitive, determined ability or Elizabeth's quick, facile skills; learning did not come easily. Beyond the royal classroom, there were his religious studies and the necessity to absorb—or at least listen to—whatever political information the Protector or council chose to divulge. Of the three children, given his youth, he was the least strong; his isolation and the restrictions of his daily environment were not conducive to a physical health such as one might have seen in a London street child. And his dedication to doing and being what everyone—his uncle, his tutor and his churchmen—wanted, had almost erased any sense of youthful individuality in the king. Edward had to be everything to so many, he'd forgotten what it was like to be himself.

The Greys returned to court about the time of the Protector's imprisonment. Dissension and an inevitable split within the Privy Council ranks had ultimately provoked Edward Seymour to action. When the French failed to retake their city of Boulogne— which Henry VIII had gone abroad in his last years to secure— the point was strongly made in the council chamber and London streets that if the Protector had paid sufficient attention, the attempt would never have been made. The sorry state of the Church encouraged even William Cecil, Seymour's secretary, to cry, "Sacrilegious avarice [has] ravenously invaded Church livings, colleges, chantries, hospitals and places dedicated to the poor!" Peasant uprisings in the West Country had led to more English deaths at the hands of English soldiers, and France was again wooing Scotland with proposals for a marriage between little Mary Stuart, the Queen of Scots, and the Dauphin. When the Protector, humiliated by failure, overwrought and overworked, had learned that secret council meetings were being held in the Ely Place home of John Dudley, the Earl of Warwick, his rash reaction was similar to that of his dead brother. Quickly, he'd taken Edward and fled to Hampton Court which, once the moat was filled, the gates fortified and soldiers placed at every battlement, assumed the aspect of a fortress. There he issued a proclamation of Dudley's disloyalty and ordered handbills to be printed and distributed throughout the area asking for the people's support of the king. Stunned by his behavior, the council had reacted, citing the Protector's numerous failures—his refusal to be guided by their advice, and that he had "in the midst of trouble and misery to build for himself in four or five places most sumptuously . . . and that his pride grew so fast, we thought we could suffer no longer unless we would in effect consent with him in his naughty doings." Seymour replied he thought they were all traitors to the king.

In the beginning, the council had assumed such remonstrating would bring the Protector to his senses. Instead, in a long wild ride through one October night, he'd taken Edward from Hampton Court to heavily fortified Windsor Castle. The delicate boy acquired a "rheum" and a bad cough and was frightened, fearful at what was happening to his kingdom and at what might happen to *him*. But he could do little but obey his uncle. Dutifully, he wrote to the Privy Council as Seymour requested, ". . . each man has his faults, he his and you yours . . . he meaneth us no hurt. He is our uncle . . . proceed not to extremities against him. . . ." The boy, frightened and ill, wandering the long corridors of Windsor, told a courtier, "Methinks I am in prison—here are no galleries nor no gardens to walk in."

Five days later it was all over. The Privy Council issued a promise to Seymour that he would suffer loss of neither property nor honor if he would submit. They were, they said, amazed that he'd reacted as though they sought only his "blood and extremity." Several councillors sent by the Protector to negotiate on his behalf had not returned to Windsor; he suspected their courage had failed and they'd rejoined their fellow councillors. At last Seymour was persuaded by Sir William Paget and Thomas Cranmer to submit.

Three days later, his Protectorate ended, Edward Seymour rode to the Tower solaced by the crowds of people who walked beside him, crying words of encouragement and cheer. When Anne Stanhope, his wife, begged King Edward for mercy, the boy was stunned. "They told me the Duke was ill!" he cried. "Why have they taken him prisoner?" It was Cranmer who tried to explain that Edward did not "know all" and that the "Lords know what they do." Stubbornly, the little king insisted, "The Duke never did me any harm," and said since Seymour had ridden voluntarily to the Tower, "it is a sign he be not guilty." John Dudley, assessing Seymour's popularity with the London throng and noticing the unusual set to the little king's jaw and the strength of his words, graciously gave way; he did not wish to incur any displeasure. The Protector would be the Protector no more, he said, but no harm would come to him. "We must return good for evil," he told his fellow councillors, and as it is the king's will that the duke should be pardoned, and it is the first matter [he] hath asked of us, we ought to accede."

It was not lost on those present—nor the king—that while there was no longer a Protector in England, the power and authority of that office had passed to John Dudley, the Earl of Warwick. He also resumed his former office of Lord Admiral of the Navy, vacant since Thomas Seymour's execution, and as a mark of esteem and gratitude, the Privy Council suggested he be made Lord Great Master of England, which title the king was pleased to confer.

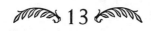

13

The assumption of the Protector's authority, if not the title, by John Dudley, the Earl of Warwick, was the latest attempt of a man who had struggled for power, wealth, respectability and security in the bubbling cauldron of court politics, where intrigue and betrayal were common. Dudley was the oldest son of that notorious Edmund Dudley, a man of shadowed lineage, who, with Richard Empson, had so skillfully served old Henry VII in raising monies for the royal use with scant royal awareness and no lamentable attacks of conscience as to how he'd acquired them. When Henry VIII came to the throne, public outcry against their activities was such that the young king, wishing no rancor to cloud his coronation, had promptly had the two hanged.

John Dudley was eight years old when his father died. He and his two younger brothers were placed in the care of Sir Richard Guildford, Lord Warden of the Cinque Ports, who managed to secure some of their father's holdings, sufficient—when increased by their mother's estates at her death—to educate the Dudley boys. Young John Dudley grew up determined to erase any lingering stigma on his name; he made an early entrance to court, where, since many families had suffered similar political disfavor or worse, he did not feel unwelcome. He became a close friend of Jane Grey's grandfather Charles Brandon, the Duke of Suffolk, with whom he served abroad, winning a knighthood for distinguished service.

That was the beginning of many years of service to Henry VIII. As Lord Lisle, he accompanied nine-year-old Princess Mary to the Welsh Marches, overseeing her household and court in that period when she'd been Henry VIII's heir and Princess of Wales. Later, he was rewarded with the posts of Master of the Horse and Lord High Admiral, which were later taken from him by the Protector for Thomas Seymour. He'd resented the loss but, typically, put a good face on it and bided his time.

It was said of John Dudley that "the faults of the father had not been visited upon the son." A soldier and diplomat, toughly ambitious, he possessed a cunning shrewdness and a refreshing lack of Edward Seymour's vacillation, skillfully concealing a deep desire for *real* power beneath a benign and polished manner. Moderately tall, with a pleasant if undistinguished countenance, Dudley spoke softly, with a coolly impartial, almost aloof, mien. His education had honed a fine intelligence; experience gave him an ingratiating and pleasing personality. In addition to his known and unquestioned personal courage and competence—invaluable in his new position—Dudley also had the support of most of the Privy Council. Many of them were the "rich landlords" of newly enclosed land whom the Protector had scorned; John Dudley did not intend to make the same mistake.

He also had the patience both Seymour brothers had lacked. While many of the "old aristocracy" at the Tudor court considered him an upstart and as much an *arriviste* as the Seymours, even his detractors had to admit his skill in diplomacy. Fighting for everything he considered important in life—from victories on the battlefield or tiltyard, where he was second to none now that Thomas Seymour was dead, to the Privy Council chamber, which he dominated—Dudley's future seemed limitless. Now that the power he'd sought for so long was his, he did not intend to use his opportunity lightly. The ancient earldom of Warwick was only the beginning of the future honors—and material rewards—Dudley intended for his family.

In 1520, at the age of eighteen, John Dudley had married his guardian's daughter. Jane Guildford was a woman of surpassing intelligence and beauty. A close friend of Queen Katherine Parr, with whom she'd studied the "new religion," Jane brought important connections and an impeccable name to the union. At a time when most marriages were made for many reasons other than love, affection or even esteem, John and Jane Dudley shared an unusual devotion. Dudley was one of the few men at court who had no mistress, nor had he involved himself in careless liaisons. The Dudleys had a brood of sons, John, Henry, Robert, Ambrose and Guildford, and at the time of the Protector's fall, marriages for Robert and Guildford, the youngest, were being considered. But the pressing question for both sons was the proper choice of bride. John and Jane Dudley were determined both marriages must bring not only wealth and an honorable name but the opportunity— through the influence of the bride's family, as well as the use of her money—to advance the Dudley sons' chances at court. Their father had risen to an earldom. He did not intend to stop there.

After six months in the Tower of London, Edward Seymour was pardoned and, with a fine of £2,000, the loss of the Protectorate and the return of some lands to the Crown, was a free man. Dudley had aptly assessed the mood of the people who still regarded the "good duke" fondly, and the young king appeared concerned for his uncle's welfare. In addition, the former Protector had several powerful, if somewhat disillusioned, friends, such as the faithful Paget and Thomas Cranmer on the Privy Council. They could prove irksome if Dudley were to abandon Seymour altogether. Caution gave way to graciousness and Dudley offered no objection when the subject of Seymour's release was debated. It was the opinion of many of the council that the duke "had received such a lesson as would have a lasting influence upon his future conduct," and Dudley "now endeavored to conciliate him as a friend and ally." The earl realized that though he might have the strongest voice in the council, it was equally important to win the support of the people and young Edward by allowing the former Protector his freedom.

Chastened and physically renewed by a not uncomfortable incarceration in the Tower, Edward Seymour returned home reflective and grateful to have suffered nothing worse than several months' imprisonment, a minor fine and the surrender of property he could afford to lose. He understood that the strength and protection of his popularity—and his relationship to the king—were the sources of his good luck, not Dudley's benevolence. He accepted that his former power was gone, at least for the moment. But he knew the problems facing England at home and abroad; in this respect he knew himself to be superior to Dudley, although their manner of handling such matters was very different. He also knew that should Dudley fail, there was no one who had his own experience. If sitting at the council table daily and watching the man who'd replaced him handle the affairs of state was a means to return to power, the former Protector did not look askance at the opportunity.

And, like Dudley, he had children. Through them, some luster might yet be reclaimed for the Seymour family. Within weeks of his release, therefore, he and his duchess were considering the marriage of their son, Lord Hertford, to Lady Jane Grey and that of their daughter, Anne Seymour, to Dudley's son Lord Lisle. Only one factor complicated the arrangement—the Marquis of Dorset obviously still hoped young Edward would marry his daughter Jane. However these tangled matrimonial schemes progressed, one dominant factor remained: Once families were tied by marriage, their ambitions—as well as their ample fortunes—were strongly intertwined. So it behooved the Seymours, Dudleys and Greys to take their time, ponder all aspects of these acts, and wait for the propitious moment to complete them.

In the summer of 1551 a double tragedy affecting the life of her stepgrandmother changed the future of Jane Grey, and henceforth Bradgate would be a small part of her life. In July, in the red brick palace of Buckden—where Katherine of Aragon had once challenged the Duke of Suffolk, Charles Brandon, to "bind me with ropes!" if he were to obey her husband, the king, and remove her to Kimbolton Castle—the two sons of the duke died of the "sweating sickness," for which there was no known cure.

Both boys had been students at St. John's College at Cambridge and, when the disease invaded their dormitories, were hurriedly sent to Buckden. There they were cared for by a kinswoman, Lady Margaret Neville. She needed all her skill when, within hours of their arrival, fourteen-year-old Henry Brandon became ill. Because of the infection, his twelve-year-old brother, Charles, was placed in another room. When the physician left Henry to see to Charles, he found the boy ill and grief-stricken. When asked the cause of his sadness, the younger boy replied, "My brother is dead. But no matter, for I will go straight after him." And inside an hour, the younger Brandon was also dead.

Their mother, Katherine Brandon, had been living at Kingston, some five miles west of Cambridge, in order to be near her sons. Since her husband's death, the duchess had thrown her considerable intellectual resources into the pursuit of a proper education for her beloved boys. Her world—once the world of the court and the splendid Suffolk estates—was now centered on Henry and Charles. When informed of their illness, the duchess rose from her own sickbed and rode hurriedly to Buckden to find that Henry had just died. Charles lingered long enough for a farewell to his now hysterical mother. Later, stunned and dazed, Kate Brandon numbly went to bed, refusing to accept the enormity of her loss or that plans for a funeral worthy of a duke's sons had to be made. As friends entered her darkened room to ask her preference, she stared at them blankly, turning her face to the wall. At last, unable to delay longer, friends made the decision to bury the boys simply in the courtyard of Buckden church. It would be several months before Katherine Brandon could return with family and members of the court to say good-bye to her boys with proper services and eulogies, to see to epitaphs for their final resting places.

Devastated by her loss, it mattered little to Katherine that the Suffolk dukedom—extinct in the male line—now passed to Frances Brandon Grey, her sons' half-sister, and through her to her husband, Henry Grey, the Marquis of Dorset.

For years, the fact that two sturdy boys stood between him and his wife's inheritance had gnawed at the marquis. Such irritation was second only to the fact that *he* had no sons at all, only three colorless girls, one of whom had the misfortune to be a dwarf. Both he and Frances had accepted that there would probably be no sons. But with a dukedom now his, their daughters assumed an even greater importance, for now they might achieve even more illustrious marriages than he'd anticipated. Certainly the Privy Council would be more amenable to—perhaps even eager for—Edward's marriage to Jane.

For the new Duke and Duchess of Suffolk now possessed one of the most renowned titles in the kingdom and with it came much that was material and satisfying. The Greys would have not only the magnificence of Bradgate but also palatial Suffolk House, that near-royal dwelling in Southwark, just down from the church where their wedding festivities had been celebrated. In addition, the dukedom held numerous manors and castles scattered through the West and North of England, with holdings run by farmers and small tenant-holders whose rents and produce contributed greatly to the Suffolk coffers. Worry over gambling debts—although not the game itself—was now a thing of the past, the marquis realized. With their new wealth and the opportunity to enhance the family fortunes by marriage or the exchange or sale of their many possessions, their prosperity was unlimited. Katherine Brandon would be the Dowager Duchess of Suffolk—a ridiculous title for one only thirty-three years old—and would, undoubtedly, retire to her own family's ancestral seat, Grimsthorpe Castle near the little village of Bourne in Lincolnshire. There she could continue her study of the "new religion" which had so interested her and Queen Katherine Parr. There she might recover from the devastating loss of husband and sons, of her friend the queen, whose child, little Mary Seymour, was still in her care. But other tangible assets of the dukedom—the properties, land, jewels, horses and wagons, the handsome books, porcelains, gold and silver objects and paintings—all belonged to Frances and Henry Grey.

To enjoy such wealth and splendor—and in so doing to shed the last shameful tinge of association with the infamous Thomas Seymour—the Greys returned to London. In the summer of 1551, when Jane Grey was fourteen, she packed her books and writing materials, fed the golden carp in the fishpond on the Bradgate terrace, stroked the mane of her favorite horse—too old to take to London—and with her family rode down the long approach lined with Spanish chestnuts. On past the old Priory of Ulverscroft and out onto the London road, she could hardly know—especially in the face of her family's happiness—that the Bradgate years had come to an end. Now more than ever, she would be part of the court.

*   *   *

At fourteen Jane was old enough to enjoy the substantial changes the dukedom had brought to her family, if only for the fact that it brought joy and pleasure to her mother's usually dour countenance and lessened the worried look on her father's face. While Jane had certainly been deprived of any parental love or attention, she'd never lacked for anything else. Bradgate in the North and Dorset Place in London were as beautiful as her father's taste and her mother's money could make them. But even they faded in comparison with the overwhelming grandeur and richness of Suffolk House.

While a desolate Kate Brandon grieved for her sons at her northern home, the court—led by young Edward, who had studied, played, wrestled and ridden with both Suffolk boys since their young childhood—went into formal mourning. But once that period passed, courtiers flocked to pay homage to the new Duke and Duchess of Suffolk. Frances Grey was radiant; her stout, flushed features beamed rosily at family and guests alike. She was overjoyed to be back in the house in which she'd grown up and to have that house *hers*. Henry Grey walked bemused through the beautiful rooms, recalling the sight of the king dancing in the Great Hall; or, picking up priceless objects, recalling his father-in-law's fondling them appreciatively. Out in the stables were the superb Spanish jennets and French stallions; in the kennels, the greyhounds awaited only his command for coursing in the woods between Bermondsey Abbey and the river; in the mews, where the prized Suffolk birds were kept, it would be difficult to make his choice.

Once again the dressmakers were called and his daughters' and wife's wardrobes were replenished with costly gowns of cloth of gold, cloth of silver and other rare and extravagant fabrics, richly laden with furs at the hem and sleeves. Jeweled caps and jackets, long rich gloves of fine Spanish leather and the famous necklaces, brooches, pins and rings of Jane's grandmother the beautiful Mary Tudor, the "French Queen," were sorted out for inspection. Table diamonds, round diamonds, big and small, vied in brilliance with rubies, emeralds, sapphires and the lustrous colors of amethyst—the little king's favorite color—garnets, creamy pearls and pastel tourmalines. All were clustered in boxes, caskets, coffers and cases nested in velvet pouches, faded over the years, for some of the jewels had belonged to the Plantagenets. Along with Katherine and Mary, Jane never ceased to wonder at their beauty. It never occurred to her to ask for any to wear or keep, nor did her mother offer unless there was a special occasion.

In addition to their distaste for such grand frivolity, the opulence of home and dress was regarded by Jane's tutor and chaplain with suspicion, compounded by the social demands made upon their pupil's time. John Aylmer and James Haddon had wrestled with the Greys' lax manner of living—the ceaseless hunting, socializing and, above all, their gambling—as best they could. In a confrontation between Haddon and Jane's father, the chaplain had thundered that he intended to make Grey's gambling the subject of a Christmas sermon. Henry Grey had capitulated, soothing the irate prelate and promising all gambling in his home would stop. Triumphant, Haddon prepared to find means to exploit or destroy other unwholesome Grey habits—only to learn that Grey had forbidden only his *servants* to gamble. The prelate and tutor remained undaunted, continuing to search for a way to protect Jane's morals from such dire influences. But it had taken almost more forbearance than either one possessed when the marquis became a duke, and they were informed that they must leave Bradgate for those twin cells of corruption—London and the court. The two men recognized that there would now be no restraining either the duke or duchess, that their already lavish style of living would only increase to a splendor approximating that of royalty.

And in the months ahead their worst fears were realized. The new Duke of Suffolk now spent more time at court for council meetings, court functions and ceremonies involving the king and his ministers. Although Edward Seymour had been reinstated as a Privy Councillor, his brooding presence was tempered by the more aggressive style of the Earl of Warwick. Dudley dominated the meetings, listened to other opinions and competently organized the council's work with great deliberation. But the problems that had faced the Protector now faced the earl. Land enclosure had increased, sending peasant families onto the road to starve or die from exposure in one of the nation's bitterest winters; the cities of London, Bristol and York were flooded with the homeless. The debased coinage had sunk to a new low and merchants complained that all "the gold was driven out of England." Now that the strongly Protestant Protector was no more, the Catholics "with renewed hope" began to fight back. The forbidden Mass was held in two Oxford chapels as Catholic prelates and councillors joined together, hoping to alleviate many of Seymour's more radical changes in favor of the restoration of Henry VIII's hybrid Catholicism. But, as both sides were to learn, "the Earl of Warwick himself was untroubled with religious convictions of any kind, and might take either side with equal unconscientiousness." Abroad, Boulogne, "ill-supplied and imperfectly garrisoned," was under diplomatic siege by the French and it was feared the city—which Henry, in one of the latter years of his life, had won—would be lost. The French opinion of the English government was evident in the succinct comment of an envoy sent by Henri II to pay his respects to Edward on his accession. Of the Privy Council, he said, "Out of twelve who kneel, seven would willingly cut the throats of both the King and the Duke of Somerset [the Protector]."

If national problems were the same for the earl as for the Protector, the relationship between John Dudley and the king was very different. Whereas Seymour had paid young Edward little attention, either personal or in government matters, the Earl of Warwick wisely kept the boy informed. Each day, a councillor was sent to brief Edward on matters facing the country, and later Dudley would ask his opinion or his understanding if the two differed. The king listened to arguments and refutations and, in time, was even allowed to present his views to the full council, a heady experience for the previously isolated and lonely fourteen-year-old. Despite John Calvin's admonition to Edward that "God does not allow anyone to sport with his name, mingling frivolities among his holy and sacred ordinances," John Dudley insisted on some alleviation of the boy's loneliness. Edward was allowed, indeed urged, to participate in running at the ring, archery and bowling contests, to play tennis and toss-ball with young courtiers or members of his chamber. For the first time, the boy joined in the sweaty, swearing competition of youth, which brought a healthier glow to his cheeks and more confidence to his manner. Dudley, the father of five sons, knew just what would appeal to the boy—how much such participation meant to one who'd been so cloistered.

With the court, Edward also attended bull and bear baitings held at Hampton Court, went abroad on the river to watch the "wild-fire cast out of boats, and many other pretty conceits." In July 1551 he wrote in his *Journal* of "a challenge made by me, that I, with sixteen of my chamber, should run at base, shoot and run at ring with seventeen of my servants, gentlemen in the court." He attended masques and balls, jousts and even a water pageant with tilting amidst a mock sea battle. When the Protector's daughter, Anne Seymour, was wed to the Earl of Warwick's son Lord Lisle, Edward was present and, the next day, watched the ceremonies that united Dudley's third son, Robert, with Amy Robsart. Impressed by the festivities, Edward wrote that "a fair dinner was made." Later, there was "dauncing" and he and the ladies went into two chambers "made of boughs" to watch a joust followed by games, "where certain gentlemen did strive who should first take away a goose's head, which was hanged alive on two crossed posts."

Edward had now emerged from childhood into adolescence. With Jane Seymour's blond hair, her gray eyes and the fair skin of the Tudors, he was a strikingly handsome young boy, sensitive to the fact that one shoulder was a bit higher than the other, and that the easy camaraderie of those his own age—such as Dudley's brood—did not come easily to him. Aware that his rank and isolation rendered him eternally apart, Edward bore all his responsibilities willingly, determined to do and give his best, a precocious attitude commenced by his father and fostered and encouraged since he was ten by tutors, clergymen and councillors. Now that he was almost fifteen and in another year would become king in fact as well as in name, Edward began—with John Dudley's help—to absorb the mystique of kingship and rudiments of power that only someone who had observed the intrigues of court life, knowing all manner of its secrets, could give.

Soon after their return to court, Frances Grey, the new Duchess of Suffolk, fell ill at Sheen, the old royal palace at Richmond. Quickly, Henry Grey left London, taking Jane with him to the venerable fortress, built by Henry VII, with its fourteen onion-shaped domes on the banks of the Thames. Explaining his sudden departure from court, the duke wrote William Cecil about ". . . my wife who . . . I assure you, is more like to die than to live. I never saw a more sicker creature in my life than she is. She hath three diseases. The first is a hot burning ague, that doth hold her twenty-four hours, the other is the stopping of the spleen, the third is hypochondriac passion. These three being enclosed in one body, it is to be feared that death must needs follow. . . ." Grey said he was, "I assure you, not a little troubled."

For Jane, the experience of an ill and suffering mother was compounded by the view of a *helpless* mother. Never before had she seen Frances Grey so vulnerable; never had she faced the fact that her mother might die. She did as the doctor advised, pressing cold cloths to her mother's feverish forehead or raising a glass of cool liquid to the woman's hot lips. Though there were terrible fevers rumored prevalent along the Thames at the time, Jane felt no fear, though her sisters Katherine and Mary had been kept in London. Obedience was so much a part of her being that it never occurred to her to be frightened or that she might become ill herself. Duty commanded she care for her sick mother, and when not at the bedside, she was on her knees praying to her own intimate God that He spare Frances Grey. Jane's normal sweetness of disposition was her main support and comfort; her place was with her mother and she would do her best. There was no sadness or worry; her heart was not involved, but conscience was. As soon as her mother improved and the complaints commenced, she was relieved and happy to be sent back to London, to her sisters and Mrs. Ellen. It was one of the few occasions when she'd been such a long time in her mother's company and there'd been no blows.

By November, Frances Grey had improved sufficiently to attend the welcoming ceremonies for Mary of Guise. The Queen Dowager and Regent of Scotland had requested a passage of safe conduct through England after her ship was stormbound on its southern coast. Disappointed as Edward was that Mary's daughter would not be his wife, the king and the Privy Council were determined to show their hospitality. Edward ordered that the mother of little Mary Stuart not only be received with a safe passage, but with "special honors." From Portsmouth to Hampton Court and then to London, where—with the full court watching—the tall, angular sovereign strode to greet Edward, to kneel before him as he sat under his canopy of estate, Mary was profusely welcomed. At dinner Frances Grey and her husband sat near the Scottish sovereign, near enough to hear Edward—who'd been prompted by his council—lament that Mary Stuart would wed the French Dauphin. He reminded the Queen Dowager of her treaty with his father, saying it should be renewed and that he would treat her daughter with great kindness. Mary of Guise reminded Edward that the Protector's bloody excursions into Scotland had effectively nullified such a contract, saying in an amused manner—to which Edward had no reply—"Such a fashion of dealing is not the nearest way to conquer a lady."

Jane, clad in one of her more splendid new gowns and wearing the Suffolk gems in her hair and on her person, watched the royal ceremonies with great interest; she was now old enough to attend such affairs and sat with the younger members of the court. Both Princess Mary and Princess Elizabeth were absent. When Jane asked why, there was no precise answer. But it was well known that Mary was still adamant about clinging to that manner of worship which had been forbidden by law. And Elizabeth, now nearly eighteen, had undergone what some of Jane's young companions said was an amazing transformation. After the Seymour tragedy and the bandying of her name and reputation with what she'd called "shameful slanders," Elizabeth had wholeheartedly embraced the "new religion," which Katherine Parr had encouraged during that time they'd lived in the same household. Pious and sober, Elizabeth now wore only plain clothing, with no adornment of ribbons or feathers or lace. She used no jewelry and her hair hung simply to her shoulders or else was captive under a small plain hood. Jane had an opportunity to see—following the Scottish sovereign's visit—just how solemn Elizabeth had become. In the days of amusement and entertainment after Mary of Guise had proceeded toward Scotland, Jane saw Elizabeth, clad in a simple gown of plain gray cloth, her slim figure devoid of jewels. She learned the princess had come to see the king, who doted on her; they were near the same age and shared the same religious beliefs, thus preventing any embarrassing situations such as Edward suffered with Mary. Both could scarce remember ever having had any mothering, which Mary had enjoyed for almost sixteen years before "the troubles" and Anne Boleyn had destroyed her mother and father's marriage. Mrs. Ellen said someone told her Edward called Elizabeth "his sweetest and dearest sister" and hated it when she left the court. He respected and admired his older sister, Mary, but her religion, staunch presence and forthright manner made him uncomfortable.

During the royal visit, Jane's days were considerably different from her old solitary life. Rushing home to change into yet another gown before proceeding to more balls, masques and hours of endless eating, held more than the lure of the forbidden for the lonely child of the classroom. The contrast between life at Bradgate and in London was no contrast at all; they were as different—and enjoyable in their own way—as possible. But the social life at court had apparently proved a temptation to Jane. The change in his pupil's days, even her dress, irritated John Aylmer, and he wrote Bullinger of his fear that Jane was being exposed to harmful practices. He lauded Princess Elizabeth as "a lady in so much gospel light to lay aside, much less look down upon gold, jewels, and braidings of the hair." As Jane's family continued to enjoy the aftermath of the Scottish sovereign's visit, Aylmer wrote another of his Swiss correspondents, begging him to remonstrate with his pupil.

It now remains for me to request . . . that you will instruct my pupil, in your next letter, as to what embellishment and adornment of person is becoming in a young woman professing godliness! In treating on this subject, you may bring forward the example of . . . the Princess Elizabeth, who goes clad in every respect as becomes a young maiden; and yet no one is induced by the example of so illustrious a lady. . . . Moreover, I wish you would prescribe to her [the Lady Jane] the length of time she may properly devote to the study of music, for in this respect the people of this country of England err beyond measure.

 14

The Greys spent their first ducal Christmas at Tylsey, another Suffolk residence, where Henry Grey threw open the doors of the vast house to entertain the whole county with a group of traveling players, including "one boy who sang like a nightingale." The duke's tenants, servants and farm laborers pursued their own forms of earthly enjoyment, including an abundance of drink, dicing, dancing and other holiday entertainment which earned Chaplain Haddon's condemnation. He considered the rites pagan and in some instances even papistical, writing his friend Bullinger, "They fancy that they are merry after this fashion on account of the birth of Our Lord. This still prevails among the vulgar . . ."; and then, thinking Bullinger might think the same tinge of the forbidden had invaded the duke's home, where gambling was openly enjoyed, said, ". . . but not in this house." But his annoyance plainly showed in his comment: "I bear this out of compulsion . . . and deal tenderly with them."

Henry Grey's brothers, Lord Thomas and Lord John, arrived with their families, and to Jane's great joy, Katherine Brandon came to visit her stepdaughter's family in a house no longer hers. Jane had always admired the duchess's humor and zest for living, her strong bent for learning and the deep loyalty she inspired in her friends. She was aware many disliked Kate Brandon, whom she'd even heard referred to as "a lady of sharp wit and sure hand to thrust it home and make it pierce when she pleased." But Jane cared little what others thought of the duchess. A special bond between the two—important to Jane, who lacked any close friend of her own—had been established in those years when she'd lived at court with Katherine Parr and the king. It was then that the duchess, sensing the child's loneliness and observing her parents' treatment, had reached out to the shy, silent Jane, including her in childish games and finding time in the court's busy day to talk with her and encourage her response.

Now, escaping from the holiday festivities, the incessant banqueting and merrymaking, the two took long walks in the unusually mild air, reminiscing about the happy days at court and at Chelsea with Katherine Parr—that life they'd both known with the queen in the days before she married Thomas Seymour. Katherine caused Jane to blush when she mentioned her attractive gown or headdress; the duchess recognized that compliments did not often come the girl's way. It was easier for both to talk of her lessons, for they were similar to those her young step-uncles, Katherine Brandon's dead sons, had been studying. Jane found their mother knowledgeably interested and it was refreshing to discuss her studies with a woman. Ever since the death of Katherine Parr—who'd shown such interest in her education—she'd been able to talk of her classroom work only with male tutors.

Inevitably their talk turned to the "new religion," the fear that John Dudley might not carry on the Protector's work in furthering the cause of the Protestant party or that he might listen sympathetically to the pro-Catholics such as Stephen Gardiner, the Bishop of Winchester, now languishing in the Tower for his defiance. The duchess told a delighted Jane there was a Prayer Book printed in English in all churches near her Lincolnshire home and that she intended to see they were placed even farther afield. The work helped her forget her loss, she said, while advancing a cause dear to her heart. Her tone indicated she was not missing the responsibilities—the homes, servants and luxuries—that Jane's family were so obviously enjoying. She was worried about Princess Mary's refusal to dispense with the Mass or accept any aspect of the "new religion." The Protector had been solicitious of Mary, for she and his wife were close friends, but the duchess did not think John Dudley would be as considerate. Jane was always startled when she remembered that the duchess and the princess were almost the same age. Kate Brandon's mother, Maria de Salinas, had come from Spain as a lady-in-waiting to Mary's mother, Katherine of Aragon, and the two had grown up together, as close friends as their mothers had been. But the duchess, sparkling in personality and robust in health, married and a mother, was so different from the princess, it was easy to forget they'd been childhood friends.

Kate Brandon explained that Mary had been summoned to London by Edward and the Privy Council after commissioners—sent by Dudley to her home, Newhall in Essex, to command her in the king's name to refrain from using the Mass—had returned to London, frustrated and unsuccessful. Mary had told them that while she was the king's most humble, obedient subject and sister and would most willingly obey all his commandments, she would lay her head on the block rather than forgo the Mass. She told the commissioners that Edward, so young, could hardly be a good judge of the laws being made in his name.

The duchess said Mary's attitude reminded her of the long years when she'd refused to accept her father's supremacy over the pope. Then Henry had ordered Mary into exile at Hatfield. She never saw her mother again and was allowed to communicate with her father only through his ministers, who used every ploy, including the threat of death, to gain her submission. Emotionally, Mary had paid a high price for her defiance, Kate Brandon said, being compelled in the end to comply with her father's orders. Now, seemingly, the same tragedy was to be played again with her brother. Jane listened with mixed feelings. She could not understand Mary's intense loyalty to a form of worship she considered abhorrent to any sensible person. And the thought that it was even *possible* to defy one's parents was so foreign to Jane's nature, she could scarce comprehend it. Was Mary being foolish, stubborn or clever?

The answer was evident sooner than anyone expected when Mary came to London, riding "unto St. John's, her place, with fifty knights and gentlemen in velvet coats and chains of gold afore her and after her four score of gentlemen and ladies everyone having a pair of beads of black." The challenging gesture, with prayer beads and the conspicuous gold cross at Mary's waist, was cheered by the Catholics who ran from their homes to greet her, calling out cries of good cheer and encouragement.

Such popularity was not lost on the Privy Council, particularly John Dudley. Unlike the Protector, he'd refused to "wink at her services." Mary's welcome was a vivid demonstration to the councillors there were still many English who preferred the old ways. William Cecil, writing a note to himself in order to clarify his thoughts when war with France threatened, said, "We are not agreed among ourselves. The majority of our people will be with our adversaries (the Catholics). It is reasonable to think that as long as the Crown can maintain tranquility, should war break out, they (the people) will listen to what they consider the voice of God calling on them to restore the Papacy. . . ."

It was less than twenty years since England's split with Rome. Her people were still divided and the council considered Mary's warm welcome as evidence of that deep schism. For several years, with the Protector's indulgence, she'd followed the manner of worship in which she'd been born and raised, writing the council that she intended to continue with "the ceremonies performed in my late father's time," saying her faith was hardly a whim, but one held "by all Christendom . . . under the late king, until you altered it with your laws. . . ." Repeatedly, she stressed the king's youth and tartly told the councillors that while she owed her brother all loyalty, "To you, my lords, I owe nothing beyond amity and good will, which you will find in me as I meet with the same in you."

Mary's sensible logic had been lost on the Privy Council, whose reaction was passed on to the king. In response to his sister's plea for understanding—that he continue, as the Protector had, to "wink at her services"—Edward asked how Mary would feel if someone in *her* household persisted in disregarding her orders? "Sister," he wrote, "consider that an exception has been made in your favor for this long time past, to incline you to obey and not to harden you in this resistance. . . ." The time had come, Edward said, "for I will see my laws strictly obeyed and those who break them shall be watched and denounced."

Such an impasse—and Mary's continued defiance—hardly made

for a friendly or relaxed atmosphere when she at last appeared before her brother and the Privy Council. It was difficult to determine who was more nervous, the king or the princess. Five years had elapsed since their father's death and in that time, as they saw less and less of each other, the warm family rapport established by Katherine Parr, the joy of a small boy in his older sister, had faded. Now *he* was the king and his council was determined—and watching to see that he did not fail—that "popery" and all its evils were swept from the land.

For all her outward stubbornness, Mary had suffered a subtle harassment from the council which had upset and frightened her. Her servants had been interrogated, at times removed from her presence for days. Under the guise of improving Crown lands, some of the more lucrative of her Norfolk lands were exchanged for others of less value, which in the end gave her less income. Mary wrote the council that she hoped the king—who she doubted even knew of the exchange—"would not seek to diminish her slender substance further." Her attitude and behavior had been so bruited about the court that many, recognizing the strong disfavor in which she was now held—and with no Edward Seymour to protect her—no longer pretended any interest in the beleaguered princess.

On the day of her appearance before the king and Privy Council, Mary's nervousness was plainly evident. It had been a long time since she'd seen Edward, and in one so young, even weeks make a difference. The king, she could see, was no longer a child; he was a young man. Inches taller, he was uncommonly attractive. His pale skin now had more color—a testament to Dudley's insistence on outdoor activities—and his light-colored gray eyes had a confident look Mary had never seen before. She'd hoped against hope that Edward's goodwill would not be turned against her and was relieved, when she advanced to kneel at his feet, to see his welcoming smile and feel the kiss of welcome on her cheek as he raised her with a firm grip, and then, smiling, sat with easy grace in his chair under the canopy of estate. Turning to greet the council, Mary saw Edward Seymour seated near John Dudley. There was an impassive look on the former Protector's face. It was a look Mary recognized, one she'd often adopted herself in time of crisis. It concealed one's real feelings as it gave one time to adapt to the situation at hand. Mary had been told that Seymour had regained a good deal of his power and influence. If so, she did not think he would endanger it by a strong defense of her.

And then the questioning began. On the religious practices of her household—the priests of the "old religion" who kept to the old ways such as celebrating the Mass, the wearing of costly copes, the intercession for saintly benevolences—all of which could no longer be tolerated. Mary did not know, or chose not to recognize, the success the Protestant party had reaped since her father's death. Spending so much time away from the court, she was unfamiliar with the true extent of the spoliation of church property—much of it by the very councillors sitting in judgment on her—and unaware that a return to the "old religion" would mean the return of those properties and their wealth to the Church. Scholarships sponsored by the Crown or the nobles had been abandoned in the universities—especially those holding any Catholic tinge—which were called "stables of asses, stews and schools of the Devil." The service of the Mass was parodied by the irreverent in plays, and Protestant ministers labeled the pro-Catholic priests as "imps of the whore of Babylon." Altars had been trampled, missals chopped in pieces with hatchets, and college libraries plundered and burned. If the contents were truly valuable, many had been taken to the nobles' homes. In St. Paul's, horses were ridden in the aisles, and the space between venerable monuments used for stabling until the stench of animal filth became unbearable. Almshouses and hospitals run by the Church for relief of the poor were abandoned and their structures plundered for their building materials.

As for Edward, for nearly five years he'd listened to his councillors' and his uncle's recommendations, buoyed and encouraged almost constantly by his ministers and advisers, who spoke of the "old faith" as a sure way to Hell's fires. Loving Mary as he did, in his young, pious and innocent mind—and not always aware of much that was done in his name—he viewed this confrontation between his sister and himself as a way of saving her soul from eternal damnation and misery.

Instead, it only proved that brother and sister were far apart. When Edward reminded Mary how long he'd suffered her Mass "against my will," she said that as a subject she would always obey, but protested again that laws made during his minority were not just laws and then, unthinking, said, "Riper age and experience

will teach your Majesty more yet." Edward, stung by her condescending tone, cried, "You also may have something to learn—none
are too old for that!"

Mary replied that it would be impossible for her to leave her
manner of worship. Had not that form also been her father's religion as he'd left it in his will? Turning to the councillors, she bitterly reminded them they'd not only disregarded Henry's will in
most respects, but had not said "Masses for the king, my father's
soul, as he commanded." The incongruity of lecturing the council
on a religious practice they and their king now denounced and
condemned caused John Dudley to laugh. Baiting Mary, he said,
"How now, my lady, it seems your Grace is trying to show us in
a hateful light to the king."

Mary ignored Dudley's jocular remark. Facing the council, she
cried, "Look at me! Do you know me? How is it you make so
small account of me? I am the daughter of Henry the Eighth and
sister of Edward the Sixth! It was a great pity that my brother's
kingdom should fall into your hands . . . !" And then, her courage breaking, she covered her face with her hands and began to
cry. Edward, seeing his sister's distress, also began to weep.

Immediately the council, not wishing to continue further under
such emotional conditions, proffered their sympathy as Edward and
Mary attempted to regain their composure. Seeing her brother in
tears, Mary said, "I would have hoped that . . . your Majesty
would have allowed me to continue in the old religion. There are
but two things—soul and body. My soul I offer to God and my
body to your Majesty's service. I would rather it pleased your
Majesty to take away my life than the old religion, in which I desire to live and die."

Edward, still nervous, clutched at his doublet with sweaty palms.
His voice wavered as he replied, "I desire no such sacrifice. . . ."
Relieved, Mary told her brother "to give no credit to any person
who might desire to make him believe evil of me, my religion or
anything else. . . ." And then, turning to the councillors, she cried,
"His Majesty has been hardened against me—God knows who were
his advisers in this!"

At which point Dudley dismissed the council, deciding there was
nothing to be gained that day. The king, without a word to his
sister, left the room, and the embattled woman departed.

* * *

Within days, Frances Grey visited Princess Mary. To Jane's surprise, her mother said she was to go also, and after inspecting her appearance carefully, the two arrived at Mary's London home, St. John's, Clerkenwell. They found Mary nervous and frail-looking, and as Jane sat quietly by, the princess told Frances Grey she had trouble sleeping, since she suffered so from nerves, trouble with her teeth and headaches. She was upset, she said, at having to defend herself before her brother and his council and protested again that the religious laws were being changed by others, not Edward, and that the Church was not the Church of her father. Jane listened to the conversation with great interest. She wanted to reply that the old king's religious practices had been cleansed, purified and were now more the original beliefs of the ancient Church fathers than the religion Mary had been taught. But she said nothing, knowing it would only incur her mother's displeasure. It was not her place—a fourteen-year-old girl—to advise a thirty-four-year-old princess. Frances Grey gave no advice either; Jane would have been surprised if she had, knowing her mother lacked any strong religious convictions. As their visit ended, Mary summoned a lady-in-waiting, saying she had presents for her guests. When the woman reappeared bearing a coffer, Mary selected a pair of crystal beads inset with gold for Frances Grey and then clasped a small necklace of pearls and rubies—the kind she'd have worn as a child—about a startled Jane's neck. Jane was delighted and warmly returned Mary's affectionate embrace. Despite all the Suffolk jewels her parents had inherited, she'd been given none and she found Mary's generosity touching.

In the weeks following the visit with Mary, Jane's family traveled constantly, either to visit their new properties or to be entertained by those anxious to ingratiate themselves with the Greys. The journeys themselves were fatiguing, necessitating overnight stops either in the homes of friends along the way or in well-known inns which gave themselves over to the ducal entourage. In most instances the ill-kept roads were muddy and dangerous, and rain, sleet or even snow often impeded progress while everyone shivered in their wagons or litters. Upon arrival at inn or manor house, where the drafty corridors and icy rooms meant one slept in one's clothes, the family would determine to make an early start to arrive at their destination by nightfall so as not to suffer another night's discomfort.

It was at the end of one such tiring and cold journey that Jane, feverish and weak—and uneasily aware she was inconveniencing her parents—took to her bed. She was now almost fifteen and not constitutionally strong. For the past year, she'd left her beloved Bradgate to visit estate upon estate she'd been told to consider another "home." She'd met and mingled with more people in one year than in all her previous life; her studies had been interrupted and her tutor and chaplain were angry and disappointed in her. She'd had little time to practice her beloved music. She'd tolerated the hazard of being almost constantly in the company of her parents, whom she'd tried—with little success—to please. It all had an effect, and, as her mother had done months before, Jane now became seriously ill. Mrs. Ellen and Mrs. Tylney spent hours at her bedside; her parents and sisters remained absent for fear of contamination.

The interlude gave Jane, verging on young adulthood, time to think. The heady life at court into which her parents, with their considerable energies, had flung themselves, was not any real temptation. Yet, emerging now from childhood, Jane acknowledged she'd enjoyed that time of unfamiliar social activity. Very feminine, she'd liked and appreciated her splendid wardrobe, the few jewels she'd been given by Mary and Katherine Parr and the compliments of friends and such as Mrs. Ellen. The game she'd played for so long to escape from her parents' carping or worse, a game which demanded only that she remove herself and keep herself from their presence as much and for as long as possible, had ended during that year when she was almost constantly in their company. Now her illness gave her time to reflect on that relationship which would end—in a material sense—only when she married. And she was now old enough to do so.

The boundaries of Jane's world actually enlarged only slightly with her father's acquisition of a dukedom. And once that year of intense social activity was over, she returned unscathed to her own. During the weeks of her convalescence, John Ulmis, Henry Grey's protégé, wrote Bullinger, "The duke's daughter had recovered from a severe and dangerous illness." Jane was now engaged, he said, "in some extraordinary production which will very soon be brought to light, accompanied with a commendation of yourself." With the enforced rest, Jane had at last been able to study and a relieved John Aylmer now gave her some books on the Psalms in Greek, Chrysostom on the Gospels in Greek and other "great treasure of valuable books." Her Swiss friends, urged on by Ulmis, Aylmer and Haddon, continued to write, their letters often being the high point of Jane's day. Her parents left her strictly alone in Mrs. Ellen's care. Ill, she was of little use to them, she knew. But the lure of a familiar and beloved world of study—with her tutor visiting her sickroom or sending daily lessons by Mrs. Ellen—was as challenging and rewarding as ever. Happily immersed in her new books and with no demands upon anything but her intellect, slowly Jane recovered.

The world to which Jane returned was still bordered by her studies, religious and academic, her devotions and the continuing philosophic dissertations with the renowned German ministers and Zwinglian disciples. She'd absorbed everything her Swiss friends had written her and hardly needed the constant encouragement of Aylmer and others to continue the correspondence. Her parents approved of the relationship, even though they never recognized it as one more bulwark in the shelter Jane had made for herself against *them*. If she was aware that her tutor, chaplain, the student Ulmis and the reformers themselves were boasting loudly of their connection with the exalted Duke of Suffolk, Jane cared little. When she told her father's protégé that she desired to learn Hebrew, John Ulmis quickly wrote Conrad Pellican, another distinguished reformer, for advice. Jane had asked, Ulmis wrote, "of the best way of acquiring that language, and cannot easily discover the path. . . ." Ulmis said he hoped Pellican would be willing "to oblige a powerful and eminent nobleman, with honor to yourself. . . ." So as not to lose Pellican, Ulmis mentioned that soon Jane might wed King Edward, for her parents still devoutly wished the marriage to take place. Then, putting pretense aside, he noted that if Pellican would help with the Hebrew, "*she* [Jane] will the more easily be kept in her distinguished course of learning, [her father] also will be more steadfast in religion, and *I* shall appear to be neither unmindful of, nor ungrateful for, the favors conferred by them on myself."

To Jane's delight, Pellican agreed and she plunged into her study of the Jewish Talmud, which the reformer had translated into Latin. And immediately, Aylmer and Haddon consulted with each other as to how they might use the learned Pellican's influence to "guide and direct persons at her time of life." Obviously, Jane's home environment—too busily self-indulgent for their conservative tastes—continued to vex both men.

It was soon obvious Jane was torn. She'd tremendously enjoyed the exchange of ideas with the Swiss ministers. They were of the same mind as she, not only upon almost any subject, but the nuances and shaded meanings of her religious and scholarly study as well. Yet they—whom she regarded with awed veneration—seemed to regard music as frivolous, whereas *she* found it comfortably inspiring, a relaxation from constant discipline. It was the same with her splendid clothing. The luxurious dresses and furs that now crowded her wardrobe, and the precious jewels she was allowed to wear occasionally, were not necessary to her happiness. But using them provided a divertisement from her otherwise normally predictable day, and they were, Jane knew, only right and proper for one of her rank, who could hardly dress like a milkmaid.

And yet, there was Elizabeth, a *princess*, garbed in such simplicity that she was always the most striking figure in any room—while the flashing jewels, lustrous satins and superb damasks, the heavy headdresses of plumes, crests and embroidery everyone else wore, appeared in ill taste. Instinctively, Jane preferred the simple; it was easier to choose and wear such a gown, for no great harm was done if it tore or became soiled. But heretofore her life had been restricted and lonely enough for her to appreciate the soft fabrics, the rich adornment and the jewels she'd been allowed to wear in the past year as she went from child to young adult. She'd been pleased that a certain becoming shade complimented her bright hair, how a certain cut of fabric emphasized the soft swell of breasts and hid her thin body in extreme fullness and folds. Battista Spinola, a Genoese merchant, saw Jane shortly after she'd returned to London and he wrote, "This Jane Grey is very short and thin, but prettily-shaped and graceful. She has small features and a well-made nose, the mouth flexible and the lips red. The eyebrows are arched and darker than her hair, which is nearly red. Her eyes are sparkling, her color good, *but freckled. . . .*"

Jane was also old enough now to recognize she had a *persona* of her own. It was not, perhaps, the kind her parents desired and certainly, as the oldest, she should have been a boy. While she would never become immune to their abuse, it was so much a part of her life, she accepted it as she accepted Mrs. Ellen's affection or the fact that her younger sister Katherine was now encouraged to participate in the more active sports the Greys loved and was proving, in every way, a more satisfactory daughter. Jane knew she was valuable to her family only as a daughter who might wed a king could be valuable.

The letters from her Swiss friends had therefore been a tremendous outlet, not only emotionally and intellectually but also because she could tell her correspondents things she'd tell no one else. "Were I to extol you as truth requires, I should need either the oratorical powers of Demosthenes or the eloquence of Cicero . . . but I am too young and ignorant for either. . . . *In this earthly prison*, you pass your days as if you were dead," she wrote to one. Jane reveled in her correspondents' fulsome praise; never before had she been so indulged and so gratified. Like Elizabeth, Jane had never had any real mothering except what little Katherine Parr had given her. Both young girls lacked that wellspring of emotional awareness, a result of the loving attention such as the Princess Mary had always had from her mother. Jane also recognized the fairness of Aylmer's and Haddon's anxieties, that living the sort of life her parents lived was not for her if she was to reach that pinnacle of intellectual perfection they sought for her. She did not understand that a pupil of her potential did not often come a tutor's way, especially one of such illustrious background who could also bestow the creature rewards of a good and comfortable living. She knew both tutors had given their best and wished only the best for her. The fortress of learning she'd constructed for herself since she could open a book had more than served its purpose, and in it she'd defended herself against her parents' emotional and physical onslaughts.

Now, each passing month brought the time when she'd leave home—and abuse—forever. She'd proven to herself she could adapt to whatever her parents wished for her. In that, she was a child of her era, when devotion and strict obedience to parental wishes was as firm a doctrine as devotion to one's Savior. And, having accomplished that and never challenging her parents or drawing attention to herself in the doing, by the time Jane had recovered, her tutor's admonitions, her chaplain's reproaches, the suggestions of her strict Calvinistic correspondents—as well as the sobering example of a pious Princess Elizabeth—had worked their way. Once she was well, Jane put aside her rich clothes, wearing them only when occasion—or her parents—demanded. She returned the few jewels she owned to their boxes and pouches. The fulsome adulation of her Swiss friends and that of such as Ulmis—heady for one so deprived of affection—was placed in perspective as tensions between pupil, tutor and chaplain disappeared. Now she no longer suffered their disapproval when she appeared for lessons plainly dressed, lacking even a ribbon in her hair; there were no longer any complaints from the two people with whom she spent more time than anyone else. The admonitions from Switzerland ceased and everyone settled down as Jane commenced the learning of Hebrew. If the fine clothes hanging in the wardrobe remained untouched, if Mrs. Ellen was puzzled by the change in her adored charge's character, it mattered little to Jane. The year's experiment with fine living had been resolved, and in many ways her illness had been a welcoming respite. She had learned where her real values lay and she did not intend to lose the comfort and solace of that world again.

15

As Jane lay ill and then, recovering, returned to her books and correspondence, John Dudley, the Earl of Warwick, conspired with several of the Privy Council to complete the downfall of Edward Seymour, the Duke of Somerset. Previously, the former Protector's popularity with the London masses, as well as his status as uncle of the king, had saved him from anything stronger than a short imprisonment and mild fines. He'd re-joined the council, chastened but hardly repentant, and ever since had proven a subtle and persistent thorn in Dudley's side. Several councillors scornfully made wagers on how long the "great love and friendship" of the two—one whose son had married the other's daughter—would last. Those "carry-tales and flatterers" who had Dudley's ear might yet be successful.

The earl accepted that most Londoners detested him as much as they loved "the good duke" and nowhere was this preference more visible than in his, Dudley's, persecution of heretics. During the Protector's reign, Joan Bocher, a Kentish woman, had been apprehended for heresy. With her fellow "gospeller," Anne Askew, who'd preached that the body of Christ was not present in the communion bread, Joan had proclaimed that "Christ did not take flesh from the Virgin Mary; He only passed through her body, as water through the pipe of a conduit, without participating anything of that body." Anne Askew, a friend of Katherine Parr's, had gone to the stake; even the queen's influence could not save her. Similarly, Joan Bocher had spent a year in prison, where persistent efforts to make her recant had been fruitless. The king, however, did not agree with the council that heretics should be burned. Along with John Cheke, his tutor, Edward argued that such a fate damned them to eternal hellfire for their misbeliefs. In this he was like his uncle Edward Seymour, who could "wink at" Princess Mary's Mass even as he sent a Catholic bishop, Stephen Gardiner, to the Tower for refusing to accept Cranmer's Prayer Book.

Now, back in his council seat, the strongly Protestant Seymour objected to Joan Bocher's and Gardiner's continuing confinement. He was so defiant that an angry Dudley told a companion, "He taketh and aspireth to have the self and same overdue an authority . . . as his Grace had . . . being Protector." Dudley had allied himself with the radical Protestant party, not from any strong religious conviction but because that was the faction the young king— whose detestation of any segment of the Catholic ritual or faith was well known—would favor when he attained his majority and ruled on his own. Then, Dudley knew, he must account for his actions, hand over the reins of power and hope the monarch would feel sufficiently grateful to reward his efforts with substantial honors and Crown lands.

In addition to his toleration of heresy, Seymour had been strongly critical of Dudley's management of foreign affairs. Boulogne had been lost, the currency remained debased and some troops were disbanded for lack of funds. Dudley had done little to improve the country's internal disorders, leaving many of the programs the former Protector had instigated at a standstill or abandoned altogether. As he regained some of his former influence, therefore, Seymour felt a responsibility to pursue those projects he considered important and to seek support for them—and himself—from within the council. But the earl, always seemingly aware of his motives, packed both Parliament and the Privy Council with his own strongest followers whenever an issue upon which he differed with Seymour was to be settled. Now their differences were more obvious than ever, particularly in religious affairs, where, as the councillors pointed out, Seymour's championing of Mary Tudor had resulted in their now finding it exceedingly difficult to make her conform. Many of the nobles remembered the staunch refusal of her mother, Katherine of Aragon, who, in the face of Henry VIII's marriage to Anne Boleyn and the birth of the Princess Elizabeth, had refused to accept that she was not still the rightful Queen of England. Katherine had gone to her grave proclaiming that right, and few doubted but that her daughter would do the same to preserve the Mass.

To combat Edward Seymour's bid for his former power, Dudley worked tirelessly against him. When the former Protector persisted in asking for Gardiner's release from the Tower, Dudley was equally determined the archbishop would remain incarcerated. And when Dudley's continuing efforts to convince Joan Bocher of the foolhardiness of her views failed, when she would not recant and would not conform, he strongly encouraged the council to pass sentence of death. When the council, particularly Thomas Cranmer, the Archbishop of Canterbury, agreed that enough time had been spent on the issue, Seymour eventually gave way. Their decision was then sent to the king.

Young Edward protested vigorously and begged Cranmer, his godfather, for another week, another chance, to save the misguided woman. When Cranmer told the boy the council and clergy had made numerous attempts to save Joan Bocher, that she still remained hardened in her views and must suffer the stake, Edward showed more compassion than the archbishop. "What, my lord?" he cried, his voice trembling. "Will ye have me send her quick to the Devil, in all her errors?" When Cranmer said it was pointless to pursue her redemption, Edward burst into tears and cried, "I lay the charge thereof upon you before God!" Shaken, Cranmer returned to the Council Chamber saying that "he had never so much to do in all his life as to cause the king to put his hand" to the execution order.

At the stake, as the sentence was carried out, Joan Bocher shouted to Bishop Ridley, "It was not long ago since you burnt Anne Askew for a piece of bread, yet came yourselves to believe the doctrine for which you burnt her. Now you will burn me for a piece of flesh and in the end you will believe this also. . . ." At the palace, Edward—giving no hint of his true feelings—wrote in his *Journal*, "Joan Bocher, otherwise Joan of Kent, was burnt for holding that Christ was not incarnate of the Virgin Mary, being condemned the year before, but kept in hope of conversion; and the thirteenth of April, the Bishop of London and the Bishop of Ely were to persuade her. But she withstood them, and reviled the preacher that preached at her death, telling him he lied like a knave. . . ."

In addition to Seymour's easy toleration of heretics, Dudley knew that the former Protector had spoken to several intimates of appealing to the country at large via the Parliament in order to curb the earl's power, "lest peradventure of one evil might happen another." He learned Seymour had even commented that Dudley's death—as well as that of several of his followers—would not be amiss. It was obvious to the earl that the duke was merely biding his time before making another leap for power. Dudley knew his own greatest asset was his rapport with the king; Edward much preferred the ebullient duke to his more withdrawn and sober uncle. But the national discontent with religious and political affairs might offer Seymour the chance to regain his former position, and Dudley realized he must meet that challenge before the duke so undermined his authority that even the king's support would mean little.

Dudley found a willing pawn in one Sir Thomas Palmer, as much a soldier of fortune as of the battlefield, where he'd had a distinguished career. With the earl's connivance and encouragement, Palmer made allegations that Edward Seymour had proposed going north "to raise the people" and, at a banquet, to assassinate John Dudley, William Parr and several other nobles. When Richard Whalley, one of Seymour's own retainers, attempted to discuss a return of the Protectorate with members of the lower House of Lords, he was quickly lodged in the Fleet Prison for his pains. Dudley called the charges against Whalley "foolish prattle" but he was, nevertheless, disturbed. When seditious bills and pamphlets "exciting the people against the council" were cast about the London streets, Dudley himself asked Whalley, "What meaneth my lord in this wise to discredit himself and why will he not see his own decay therein? Thinks he to rule and direct the whole council as he will, considering how his late governance is yet misliked?

Neither is he in that credit and best opinion with the king's majesty, as he believeth—and is, by some, fondly persuaded." To emphasize his distress, Dudley's eyes filled with tears.

Later, Palmer further alleged that Seymour had several accomplices who proposed to "incite the people" and "raise the North." One supporter, Lord Arundel, would take possession of the Tower while Sir Miles Partridge would "raise London and possess the Great Seal with the aid of the City apprentices," Palmer said. And then Edward Seymour's daughter, Jane, would be married to the king. When Dudley learned that yet another Seymour confederate, Sir Ralph Vane—who'd suffered humiliation and loss of property at Dudley's hands and was yearning for revenge—could muster two thousand men to deal with any retaliation, Dudley knew he must act, and soon. There was just enough truth in the disgruntled Seymour's own comments—such as the fact that Dudley and his colleagues would probably die in any insurrection, which no one disputed—to lend some substance to what were, in truth, enormously wild accusations mixed with a tinge of the absurd.

But before he could accomplish Edward Seymour's destruction, Dudley had one more card to play. The opportunity came with the ceremonies elevating Jane Grey's father to the dukedom of Suffolk. Though he'd enjoyed its privileges for the past four months, Henry Grey's formal investiture had yet to take place. When the "sweating sickness" invaded the Westminster area, carrying off one of the king's gentlemen of the bedchamber and a groom, the court fled to Hampton Court. There, in Wolsey's palatial Great Hall, on October 11, 1551, the ceremony that made Henry Grey Duke of Suffolk also elevated John Dudley to the dukedom of Northumberland. Jane was still recovering from her illness as Dudley received the ancient title of the Northern Percys. At the same ceremony, William Cecil, Edward Seymour's secretary, and John Cheke, Edward's tutor, were knighted; old Will Paulet became the Marquis of Winchester; and Katherine Parr's brother-in-law, Will Herbert, was made the Earl of Pembroke. Observing the ceremonies, which elevated his adversary to a rank equal to his own—one of only four dukes in all England—Edward Seymour remained silent and expressionless. Shortly after the lavish ceremonies were complete, he left for Syon House, a nearby residence at Isleworth.

There he found the sickness had invaded his home, and several servants were ill. There was no question of his leaving; he must remain at Syon House for fear of infecting others. Thus he was absent for several days as the Privy Council went about its business at Hampton Court, where reports of his alleged misconduct and intrigues were openly discussed. The new Duke of Northumberland, feeling his power and certain of the support of the majority of the council, now decided the time had come. A scapegoat was needed, one who could be blamed for everything that he, Dudley, had not accomplished in the past year. If nothing else, accusations leveled against Seymour would divert attention from the council's shortcomings. Dudley felt he now had sufficient evidence to accuse, and whatever he lacked to attain the final sentence could be gained later. It was important to settle the matter of Edward Seymour's final destruction while the former Protector was absent.

Returning to London and his council duties several days later, Seymour was immediately aware of a change. There was a cool confidence in the new Duke of Northumberland's manner and an equally cool aloofness on the part of his fellow councillors. Seymour was wise enough to know that absence from the court rarely made for security; one must be constantly present to defend one's possessions and privileges. He was no fool and recognized the recent elevations for what they were. Henry Grey's had come about on the death of his wife's half-brothers; the others were nothing but bids for power and rewards for supporting the new duke. For the first time, Seymour experienced a vague uneasiness, and warily he approached the newly knighted Sir William Cecil, his secretary since the days of his Protectorship. He described his absence and the atmosphere in the Council Chamber, saying, "I suspect some ill. . . ." Cecil's reply revealed that Seymour indeed *did* have something to concern him. "If your Grace be not guilty, you may be of good courage. If you are, I have nothing to say but to lament you," the secretary had written.

Cecil's patronizing tone told Edward Seymour all he wished to know. Later, he wrote Cecil a letter bitterly denying any wrongdoing, knowing that since his secretary had now abandoned him for the more powerful Dudley, the letter's contents would be revealed. Then he returned to the council meetings as if nothing had happened. Remembering the consequences of his wild flight with Edward which had preceded his loss of the Protectorate, Seymour reasoned that any rumors would be negated by his presence and seeming unconcern; to flee would be an admission of guilt. He was certain the king had been kept in ignorance of any charges of sedition, treason or rebellion. It was not Dudley's way to tell Edward—or anyone else—anything that might be construed as meaning he was not in complete control of a situation. It would be more the duke's way to have a *fait accompli* to convince the king than risk having Edward demur at—or even refuse to consent to—his uncle's detention.

Seymour had about convinced himself he was worrying needlessly when, after attending a Privy Council meeting on October 16, he joined the other nobles as they left the chamber for their midday meal. At the table, the Lord Treasurer suddenly rose and accused the Duke of Somerset of high treason. Stunned, Seymour noted guards waiting at the door. Then it was all clear. The Duke of Northumberland had won—again. Seymour said nothing but rose to join the guards. It was then he realized John Dudley was absent. Undoubtedly the new duke was even now with the king, describing the treasonous activities of yet another uncle. Remembering what had happened to his brother Thomas—and that he'd not raised a finger to save him—Edward Seymour wondered if the king would be as impressionable at fourteen as he'd been at eleven.

Jane Grey's father, the new Duke of Suffolk, and Paulet, the new Marquis of Winchester, escorted the former Protector to the Tower. At once the Privy Council summoned "the Lord Mayor and aldermen . . . to the King's Majesty's place at Whitehall" to deal with any local disturbances which might be expected when the imprisonment of "the good duke" was revealed. The council sent out orders for all "householders to be kept in every ward from nine o'clock at night til five in the morning." The following day several of Seymour's alleged accomplices were arrested, and on the eighteenth, his wife, Anne Stanhope, the Duchess of Somerset, "a woman of haughty stomach," was brought by water from Syon

House and also lodged in the Tower. Only then, with the Seymour family and their followers imprisoned, did Dudley commence to deal with citizens, council and king alike.

On the night previous to Seymour's arrest, Dudley had visited Edward. The king did not consider it unusual; the duke often came to the palace in the evening. Much to tutor John Cheke's disappointment and dismay, Edward was often kept up past his bedtime, or delayed in studying, while his visitor informed him of state affairs. On the night before Seymour's apprehension, Dudley told the king his uncle had planned to incite the people of the North and London to rebellion, to assassinate council members as well as Dudley himself and then marry the king to his daughter, Jane Seymour. In the matter of religion—in which Dudley knew Edward to be strongly pro-Protestant—he warned that Seymour would probably work for a return to a "popish" worship. Hadn't he refused to deal with the Princess Mary's Mass, making it equally difficult for her brother, the king, to resolve also? Edward, shocked and bewildered, reacted as Dudley hoped he would, saying little but neither condemning nor defending his uncle's actions. The duke then left the boy with his uncertain thoughts.

During the following days, as he had more time to think, Edward wavered in his belief that his uncle was as guilty as Dudley claimed. When news of Seymour's arrest became public, the hot mutterings in taverns, inns and homes were firmly in Seymour's favor. Demonstrations, fiercely and promptly quelled, preceded the trial, which Dudley hoped would be held as soon as possible. To his great disappointment, Edward would not be hurried. When petitions were presented to the king—and for the first time he realized he might be forced to send another uncle to the scaffold— he was reluctant to sign. When Seymour's supporters in the Tower refused to give evidence, they were threatened and eventually tortured. Others were indignant—such as Lord Arundel, who admitted he and Seymour had planned only to arrest Dudley and William Parr to compel a change in the government. "None of my race have been traitors," cried the noble, "but we all know who have!" a reference to Dudley's father's ignominious end on the scaffold.

When a week had passed and Edward gave no sign of being completely convinced of his uncle's deception and was considering exile on the Continent as an alternative to imprisonment, Dudley made one last attempt. Repeatedly he emphasized the "large vanity and languid intellect" that so characterized Edward Seymour. Again, the uncle was blamed for everything from the bad currency to the bad weather. How sincere was Seymour in the matter of religion, he shouted to the king, when he could neither free a Catholic bishop from imprisonment nor save a deluded woman of Kent from the stake? Hadn't Seymour grown "lukewarm and had scarcely anything less at heart than religion"? When Edward remained pensive but firm, Dudley at last lost his temper and could be heard shouting at the king and banging his fist on the royal desk for emphasis.

Soon it was obvious the duke would have his way. Only those who hated Seymour were allowed about Edward and, to a man, lost no opportunity to revile and excoriate the former Protector. Edward Seymour was deemed an "apostate and backslider" in religious matters while John Dudley was glorified "as a champion of the Lord." The nation's general discontent was blamed on the Protector's poor administration. Jehan Scheyve, the Spanish ambassador, openly said the young king's mind was slowly being poisoned by the Duke of Northumberland and his adherents. In the meantime, the government was at a virtual standstill while the play of wills between the duke and the king continued.

It took some six weeks to convince Edward of his uncle's base intentions. He'd never had any real affection for—or from—his uncle. As Protector, Seymour had paid little attention to Edward Tudor, while Dudley had soothed the king's hurt pride with attention and flattery. Every man of substance still free now blamed the king for misunderstanding the situation, for disloyalty to John Dudley, who'd uncovered the former Protector's insidious plot. At last, emotions battered, his boyish pride stung, Edward—exhibiting an almost icy calm—signed the necessary documents and the trial was ordered to proceed.

But Dudley still did not trust the Londoners' mood. Their hatred of him had deepened and was openly expressed during the weeks Seymour had remained in prison. Thus it was five o'clock in the morning of December 1, 1551—at a time when the City was normally just awakening—that the former Protector's trial commenced. Dudley had hoped the early hour might be kept secret, with sentence passed by midday. But word of what was occurring had spread, and, ignoring curfew restrictions, the citizens of London took matters into their own hands. In the wintry darkness they lined "the streete" at Whitehall, and Old Palace Yard was alive with the shouting, surging throng when Edward Seymour arrived by barge at Westminster Hall. One thousand halberdiers ringed the area, but even so the people shook their fists, shouting and cursing, as women screamed invective at the captors of the "good duke." Everyone reviled Dudley and his Privy Council; some even spoke harshly of the king's failure to protect his uncle.

Inside, under the great vaulted hammer-beam ceiling, wooden angels gazed down on the scene where Sir Thomas More had stood before a similar jury less than a quarter of a century previously, as Seymour now faced his accusers. Will Paulet, the new Marquis of Winchester, presided as High Steward. The other twenty-six peers were all well known to the prisoner; they'd worked with or against each other for years. Seymour was aware of their thoughts. Many owed their new prosperity and influence to John Dudley. Should he be pardoned and returned to power—as the shouting populace outside clearly wished—he would deal with them as he was now being dealt with. What chance could he possibly have?

There were few witnesses to speak, for traditionally, only their depositions were read. Listening to the five counts with which he was charged—assassination, sedition, rebellion, interfering in foreign affairs and encompassing the king's marriage—Edward Seymour knew himself a lost man. Though he had the right of rebuttal and could question his accusers, he refused to do so. He called Sir Thomas Palmer, whose testimony had been so invaluable, a "worthless villain" and a scoundrel, indicating by his contempt that the allegations were of no account. He admitted discussing the arrest of Dudley and Will Herbert; no more. He'd changed his mind, he said, and decided he "would meddle no further with the apprehension of any of the council" and said he was sorry he had gone so far with the Earl of Arundel. He denied all other charges except wishing for a change or alteration in the administration. And that, said Seymour, had been discussed in open council meetings which he'd attended in the company of several of the jurors.

At last the judges retired to consider the verdict, returning six hours later to pronounce Edward Seymour guilty. At once, the

Sergeant-at-Arms, who traditionally accompanied the prisoner with the axe, was dismissed. As he left Old Palace Yard, the waiting throng misinterpreted the departure to mean Seymour had been acquitted. Immediately, down "the streete" and up to the Strand, a great cry went up, stunning those inside the Hall, where the remainder of the verdict was still being read. Women wept and men threw caps in the air. Later, Edward would write in his *Journal*: "The people, knowing not the matter, shouted . . . so loud . . . that from the Hall door it was heard at Charing Cross, and plainly, and rumors went that he was quit of all." Church bells began to clamor as citizens ran to start preparations for celebratory bonfires.

But the Duke of Northumberland had not gambled so seriously to have all lost on one or more charges. There were still others. Though Seymour had been found not guilty of treason—being acquitted of the charges of planning the assassination of Dudley and other council members—he was guilty of "felonious intent" in the other three, and the penalty was the same as for treason: death. As the verdict was read, Seymour paled and his shoulders sagged. In quiet dignity he fell to his knees as Winchester, Dudley and Pembroke, by tradition, turned their backs to him. Dutifully he thanked the judges for his open trial and asked mercy for his wife and children.

As he rose, so did John Dudley. Now that the death sentence had been passed, the Duke of Northumberland desired to appear in the best possible light, particularly to the crowds waiting outside. Raising his voice so all in the vast Hall could hear, he cried, "Oh, Duke of Somerset! You see yourself brought into the utmost danger, and that nothing but death awaits you. I have once before delivered you from a similar hazard of your life; and I will not now desist from serving you, how little soever you may expect it. I desire you therefore to appeal to the royal clemency, which I doubt not will be extended to you." Having held out the hope of Edward's charity, he then ended, "As for myself, I shall willingly forgive you everything and will use every exertion in my power that your life may be spared."

Only after Seymour had left the Hall—at which a great groan went up from the waiting crowd, where premature joy had turned to a dangerous enmity when the correct verdict was known—was the full impact of that decision realized. As a mounted Dudley left the Palace Yard, enclosed on all sides by guards, the shouts and curses of the crowd followed him up "the streete." The people were not accepting the verdict with equanimity, but Dudley was not fearful. He could deal with crowds. What bothered him most was how to deal with the king.

The Duke of Somerset's imprisonment, under sentence of death, was hardly unexpected in the home of the Duke of Suffolk. Violence, with its attendant hazards and heartbreak, was so much a part of everyday life, especially at court, that the Greys were neither alarmed nor surprised. There were those, more caring, who lamented the power struggle between the dukes—whose families were united by marriage—if for no other reason than that it affected the Privy Council. Still others wondered if Dudley, with no scapegoat to blame for his own shortcomings, could recoup his prestige and become the able administrator the country so desperately needed. Many, recalling the unstable Thomas Seymour, pointed out that while all the Seymours were ambitious, they lacked the cleverness, perception or strong common sense to ensure their success. Sir Thomas More had once defined a government as "a certain conspiracy of rich men procuring their own commodities under the name and title of commonwealth," and many thought the late Lord Chancellor's comment apt for John Dudley and his colleagues.

The same was not true of the people of London, quick to give their loyalty to anyone they regarded as decent and having their welfare at heart. They could be equally disdainful of one who was neither, whether he was king or commoner. For all his shortcomings, they'd loved and trusted their "good duke" as much as they'd hated John Dudley. Their unrest was so flagrant that, two days after Seymour's trial, it was thought prudent to have a parade of the gendarmerie throughout London. And a week later, "there was a muster before the King's Majesty in St. James's Field beyond Charing Cross." With banners flying and drums beating, trumpeters preceded the king's pensioners, each on horseback. Behind them walked the servants, each clad in their master's colors and carrying a spear. Then the nobles' retainers and those of the Privy Council paraded—each a group of over one hundred, sumptuously garbed in richly glowing colors. A loud blaring of trumpets announced the arrival of each group and then, with strict precision, the wintry sunlight gleaming on their weapons and the gold and silver thread on the horses' bright caparisons, they marched briskly past the king. The opulence of the standard-bearers' dress and the spearmen's agility brought loud cries from the assembled throng as they shouted for their favorites. For hours, as Edward watched, "sitting on horseback on a hill by St. James's with his Majesty's Privy Council" the parade continued. Then everyone walked to Hyde Park, where "the lords' servants were set in array . . . which was a goodly sight."

At Suffolk House, Jane listened as her parents discussed Seymour's imprisonment, expressing their opinions as if she were not in the room. Their main concern seemed to be that should she not, as they'd hoped, wed the king, then she might have married one of Edward Seymour's sons. But now, with the father accused of treason and likely to suffer a stronger penalty than imprisonment, how could a daughter of the house of Suffolk wed into such a family? If there was no king or a duke's son, who else might the maiden of such an illustrious family, one noted for her piety and education, wed? It was the first time Jane had ever heard her parents speak of her in such a way; usually there was only criticism and, inevitably, another "nip and bob."

She said nothing, however, knowing that Frances and Henry Grey were not interested in her opinions and that to express them might only provoke her mother's unpleasant temper. It was always a great relief to Jane when the family meal—or an excursion on the river or down "the streete"—ended and she was dismissed to return to the refuge of her classroom or chamber. There was nothing she could do about her marriage.

She was, however, sympathetic with her parents' ambitions when they learned John Dudley and the Privy Council were pressing for Edward's marriage to Princess Elizabeth, the daughter of Henri II of France. Remembering Thomas Seymour's insistence that he'd bring about *her* marriage to Edward, she understood the Greys' deep disappointment. For herself, she cared little. She'd seen few happy marriages: Charles Brandon and his Kate's had been one; Katherine Parr and Thomas Seymour's, another. Jane had always been glad the kindly queen had not lived to see her husband's shameful end. She knew her father would marry her to one worthy of her rank and upbringing and refused to concern herself over something in which she'd have no choice. When it was right and proper—and approaching fifteen was right and proper—she would marry as her parents chose.

In the meantime, there were the daily sessions with her beloved "Mr. Elmer" and, above all, the rewarding and enjoyable correspondence with her Swiss friends. It was the one way Jane could reveal—by thought and later in writing—the depth of her religious commitment, which meant so much to her. The correspondence had given a new intensity and a deeper meaning to her spiritual beliefs. She was aware that everyone did not believe as she did, but that she was—like many seeking English people, mostly young—a perfect representative of the sort John Cheke, the king's tutor, had in mind when he wrote: "In hearing the word of God, whether it be by the voice of others *or by yourself reading*, you are ever to think that God speaketh to you. . . . You are to remember that you speak to God. . . . You walk in the eye and sight of God . . . when you speak to God, know that you speak to Him who understandeth the bottom of your heart."

Jane was not unlike many others, young and old, who thrived on the intellectual stimulation of theological argument. Such debates—when carried to the extreme, often followed by imprisonment, agonizing tortures and eventual burning—were engaged in by people of all social strata in all parts of England. The Virgin Birth, the Real Presence, the pope and all the Catholic rituals and doctrine so scorned by the Protestants—and their advanced counterparts on the Continent, such as Jane's correspondents—provided an outlet for emotions and convictions not present in any other aspect of life. The average Englishman had no opportunity to choose who would lead the government. No one asked his opinion about the price of wool or whom the king might marry, or about a foreign war in which he or his son might lose his life. Only in their spiritual life, in the sanctity of their churches and the haven of their homes, did some opportunity for self-expression exist. While most conformed to whatever government policy prevailed at the time, many did not. And these nonconformists provided fuel not only for the stake but for the theological debates that were so alive to Jane Grey and her contemporaries. Few women, however, possessed the time or the education to devote to religious study—or argument—that Jane did.

Jane Grey considered herself fortunate to have escaped the fate of such as Princess Mary—to have been born, as Mary had been, in a Catholic England where the excesses of that religion were well known, yet tolerated by otherwise decent, sensible people. She did not understand the willingness and devoutness of those who believed that Christ's body was present in the communion bread, that His blood was present in the communion wine. Certainly, the Protestant view—that since it could not be proved by Scripture, it was only symbolic—made more sense? Yet the "Henricians," those survivors of Henry VIII's schism with Rome, insisted *that* was not what the old king had believed, nor what his daughter believed. He'd bequeathed the doctrine of the Real Presence, as well as many other beloved rituals, to his kingdom, to be celebrated in the churches their ancestors had known. Who were the upstarts—encouraged by Edward Seymour and John Dudley—who could set aside a king's mandate and destroy and plunder English churches and change a nation's beliefs so radically in five years?

This "Henrician" view, Jane knew, was also Mary Tudor's heartfelt belief, which she rarely lost any opportunity to present as a strong defense to anyone insisting she forgo the Mass. Jane had heard her parents say that Mary's insistence that the king, her father, had left the Church as he wished the realm to have it, would only make trouble for her. Her brother was also a king and *his* religious beliefs, fostered by his godfather Archbishop Cranmer, the Seymours and John Dudley, were hardly sympathetic to their dead father's views.

It is doubtful it ever occurred to young Jane Grey, critical and judgmental, that her reaction only mirrored the deep conviction of others who were as firm and certain in their beliefs as she was in hers. Contemptuous, even mocking, of the Real Presence, she could write to a friend, "Wilt thou torment again, rend and tear the most precious Body of our Saviour Christ with thy bodily and fleshly teeth?" The Redeemer, she insisted, "was ascended into Heaven and placed on the right hand of God the Father; therefore it could not be situate upon earth in the sacrament of the altar."

Jane's pride in her theological knowledge—encouraged by John Aylmer and Chaplain Haddon and stimulated by her Swiss correspondents—was further enhanced when, shortly before the Greys left for Greenwich to spend Christmas with the king and his court, where John Dudley intended a celebration to take Edward's mind off his uncle's as yet undecided fate, she received an anonymous letter from a court lady extolling the virtues of Basil the Great. A small book of the fourth-century Bishop of Caesarea's work, denouncing the claims of the See of Rome to primacy in the Christian church, was enclosed. A letter described the gift as worthy of one of "your noble birth, and on account of your learning and holiness. . . ." That the writer was older than Jane was evident in the words, ". . . hoping that the perusal of these words will be no less agreeable and delightful to you than they have been to me throughout my youth . . ."

Jane was enchanted, not only with the gift and the flattery of the donor, but because it acknowledged that her hard work—her studies and her devout insistence on the truth of the reformed faith—had crept beyond the door of her family home. For the young girl who'd won so little acceptance from her family, whose only approval—and even that limited to conforming to *their* wishes— had come from Aylmer and Haddon, such outside recognition of her accomplishments was heady and invigorating. That others might not share her beliefs, and those of the author of the letter, was of little importance. Tolerance of anything like the Catholic God, whom she described as "a detestable idol, invented by Romish popes and the abominable college of crafty cardinals," was abhorrent to Jane. She, as well as many of the younger generation of English people, felt it a sacred duty to correct and inform. That a thousand-year-old belief was being challenged and could only end in destruction—or that others as devoutly enthusiastic as she in their spiritual life might perish for their convictions—mattered little to Jane. Typical of her generation, she sought constantly to perfect herself and hoped that in the doing she might inspire others to do the same. That a tinge of the very bigotry and self-delusion she derided in others might cling to her *own* strong opinions never entered Jane's mind, convinced as she was that the Catholic form of worship was of the Devil.

Jane viewed her own strong religious convictions in much the same manner as did any of her intelligent, seeking contemporaries, relishing the fact that at last the English nation, free of Roman shackles, had the opportunity to worship in the manner of the ancient church fathers. The old king had commenced the process when he'd broken with Rome, they admitted, but he'd not gone far enough. That had been left to his son, and under the supervision of a Protector, an archbishop and a duke, the process of reforming and cleansing the church had been carried out. That there was still a long way to go, Jane realized. And if she ever wondered how far the distance would be, she had only to listen to her Swiss friends, her tutor and chaplain, who reaffirmed that *she*, with her staunch faith, her superior intellect, prestigious family and its connection with royalty, might shorten the way. The "new religion" had, at last, gained firm ground. How could it not be true that after years of misguided allegiance to a false faith, England was now ready to emerge into a brighter day?

The Duke of Northumberland was determined the Christmas and Twelfth Night celebrations at Greenwich would uplift the spirit not only of the court but of the king as well. Thus, as Jane and her parents arrived at the old riverside palace of Placentia, the corridors and hallways were thronged with courtiers, foreign ambassadors, Privy Councillors, household officials and their families. Abroad in the streets of London it had been rumored that though Edward Seymour and his family remained in the Tower, John Dudley was working with king and council to effect his pardon and decide his future. Once the festivities were over, presumably the duke would be released.

Therefore, those sympathetic to the former Protector put concern behind them and enjoyed the celebrations, which, as Edward later wrote in his *Journal*, were "well and merrily passed." The king, like his father before him, was happy at Greenwich. It was near London, yet the formalities of court life were relaxed. There he could see his old nurse, Sybilla Penn, and his father's Fool, craggy-faced Will Somers, living out their days in comfort on generous pensions and a boy-king's affection. There, as fog lifted from the river, Edward could race with younger courtiers across the park to plant his standard high atop a hill. Though he was never far from books, his study time was less regulated, but there were still the inevitable council meetings to attend and administrative duties he must deal with. John Dudley was always present, subtly reassuring, to take much of the burden from Edward's shoulders, even as he made certain that Christmas kept the boy pleasantly occupied, with no time to think of an incarcerated uncle.

As the hunting, the archery contests and running at the ring kept Edward busy outside, the court reveled inside in the mumming and masques that had kept the Wardrobe and the Master of Revels busy for months. While most entertainments went smoothly and enjoyably, some disgusted and angered the onlookers' sensitivities. The Lord of Misrule, disregarding diplomacy and taste, supervised several pageants which were nothing other than religious parodies, anti-Catholic in tone and demeaning in performance. The fact that the king participated in these left the Spanish, French and Venetian ambassadors appalled and angry. While actors dressed as the pope, nuns, monks or priests paraded drunkenly and wantonly before the court audience, which roared its approval, Princess Mary's absence was commented upon. The relationship between young Edward and his sister had deteriorated, it was explained, as she realized her brother was determined that she give up her heathenish devotion to the Mass.

While Mary's many friends—Frances and Henry Grey among them—lamented her absence, they also accepted that her presence would have been awkward, diminishing others' pleasure in the festivities. An impasse had been reached and must soon be resolved. After attending one meeting between Edward and Scheyve, the Spanish ambassador, Henry Grey told his wife that when the ambassador pleaded that Mary be allowed to follow the only form of worship she knew, Edward replied, "It would be against my conscience to allow the Mass." He promised to treat Mary "as my good sister in other matters," but insisted she must obey the laws of the realm. Scheyve noted that during the conversation Edward often glanced toward John Dudley, as if seeking approval. In the report sent that evening to the Spanish emperor, the ambassador cannily observed, "His Majesty is an intelligent lad, of quick, ready and well-developed mind, remarkable for his age. If he were well taught [i.e., in the Catholic faith] he would be a very noteworthy prince. The Duke of Northumberland—whom he seems to love and fear—is beginning to grant him a great deal of freedom in order to dispel the hostility felt for himself and to cause the king to forget the Duke of Somerset as quickly as possible."

In the meantime, however, the merrymaking and conviviality might be enjoyed, as the new Duke and Duchess of Suffolk basked in well-wishers' congratulations on their good fortune. For Jane, the thumping music and rich food, the revels and the dancing to tabor, pipe and drum were exciting. Conscious now of her almost grown-up status, she emerged from a natural shyness to dance with younger members of the court and talk to the king as he sat, resplendent in the pastel satins he so loved, in his chair of state with the canopy overhead. Jane saw her parents, always at the center of a group, and on the sidelines Aylmer and Haddon waiting, disapproval written all over their faces. Anticipating the riotous merrymaking of a court holiday, and remembering the previous year's wanton excesses, the tutor had written Jane's Swiss friend Heinrich Bullinger, asking that he advise Jane how best to spend her time during the festive season. Aylmer dreaded the frantic, almost pagan jollity of Christmas which might cause his pupil, now well advanced in her Hebrew studies, to fall from grace. "Whatever she has begun," Bullinger was told, "she will complete—unless diverted by some calamity." Clearly, Christmas was a calamity.

But the two gentlemen need not have worried. Upon returning to her chambers and to her sister Katherine's insistence that Jane tell *everything* that had happened that evening, she quickly put her rich gown aside, even as Mrs. Ellen chattered about the dress she might wear on the morrow. Jane had enjoyed her evening of celebration—particularly because there'd been no confrontation with her parents. Now she could happily return to her books and just as happily enjoy whatever the court had devised for her pleasure the next day, knowing that each day brought her nearer her return to Suffolk House—and reality.

Once the court had returned to London, the most important matter facing the council was the fate of the Duke of Somerset. The "mirth and good pastime" of Christmas was over, and Edward, it was noted, was depressed. No longer would the diversions—the jousts, the excitement of the tiltyard and mumming in the evening—prevent his acknowledging the fact that another uncle's life depended upon *him*. Continuing imprisonment, exile, even pardon—Edward had discussed them all with John Dudley. The duke had exhibited enormous patience, knowing the boy would not be

Queen Mary I
Daughter of Henry VIII and
Katherine of Aragon

(From the Studio of Antonio Moro)

Princess Elizabeth
Daughter of Henry VIII
and Anne Boleyn

by an unknown Flemish artist

Edward Seymour
The Duke of Somerset
Protector of England

by Corneille de Lyon

This portrait was painted in 1537,
the year Lady Jane Grey was
born. At that time, Edward Seymour was about thirty-one years
old and the Earl of Hertford.

John Dudley
The Duke of Northumberland

Sir John Cheke
Tutor to Edward VI

Artist Unknown

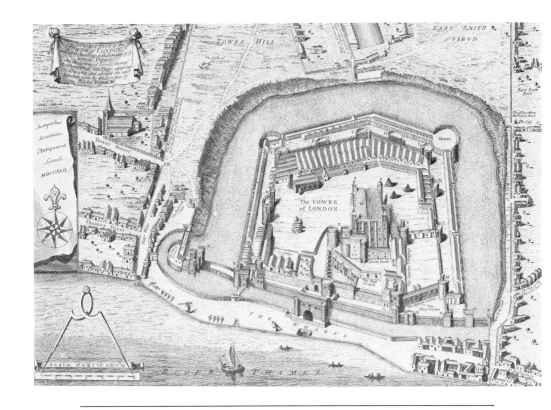

The Tower of London
Survey of 1597 by Hayward and Gascoyne

All these buildings were in existence during Lady Jane Grey's incarceration in the Tower. "The Queen's Lodgings" show the royal apartments and the Privy Garden in which she walked. Later, she went to the row of houses known as the "Master Gaoler's Lodgings" just to the left of the houses marked "The Lieutenant's Lodgings." The execution site was in front of these buildings where the small cluster of houses appear on the Green. The other execution site, outside the Tower on Tower Hill, is shown in the top left marked "The Posts of the Scaffold."

Lady Katherine Grey
and Her Son

Artist Unknown

| Stephen Gardiner The Bishop of Winchester | Thomas Howard The Duke of Norfolk | Henry Fitzalan The Earl of Arundel |

Stephen
Gardiner
The Bishop of
Winchester

Thomas
Howard
The Duke of
Norfolk

Henry Fitzalan
The Earl of
Arundel

by Hans Holbein

Sir William Paget
Lord Privy Seal Under
Mary I

by Hans Holbein

Thomas Cranmer
The Archbishop of
Canterbury
Edward VI's godfather

by G. Flicke, 1546

Sir William Paulet
The Marquis of
Winchester
Lord High Treasurer

Artist Unknown

Thomas Wyatt
Leader of the Wyatt
Rebellion

Artist Unknown

pressured or pushed; Edward must come to a decision on his own. Relentlessly, however, he hammered home Seymour's deficiencies—some real, some imagined—as well as their effect upon the safety of the realm and its reformed faith. The duke told Edward that if Seymour was spared, the French king would undoubtedly break the betrothal contract with his daughter. Later, he made certain the French ambassador approached Edward with the same cautionary warning. To lose the marriage with France was more than the king had bargained for. He was disturbed at his helplessness, hating to acknowledge that a fourteen-year-old boy was no defense against the sophisticated maneuverings of a duke and an ambassador.

In the end, Dudley and the Privy Council had their way. At a council meeting on January 18, 1552, two weeks after the Greenwich celebrations had ceased, Edward signed a document that referred to the prisoners and noted that "by their punishment [an] example may be showed to others. . . ." Now the council had the authority to act against Seymour and his confederates. Later, mysteriously, an insert was made in the document, so that it now read: "that by their punishment *and execution according to the laws* [an] example may be showed. . . ."

Three days later, when Dudley insisted Edward be more decisive, all the boy would say was, "Let the law take its course," clearly indicating—by what he remembered signing—that punishment must be made, exactly what he did not know. It was all the duke needed. If, when the final writs were presented to Edward for his signature—and he noticed the sentence for punishment—he gave no indication. Wearily, he signed the papers and left the room.

The following morning, January 22, at eight o'clock, Edward Seymour, the Duke of Somerset, left the Tower for the last time. Bareheaded, his long beard and black cloak—to which he'd pinned all his decorations and medals—lending to the tall figure a sober dignity that even the pallor of weeks of confinement could not diminish, he strode up Tower Hill, where more than one thousand men-at-arms and sheriffs waited. Though the council had ordered Londoners to remain in their homes, the area was one enormous mass of angry, shouting citizens. Indignantly they hooted from the rooftops, tree limbs and the walls of the Tower moat. Those on the ground were no less vocal, even as halberdiers pressed them back from the scaffold with poleaxes. When Lord Arundel—who'd previously cried he was no traitor, then later given evidence against Seymour to secure his own release—was seen waiting at the scaffold, the crowd's protests became even more threatening.

If Seymour saw Arundel he gave no sign; the former Protector's mien was almost serene. Leaning against the scaffold's railing, as the multitude surged angrily forward, roaring its protests, he commenced his farewell. He raised his hand and there was immediate silence; no one wished to miss a word. "Masters and good fellows," he said in a strong voice, "I am come hither to die, but as true and faithful a man as any was unto the King's Majesty." After more traditional pieties, he noted, "Concerning religion, I have been always, being in authority, a furtherer of it to the Glory of God, to the uttermost of my power, whereof I am nothing sorry . . . beseeching you all to take it so and follow it on still; for, if not, there will follow and come a worse and great plague."

Suddenly there was a great rumbling around All Hallows' Church, and a band of soldiers on horseback—latecomers sent by Dudley to prevent any rioting—appeared. The crowd, thinking they bore a reprieve from the king, shouted and cheered, throwing caps in the air. So great was the disturbance that several standing on the moat's walls fell into the foul water; others were trampled on. For a brief moment the crowd's joy spread to Seymour, and his cheeks flushed with seeming relief. Then, spying Sir Anthony Browne, the Master of the Horse, and realizing the true mission of the soldiers, he again called for silence.

"Beloved friends," he said, "there is no such matter as you vainly hope and believe." As several made for the scaffold, as if to carry him off, he motioned them away, cap in hand, asking them not to grieve for him and to make no further disturbances. Instead, they might "pray for the King's Majesty . . ." he ended. Then, with loud groans and lamentations, the crowd watched as Seymour withdrew his rings and presented them to the executioner. Next, he handed his sword to a Tower official and then, loosening his shirt-collar, knelt at the block, covering his face with his handkerchief and crying, "Jesus save me, Lord Jesus save me . . . !" The executioner brought down the sword, neatly severing the head—which he quickly held aloft—at the first blow. Weeping, those nearest the site sent their children under the scaffold to dip handkerchiefs and cloth torn from their garments in the blood of the "good duke."

The noise of the spectators and the clatter of the unusual number of soldiers and mounted guards drifted back along the river. It was heard across the river at Suffolk House, where the Grey family had gathered in the chapel to pray for Edward Seymour. With the former Protector's death, John Dudley was now predominant in the Privy Council, and second to him would be Henry Grey, the Duke of Suffolk. The noise spread along the arc of the river, gleaming in the wintry sunlight, to Westminster, where Edward sat with Scheyve, the Spanish ambassador. Listening to the loud tumult, the king asked his guest what could be causing the noise? In hushed tones, Scheyve explained. Edward sat silent for a long time and then, his voice hushed, remarked, "I would not have believed he would have been a traitor."

Later that evening, after his uncle had been interred with rites "hurried and simple as for a pauper" in St. Peter's-ad-Vincula, the church within the Tower, in the same area where the dead queens Anne Boleyn and Katherine Howard lay, Edward wrote in his *Journal*, "The Duke of Somerset had his head cut off upon Tower Hill between eight and nine o'clock in the morning."

The reign of the Seymours—Jane, Thomas and Edward; queen, Lord Admiral and Protector—was over.

16

In the year following the former Protector's death, John Dudley, now the Duke of Northumberland, reaped the rewards of his duplicity. He had the trust and affection of the king and he was supreme in the Privy Council. There, where his colleagues regarded him with apprehension and fear, he had disdained the title of Protector. Already, though lacking the goodwill or affection of the English people, he had as much power as Edward Seymour had once possessed; a Protectorship was unnecessary. That he had little admiration—or even the barest respect—from his fellow councillors did not matter. Power came from the king, and John Dudley had no doubt but that he could manage the boy.

As for Edward, the new duke was a trusted, likable and willing servant, eager to do the royal bidding, to protect the monarch from his nobles' intrigues—had he not just rescued him from the warped ambition of yet another treasonous uncle?—and, above all, to foster and secure the "new religion" which Edward regarded with a passionate obsession as his true mission in life. That his devotion to the reformed faith bordered on the bigotry of which he accused the Catholics—and particularly his sister Mary with her staunch devotion to the Mass—eluded the boy, as it had his priests, bishops and council. Edward was confidently fearless in his appraisal of the garb his priests wore, the context of their sermons and religious ceremonies, even the wording of their oaths and blessings. When Bishop Hooper was given the See of Gloucester, Edward immersed himself in plans for the ordination. Hooper had dispensed with the rich episcopal garments and what he considered a "popish ceremony," but Edward could still find fault. Reading the service of consecration, the young king's eyes fell on the oath, which contained the words "So help me God, all saints and the holy evangelists." This was too much for the boy and he exclaimed excitedly, "What wickedness is here, Hooper? Are these offices ordained in the name of the saints or of God?" A chastened Hooper watched as Edward wrote, "So help me God through Jesus Christ," in place of the offending phrase. It was later carried in the Second Prayer Book of Edward VI, which set the standard for religious worship in England.

Edward's desire—to lead his people from the clutches of the Roman Church and all it symbolized—was also encouraged by Henry Grey, the Duke of Suffolk. Jane's father, "the thunderbolt and terror of the papists," through his acquisition of a dukedom and his alliance with John Dudley, at last enjoyed the influence he'd envied in others all his life. Prominence had always been his; the husband of Henry VIII's niece could hardly be overlooked. Henry Grey was now old enough, however, to understand how much his uneven temperament, excessive extravagance and weak personality had cost him in the respect and friendship of his peers. But with Dudley's support, all that was in the past. Now, even his protégé John Ulmis could boast to Jane's Swiss correspondent Heinrich Bullinger, "He [Dudley] almost alone, with the Duke of Suffolk, governs the State and supports and upholds it on his shoulders."

It was not an idle claim. With Edward Seymour's death, the last deterrent to both Dudley's and Grey's ambition was removed, and the king—who would be fifteen in a few months—admired and trusted them both. Of all his family, Edward had left only two sisters. One was foolish enough to be troublesome with her stubborn devotion to her faith, while the other, Elizabeth, by her silent cooperation in dress, manner and deportment, had seemingly embraced the reformed religion and would be no deterrent to their ambition. Though Edward's tutor, John Cheke, now sat on the Privy Council, he would present little problem to the dukes' activities providing they did not overtire his pupil, keep him from his studies or ask anything morally wrong of him.

Within months of the former Protector's execution, therefore, a fury encouraged by Dudley and Grey and sanctioned by Edward was unleashed upon the religious houses of England. With no Protector to promulgate compromise or tolerance, the cathedrals, churches and abbeys that had escaped Thomas Cromwell's depredations in Henry VIII's day now fell victim to destruction, defacement and looting by Edward's trusted officials. Walls vivid with ancient wall paintings were hurriedly whitewashed in an orgy of pious endeavor, lest they corrupt the ignorant. Statues, chalices, ornaments, colorful window glass, rood lofts, screens and heavy altars—anything that escaped whole in the general smashing, looting and burning—were carted to London and shipped abroad to Catholic countries where the English "imaugys" fetched respectable prices.

But some remained in England, and soon "the halls of country-houses were hung with altar-cloths; tables and beds were quilted with copes; the knights and squires drank their claret out of chalices and watered their horses in marble coffins." In the counties adjoining London, thick piles of church linen burning on street corners so enraged and disgusted the citizens that a petition was sent to John Dudley to secure whatever had been taken for use in the hospitals. Whatever "jewels, plate, ready money, copes, vestments with other metals of brass and copper . . . and other jewels of gold and silver . . ." remained were delivered to the King's Majesty at the Tower, and there was "reserved to every cathedral and parish church, a chalice or cup, or more, with tablecloths for the communion border"; nothing else was allowed. The priest became minister, the altar a plain bare table, and the Eucharist a commemoration only. Many churches, crumbling and ruined, were not replaced; some parishes had no ministers, only curates who could barely read or write. "A thousand pulpits were covered with dust . . . ," lamented one Englishman. When the "new suppression" was over, the anguished parishioners could only gaze at the desecration and the lack of color, statuary and treasures which the reformers considered superstitious. Their barren, defaced churches and cathedrals no longer resembled the familiarly warm buildings that had been havens of spiritual comfort for centuries.

And, since Edward Seymour's properties had now reverted to the Crown, his manors, farms, castles and vast acreages of land were all in the king's gift, to bestow on his favorites for loyal service. That it was actually John Dudley who was responsible for the largesse now distributed was no secret, causing one loyal Hampshire gentleman to say of the king, "Alas, poor child, unknown it is to him what acts are made nowadays; when he comes of age, he will see another rule and hang up a thousand knaves." As councillors and nobles alike scrambled for the loot, one of the most substantial gifts was to the Duke of Suffolk, and in the spring following Seymour's execution, Henry Grey brought his family to the old Priory of Sheen, one of the Protector's many homes. The Priory, formerly a Carthusian monastery, adjacent to Richmond Palace, had been given by Henry VIII to his brother-in-law in the months following Jane Seymour's death. Syon House, a former Bridgettine convent before the dissolution, was opposite on the riverbank; it, too, had been a favorite Seymour residence. Now, with the gift of Sheen to Henry Grey, Syon House was confiscated from Seymour's estate by John Dudley. Thus the two families had dwellings near each other and, more important, a proximity to the king when he was at Richmond. At last Henry Grey had a closeness to the monarch he'd never enjoyed before and, in his alliance with John Dudley, a source of power he'd never envisaged. For the Duke of Northumberland, son of that hated Edmund Dudley whom the present king's father had hanged for his confiscatory practices, time had balanced the scales of justice. Now he had everyone—king, councillors and nobles—in his hand.

With the assumption of their new titles and authority, it followed that both Dudley and Grey should regard their families' future with a new optimism. There was virtually no limit to what might be obtained through marriages for the remaining four Dudley sons; Robert was already wed to Amy Robsart and still, seemingly, besotted with the girl. And Henry Grey had three daughters, one of whom had gained an enviable reputation for learning and religious piety. The other was pretty, though somewhat emotionally high-strung, and the third was a dwarf. The Dudley boys were devoted to their parents and to one another. Close-knit and loyal, ambitious for themselves and their father, they were regarded as formidable opponents with a limitless desire to succeed and achieve. The Grey girls, on the other hand, were more aloof; they did not mingle with or appeal to everyone.

Both John Dudley and Henry Grey knew, however, that their backgrounds, or the suitability of their offspring, mattered little to those seeking a marital alliance. Wasn't Anne Seymour, whose father had just had his head cut off on Tower Hill, married to one of John Dudley's sons? What counted was power, influence, money and those other forms of wealth—lands, castles, manors and the profitable perquisites of government offices—within the gift of the Crown. Both men were now predominant in the court and council; there were still almost two years before young Edward would attain his majority and rule alone. Within that time—before they had to hand over their stewardship to the king and accept the gratitude which would surely be forthcoming and accompanied by further honors—there was no limit to what glorious indulgences both dukes might obtain for themselves and their families.

The subject of her eldest daughter's marriage now occupied the thoughts of the Duchess of Suffolk. At Sheen, at Suffolk House or visiting her friend Jane Dudley, Duchess of Northumberland, at Syon House, the question of Jane Grey's marriage to King Edward—so long encouraged by that rascal Thomas Seymour—still rankled. Though Edward was now engaged to a French princess, engagements had been broken before. Hadn't her own husband broken a contract with Lord Arundel's sister to marry *her* instead? France had agreed to a bride for Edward, but who else on the Continent—except that hotbed of reform, Germany—would send a bride for such a fervid advocate of the "new religion" as the king? Who else in all England but her own daughter Jane would be the most suitable bride for the young boy? The girl had matured nicely in the past year, was presentable if one overlooked her freckles and the fact that she preferred books to horses. The only trouble—and Henry Grey had refused to interfere—was that John Dudley supported the French alliance and, failing that, still wished a foreign bride for Edward. Such a marriage would not only enhance English status abroad, it might lessen the risk of a war with Spain. Surely even the very Catholic Charles V, the Holy Roman Emperor, would think twice before attacking a country with such a strong ally. And lastly, but most important, a foreign bride's dowry would be richer than any English bride might bring.

Frances Grey was a realist. Anything might happen if one had patience, which even she recognized was not her most sterling quality. One must be ever on the alert for opportunities, make as few enemies as possible and, above all, be continually present at court, where, literally, life-and-death decisions were made.

So Bradgate was closed and left in the care of a few servants. The duchess informed her family they would follow the court and when in London live at Suffolk House or Dorset Place, depending upon how many guests the new Duke of Suffolk with his weighty court duties wished to accommodate. In the country there was the old Brandon home, Westhorpe in Suffolk, and now the Priory of Sheen on the river at Richmond. It still seemed miraculous how much the deaths of Kate Brandon's two sons and now the Protector had enlarged Henry Grey's coffers, tinging his name with a luster unimagined only a few short months ago.

Both Greys were eager to enjoy such largesse, and the opportunity soon arose when the council decided the English counties should see their young king. For weeks following Seymour's execution, Edward had been introspective and moody, although "his lords did much to help dispel any dampy thoughts which the remembrance of his uncle might raise, by applying him with great variety of exercises and disports." But Dudley had ample proof that Edward had not forgotten. While shooting at the butts with several younger companions, Edward scored a bull's-eye. "Well aimed, my liege!" Dudley complimented the boy. Edward, removing the arrow, replied tersely, "But you aimed better when you shot off my good uncle Somerset's head."

Dudley made no reply. Edward had begun to assert more of the royal prerogative than the duke had anticipated. In religious matters, he and John Dudley thought alike. But the king had lamented the tampering with the currency which now threatened England with bankruptcy. Constantly he asked for some remedy for the "fairy money" so scorned by the Continentals. Only recently, he'd insisted on being informed of what went on in the Council Chamber, so that now a weekly account was prepared for him. Edward scrutinized who got what, how his revenues were spent, and was as indignant at the excessive table allowances in his own court as he was at the cost of expensive garrisons maintained in Ireland.

To take Edward's mind off matters Dudley thought better handled by the council, he urged the royal progress to commence. The father of five sons, the duke knew just how much the games and entertainment attending any monarch's visit would be enjoyed by the boy. The English cities and countryside, the pageants and spectacles provided for his diversion as well as the luxurious castles and noble homes in which he would stay, would lull Edward's suspicions. And with the plaudits and loving welcome of his subjects ringing in his ears, any disillusionment concerning his uncle's death would soon be forgotten.

As plans were being made, however, Edward sickened. "I fell sick of the measles and small-pox," he wrote, somewhat proudly, in his *Journal*, ". . . and the Parliament brake up." Within three weeks he had recovered and in order to dispel the Londoners' fears for his condition, Dudley had him ride through the streets before taking the royal barge to Greenwich. There he resumed his archery practice, spent mornings hunting and running at the ring with young courtiers, and the twilight hours conferring with Dudley and his councillors.

In a month Edward had recovered, and the progress plans resumed. The king was excited; he'd seen so little of his realm! John Dudley, recognizing his own unpopularity, wisely decided to remain in London where his hold on the council would remain firm. John Cheke, Edward's tutor, was placed in charge of the long royal cavalcade, which wound southward to Cowdray and Petworth, where Edward wrote, "We have been occupied in killing of wild beasts, in pleasant journeys, in good fare, in viewing of fair counties." At Portsmouth he commented, "The town is handsome and for the bigness of it, as fair houses as be in London. The citizens had bestowed for our coming great cost in painting, repairing and ramparting of their walls." Edward inspected the outmoded, moldering dockyards and fortifications, agreeing they must be modernized or replaced. Everywhere he went, people ran along the roads and lanes to acclaim the tall, slim boy, dressed in his favorite pastel velvets and satins, the long-plumed hat set somewhat rakishly atop his wheat-colored hair. At times their ac-claim—the tears of pride and love, the excitement at seeing their monarch there before them, waving in response to their cries—almost overwhelmed Edward. Then he would rein in his horse and slowly proceed along the freshly graveled streets gay with banners and bunting, so none would miss him, careful always to respond to mayors, sheriffs or even the local squires who came bearing gifts or plaques.

He hunted in the New Forest for one day, continuing on to Christchurch and to a ceremony in the vast splendor of Salisbury Cathedral. There, a worried John Cheke insisted that the progress halt to give Edward a much-needed respite from the rich food, cheering crowds, the constant pageants and festivities which had almost numbed the boy's senses. During the four days he rested, it was decided to shorten the progress. When finally his fatigue had abated somewhat, Cheke arranged a hunting party, and as the small group separated, looking for sport, Edward suddenly real-ized no one was about. It was a unique experience for the boy; he was alone in an unfamiliar country lane where everything was su-premely quiet and lovely. Savoring the experience, he rode on, soon encountering a little girl. Edward nodded courteously, aware of the awed gaze of the child, who never before had seen such mag-nificence. In a moment his companions, worried and embarrassed at losing their king, rode up to lead him back to the hunting party. The little girl, struck dumb by the events, never forgot that day and in 1649, at the venerable age of 103, "Old Good Wife Dew" could still recount the day she'd encountered the last Tudor king, lost on Falston Lane.

Edward Seymour's execution revived for Jane Grey the memory of those many months when she'd lived in a palace with the old king and Katherine Parr, later moving with the queen to the little manor house at Chelsea when Katherine had married Thomas Seymour. Though that life had begun only five years ago, there were times when it seemed as though those days had never been. In the palace she'd seen Mary, Elizabeth and Edward often; they were the king's family and she'd been part of it. Later, at Chelsea, she'd studied with Elizabeth until that mysterious time when the girl had been hastily sent away. Mary Tudor had often visited the manor house and there'd been those happy occasions when Edward had stayed for days with his stepmother.

Then everything changed when the old king died. Jane now understood Thomas's jealousy of his brother, the Protector, whom she remembered as a tall, forbidding presence, so solemn and imperious in contrast to the more jocular Thomas. Yet even Queen Katherine had never underestimated Edward Seymour's competence or integrity. Jane never quite understood why Thomas had been executed and she understood even less why one as powerful as the former Protector had to die. She knew that John Dudley, the Duke of Northumberland, had taken Seymour's place and was the most influential man at court. She realized her father had reaped enormous benefits from the Protector's execution and she accepted it in much the same way she'd accepted the largesse received when poor Kate Brandon's boys had died. The title—and all it conveyed—had rightfully come to Henry Grey through his wife's inheritance. And since the estates of anyone deemed a traitor were inevitably confiscated by the Crown, it was only right and proper the king should honor her father with part of his dead uncle's property. She missed Bradgate but recognized her parents' obvious pleasure in their new wealth and honors. Almost immediately, she'd noticed a new sense of purpose in her father, whose court duties had heretofore been largely ceremonial. Now he spent more time at court with the council, the king and, above all, with John Dudley. The possibility of religious rebellion, the bad currency which threatened national bankruptcy, and the worsening relations with France with the possible loss of the French marriage—even Calais—were nightmares for Dudley and caused his usually calm temper to explode in scenes reminiscent of the Protector when pressures had mounted beyond tolerance.

During those first few months at Sheen, Jane often saw the Dudley family. Her mother and Jane Dudley, always good friends and now newly elevated duchesses, were closer than ever. For years Jane had watched the Dudleys either at Bradgate, where the parents, with their brood of handsome sons, hunted over the Leicestershire countryside, or else in London, where, resplendent in their finest clothes, they enjoyed the festive evenings at Dorset Place. Then they'd ignored her, a thin, small child, usually hiding behind Mrs. Ellen's ample skirts. Then their rough vigor and good humor had fascinated Jane. Their vitality, however, was not that of the uncouth or ignorant; all the Dudley boys had received a fine education from tutor John Dee, an intellectual who'd studied on the Continent. Dee was as demanding as John Dudley; he insisted the boys be disciplined scholastically as well as socially and they shone in any competition, even among themselves—at court, in the tiltyard and, as some gossiped, even in the boudoir. They were at their best working within the framework of the court, where in essence they acted as their father's unofficial deputies.

The Dudley men had received the best of each parent: their father's darkly handsome mien, charm and proud bearing as well as their mother's quietly purposeful elegance. Jane Dudley was as aggressive in her own way as her husband, though she would have considered it improper to show such forcefulness. In addition to their striking appearance, an ambitious energy characterized all the Dudley boys, even Guildford, the youngest, more nearly Jane's age. But being the youngest, Guildford had been spoiled and, it seemed to Jane, possessed a willful insolence which the others lacked. Guildford, along with his brothers, had ignored Jane and she'd been grateful for the slight, never being as at ease in any personal confrontation as when, with pen and paper, she might bare her innermost thoughts to her correspondents.

But now, just a few months shy of fifteen, Jane was no longer ignored. At the evening meal she was expected to dine with her parents and their guests and remain for at least part of the festive entertainment—the dancing, mumming, the music and gambling—for which the Greys were noted. Jane never entered into any conversation unless she was spoken to directly and then answered as politely as she could. As she grew older her parents' abuse had not lessened, and she knew that whatever she said or however she bore herself, it would never meet with her mother's approval. If she spoke out of turn, she was too forward; if she remained silent, she was too shy, possibly even stupid. The stoic face Jane Grey presented to her parents' guests bore no trace of any inner torment. But it was always a relief to be excused and to walk slowly, with poise and soft tread, out of the Great Hall. Once out of sight, she would flee on tiny sandaled feet down the corridors to her chamber or, if she wanted company, to Mrs. Ellen's.

The greatest pleasures of Jane's day were still her religious studies, her work with John Aylmer and her correspondence. On her last visit to Bradgate she'd sent beautiful gloves to the wife of Heinrich Bullinger, and later Conrad Pellican, another of her reforming friends, would write in his journal: "On June 19, 1552, I received a Latin letter, written with admirable elegance and learning, from the noble virgin, Lady Jane Grey, of the illustrious House of Suffolk." The fact that the "new religion," Protestantism, was not as appealing to or favored by the majority of the English people, did not disturb or puzzle Jane. The now colorless churches, devoid of statues or paintings, with their plain tables for altars, the sermons excoriating the Real Presence and other "Romish" beliefs were, in Jane's mind—as in the minds of many of the younger generation—a true expression of the worship of God.

For Jane Grey it was all so simple, and in the isolated austere world she'd made for herself with tutor, chaplain, servants and her correspondence, it was impossible that others should believe differently. Her foreign friends, self-appointed apostles of the reforming movement, were as bitter in their denunciation of unbelievers as they often were of one another. Confident *their* dogma was the Truth, they constantly betrayed their own doctrine. The Mercy of Christ and the Love of God which they so confidently preached were mercilessly violated in their intense hatred of their presumed enemies; Jezebel, Satan, the Scarlet Whore, even the Devil, were labels identifying those in power who did not accept the fundamentals of the reforming movement. A good deal of this brushed off on Jane, whose intolerance equaled that of her mentors. It was comforting that the king was also such a staunch believer, and with the issuance of his new Prayer Book, Jane felt Edward had set a firm standard of worship for the nation. If it was regarded with misgiving by many—as she knew it to be—time would show the unbelievers the true way.

That two teen-aged children, lacking any close friends, with little affection from any except household officers or servants, should have such firm ideological beliefs and a willingness to combat any attempt at tolerance or understanding for those who believed differently, was regarded with admiration by all who knew Lady Jane Grey and King Edward. None held them suspect of bigotry or self-delusion; no one regarded them as arrogant or narrow-minded.

Their lack of love or parental interest, the loss of any real childhood, the absence of close friends and the mere enjoyment of normal childish pastimes and pleasures—none of these was ever considered important. Certainly Katherine Parr had fought for a real home life for her stepchildren and Jane; those few years with her were all the Tudor children or Jane Grey were ever to know of warm family intimacy. It is doubtful if any of them—with the exception of Mary Tudor, who was old enough to remember her younger years with her parents—missed what they'd never really had. Edward had been too young to recall much of those days with the queen, and for Jane they'd already faded into a yesteryear reality, replaced now by her dedication to advancing her religious studies to the utmost, to mastering Hebrew, to paying strict attention to her Continental correspondents, whom she revered, and above all, to maintaining or even furthering the brilliant reputation she'd won for herself with her scholarship.

Jane's strong insistence on her own beliefs, her lack of that simple tactfulness which even the most seasoned courtier or churchman employed in difficult situations, often made for needless dissension or even outright hurt. It is doubtful, however, that Jane would have understood or admitted such a lack, even when it involved one she had been taught to regard with the respect due royalty.

In midsummer of 1552, as the royal progress and Edward neared home, "riding through Greenwich Park unto Blackheath, with my Lord Derby, my Lord of Warwick, my Lord Admiral Clinton and Sir William Herbert, the trumpeters playing . . ." Jane and her parents traveled to Beaulieu, the Newhall Boreham home of Mary Tudor in Essex. Mary had special reasons for not wanting to visit the court since the last unhappy confrontation with her brother and his council. Since then, she'd thought of escape, and ships of her Spanish cousin, the Holy Roman Emperor, and the Queen Dowager of the Netherlands had actually been sent to lie off Maldon on the Essex coast to rescue the beleaguered princess.

But Mary, alone and virtually penniless, had been distraught at the thought of leaving her country for a foreign land. She was the last royal link with that ancient faith of her mother, even of her father, for the religious doctrine advocated by Edward and Dudley had not been that of Henry VIII. Did she not owe it to their memory to fight for her beliefs as her mother had fought for hers? And while undoubtedly Edward would live a long life—she prayed for it daily—should anything happen to him, if she absconded, the crown would go to Anne Boleyn's daughter. In the end, wavering and indecisive, with no trusted friend to advise her, Mary had waited too long. The ships, floating idly off the coast, had excited suspicion and suddenly their purpose was revealed. As Edward later wrote in his *Journal*: "Sir John Gates was sent into Essex to stop the going away of the Lady Mary."

Since then, soldiers had been posted at Newhall Boreham to deal with any further attempt to rescue Mary; the specter of a princess of England forced to flee her country because of persecution did not enhance their reputation abroad, the Privy Council recognized. The emperor, inwardly relieved he'd have no Spanish Tudor on his hands, had nevertheless asked Dr. Wotton, the English envoy at the Spanish court, "Ought it not to suffice that ye spill your own souls, but ye have a mind to force others to lose theirs, too? My cousin, the princess, is evil-handled among you . . . !" The Queen Dowager was more clever. She had denied everything, throwing it back in the council's face that it was *their* shameful treatment of a princess of England that had provoked the situation in the first place. What had frightened Mary most of all was the remark of Scheyve, the emperor's ambassador, that the council was spreading news of her intended flight, undoubtedly to give them cause for a new severity regarding the king's unruly sister. As the days passed—and Edward's remark that his "conscience will receive a stain if he allow her to live in error" was passed along to her—Mary had wondered how long it would take John Dudley and the council to convince her brother he must act.

She'd not had long to wait. After one of her priests, Francis Mallet, had fled into Yorkshire when threatened with arrest, and another chaplain, Barkley, had disappeared, the council had said Edward Seymour's promise to "wink at" her continued use of the Mass could no longer be tolerated; she must conform. Not only was she breaking the law herself, she was assisting others to do so, as had her priests. It was well known that Mary welcomed anyone to the old service, anyone from old Sir Anthony Browne, her father's Master of the Horse, to any local squire, soldiers or just friends or acquaintances who timed their visits to Mary to coincide with the hour when they knew the Mass would be held. They had the comfort of the ritual; Mary accepted the danger.

So the council had sent commissioners—Lord Chancellor Rich, Secretary William Petre, and the king's Comptroller, Sir Anthony Wingfield—to visit Mary in order to resolve the impasse. These were men, as were others on the council, whom the princess had known for years; she had feasted, danced, worshiped and ridden with them; in some instances she was godmother to their children. As much as they agreed with Dudley and their colleagues that Mary was indeed breaking the law, it was another matter to confront the princess in her own home with accusations of religious disobedience.

Mary, her nervousness apparent, had greeted her visitors warily, suggesting to the verbose Rich as he read the charges that he hurry. "I am not well at ease . . . and I will make you short answer." When they told her of those at court who now accepted the restriction of the Mass, Mary had been contemptuous, saying she cared not to hear their names; she repeated that any religious changes should wait until Edward "shall come to such years that he may be able to judge these things himself." Her conviction that Edward had little or nothing to do with the momentous differences in church ritual and law that so depressed her, poignantly illustrates how far brother and sister had drifted apart since their father's death. When the commissioners had advised her that Wingfield would remain in her home to see that the Privy Council's orders were obeyed, Mary replied tremulously, "If my chaplains do say no Mass, I can hear none, no more can my servants. But as for my servants, I know it shall be against their will, as it shall be against mine. . . . And as for my priests, they know what they have to do. . . . But as for your 'new service' none shall be used in my house, and if any be said in it, I will not tarry in the house."

Inevitably, Wingfield had been recalled to London, the priests had come out of hiding and Mary, for the moment, had her Mass.

And so the visit of the new Duke and Duchess of Suffolk to Beaulieu was doubly welcome to Mary. She'd had few visitors during the past dreary months; not even close friends cared to visit someone at such odds with the king and his council. Mary was now a spinsterish thirty-six and she greeted the Greys affectionately, determined to put from her mind all thoughts of John Dudley, his council and her fear of what the future might bring. Mary and the Greys had always been close—they were relatives, after all—and she delighted in happy anticipation of the days of hunting, the card games and long musical evenings she so loved. Increasingly she'd suffered from headaches and toothaches and failing eyesight. But having company meant she could wear her brightest clothing and jewelry and forget for a few weeks that her brother's return to London would undoubtedly mean a summons to court.

The princess did not, therefore, take it kindly when she sent a "rich dress" to Jane Grey's chamber and the present was refused. As the lady-in-waiting laid the dress on the bed for her inspection, Jane only gazed at the garment. It was similar to the ones at home which she wore—to the continued disapproval of chaplain and tutor—when the occasion demanded. It was very like several Mrs. Ellen had packed for this visit to Beaulieu, for never would her mother see her other than appropriately dressed. Why did the princess think she needed another elaborate costume?

"What should I do with it?" she asked the lady-in-waiting, thinking more of the gift than the generosity and affection it represented.

The woman gazed at the young girl as if she'd not heard correctly. "Marry," she replied, "wear it, to be sure!"

"No." Jane handed the gown back to the lady-in-waiting. Mindful of John Aylmer's constant praise of the Princess Elizabeth, who wore no jewelry and only plain garb, she said, "That [it] were a shame to follow the Lady Mary, who leaveth God's word, and leave my Lady Elizabeth, who followeth God's Word!" Silently, the shocked lady-in-waiting took the gown and left the room, angered by a piety that overlooked generosity. Later, when she saw the princess, Mary made no comment.

But in the following days, as her parents and Mary, accompanied by other guests, rode out each morning to hunt, Jane walked the grounds of Beaulieu for exercise, later returning to her chamber for study and meditation. Alone, as usual, she thought about Mary's insistence on observing the Mass, on allowing her household to worship in direct disobedience of the standards set forth in Edward's new Prayer Book—that book for which he, Jane and all who practiced the "new religion" had such high hopes. Although there was little chance of Mary's ever ascending the throne—certainly Edward would live a long life and have many sons—she *was* next in the succession. How, then, could anyone in such a position deliberately break her brother's laws? Did she know the trouble that might result from her insistence on her old-fashioned and misguided beliefs? Knowing how stalwart she was in her own spiritual devotions, it never occurred to Jane that Mary might be as stubborn. Surely time, proper instruction—and some advanced reading—would help the princess see the error of her ways?

That Jane Grey perhaps thought herself equal to suggesting that Mary Tudor examine her conscience more fully was soon demonstrated. Shortly after the refusal of Mary's gift, Jane passed through the Beaulieu Chapel, where the princess worshiped each day. She was accompanied by Lady Wharton, as zealous in her Catholicism as Jane was in her Protestantism. As they passed the Host at the altar, Lady Wharton made a deep obeisance.

Looking about her, Jane asked, "Is the princess in the chapel?" When Lady Wharton shook her head, Jane asked, "Then why do you curtsey?"

"I curtsey to Him that made me," replied the woman, her tone exasperated, as if she were addressing a stupid child.

"Nay." Jane shook her head and, referring to the Catholic belief of the Body of Christ in the communion wafer, said tartly, "But did not the baker make him?"

Ignoring the stunned and angry look on her companion's face, Jane then turned and left the chapel. Her thoughts were a mixture of triumph—she could have said nothing else—and foreboding. If the remark was passed along to Mary and the princess told her mother, she would be punished. No one would understand that what some might regard as bad manners was, in reality, an opportunity Jane had seized to show by example her dedication to her religion. Why was that so difficult to grasp?

That evening, as the guests assembled for dinner, Mary paid no attention to Jane. Usually kind and commenting on the girl's dress or asking about the day's activities, on this occasion the princess ignored her young guest. Lady Wharton had lost little time in repeating Jane's remark. For Mary, it was one more painful reminder of how much ground the "new religion" had gained since her father's death. Everything had gone wrong since that time.

Yet the princess did not blame Edward, and in truth, she did not blame Jane. They were the unfortunate victims of people who'd lusted after the Church's power, influence and its wealth, who were willing to turn the spiritual life of England upside down to gain their own ends. The Greys, she knew, would support whatever religion the state demanded, but they at least had the common sense and good manners not to goad her about her own beliefs. That Jane had thought differently saddened Mary. She'd loved the little girl, but now that child had grown up and the sweetness, the desire to please, the sunny disposition Katherine Parr had so admired and fostered in Jane were no longer evident. Mary had suffered enough heartache in her own young years—her "troubles" had started when she was about Jane's age—to know the tremendous emotional cost. She'd also had years of observing Frances Grey's treatment of all her children and could admire the manner in which Jane had reacted to such harshness. But nothing—parental abuse or the severely solitary life Jane endured—merited such tart and caustic response to her generosity and her lady-in-waiting's simple pious gesture. In her spontaneous remark, deemed almost flippant by both Mary and Lady Wharton, Jane lost more respect and affection than, undoubtedly, she ever realized she'd had.

17

In the months following his return to court, it was obvious to many the young king was not himself. Never a robust child, Edward had suddenly grown taller, the added height and slimness emphasizing the disparity in his carriage, with one shoulder blade higher than the other. The king had inherited Jane Seymour's paleness and now the pallor seemed intensified. After Edward had spent hours of study at his desk or absorbing the numerous documents the Privy Council now sent him, John Cheke noticed how quickly his attention drifted away, how easily he tired. Some said the progress had been too demanding, the distances too far and undertaken before Edward had regained his strength after his bout with the measles. Others said that "he mourned and soon missed the life of his Protector, thus unexpectedly taken away, who, now deprived of both uncles, howsoever the time were passed with pastimes, plays and shows to drive away dumps, yet ever the remembrance of them that sat so near his heart, that lastly, he fell sick."

John Dudley, concerned at Edward's condition, advised he spend more time outdoors. In the following weeks he presented the king with expensive presents, a new Spanish jennet to ride and a teacher to explain and instruct him in the use of various weapons—anything that might hold the king's interest and improve his health. With the Privy Council's approval, he decided that the boy would be given his majority before it was due; at fifteen, Edward would be king in substance as well as in name. But the boy's languor and tiredness persisted and, as Parliament sat, it was decided that "The king being a little diseased by cold-taking, it was not thought meet for his Grace to ride to Westminster in the air," to preside at the final session. Thus on Good Friday the ceremony was enacted at the palace, where the Lords Spiritual and Temporal waited upon Edward.

By early 1553, four months after his return from the progress, there was no denying that something more serious than a "cold-taking" plagued the king. It perplexed and worried John Dudley, Henry Grey and the Privy Councillors who heretofore had managed the king and his realm in ways profitable to themselves and their families, but seemed unable now to help the boy himself.

But Dudley tried. The court physicians, Dr. George Owen and Dr. Wendy, were called in, but whatever they saw in Edward after examining him, they did not commit themselves. To proclaim the monarch mortally ill virtually amounted to treason; to admit he was incurable reflected upon their skill. Anyone could see that "It was not only the violence of the cough that did infest him, but therewith a weakness and faintness of spirit which showed plainly that his vital parts were strongly and strangely assaulted."

Dudley then summoned Dr. Girolamo Cardano, a distinguished Italian physician, a friend of John Cheke's, to see Edward. Cardano later described the king "as of a stature somewhat below the middle height, pale-faced with grey eyes, a grave aspect, decorous and handsome." Cardano was also a noted astrologer and mathematician, and the king, piqued by his visitor's knowledge of the concourse of the planets and the cause of comets, exhibited more interest than he had in days. But Cardano was not deceived, even when Edward offered to play for him upon his lute. After a later visit, when they discussed Edward's hopes for his country—its government and religion—Cardano said, "In his humanity, he was a picture of our mortal state. . . . this boy of so much wit and promise was nearing a comprehension of the sum of things . . . and there was the mark in his face of death that was come too soon." Years later, he would call Edward "a boy of wondrous hope, who, if he had lived, would have done much for the betterment of his kingdom." Cardano, ever the mystic, later wrote, "It would have been better, I think, for this boy not to have been born, or if he had been born, not to have survived—for he had graces. . . ."

While the court was aware of Edward's condition, Londoners knew little except what tavern gossip revealed, and no word of the seriousness of his illness was sent to his sisters, Mary and Elizabeth. Following the king's return from his progress, Mary had ventured to London to see him. Aware he did not stand too highly in the estimation of the woman who would replace Edward if he did not survive, John Dudley had ordered the full court to greet the princess. Mary was obviously surprised when, as she "rode from St. John's, Clerkenwell, with a great number of lords and knights and all the great ladies to Westminster," she saw the familiar faces of many of her old friends—the Northamptons, the Winchesters, the Bedfords, Shrewsburys and Arundels—waiting "with my Lord Duke of Suffolk [Henry Grey] and my Lord Duke of Northumberland [John Dudley] . . . and a vast train of knights and gentlemen. And so she went up to the Chamber of Presence."

But Edward was too ill to see her and Mary had to wait three days before being admitted to his bedchamber. The king had asked his Master of the Revels to provide entertainment for his sister, and a masque was to be performed that evening. But the boy's fevered breathing, the lung congestion and his frail, weakened condition so shocked and frightened Mary, the performance was cancelled. After a few days the distraught princess left for Newhall Boreham, writing her brother "that as hearing of your highness' late rheum and cough was as much grief as ever was any worldly thing. Even so, the hope which I have conceived since I received your Majesty's last token by my servant hath not been a little to my comfort. Praying God Almighty . . . to give your Majesty perfect health and strength, with long continuance in prosperity to reign. . . ."

In the days that followed, since *she* was next in the succession, it would have been impossible for Mary not to have wondered what would happen if Edward should die. Would John Dudley, the Privy Council and that embattled clergy allow her to receive the crown without hindrance, without those religious conditions she knew she could not tolerate? Mary loved her brother. She wanted him to live and marry and have many sons. She still believed that when Edward ruled alone, he would accept at least some rudiments of the Catholic belief, such as the Mass, which had survived at their father's death. Being away from the court as she'd been for so long, the princess never realized the depth of Edward's passion and conviction for the reformed religion. To her, he was still a little boy whom others had misled and misinformed ever since he'd been king. Mary was aware there was little she could do and she retired into the peace of Beaulieu, disturbed, frightened and sad. Now more than ever, she understood the welcome she'd received. Among the dukes, earls, knights and their ladies, there had been genuine friends. But most had been there to curry favor with one who might be their monarch sooner than they'd expected. Apparently, her past sins would be easily overlooked.

But John Dudley could not tolerate the thought of the Catholic Mary as his queen. Already he'd dispensed with Convocation and in some instances even the consent of the council in his measures to reform the Church. In his zeal, Dudley knew he could always count on Edward's support. Often he decided an issue or a question by sheer force of his personality, for authority came naturally to him. As the cleansing of the English Church and the repression of the Mass continued, when the question of Mary's use of the ritual arose in the Council Chamber, Dudley leapt to his feet, shouting angrily, "The Mass is either of God or of the Devil; if of God, it is but right that all of our people should be allowed to go to it; but if it is not of God, as we are all taught out of the Scriptures, why then should not the voice of this fury be equally proscribed to all?"

Religion apart, Dudley considered he'd worked too hard to lose everything he'd accomplished if Edward Tudor should die. He'd been a major force behind the deaths of both Seymours—the Lord Admiral and the Protector. He'd parried the thrusts of any on the council so presumptuous as to think he would share power or condone religious compromise. He knew who his enemies were and was confident he could deal with them; he knew he had few true friends. He'd made certain of young Edward's trust—even his affection—and, had the boy continued in good health, doubted not that he'd have remained the king's most influential minister. He knew Mary Tudor's opinion of him and realized she blamed him for most of her troubles. She would not be any more tolerant of him if she gained the crown than he'd been of her. No matter what the cost, Dudley knew she must be prevented from becoming queen, and somehow he must conserve his power should Edward die. Mary had genuine friends on his council; Frances and Henry Grey were good examples of those who, despite differing religious beliefs, were still close to her. What would Grey do if Edward died? How could he, the next most powerful man to Dudley, be persuaded to forgo that relationship of blood and a friendship commenced when, as children, his wife and the princess had shared the royal classroom?

In the months since Edward had returned to London, the Dudley and Grey friendship had deepened. Henry Grey had helped the duke deal with the myriad problems facing England: attempting to salvage the currency and to appraise the balance of power between France and Spain, keeping firm the match between the little French princess and Edward as a hedge against the Spanish power of the Holy Roman Emperor, Mary's cousin. Together they'd worked to abate the ambitions of the clergy, who were still striving to maintain some degree of influence in the England they'd once ruled as much as their monarch had. Dudley had harassed the most powerful prelate, the Archbishop of Canterbury, in open council. When Thomas Cranmer made some mild suggestions for improving Canon Law, Dudley had again leapt up, shouting, "You bishops! Look to it at your peril that you touch not the doings of your peers! Take heed that the like not happen again, or you and your preachers will suffer for it!" Only the shocked faces of Cranmer and his fellow councillors made Dudley realize he'd gone too far. The thought of anyone, even the clergy, sharing any of his hard-won authority was almost more than he could bear.

During that early spring before Edward had become so desperately ill, as he'd dutifully ridden, then practiced his archery or learned the intricacies of the longbow, the Dudleys and Greys spent much of their time at their river homes. Frances Grey at the old Priory of Sheen and Jane Dudley at the old Convent of Syon often visited each other, crossing the river in barges filled with children, companions and servants. There were archery contests on long green lawns at which the Dudley boys excelled. If the weather was inclement, they might all wander the long halls and cloisters of the two old religious houses, marveling at the spaciousness, the beauty of the carvings, the majesty of the stonework. Already Frances Grey, the Duchess of Suffolk, owned more of the former Carthusian properties than anyone else. In addition to Sheen, she'd just been given the Charterhouse, a former monastery taken by her uncle, Henry VIII, from which he'd hung parts of dismembered monks' bodies. It mattered little to the Greys that their homes were formerly residences of those in the service of God; all of their friends had received similar gifts from Dudley and the king. Who else should have them if not the nobility of England?

In the evening, there was music and dancing. Before the performance, the long tables in the Great Hall were filled with family and guests, and servants brought in platter after platter of steaming food and refilled the jeweled goblets with "malmsey, romney and muscadell." Then, much to the disgust of Jane Grey's tutor and chaplain, strolling players, mummers or even Lord Oxford's distinguished troupe of performers might present the latest play. Present at one such gathering was one of Jane's favorites—Katherine Brandon, the Dowager Duchess of Suffolk, her stepgrandmother. For almost a year Kate Brandon had mourned her two lost sons at Grimsthorpe, her Lincolnshire home. One who had understood and helped the duchess through that difficult time was Richard Bertie, a man of good birth and lineage who'd served as a Gentleman Usher in the Brandon household. In early 1553, Katherine married Richard Bertie and during those spring months, as the king lay ill and the Dudleys and Greys entertained in the former Protector's homes, Katherine and her husband were often guests. They watched the "romps, games and dancers," the performers disguised as "four hobby-horses, two dragons, four men as monkeys, a giraffe and a man that swallowed fire," who filled the Dudleys and the younger Greys with awe. Those evenings were preferable, everyone agreed, to the questionable entertainment John Dudley's sister, Lady Audley, provided at *her* home at Saffron Walden where a preacher ended the evening meal with a long sermon on improving their manner and morals. At Syon or Sheen, as the wine bottles were emptied, the conversation loosened, the minstrels' music thumped louder and the dancing became more abandoned. Then the matter of the king's health and the complex problems facing England were put aside for the moment. Then even Dudley—in the refuge of his luxurious and comfortable home, surrounded by his elegant duchess and handsome sons and daughters—could forget that much, perhaps all, of it depended upon the health of that frail boy, so obviously dying back at the palace. Suspense and strain had begun to tell upon John Dudley also, but he attempted to put it from him as good-byes were said at the darkened waterstairs, as oars splashed through the moonlit night, taking one family home across river.

As Dudley brooded on Edward's illness and the challenge his death would present to his own authority and power, he turned again to Henry Grey, Jane's father. Despite all his surface affability, Dudley considered Grey an unimaginative weakling, easily led, strongly dominated by his wife and too conscious of his rank to scheme as blatantly as one must to reach or maintain any autocratic position at court. Dudley, the man who had been described as having such a "head that he seldom went about anything but he conceived three or four purposes beforehand," suddenly had the answer. There *was* a way to maintain his influence and it was all very simple. It would involve Henry Grey's cooperation, but never once did Dudley doubt that the Duke of Suffolk would do as he was told; he'd have as much—even more!—to gain as Dudley. The clergy, loath to lose any more of their diminishing authority, would give him little trouble. Many older nobles—several of whom had left court since the Protector's death—were all fearful of what he, Dudley, would do should Edward die. The Privy Council, among whom he had few real friends, might be quarrelsome but Dudley felt he could browbeat them into submission. The only real problem might be the king himself.

In the end, however, Dudley felt that Edward would see the wisdom of this plan. Frail now and in genuine discomfort, the king presented no real challenge. Dudley recognized he'd have to maintain a patience he was far from feeling. How often in the past had he won Edward over with detailed explanations when they thought alike or with half-promises and half-truths obscuring any issue of which he knew the king would not approve? But Edward was older now and not as gullible or as trusting; he was king in fact as well as name. Only recently, at a council meeting at which he'd insisted upon presiding, Edward had lost his temper over a matter on which he and his councillors disagreed. Frustrated and angry, the king had shouted, "You pluck out my feathers as if I were but a tame falcon. The day will come when I shall pluck out yours!" The incident had served notice that Edward had found his independence and—once his health allowed—would not hesitate to use it.

But John Dudley knew his plan was the only way to save himself and the great wealth and authority he'd lose if the king were to die. He had little doubt, therefore, that he could make a convincing case for the scheme, which in essence would set aside the legitimate claims of two princesses and a duchess in order to make Henry Grey's eldest daughter a queen and his own son a king-consort. And religion would be his reason.

There had been talk at one time of Jane Grey's marrying Lord Hertford, the dead Protector's son, while twenty-year-old Guildford Dudley would wed Lady Margaret Clifford, the daughter of Frances' Grey's younger sister, Eleanor. But with Edward Seymour's ignominious end—and the confiscation of his estates—the Greys had changed their minds. And Eleanor Brandon Clifford, whose mother had been Henry VIII's sister, thought her daughter infinitely more worthy of someone other than one of the upstart Dudley's brood.

However, Dudley had not given up easily. He'd then suggested that his brother, Sir Andrew Dudley, wed Margaret Clifford. When her father, the Earl of Cumberland, heard that Dudley intended to commence negotiations for a marriage contract, that Sir Andrew had even gone to the Wardrobe to look over which splendid outfit he might wear at the ceremony, the earl simply removed his family to their country seat far from court and refused to consider the matter. It was a slight Dudley found difficult to forgive.

But should his son wed Jane Grey, of the same blood as Margaret Clifford, the haughty earl might yet regard the matter differently. Dudley knew that Henry Grey, now that the union with the Protector's son had been abandoned, still wanted a desirable marriage for Jane. Since all such marital alliances had to be approved by the king, it was paramount that Edward, in poor spirits and temper, not upset any arrangements.

By March, the boy's health had not improved and he undoubtedly had faced the fact that he might die. Edward had been ill for nearly five months and his doctors seemed unable to cure him or even relieve his discomfort. He was rebellious at the loathsome medications fed him, for none had helped. He hated the weakness and frailty that enveloped him and, frustrated, remembered all the matters that, as king, he should be dealing with: those charitable institutions in London for orphans, widows and the truly poor, and his schools and hospitals; the currency, which young Sir Thomas Gresham, thankfully, seemed to be coping with at last; the coastal defenses about England which hadn't been properly maintained or improved since his father's time. On his progress, he'd tried to set things right. Were Dudley and the Privy Council following his orders? Thinking of his father, Edward contemplated the Church. To the best of his ability and that belief carefully fostered and nurtured by the Protector and his councillors, he'd attempted to further the cleansing process his father had initiated but not lived long enough to complete. Edward still missed his father, and the executions of his mother's two brothers bore heavily upon him. And what of his sisters—all that was left of his family? Elizabeth had written him letters solicitous of his health, and only recently he'd sent Mary, whom he dearly loved, a table diamond even though her obstinacy in religious matters angered him. And *she* would succeed him if he did not recover.

By April the royal physicians decided the spring air of Greenwich might he helpful to Edward's worsening condition and depression. Even the short trip down the Thames from Westminster and the new surroundings might lift him from the lassitude and languor of the past months. At Placentia, that old palace so beloved by all the family, he might yet regain some vigor.

On April 11, therefore, the royal barge was prepared and Edward Tudor left London for the last time. The Thames was crowded with wherries, barges and ships being outfitted for voyages to the New World. Their passengers watched as the great barge glided smoothly past and then, aware their king was aboard, broke into cheers. People ran to the riverbank to call out their affection; others remained silent, knowing how ill the boy was. At Southwark the inns and taverns emptied as citizens rushed to the shore, and a farewell salvo of guns from the Tower boomed across the river and the oarsmen lifted their oars for a moment in salute. The stricken king lay on a couch on the deck, shaded from prying eyes by a rich velvet canopy. If Edward thought this short river voyage might be his last, he gave no sign.

By early May he'd rallied somewhat and could walk in the palace gardens and enjoy the fresh air. His doctors accompanied him to see he did not overdo—which, weak and listless as he was, seemed hardly possible. Since he could no longer participate in any sports or vigorous exercises, Edward received as many foreign ambassadors as his strength allowed, listened to his advisers and dutifully read the weekly résumé of the council's activities. The young king's sweet disposition, so much a part of his temperament, had disappeared with his illness, and now, rebellious and irritable, he was often impatient with his councillors. John Dudley, who visited Edward daily, realized that discomfort was partly to blame for his obstinacy. But it was also true that the boy's intelligence, almost adult now and seasoned by years of observing his courtiers in action, was disappointed and critical of what he viewed as Dudley's and the council's mismanagement. The king's attitude did not help Dudley, whose own nerves were frayed by the magnitude of his duties and the worriful suspense of what would happen if Edward should die. At times, the strain often sent him to his own bed for days.

Edward's doctors were encouraged by what appeared to be an improvement; they regarded any positive change with relief. The young king often sat in the sun and watched the arrivals and departures at the palace waterstairs. Some semblance of color reappeared in his cheeks. But several of the doctors scoffed at their colleagues' suggestion of a permanent improvement. The color was due to increased fever, they said. What of "the matter he ejects from his mouth . . . sometimes colored a greenish-yellow and black, and sometimes the color of blood?" Was he not tiring more easily, and was he not more weak every day? No one mentioned it was also true that there was little anyone could do for the boy. All of them dearly loved Edward Tudor; some had attended him since birth. But the position of a royal physician, which many envied, was not a comfortable one. Especially when their patient was dying—and taking such a long time in doing it.

18

John Dudley's scheme to alter the succession was almost certainly conceived when, after cornering Edward's physicians, Dr. Wendy and Dr. Owen, he demanded to know whether the king's consumption "was mortal, and for how long a period in their judgment his life might last." They, having consulted together, determined that the king was sick of consumption and the disease mortal; but they still reckoned upon his surviving until the following September. The finality of the statement made Dudley realize there was not much time to waste; otherwise Mary Tudor would be his queen. He knew there were some on the council also fearful of that possibility, for not only would Mary deprive them of their lucrative posts, perhaps even their lives, but she would attempt to return the country to the "old religion." Then, valuable possessions more important than faith would have to be relinquished. Lands, castles, manors, the monasteries and abbeys—those that hadn't been destroyed, as well as the jewels and treasures stripped from them—all would be reclaimed by their former owners and the church. Dudley knew his colleagues' fear would be his most important advantage if the scheme was to succeed.

Within weeks of his meeting with Edward's doctors and after

talking with Frances and Henry Grey, it was agreed that Lady Jane Grey, now a few months short of sixteen, would marry twenty-year-old Guildford Dudley. At the same time, the betrothal of her thirteen-year-old sister Katherine to Lord Herbert, son of the Earl of Pembroke, and her nine-year-old sister Mary to Arthur Grey, Lord Wilton, would be announced. In addition to affiancing all the Grey girls, John Dudley also promised his daughter Katherine in marriage to Lord Hastings, son of the Earl of Huntingdon.

Dudley had chosen well. In the wholesale betrothals, he'd allied one son with the Tudor line and one daughter with the Plantagenets, for young Lord Hastings was the grandson of the redoubtable Margaret Pole, Mary Tudor's beloved governess, whom Henry VIII had beheaded for treason some twelve years previously. Katherine Grey's engagement to Lord Herbert assured Dudley of the support of the Earl of Pembroke, whose wife, Ann Parr, was a sister of the late Queen Katherine. Both Pembroke and Huntingdon were firm allies of Dudley's; they had helped in the Protector's arrest and persecution and been generously rewarded with some of Edward Seymour's lands and other possessions. Both were members of the Privy Council, where their prestige and influence would help convince those other councillors who might be troublesome regarding what John Dudley—whom many still regarded as an opportunistic "new man"—knew he must do. When the king died and his scheme would go into effect, those who'd amassed great riches in the years since Henry VIII's death would be forced to cooperate—for their own gain if not for his. Dudley had told no one of his plan. At that moment, it was enough to lay the groundwork with the four betrothals. After the king died, everything would depend upon how quickly he could carry out whatever alternative then seemed feasible. The marriages would be the first step.

Frances and Henry Grey were pleased with John Dudley's offer of Guildford as a husband for Jane. It would bind the two families even more closely, and Dudley would certainly be the one who would have to cope in the still-shocking eventuality of the young king's death. When Mary Tudor succeeded, they would not only be close to the throne, related to the queen by blood and years of friendship, they would also be equally close to the man who would still, they doubted not, remain the most powerful man in the government, the true head of state. By allying their children as they had, the Greys and the Dudleys had closed ranks, banding together so that Mary or her advisers would hesitate to challenge their impregnability. It was also comforting to know that each would find it difficult, though not impossible—as Edward Seymour had found—to betray the other; outwardly, the unions bound them all together.

It was in early May, as Edward walked the palace gardens at Greenwich, that Jane Grey was called to her parents' presence. She thought little of the summons; it was only by such means that she ever saw her mother and father, other than those times when they shared a meal. Dutifully, she submitted to Mrs. Ellen's last straightening of hood and collar, a smoothing of her skirt, and then proceeded with her governess to where the duke and duchess waited. There, her father informed her it had been decided that she was to marry Guildford Dudley. And there for the first time in her life, Jane refused to do her parents' bidding.

The Greys were stunned. Never had their daughter challenged them. Never had she been anything but compliant, respectful and submissive. It was that attitude which had so often aroused Frances Grey's fury. It was difficult to believe anyone as insipid, colorless and meek as Jane could be *her* daughter; to strike out at the girl had been a release of her own emotions. And then it had become a habit. The duchess liked to be obeyed. Tolerance or compassion was not part of her temperament; it was easier to browbeat than to waste time attempting any understanding.

The duke spoke again, telling Jane that not only did he, her father, desire the marriage, but that Edward had also approved. Was she to refuse her king as well as her father? How dare she disobey! At which Jane, pale with nervousness, again refused. Dipping a slight curtsey and begging their understanding, she said she could not wed anyone other than Lord Hertford, the Protector's son. *That* was the boy her parents had always said she was to marry. If she'd been contracted to Hertford, how could she marry Dudley?

Loudly the duke swore, shouting that he knew more about such matters than she did. Contracts were often made and contracts were just as often set aside; the one with Hertford no longer existed.

The boy did not even have a home, he cried, and her mother, the Lady Frances, had taken him under her care. His father, the Protector, was dead, and while his own mother still remained in the Tower, the remaining Seymour children had been parceled out to various families. How could she marry one of that station and situation? She *would* marry Guildford Dudley and he wished to hear no more of the matter.

The duchess, standing by, watching her daughter, saw Jane shake her head again. All that the duke had said was true, but the girl was looking at them in a way that showed she still disagreed, that she did not think her parents had done the right thing. Though her lips and hands were trembling with nervousness, she was prepared to stand her ground and assert her own desire, something her mother had never witnessed before. Enraged, the duchess swung out her full palm and slapped Jane across the face. Frances Grey was stocky and broadly made; the force of the blow almost swept Jane to the floor. Steadying herself, tears in her eyes, Jane only shook her head, saying in good conscience she could not marry Guildford when she knew she'd been contracted to Lord Hertford.

Henry Grey swore loudly at his daughter and brought down his own palm against her shaking shoulder, his oaths punctuating each blow. By now, Jane was crying openly, holding her hands up to shield herself. As he continued to strike, Frances Grey screamed at Jane, slapping her face, her back, anywhere she could lay a hand on the thin child who dared question their decision and authority. At last, Mrs. Ellen, hearing the screams as she waited patiently outside in the hall, appeared in the doorway. Gesturing to Jane to leave, the disgusted parents turned their backs on their weeping daughter, almost hysterical now with fear and shame as she sped out to the hallway to Mrs. Ellen's waiting arms.

In the following days, after talking with Mrs. Ellen and her tutor, Jane realized there was no way she could challenge her parents' decision. She'd not told them or anyone else how much she disliked all the Dudleys, particularly Guildford's domineering mother, the Duchess of Northumberland, and even Guildford himself. She thought the slim boy as handsome as his brothers, with the same chestnut-brown hair and eyes. But Guildford was conceited and petulant. Jane had always regarded the Dudley family as too assertive and so arrogantly contemptuous of others, with such strong, forceful characters that they made others feel insignificant and uncomfortable in their presence. That all the Dudleys were magnificent, with an overabundance of good health, charm and elegance, was certainly true. But that did not alleviate her distrust or dislike, and the thought of being Guildford Dudley's wife was too terrifying to contemplate.

Yet the consequences of objecting were equally horrifying, and Jane accepted that she could not defy her parents, who were certain to have their way. They had subdued her once and could do so again. Though they had not told her directly, she was relieved to hear that once the ceremony was complete, both she and Katherine would return to their own home and not be left with their husbands. In an effort to lessen Jane's terror, Mrs. Ellen stressed that nothing would be changed. She would be married to Guildford Dudley, but would not have to live with him as part of his family for perhaps several years. Jane knew she was old enough to live with her husband; some girls her age already had children. But Katherine was too young, and that—plus the unsettled times, with the king so desperately ill and no one daring even to mention the possibility he might die—had made her parents agree to this marriage of convenience, which Jane knew was hardly unique. And so she convinced herself that once the wedding ceremony was over, her life would be much the same as it had before.

But even in the following days, it proved otherwise. Now for the first time her studies had to wait while she endured fittings for her wedding dress or discussion of the jewels she would wear. She listened patiently to her parents' plans for the ceremony, which would be held in old Durham House. The mansion, in the curve of the river just below the Strand, was a former residence of the Bishop of Durham but now it belonged to her father. As the nearest church, St. Mary-le-Strand, had been pulled down by the Protector for building materials, Dudley reasoned that the old chapel in Durham House would be fitting and easier for Edward to reach than either Syon or Sheen. Jane was disappointed that neither Princess Mary nor Princess Elizabeth would be present, yet dared not ask her parents why. Since the "nips and bobs" she'd received at their hands—the bruise marks of which were still visible on her face and aching body—Jane had been docile and attentive, realizing she had no other choice. Once she knew she'd be returned to her own home and Mrs. Ellen after the marriage ceremony, she put Guildford Dudley from her mind and determined, with a patience she thought even a saint might admire, to enjoy the festivities.

Again Sir Andrew Dudley approached the Wardrobe, that royal repository of rich clothing and costumes used in court masques and plays, with its hoard of precious materials, of gold, silver or embroidered trim, colorful scarves, gloves, boots and shoes of Spanish leather and sandals of the softest velvets. He carried a warrant for "wedding apparel, certain parcels of stuffs and jewels . . ." from the king at Greenwich, and soon after, the materials were delivered to Frances Grey.

Henry Grey discussed Jane's dower with John Dudley, for so noble a bride bringing a generous dowry must receive a like gift from her intended husband's family. Among the many manors and domains Jane would have after her marriage to Guildford, the two agreed, would be Stanfield Hall in Norfolk, part of a monastic holding which had once belonged to Princess Mary. Stanfield had originally been part of the Knights Hospitallers, whose St. Lazarus of Jerusalem monks lived there and cared for the destitute poor of the area. The Plantagenets had appropriated it for a hunting lodge, and though Jane could not know it, Stanfield had been partly responsible for the rebellion of Robert Ket, the Norfolk tanner, in the early years of the Protectorate. Then it was Ket who'd objected when John Dudley bought the adjacent Wymondham Abbey, which he intended to tear down. The rebellion had followed upon Dudley's refusal to save Wymondham. Ket had been executed and the body of his brother William, the monk, preserved in the blackened pitch in which it had been dipped, still hung from the church tower and could be seen from the windows of Stanfield Hall.

By mid-May, Edward's doctors announced he was too weak to attend the multiple weddings. But even the king's absence could not detract from the opulence of the ceremony which took place on Whitsunday, May 25, 1553, at old Durham House. There Jane Grey, "a lady of as excellent qualities as any of that age, of great parts, bred to learning and much conversant in Scripture and of so rare a temper of mind, that she charmed all who knew her," was wed to Guildford Dudley. Her headdress "was of green velvet, set round with precious stones. She wore a gown of cloth of gold and a mantle of silver tissue. Her hair hung down her back, combed and plaited in a curious fashion." The plaiting had been done by Mrs. Ellen, who was determined that Jane would shine despite the beauty of the other brides, Katherine Dudley and Katherine Grey. Mary Grey's wedding was not to take place for another few years, since she was only nine. Sixteen young girls— one for each year of Jane's age—dressed in purest white preceded the pages, chosen for their comeliness, with bride-lace and rosemary tied to their sleeves, as they escorted Jane along the Turkey carpet to an altar resplendent with a new cloth sewn with exquisite seed pearls. Jane's face was expressionless. It bore no similarity to the tear-stained, bruised and fearful countenance of only a few weeks earlier.

Some thought the wedding ceremony was too "popish," for the church hierarchy, in the process of being reformed and cleansed, had not as yet formulated a ritual appropriate to the occasion. That did not deter the ceremony from being "very splendid and royal and attended by a great concourse of people and the principal persons in the kingdom." That much of the borrowed finery—from the garments the bridal party wore to the jewels that adorned their clothing or persons—was all from the confiscated estates of the Protector bothered no one, least of all the participants. Certainly neither Jane nor her sister ever questioned the source of the splendidly rich costumes and the gleaming jewels. Their parents had provided them and Jane wore them without question.

As church bells pealed along the river, the London populace crowded Durham House's back entrance on the Strand and even the waterstairs—eager always to view the finery, the pomp and pageantry of the nobles and their entourages. There were those who thought that the ceremonies might have been less public, out of deference to their young king's illness. Many were at last beginning to suspect that Edward's absence provided proof he was more seriously ill than they'd been told. Everyone was pleased with the comely brides: tall, chestnut-haired Katherine with her strong Dudley features; the other Katherine, Henry Grey's daughter, blond hair shining from Mrs. Tylney's brushing, her exquisite complexion in such contrast to the freckled skin and deep red-gold hair and brows of her sister Jane, who was so tiny, almost like a child too young to be married. All the girls walked slowly, burdened by the extraordinarily heavy gowns and the sparkling jeweled hoods, which they found difficult to balance properly.

All day in the spacious rooms of old Durham House, hung with long lengths of crimson and gold tissue from the Wardrobe, the feasting, mumming and dancing continued. The numerous residences of both the Greys and Dudleys were overflowing with guests and their servants who would remain for a week or more after the weddings. For days the family granaries in the country and the town bakehouses, breweries, dairies and storehouses for cheese and fish had been emptied for the wedding feast. What the family estates could not provide, the "acaters," those purchasers who bargained with purveyors of outside provisions, did. For weeks they'd been busy with their lists and tallies, and now course after course of beef boiled and baked, of lamb, kid, buck, goose, cygnet and capon were followed by pheasant, rabbit, partridge and quail. Beer and ale from hogsheads in the courtyard and French, Rhenish and Spanish wines from the Durham House cellar flowed liberally in the Great Hall, where toasts were made to the three bridal pairs sitting under clusters of thick, brightly burning candles. After a masque during which each bride danced with her husband, the three grooms took their leave and, with several younger courtiers, left to joust in the royal tiltyard at Whitehall.

Soon the church bells along the river quieted, the observers departed, and by horse, coach or river, the guests began to leave. Then Jane, Lady Dudley, and her sister Katherine, Lady Herbert, and John Dudley's daughter, now Lady Hastings, re-joined their parents, each anxious for the familiarity and peace of her own chamber. Jane and Katherine were eager to discuss the day's events with Mrs. Ellen and Mrs. Tylney, who were waiting to relieve them of their heavy borrowed finery, which had caused heads and shoulders to ache. While all three agreed it had been an exciting day, they also admitted they were happy now to return to their homes.

As Jane returned to the security of her classroom and correspondence with her Swiss friends, John Dudley recognized that Edward's illness was progressing so swiftly, the boy might not live until September. He knew, in view of the king's diminishing strength, that Antoine de Noailles, the French ambassador, and Scheyve, the Spanish ambassador, were writing their home courts that there was little chance of the king's recovery. Already, he'd insisted that the Privy Council meet in secret sessions and later had refused to divulge what had occurred, thereby frustrating the ambassadors, who prided themselves on ferreting out information which their king and emperor expected by the first courier. When Edward died, it would be of paramount importance that France, particularly, do everything to prevent Princess Mary from attaining the throne. Her mother, Katherine of Aragon, had been a niece of the Spanish emperor and there was no doubt but what Mary would immediately ally herself with Spain—which the French would do anything to prevent. Edward's engagement to the little French princess had made England their ally. Now, suddenly, when the king died, the entire political balance of power would be shifted.

What worried the perplexed ambassadors also was the extraordinary activity in the City. Commencing with the multiple weddings within the Dudley and Grey families, there'd been an intense movement of soldiers—with five hundred alone under the command of William Parr, the Marquis of Northampton, sent to Windsor Castle. The fleet at sea and the small standing army on land were on the alert, and large amounts of ammunition and weapons had been seen arriving at the Tower of London. Even the treasury—that source of so much misguided endeavor since Thomas Seymour's manipulations of the currency—had come firmly under John Dudley's control. Any unusual military movements were always of prime interest to the ambassadors and when De Noailles frankly told Dudley he was suspicious of the naval activity, the duke only laughed. The ships were intended for an expedition to the Barbary and Spice Islands, he said, a reply the ambassador did not believe because of the number of ships involved.

Three weeks after Jane's marriage, John Dudley at last broke the silence with which he'd surrounded his actions since Edward's illness had worsened. When the physicians agreed the boy might not live even until September, and after he'd persuaded the council to agree to extraordinary military preparations to deal with any crisis deriving from the king's death, Dudley knew the first part of his plan must be put into effect. It depended upon the cooperation of Frances and Henry Grey, a fact the duke viewed with some misgiving and alarm. Of Henry Grey, he had little doubt; of the duchess, he was not so certain.

By the terms of Henry VIII's will, the succession had gone to Prince Edward, then to Princess Mary and finally to Princess Elizabeth. Failing that, the crown devolved on the heirs of his sister Mary, the wife of Charles Brandon, the late Duke of Suffolk. Mary's children were half Tudor with Plantagenet blood from Henry's mother, Elizabeth of York, the daughter of Edward IV. It was a claim none could question, excepting of course those of Plantagenet blood who'd never ceased to lament the Tudor ascendancy over Richard III in 1483. Seventy years was not a long time in an established monarchy; in a new one, the perils of the victor were perpetual, with claimants from the older, vanquished line constantly contending for supremacy. Continuation of the Tudor line had hung on the slim, handsome youth now so near to death at Greenwich. With no male heir and facing an undeniable death—possibilities few could have foreseen as the boy matured—the crown would go to half-Spanish Princess Mary with her ties to her mother's country and its staunch Catholic Holy Roman Emperor, Charles V. No one knew better than John Dudley how impossible it would be for England—after almost twenty years of religious upheaval, of papal schism and excommunication, of martyrs, confiscation of land, both private and ecclesiastical—to accept Princess Mary as their queen.

As for Elizabeth, Dudley gave little thought to Anne Boleyn's twenty-year-old daughter, for there were many who still regarded Henry's marriage to her mother as spurious. At the time he married Anne, the king had not secured a divorce from Katherine of Aragon. Elizabeth—conceived before the secret ceremony that united her parents in their doubtful marriage—had always had a tinge of the illegitimate, which her father had buttressed by declaring her so when it suited him. The true Catholics did not consider the Boleyn marriage valid, since there'd been no papal divorce, only Cranmer's annulment of the twenty-five-year Spanish marriage. Dudley, along with others at court, knew that Princess Mary, for instance, did not even consider Elizabeth to be Henry's daughter, but actually the offspring of one of the lovers accused with Anne Boleyn at her death.

In addition, Dudley had never liked Elizabeth. He'd known both princesses since their birth, and when Mary, as Princess of Wales and Henry's only heir, had been sent to live in Ludlow Castle in the Welsh Marches before she was ten, it had been to young John Dudley that the king had entrusted her care and the running of her household. He'd had little opportunity to be as close to Elizabeth, seeing her most often in the years when the king was married to Katherine Parr and the queen had all three of the royal children together under one roof. Later, at Chelsea, he'd disliked and distrusted the younger princess with her bright intelligence, and he remembered well the reason she'd been sent away from the Seymour household. In contrast to Mary's dependable predictability, Dudley thought Elizabeth much too close-mouthed, dissimulating and clever, the exact opposite of her sister. No one would ever call Mary Tudor clever. She was too honest and open, as anyone who'd watched her battle for the Mass during the last several years could testify. Elizabeth, on the other hand, had quietly assumed the demeanor of a pious and learned princess, one twice removed from the crown, eager only to learn, to conduct herself as befitted her position and, above all, to give neither the council nor anyone else responsible for her well-being any reason to bother her. Dudley considered her attitude false, but of little threat to him.

So, with the setting aside of Mary's undeniable claim to the throne for religious and political reasons, it would be easy, Dudley felt, to set aside Elizabeth's also. The girl was young, untried, untested and above all, an unknown quantity. If Mary could be set aside in the succession, Elizabeth should present no problem. If one arose, he could deal with it.

19

The three weeks following Jane Grey's marriage were crucial to the success of John Dudley's plan. When he could not visit the king himself, daily reports of Edward's condition were sent to him, not only from the physicians but from his son. Robert Dudley, a few years older than Edward, was a member of the king's Privy Chamber and held the appointment of Carver as well; he spent much of his time at Greenwich. There were days when the reports filled Dudley with dread: The boy was "steadily pining away. He does not sleep except stuffed with drugs. . . . The sputum which he brings up is livid, black, fetid and full of carbon; it smells beyond measure. . . . His feet are swollen all over. . . ." The best guarantee of his own power and authority was Edward Tudor's life, and it was slipping away too quickly, before he had time to effect those momentous changes to resolve the eventual crisis. Through the marriages of his son and daughter, he now had the support of at least three of the most powerful families at court, and others would be forced to fall into line. But how long would he keep that support if Edward died before he'd completed his plan?

The multiple weddings, he knew, had increased the public's dislike, for "the noise of these marriages bred such amazement in the hearts of the common people apt enough in themselves to speak the worst of Northumberland [Dudley] that there was nothing left unsaid which might serve to show their hatred against him, or express their pity for their king." The weddings had also excited the foreign ambassadors' suspicious interest. None had been invited to the ceremonies nor had they been given any explanation of the extraordinary event. Yet Dudley felt that Antoine de Noailles, the distinguished French ambassador, had probably guessed the unions were connected with setting aside the Catholic Mary in the succession. But even the ambassador would never guess Elizabeth was also to be set aside in favor of the duke's new daughter-in-law, Lady Jane Grey Dudley. Even the girl herself had not realized the motive behind her sudden marriage and had settled back into her classroom routine, resuming her Swiss correspondence and Hebrew studies. Many of those Swiss reformers—or friends of Jane's correspondents—had arrived in England in answer to Thomas Cranmer's request to lecture at Oxford and Cambridge. While they all regarded the pope as their common enemy, they often hated each other far too heartily and quarreled often enough among themselves on vital points of the Christian faith, thus creating a dissension that had not endeared them to their followers nor helped their cause. But their influence would be one more counterbalance to Mary's gaining the throne, for they were capable of stirring up religious controversy at will.

Jane had been delighted to return to the correspondence with her Swiss friends, and their letters were deeply valued by the lonely girl. They provided a welcome diversion from her normally restricted days of study and devotions, containing as they did an immeasurable amount of praise for her intellectual abilities—heady satisfaction for one whose own ego had been so savaged during her short life. Jane did not need the oft-repeated encouragement to remain faithful to her deep Protestant belief, though others such as Dudley and Henry Grey desired her interest be kept at "fever heat" to provide that strongly emotional zeal she would need in the days ahead.

Dudley, too, especially in face of public suspicion that his interest in Church reform was largely opportunistic, took particular pains to emphasize the depth of his own religious commitment, writing William Cecil, "I have for twenty years stood to one kind of religion, in the same which I do now profess; and I have, thank the Lord, passed no small dangers for it."

Religion aside, Dudley had other worries where Edward was concerned. He'd been present at court in the days of Henry VIII when Thomas Wolsey and Thomas Cromwell had enjoyed their great power. And he'd seen them fall. He himself had contributed mightily to the Protector's destruction. It was easier to fall than to rise, a maxim observed by several at court including milords Derby, Oxford, Sussex, even Henry's old war-horse adviser Lord Paget— all of whom had absented themselves from court at their county seats when Dudley became dominant in the council. It had worried Dudley that—long before he'd have the opportunity to plan on such an eventuality—Edward's death would call for an accounting of his stewardship. The national debt, the corrupt jurors and judges, continued robbery of the poor by land enclosure, the ineptness of the new Protestant clergy who vied for dereliction of duty with many of the venal Catholic clergy, the magnitude of the land sold far below its true value or stolen outright by the nobles—all would be revealed with Edward's death, and his successor would be pitiless. The daily stress and tension, the necessity of keeping his hold over so many varying factions strained Dudley's nerves to the utmost, and again he often took to his bed. Edward had to be kept alive at all costs and the public's concern abated until he had set in motion the measures by which his cupidity and duplicity might be concealed. For the moment, his greatest hope of security lay with those on the Privy Council and other influential nobles who'd shared in the stolen loot.

During a short rally in the king's health, Dudley ordered that Edward be carried to a window at Greenwich palace so that the populace which remained night and day in the courtyard might see their king was still alive. Trembling and white-faced, wasted to skeletal proportions and too weak to wave in response to his subjects' affectionate cries, the boy was held up to the throng. Then, subdued and silent, with many in tears, the people returned to their homes, realizing their monarch would never recover.

The king's condition was now such that ulcers had broken out over his body and the agonizing cough still strained his infected lungs. With the constant high fever, swollen stomach and feet, it was impossible for him to leave his bed. Often delirious, he would be revived with stimulants to suffer another day, causing William Cecil to write to a friend, "God deliver you from the physicians."

Now that the public had seen Edward, it was impossible to conceal the seriousness of his condition. Even his sisters had not been advised, though Dudley had little doubt but that they'd heard rumors of his deterioration. Now, formal bulletins were sent to Mary and Elizabeth, and to avert the elder princess' suspicions, the duke ordered that Mary have the royal arms and quarterings of her mother—which she'd borne as heiress-presumptive before Elizabeth's birth—restored. If nothing else, it would show the foreign ambassadors, the unfriendly populace and members of the Privy Council that he, Dudley, was preparing for the succession in a normal manner.

Within ten days of Jane's marriage, John Dudley met the Duke and Duchess of Suffolk and revealed the plan that had commenced with the marriage of their children. If the Protestant religion was to be maintained in England, he stressed, the accession of Mary Tudor must be avoided at all costs. Mary was now thirty-seven, frail, emotionally and physically unstable and unlikely to bear an heir. Elizabeth's claim must also be set aside. Dudley did not say that, in addition to the legal obstacles, he doubted he'd have any better luck in handling Elizabeth than he'd had in handling her older sister. Both were Tudors and regarded his family with distaste; both were as firm in their religious commitments as he was in his political ambitions. But Elizabeth, who had piously followed the dictates of council and clergy, would have to be set aside for reasons other than religion. First there was the tinge of illegitimacy which a large proportion of the English people, most Catholics, believed valid, since the pope had never divorced her father from Mary's mother. Also, Elizabeth was twenty and just the right age for marriage, but did the country want a foreign prince for their king? Dudley had once considered Elizabeth as a bride for his son Guildford, but recognized he could never manipulate or dominate her as easily as he could Jane Grey.

But the duke's main concern now was how long would all of them—the Greys as well as the Dudleys—remain in their full power under the command of either princess, both of whom they'd been only too anxious to keep away from the court in the years since Katherine Parr's death?

Dudley's assessment was a sobering one. Both Henry and Frances Grey, well advised of Edward's condition and holding no hope for his recovery, had accepted that Mary would succeed. For the "thunderbolt and terror of the Papists," which Henry Grey considered himself, it was unfortunate and disturbing that she was so stubbornly Catholic. Yet Mary was a blood relative and there were ties going back many years, and neither felt, at first, it would be easy to set her aside. It was then that John Dudley told the duke and duchess that the two princesses would be set aside for their daughter—*his* new daughter-in-law—Lady Jane.

But first Frances Grey had to be dealt with. If Mary and Elizabeth did not succeed, then *she*, the daughter of Henry VIII's sister, certainly viewed herself as heir. But Henry, who'd considered his will inviolate, had envisioned a long life for Edward, with those sons the boy would undoubtedly have to follow. Any eventuality of the succession going further than his son, two daughters and *their* heirs was almost impossible to contemplate in 1546. So Henry, anticipating that either Edward's children or his daughters' children would occupy the throne, had stipulated that only the *heirs* of his niece Frances should inherit. Presumably, after that long procession of possible heirs, the duchess herself would likely be dead. It was difficult for Jane's mother to admit that her chief heir was indeed her meek and pale-faced daughter, Lady Jane. That there would be political, possibly even legal, obstacles put in their way, everyone agreed. But Henry VIII's will gave the duchess's daughter a claim after Mary and Elizabeth. Though the king had never considered that his will would ever be tampered with, there was no denying that if they could legally set aside Henry's other designated heirs, Jane Grey's claim was valid.

Dudley then approached the king at Greenwich. Edward was the weakest the duke had ever seen, plagued with bed sores and vomiting the food the physicians insisted he eat. John Cheke told Dudley he'd heard the boy whisper, "I am glad to die," and that when alert, Edward had composed a prayer which he'd committed to memory. Dudley, despairing that the king might die before his plan could be accomplished, wasted little time in indicating to

Edward that he must make a will. In so doing, if the boy was to
justify that deep religious faith to which he'd committed his short
life, then his sister Mary—that staunch advocate of popery and all
the offenses and sins its return to England would mean—must be
omitted from her brother's will. It also followed, Dudley said, that
if Mary was eliminated, then Elizabeth must be also. The position
and right of one depended upon the other. No matter how deep
Edward's affection was for his sisters and despite what their father
had thought six years ago, their accession would be a national
calamity. Mary would return England to the Catholic fold and
Elizabeth would marry a foreign prince whose country might
"extinguish at last the very name of England." Dudley was at his
most convincing in hammering home to the boy—worn by his disease, yet still conscientious to a fault—what the religious reversal
would mean, saying it was Edward's duty to prevent it. "It is the
part of a religious and good prince to set apart all respects of blood
where God's glory and the subjects' weal may be endangered," he
stressed. "That your Majesty should do otherwise were, after this
life which is short, to expect God's dreadful tribunal."

For one of Edward's deep religious conviction and complexity,
facing "God's dreadful tribunal," the thought must have been
chilling.

Having put the seed of doubt in his mind, Dudley continued
the discussion in other short visits to the king—occasions determined by the boy's ability to tolerate the demands of his deteriorating condition. Weak and diseased though his body might be,
when his mind wasn't hazy with drugs, Edward was alert. He
considered Dudley's reasons for eliminating his two sisters from
the succession and at last accepted such a dire procedure as necessary and in the country's best interests. Soon thereafter, Frances
Grey arrived at Greenwich and, kneeling at Edward's bedside,
swore she had no claim to the throne. Then it was easier for the
king to consider it was *her* heirs who would inherit his crown. Edward had always been fond of his cousin Jane, and as Dudley told
him, "She hath imbibed the reformed religion with her milk and
is married in England to a husband of wealth and probity." He
reminded Edward of his "affectionate sympathy with that excellent lady" and reiterated, "You are bound by your duty to God to
lay aside all natural affections to your father's house."

But, still not trusting that Edward might not change his mind, upon leaving he asked Sir Henry Sidney, husband of his eldest daughter, Lady Mary Dudley, to remind the boy constantly of Jane's sterling qualities of mind, religion and heart and "the high esteem in which she was held for her zeal and piety."

Dudley's apprehension was understandable. Before his illness, Edward had exhibited traits of the mature king he'd hoped to become. He often questioned his ministers' intentions and methods of dealing with public affairs and, with diminishing patience, would argue or reprimand if the answers were not to his satisfaction. And it was very obvious to many, particularly Sir Nicholas Throckmorton, a close friend of the king's and member of the Privy Chamber, that soon after the Protector's death, the boy had begun to distrust and dislike John Dudley.

But the duke's arguments were persuasive and the king's strength waning. At last, too weak to argue, subdued yet apprehensive, Edward agreed that perhaps it was all for the best. Dudley knew then he had won. But would the king live long enough for him to make Jane's claim legal? The Privy Council must be dealt with; not everyone there was his friend. Princess Mary's suspicions must not be aroused and her very person secured if his plan was to succeed. Exhilarated, Dudley left Edward, knowing that sick as he was, the conscientious boy would expend his last breath working at what he considered best for his kingdom's future. The duke had been more successful—and in shorter time—than he'd anticipated. But he needed one more string to his bow and he intended to secure that as soon as possible.

As Edward took advantage of those intervals when his mind was clear and his discomfort bearable to work on his "Device," that instrument by which he intended to alter the succession his father had willed, Jane Dudley, the Duchess of Northumberland, talked with her husband and agreed that their original decision to let Jane remain at home in an unconsummated marriage had been unwise. If she was to be queen when the king died, she should be Guildford Dudley's wife in fact as well as name. A pregnant queen— the last one in England had been sixteen years ago, when Jane Seymour had given birth to Edward—would make acceptance easier, for the child might be a son. With only women in line for the succession—one too old for childbearing—that in itself was an emotionally powerful argument for Jane's queenship.

When the duchess insisted the nuptial agreement be changed, Guildford Dudley was told his bride would be coming to live at Durham House. He accepted the news with mixed feelings. His dislike of Jane Grey was as strong as he knew hers to be for him. His taste did not run to subdued, freckle-faced girls with soft voices, thin bodies and little spirit. He was not impressed with Jane's knowledge and other accomplishments. Though he'd received the respectable education befitting a duke's son, the love of learning for learning's sake did not exist in any member of the Dudley family. What pleasure would he have in a wife of such character and unpleasing physical endowments? His parents, both handsome and knowledgeable, had enjoyed a marriage of extreme compatibility in a court where unions were made for every reason other than love. His brothers, too, seemed satisfied with their brides. Petulant and almost unreasonable, Guildford sulked at his misfortune.

But when his father told him—insisting he remain silent until the Privy Council had been told—that his wife would be the next Queen of England, Guildford put his exasperation and disappointment behind him and accompanied his mother to Jane's home.

She was waiting with her own mother when they arrived. No one had told her what the meeting was for. But after a short greeting, Jane Dudley minced no words, telling Jane she must accompany her to the Dudley home, where she would live as Guildford's wife. Guildford, lounging nearby, said nothing.

Jane looked at the tall boy, elegant with the reed-slimness of all the Dudleys, his plumed cap held at just the right angle under his arm, dressed with the exquisite taste for which his family was noted. She sensed his dislike and wondered why it was now so important for her to leave her family. She looked at her mother, who appeared puzzled, and was encouraged that apparently Frances Grey knew no more than she.

In a soft voice Jane told the duchess that before her wedding she'd been promised she might remain in her own home. She avoided Guildford's stare, now almost bold, caring little what he thought. It was almost as if he were enjoying her dismay. Again she looked to her mother for help. Frances Grey's expression was now guarded; still, she said nothing.

Jane Dudley, tense and showing her exasperation, then told Jane "it was publicly said that there was no hope of the king's life . . . and that when it pleased God to call King Edward to His Mercy," Jane should hold herself in readiness: She might have to go to the Tower, since His Majesty had made her, Lady Jane Grey Dudley, "heir to his dominions."

At first, Jane did not grasp the duchess's meaning. She saw her mother's eyes narrow and knew she must do whatever possible, make any appeal necessary so she would not be forced to go with the Dudleys. When the two women began to argue loudly, Jane realized her mother did not want her to go. She knew it was not out of consideration for her that she'd been allowed to remain at home; it simply had not been important that she live with her husband. Obviously there'd been some change in plans, but she was encouraged that her mother apparently *did* want her to remain in her care.

Jane had been so upset at the thought of leaving her family, and by Jane Dudley's comment on the king's health and his plan for her, that moments passed before she realized their true meaning. As she was later to write, "These words, told me offhand and without preparation, agitated my soul within me, and for a time seemed to amaze me. Yet afterwards, they seemed to me exaggerated and to mean little but boasting, and by no means of consequence sufficient to hinder me from going from my mother."

When she told the duchess so, intimating it must all be a joke of questionable taste, "the Duchess of Northumberland was enraged against my mother and me." It was then Jane realized why her mother didn't want her to leave. It was not from any maternal consideration, but because *if she were to be queen*, it was to be from Frances Grey's home that she should leave. Her suspicions were justified as the two women began to shout at each other, Guildford's mother crying that she meant to have Jane in her care, insisting it was her duty "at all events, to remain near my husband. . . ."

So violent did the duchess become that at last, waving her daughter away, Frances Grey consented. Shocked, Jane ran from the room, too frightened to speak. In her chamber, she wept as Mrs. Ellen, tight-lipped and trembling, packed a small trunk which the waiting Northumberland porters would take to her new home.

There was one last embrace and then, her own tears starting, the governess pushed Jane through the door. Her mother was nowhere to be seen and Jane knew any appeal would be fruitless. Slowly, she followed the porters down the stairs to where her mother-in-law and husband were waiting.

It was dusk when the Dudleys arrived back at Durham House, where she'd been married only a few short weeks ago. Jane was told that Guildford's father was with the king at Greenwich. He expected the new will naming her queen to be passed through the Privy Council within a few days and then a Parliament would be called to ratify the changes. But Jane must hold herself in readiness for whenever the duke or the council wished to see her.

The enormity of the event at last aroused Jane from her frightened state. Of course a Parliament would need to be called if Princess Mary and Princess Elizabeth were to be set aside. Repeatedly the thought coursed through Jane's brain: How could two princesses, daughters of Henry VIII, be overlooked and the crown come to *her*? No one had told her; she doubted that anyone would. But why had Edward named her when he had two sisters his father had designated as heirs?

And why had no one ever mentioned that Edward might die? Jane had known of his illness, but no one had ever intimated he was so sick. The questions flew about in her brain and she wished for her mother, for, even risking a blow, it would be better to know than to be so ignorant. She dared not ask Jane Dudley. There must be some very good reason why Edward was willing to overlook sisters he cared for in favor of someone else. Jane had always known of her place in the succession. But with a king and two others preceding her, never once had she thought of becoming queen. She longed to ask Jane Dudley also what had made Edward change his mind and wondered what Mary and Elizabeth thought of his decision. But she could not bear to involve herself in discussion with any of the Dudleys. The less she had to do with them, the easier it would be for her.

By nightfall, however, it was obvious that she was expected to have a good deal to do with Guildford. The porter had placed her trunk in a corner of the room to which a steward, bearing a large flaring candle before him, led her through long corridors. An impressive canopied bed was in the center of the chamber and a fire blazed at the opposite end. Jane had never ever been away from home before *alone*. Always, whenever she'd been in strange houses, or houses of relatives such as Princess Mary at Newhall, her parents and sisters, Mrs. Ellen and Mrs. Tylney and other Grey servants had been nearby. Now there was no one, no one at all, only a house full of strangers, a family she didn't like, under conditions she'd never thought possible. It was unreal that Edward, her own age and a king, was dying.

Busy as she was with her thoughts—and that first sadness for Edward which the very immensity of the day's events had prevented her from feeling before—she was not aware of the fact that Guildford had entered the room. Along with those other feelings she could not bear had been the presence of her husband himself. Jane had almost convinced herself that though it was strange to be away from the familiar rooms of her own home, it would be bearable if that was the only change. But the fact that Guildford was in his nightrobe and preparing to enter the bed left little doubt that something more was expected of her. Almost dizzy with fear, the long events of the day racing through her mind, the unbearable presence in the bed demanding she undress and join him, Jane hoped she would not faint, for her mind seemed to have left her.

But there was no one she could turn to, and to flee would be not only foolish but would earn her a physical beating she wondered if she could stand. Perhaps it would be better to take the other kind of beating and hope that God, in His mercy, would help her endure. Silently, gulping back the nausea in her throat, she began to remove her sandals. Trying to occupy her mind, she wondered if that was what Mrs. Ellen had always done first, for she'd never undressed herself before.

The following three weeks were emotionally draining for everyone at court, particularly John Dudley. His plan to alter the succession had been received with little enthusiasm by those he needed for its passage. On June 11, Sir Edward Montague, Chief Justice of the Court of Common Pleas, with other court officials, as well as Sir William Parr, the Marquis of Northampton, and Sir John Gates, a close friend of Dudley's, had been present when Edward told them that, considering the state of religion in his realm and since he would die without heirs, he wished them to "make a book" of the "Device" over which he'd labored, weakly crossing out words and inserting others so there'd be no mistaking his intent once he was gone. Already such powerful nobles as Winchester, Bedford, Shrewsbury and Arundel had voiced strong objections to Dudley's intent, stating that even when Henry VIII had bequeathed his crown, he had needed the confirmation of Parliament. How could a weak and dying boy, lacking those years of maturity needed to reach such a decision, expect to dispose of the crown at will? Everyone knew that while Edward undoubtedly believed his proposal to be in his country's best interests, the original intent had not been his.

Montague and the other court officials demurred. They also said Edward's request was illegal; only a Parliament could effect a change in the succession. Edward, rising above his discomfort, told them sharply they were to read his "book," as he called it, that he would tolerate no objections, and he ordered them to "draw the letters patent forthwith." Troubled by the royal obstinacy and frightened at the responsibility, the justice said he and his colleagues would read the "Device"; then they left for London.

At the Ely Place home of Sir William Petre they reported, to the assembled councillors and nobles awaiting their decision, that to comply would be tantamount to treason, and they themselves wished no part of the affair. As they finished speaking, John Dudley, arriving late and hearing their words, shouted at the assembly in "a great rage and fury, trembling for anger and, amongst all his outrageous talk called Sir Edward Montague traitor and further said he would fight any man in his shirt in that quarrel." Later, Montague was to say he was "in dread then that the duke would have stricken one of them."

In the following days a test of wills emerged. Again Montague visited the king at Greenwich and Edward angrily demanded why his orders had not been followed. "Where are my letters patent?" the boy asked, cheeks flushed with the effort. Montague fell to his knees beside the bed, stating in a quavering voice that to comply would be "to put the Lords and us in danger of high treason—and yet be nothing worth." Without Parliament's approval, he said, the document was useless. Scornfully Edward replied, throwing the justice's words back in his face, that "to refuse were treason." At the back of the room, an associate of Dudley's whispered smoothly that to do any but the king's bidding might also be treasonous. Irrelevantly and in obvious despair, Montague said he was "an old man and without comfort," that he'd served Henry VIII and Edward for nineteen years and was "loath to disobey" the king's commands. Later, in the dining hall, Montague and his fellow justices were openly snubbed by other courtiers who "looked upon them with earnest countenances, as though they had not known them."

Montague, "in as great fear as ever he was in all his life before, seeing the king so earnest and sharp and the duke so angry," now looked for a way out. After conferring with his colleagues, he at last convinced himself it would indeed be treasonous to disobey his king while he was alive; later, he privately told others, "he would meddle no more." He told Edward he would sign his "Device," "if Your Majesty would grant me a license under the Great Seal and a pardon for having signed." Edward, aware of Montague's timidity and recognizing a means by which his own intent might be accomplished, immediately agreed. Whereupon John Dudley jumped to his feet, shouting, "I will have no man in better case than myself!" When someone then suggested that everyone who signed the "Device" should share in the general pardon, it was wearily agreed and the terrified judges—Montague weeping openly—left the palace.

Within days, the Privy Council, threatened with the loss of their church spoils should Mary succeed and terrified into compliance by the extent of Dudley's success—and his fury if they should disobey—had acquiesced. Still not trusting his colleagues, however, Dudley forced them to sign a promise to support Lady Jane Grey as queen and "never to vary or swerve during our lives from the said limitations of the succession, but to . . . defend and maintain."

By June 15, all had been accomplished. One hundred and one signatures of councillors, peers, judges, Crown and Church officials attested to the validity of the instrument by which Princess Mary and Princess Elizabeth were deprived of their inheritance. With his goal almost in sight and the strain of the past months clearly evident in his erratic behavior, John Dudley had insisted all must share in the responsibility for altering the succession. On the following Sunday, prayers for Princess Mary and Princess

Elizabeth were omitted from all London churches. The duke's manipulation and the strong will of a dying king had been triumphant.

In order to sooth bruised feelings and hurt egos, Dudley ordered a court celebration. To lull suspicions and convince everyone of his good intent, he also invited the foreign ambassadors De Noailles and Scheyve, confiding in them that the king, deathly ill on the preceding Tuesday and Wednesday, was now much improved. The fever had left Edward and a merry celebration was in order, he told De Noailles. But the French ambassador—openly marveling at the trumpets at dinner and the festive decorations, with the nobles "more content and easy in their minds" than they'd previously been in the months of the king's illness, when the court had become a silent and empty place—was not fooled. He wrote his home court that the festivities arose more "from the satisfaction taken by the lords on finding themselves agreed in one counsel," as the Duke of Northumberland "had since united them and bent them to his own opinion." De Noailles's spies had informed him that the nightly watch had been increased at the City gates and those illustrious prisoners in the Tower—the old Duke of Norfolk and Anne Stanhope Seymour, the Protector's widow—had recently been denied their daily exercise on the leads and in the Tower gardens. Certain courtiers and nobles who'd openly disagreed with Dudley, the ambassador said, were under surveillance. De Noailles had also learned of Edward's "Device" and on June 26 wrote the French court, "It is now nine days since the king made his testament by which he ordains and wills that his crown shall devolve on Jane of Suffolk; and the Parliament at Westminster has been postponed until the end of September."

Scheyve, the Spanish ambassador, had also written the Spanish court that should the duke kidnap Princess Mary, his "party may desert him. He is hated and loathed for a tyrant while the princess is loved throughout the land." He attributed Edward's illness and coming death to punishment by God for a nation that had strayed so far from the true religion.

Now that Dudley had successfully and legally forced the king to alter the succession, it was imperative that Edward live until the September Parliament had ratified his will. The duke accepted that Jane Grey's accession might not be popular with the people, that a rebellion might arise when they learned Princess Mary had been set aside. While acknowledging his own personal unpopularity, the duke knew that Mary was greatly loved. The sufferings of her mother, Katherine of Aragon, and the persecution Mary herself had undergone in her youth had endeared her to the common people and earned her their sympathy. Mary had accepted the reformed religion of her father, as had a large part of the English nation. It had been the further tampering with ritual and creed—and the elimination of the Mass—encouraged by the Protector and Dudley and insisted upon by Edward, that Mary and many Catholics found difficult to accept. What would happen when the nation found that Jane Grey and not Mary Tudor would be queen? It was imperative, Dudley felt, that Edward be alive when Parliament dealt with the succession; a living king would promote his own intent more strongly and the onus of much that had happened would not fall upon the duke.

In the following days, as Edward continued to fail, "a gentlewoman, unworthy to be named, but accounted to be a school-mistress . . . offered her service assuredly to cure him, in case he were committed wholly to her hand." When the king's physicians objected, saying she would "give no reason either of the nature of the disease or of the part afflicted . . . nor would she declare the means whereby she intended to work the cure," Dudley took the matter to the council. They, aware of his intent as well as the fact that it was now also *their* responsibility, deliberated and "it was resolved that the physicians should be discharged and the case committed to her alone."

Edward's physicians, Dr. Owen and Dr. Wendy, had been at Henry VIII's bedside when he died; Dr. Owen had brought Edward into the world. Both were shocked by the order to hand their mortally ill patient over to an unknown. Yet they could do nothing but obey and so, incredibly, the life of the sixteen-year-old king of England was put into the hands of a woman of no demonstrable professional skills, of unknown reputation and, not unlikely, a quack.

Within a few days, however, it was announced that her "treatment was injudicious, bringing the king to the verge of his life, through the restringents that she employed, which in a brief space of time puffed up his limbs, and burdened his person much more than before." Edward's blond hair began to fall out and his pale skin darkened. Gangrene now appeared on his fingertips and toes. No longer did he dwell upon his "Device," his hospitals and institutions; no longer did he hear the throng below in the courtyard or the ships of his Merchant Adventurers being "towed down the Thames by boats manned with stout mariners, apparelled in watchet or sky-blue cloth." Opposite the palace, the ships' guns were discharged, "so that the Kentish hills resounded, the valleys and the waters gave an echo." Alone with the woman who, innocently or deliberately, was slowly poisoning the boy with arsenic, Edward, mercifully, was now delirious much of the time. When "the apparent defect both of her judgment and experience, joined to the weightiness of the adventure, caused many to marvel, and some deeply to suspect that she was but an instrument of mischief," Dudley and the council became alarmed. On July 1 the duke dismissed the woman. The physicians returned and, appalled by Edward's further deterioration, dedicated themselves to relieving his suffering for the little time that remained.

While Edward was enduring the "gentlewoman's" deadly ministrations, Jane Grey was enduring her own particular hell at Durham House. The marriage bed had proven a shock; nothing had prepared her for the assault on her senses, much less her body. Her nature, gentle to the point of timidity, was outraged at the behavior expected of her, even when Guildford told her his conduct was no different from that of any other man with his wife or, indeed, any other man and woman. He was her husband, he told Jane, and he had his rights, which he chose to exercise at will, saying she was lucky he did not beat her. For a girl who'd been beaten all her life and knew of wife-beating—in the upper as well as the lower classes—her husband's words did not sound odd. She supposed she was lucky that she was not beaten, and as long as she lay and let Guildford do his will, she supposed she would not be.

But marriage had taken its toll. Often, after Guildford had satisfied himself and slept beside her, Jane lay awake for a long time, wondering what her future life would be. She missed Mrs. Ellen and her sisters, the classroom and those letters from her foreign friends which had meant so much. She even missed her mother and father and the familiar rooms of her home where she could find refuge, if she was fortunate, from their recrimination. At Durham House itself there was little to do and no refuge at all. She must spend her days with Guildford's mother in an unfamiliar routine in strange rooms with people and servants she hardly knew and with whom she had nothing in common. There was little opportunity to read, and for one so used to solitude, the presence of so many people—while dining or even exercising on the well-trimmed paths leading down to the river—was disheartening. Jane had never been proficient in the small talk at which those of the court were so clever. The latest flirtation or scandal, the newest fashion in dress or coiffure did not interest her. She could relate to little at Durham House, including the husband who was absent during the day with his father or out hunting. Worst of all, during the evening meal, as she pushed the food about her plate and watched Guildford with those who had more pleasure in the dance than he felt his wife possessed, there was nothing to anticipate except what would happen when she joined him in the large canopied bed upstairs.

Within a week, the emotional strain under which Jane lived was evident. After being assured by John Dudley that now that the king's "Device" was accomplished, it made little difference where Jane lived as long as she remained in *their* possession, his wife agreed that her daughter-in-law might spend a few days away from Durham House. There were several other places she might go, and Mrs. Ellen might be brought from Sheen to attend her former charge. There was a Dudley residence right there on the river at Chelsea, the duchess said; it was not far from Durham House by barge and Jane could be easily reached if she was needed. So she was free to go, although a steward and other Dudley servants would accompany her, of course.

Jane could scarcely believe her good luck. *Chelsea.* The little manor house on the river where she'd lived that short span in her life she would always remember as her happiest. That summer with her cousins Mary and Elizabeth and with Queen Katherine Parr; those golden days when they'd picked reeds at the river's edge and gone with Katherine and her friend Kate Brandon on the river to picnic in their barge and throw bits of food to the kingfishers and herons.

Where Thomas Seymour, arriving by horse or barge, would sweep the blushing queen up in his arms and carry her off. Where, with Mary Tudor and Kate Brandon, she remembered watching the queen sitting on the seawall, all three eating cherries Mary had brought from Newhall, vying to see who could throw the pits the farthest out into the river. Where there had been little protocol, much affection and warmth, with songs on the terrace in the evening and those loud early-morning romps in Elizabeth's bedroom which had made her governess, Cat Ashley, so angry with Thomas Seymour and had resulted in Elizabeth being sent away. Jane now had some understanding of what might have happened or perhaps *had* happened at that time, but could not bring herself to think of it too much. It was enough that she was going to Chelsea, with no husband, no mother-in-law—only her memories.

While Jane was at Chelsea with her mother and Mrs. Ellen, Dr. Owen and Dr. Wendy remained in the bedchamber of Edward Tudor at Greenwich palace, aware the boy's long agony was coming to an end. It was July 6, an overcast day, and the room was gloomy and gray. Near the physicians, Sir Henry Sidney and Sir Thomas Wroth also kept the vigil, watching the emaciated figure on the bed. In a corner, Christopher Salmon, a groom, once a barber to Henry VIII, waited; he'd been in Edward's service all the young boy's life. The room was fetid with the smell of rotting flesh and sweat, but none would leave. All loved the king, each in his own way, and none would desert him now.

Edward lay quietly, his eyes closed. At last, "as if speaking to himself and thinking none to have heard him," he whispered the prayer he'd committed to memory: "Lord God, deliver me out of this miserable and wretched life, and take me among thy chosen: howbeit, not my will, but thy will be done! Lord, I commit my spirit to thee. Oh, Lord! thou knowest how happy it were for me to be with thee. . . ." As Edward continued to pray, he became aware of his companions, hovering now nearer the bed. Turning his face, he said, "Are ye so nigh? I thought ye had been further off."

Dr. Owen brushed the sweat from Edward's forehead. "We heard you speak to yourself, but what you said, we know not."

"I was praying to God," the boy replied quietly. Then, wearily, "I am faint, Lord, have mercy upon me and take my spirit. . . ." As he closed his eyes again, Christopher Salmon sobbed and Dr. Owen gathered the wasted form in his arms. Then everyone dropped to his knees by the bed, tears intermingling, to pray for the soul of the last Tudor king, who had gone to the God he'd labored so hard to serve.

As the fateful day drew to a close, Londoners began to clear the debris that a giant hailstorm had blown throughout their streets and parts of southern England. Much of the City's lower sections was flooded with "cataracts of water, turning the streets into rivers"; everywhere, uprooted trees, roofless houses and cottages, dead animals and injured citizens attested to the storm's ferocity. Gardens and orchards had spilled their damaged harvests, and in a daylight as black as night, people sought to salvage what they might, comparing their experiences in the most devastating storm within living memory.

At Hatfield, Princess Elizabeth watched the black fury—sheets of rain hammering on window and leads, the gardens flattened by the hail—and wondered if Edward was alive, whether England had a king or not. Only a few weeks before, she'd attempted to visit her brother and—making certain her visit, for which she'd not sought permission, was well-publicized—had proceeded slowly on the journey. Within two days a messenger had intercepted her entourage, ordering her *at the king's command* to return to Hatfield. Silently, Elizabeth had obeyed, for she'd learned all she wanted to know. Edward was either dead or dying. Never before had he refused to see her.

Upon arrival at Hatfield, she'd written her brother, ". . . of my grief I am not eased," asking his forgiveness for attempting a journey without permission. Then, just a few days ago, when another message summoned her to Greenwich, Elizabeth guessed her brother was gone. Now Mary was queen and it would be proper—and more tactful—to wait until her sister asked for her presence. Still apprehensive at something she could not name, Elizabeth told her doctor that suddenly she felt unwell. She asked him to write the king and send her apologies, promising she would visit as soon as she'd recovered. And then, satisfied she'd done all she could to avoid participating in whatever was happening in London, she promptly took to her bed.

* * *

At the village of Hoddesdon in Hertfordshire, an unsuspicious Mary Tudor, answering an appeal "that her brother, who was very ill, prayed her to come to him," was stopped by the force of the storm. But broken branches, lying in the lashing rain—a hazard to horse and rider alike—did not deter a messenger, a goldsmith familiar to the princess, from handing her a message. *Turn back. Do not come to London*, the letter warned.

Mary felt her throat constrict. So Edward was dead. Her father's "precious jewel" was gone. The handwriting was familiar, that of Sir Nicholas Throckmorton, a member of Edward's Privy Chamber and a devotee of the "new religion." Was the message, allegedly from Edward, a ruse to get the Catholic heir into custody before he died? Aware that proclaiming herself sovereign while a monarch lived might be considered treasonous, yet feeling that not to go to Edward, especially if he was near death, was heartless, Mary was torn and frightened. She asked the goldsmith if he knew "for a certainty, the king was dead," and the man nodded.

Something had gone wrong. Over the last several weeks, Mary had wondered why John Dudley refused the permission she sought to see her brother. And she'd wondered why Elizabeth had been ordered back to Hatfield. Why had the duke not wanted either princess to see their brother while he was still alive? A few trusted friends in London had sent messages telling her Edward was a very sick boy and she must hold herself in readiness. Why now, of all times, shouldn't she, the heir to the crown, go to London? What could happen to her now that she was queen?

"If Sir Robert were at Greenwich, I would hazard all things and stake my life on the leap," she told the messenger. Sir Robert Throckmorton, the older brother of Sir Nicholas, was one of Mary's staunchest friends and had clung to the Catholicism his brother had put aside.

Shaken, Mary wondered what to do. But only for a moment. Wiping the tears from her eyes, the princess quickly ordered her steward and companions to make for old Kenninghall Castle in Norfolk. But the storm was such that they must find shelter first, she said, and her steward rode off in the direction of Cambridgeshire to look for accommodation. Then Mary gathered the small group about her and, voice quivering with emotion, told them Edward Tudor was gone. When all had bent their heads in prayer while the princess prayed for her dead brother's soul, one of her companions, the daughter of Margaret More Roper, noted it was on the same day, seventeen years ago, that her grandfather Sir Thomas More had walked up Tower Hill to his execution.

The prayer finished, Mary urged they all follow the steward, for they must find shelter and protection until she learned what was happening in London. It would be wise, she knew, to stay near the coast for flight abroad to Holland or Spain, if that hazard ever became necessary. But if God was on the side of justice and honor, Mary grimly told herself, when she next rode for London it would be as the rightful Queen of England.

The
Drama

20

Edward had died on Thursday, July 6. From that moment on, until Mary Tudor was in custody it was imperative his death be kept secret. Physicians and members of the Privy Chamber were sworn to secrecy and the Privy Council labored far into the night deciding how details of the king's death and Lady Jane Grey's accession would be made public. There was little doubt but what Robert Dudley and his three hundred soldiers would bring Mary, unaware and unsuspecting, to the Tower, and to a man, they considered they'd dealt with any emergency that might arise. The French and Spanish ambassadors must be informed, but not until both Mary Tudor and Jane Grey were in the Tower—one as a prisoner, the other to wear her crown. In the meantime, the public must be kept ignorant of Edward's death while council business continued to be carried on in his name.

But when John Dudley canceled an appointment and dinner with Antoine de Noailles, the French ambassador guessed the truth. And when the Marquis of Northampton and the Earl of Shrewsbury visited the Tower, leaving Admiral Clinton behind as Constable, while the Tower guns were hauled to the top of the White Tower by sweating soldiers, and carts "full of ordnance, great guns and small, bows, bills, spears, Morris-pikes, arrows, gunpowder, victuals, money, tents and a great number of men" appeared, many realized what had happened. Even the recently arrived Simon Renard, the new Spanish ambassador, guessed Edward had died. Quickly, in the emperor's name, he wrote Mary, advising her not "to venture upon a course from which I anticipate inevitable ruin." The notion of a female sovereign—which even memory of the great Spanish Queen Isabella did little to dispel—was abhorrent to Renard. But the Spaniard's message never reached Mary. By the time it was delivered to Hunsdon, she'd already fled.

By July 9, the cautious council divulged the news to a selected few. Sir John Gates, Captain of the King's Guard, told his archers that the king was dead and Lady Jane Grey would be queen, and swore them to her cause. Soon afterward the Lord Mayor, accompanied by London aldermen and representatives of the London Guilds, were summoned to Greenwich, "unto whom . . . was secretly declared the death of King Edward, and also how he did ordain for the succession of the Crown . . . to the which they were sworn and charged to keep it secret." Official word was then sent to Princess Elizabeth, ill at Hatfield, and to Princess Mary at Hunsdon—a formality, since it was now known she'd eluded Robert Dudley. Within days, Bishop Ridley would be ordered to preach at Paul's Cross against both Mary and Elizabeth, declaring them illegitimate and denouncing Mary particularly for clinging to her popish ways. So bitter were the bishop's words that many of the congregation would leave in disgust. If either Ridley or his parishioners wondered what had happened to the king's body—why Edward was not lying in state for a grieving public to honor—nothing was said. Rumors were flying about London that the king's body had been so corrupt that proper embalming was impossible, that it had been taken secretly from the palace bedroom and thrust into a hastily dug grave in a paddock near the palace gates. If and when there was a funeral, it would not be difficult to find a body to put into a sealed coffin.

Having thus taken care of the Tower, the army, navy and officials of the City of London as well as the Church, John Dudley agreed with the council that, since "London was the hand which must reach Jane the crown," it was time to inform the queen herself of her cousin's death. Though she must be carefully coached in her behavior before being brought to London, neither Dudley nor his colleagues expected any surprises. Jane Grey was a docile creature. She was the duke's daughter-in-law and her father was one of the most prominent nobles in the land. The girl would do as she was told, but first she must be informed of her accession.

As Mary fled into her refuge at Norfolk, Jane remained at Chelsea. Walking through the little manor house's pleasant rooms and garden, with their treasured memories, she felt a great burden fall from her shoulders. Her mother and Mrs. Ellen soon joined her, but she was still left much alone. Frances Grey, accompanied by several of her ladies, coursed almost daily in the woods up past "the King's Road," riding through the back part of Sir Thomas More's old home to reach the paths where her greyhounds might be freed. Henry Grey was either at court with John Dudley or visiting the king at Greenwich, and Jane supposed that was where Guildford was also.

Now, for the first time in almost a month, Jane could be by herself and sit quietly on the old seawall and wonder at how greatly her life had changed. She still found it difficult to believe Edward had chosen her as his successor and fervently she prayed he would live. She could not imagine why Mary would not want to be queen. Had she obstinately refused to give up the "new religion," and if so, then what about Elizabeth? Jane did not think either of the princesses would voluntarily relinquish the crown. How had Edward made that possible?

The mystery worried her so that in the following days she found that Edward's intent—and the threat it was to her future—had superimposed themselves on the anxiety she'd felt while living with Guildford Dudley, and she wondered how she could face living with him for the rest of her life. If she were to be queen, would Guildford be king? It would have a strong appeal to her husband, Jane knew. But immediately, the memory of old Henry and young Edward and the thought of Guildford wearing their crown caused a revulsion so deep, she felt almost physically ill. She realized John Dudley would dearly love to see his son king and knew—should God ordain she must be a queen—she'd *never* let a Dudley wear Edward's crown.

Her distress continued each night when she tried to sleep and thoughts revolved in her head, seeking a way out of her marriage as well as a queenship. *I don't want to be a wife and I won't want to be a queen*—the thought brought tears and again, as at Durham House, Jane found sleep elusive. When she did wake from whatever bad dream possessed her, she dreaded what the day might bring. The tears came too easily and she trembled whenever a barge landed on the sandy beach below the manor house. Each horseman that galloped into the courtyard might bring the news she dreaded—either Edward had died or Guildford was coming to join her. Jane became snappish with Mrs. Ellen and the servants, then was disappointed in herself that she wasn't more resolute or accepting of the position so many others might regard with satisfaction, if not awe.

Within a few days as the strain persisted, Jane became so ill that Mrs. Ellen put her to bed and slept nearby on a pallet during the night. Jane vomited constantly, lying back on her bed exhausted, wishing for sleep to escape the nausea. She ate little, for her stomach, it seemed, was one large knot and hurt when Mrs. Ellen probed gently. Her whole body ached, and more than once the suspicion came that she might be poisoned. Had someone given her something at Durham House and then sent her to Chelsea to avoid being blamed? There *were* poisons, she knew, that did not act for several hours or several days. But why would anyone wish to poison her? The suspicion, however, would not go away but mixed with all the other black thoughts that filled her mind. Jane continued to lie weak and ill, wondering what was happening at Greenwich and almost not wanting to know. Even her books or letters failed to interest her now. What she wanted more than anything else was relief—blessed relief from any expectations of a husband or a crown—and a return to the quiet refuge of her classroom and tutor. It was such a simple desire, she thought as she turned restlessly in bed, seeking sleep and the absence of the worry that filled her mind. But one so difficult to attain.

At last, as news of the king's death spread outward from London, Jane began to improve, becoming stronger each day. Mrs. Ellen said it was only her nerves which were frayed and no one was trying to poison her. Think of how much had happened in one month!

Her mother, who looked in on her each morning before hunting, agreed and told her daughter there was nothing wrong with her; she must make every effort to get well. Jane still prayed daily for Edward's recovery, for then she might be permitted to return home and the nightmare of the past month would gradually become only a bad memory. The fact that sometime in the future she would be forced to return to her husband, that they would live together in their own home and perhaps even have a family, was something Jane felt she could not afford to think about, and forcibly she put it from her mind.

She had recovered enough to walk with Mrs. Ellen in the garden when, three days after Edward's death, a barge brought Lady Mary Sidney, wife of Sir Henry, who had been at the dying Edward's bedside, to Chelsea. Mary was John Dudley's daughter and one of the few of that family whom Jane did not dislike. When Lady Sidney, "with more gravity than usual," told Jane there was news of the king, that her mother and father were now at Syon and wanted her to join them there, Jane's feelings were a mixture of relief and dread. Even with her illness, Chelsea had given her some semblance of emotional peace, but she knew she could not remain there forever. Syon, a former home of the Protector, was just across the river from Sheen and perhaps would be the first step toward a return to her own house.

It took almost two hours, as the rowers skimmed along the river and the two ladies chatted amiably, for the barge to reach Syon House, where the council and John Dudley were nervously discussing his son Robert's failure to arrest Mary Tudor. They learned that the princess had spent the first night of the great storm at Sawston Hall, the home of John Huddlestone, a loyal Catholic known for his partisanship toward Mary, and whose brother Andrew was a gentleman of her household. After hearing Mass the following morning, several of the princess' retinue had left singly in disguise, after which Mary, wearing the clothing of a market woman, had ridden docilely behind Andrew Huddlestone, humbly dressed as one of his own retainers. Robert Dudley had missed her by moments, and when he arrived the princess and her companions were already lost in the Gog Magog hills. Instead of riding on to overtake her, Dudley had taken out his frustration on

Mary's host, and after plundering Master Huddlestone's home of valuables and "Popish books used in celebrating the Mass," he burnt it to the ground.

While it was equally frustrating to the council not to have captured the princess, each felt it was only a matter of time before that was accomplished. What mattered now—since the news that Edward was dead had begun to reach the counties—was that Jane's accession be secured. Dudley knew he had little time to deal with Renard, Scheyve or De Noailles and those two French envoys waiting at Boulogne to see which way England would go—to Spain or France—now that its king was dead. Religion would play a large part in the casting of the dice; with Mary there would be an orderly return to Catholicism, and the English persistence with its new toy—the "new religion"—would become a thing of the past. With Jane Grey, or even Elizabeth, Rome would continue to be an archenemy, with the English Church professing its own independence and ritual. Everyone—Dudley, council, ambassadors and nobles—realized that the government's edicts of the last ten years had not strongly influenced the majority of the English people, especially in those counties far removed from London and the south which remained staunchly Catholic. Mary's popularity alone might carry her to the throne.

Just how much was at stake, and the emotion it engendered, was shown when a letter from Princess Mary arrived as the Privy Council sat at Syon House awaiting Jane Grey's arrival. The letter was impressive, yet cautious. The princess' hatred of hypocrisy—a gift from her mother, Katherine of Aragon—was well known and she did not mince words, stating that she was aware of the king's death, "albeit this so weighty a matter seemeth strange, that our said brother, dying upon Thursday at night last past, we hitherto had not known from you." Mary said she was not "ignorant of your consultations to undo provisions made for our preferment, nor of the great bands and provisions forcible, wherewith ye be assembled and prepared, by whom, and to what end, God and you know, and nature can but fear some evil."

One of Mary's favorite phrases, so indicative of her character, was to preface a remark with "to be plain with you" and she was now "plain" with the Privy Council. Once they'd proclaimed her queen, she said, she would overlook their lack of support and would "fully pardon the same and that freely, to eschew bloodshed and vengeance against all those that can or will intend the same." At the conclusion of her letter, she was not only plain but blunt. If they did not accept her offer of amnesty, and "take and accept this grace in good part . . ." then she would be "enforced to use the service of other of our true subjects and friends, which in this our just and right cause, God, in whom our whole affiance is, shall send us." Mary then required, upon the allegiance which the council owed to God "for our honor and the surety of our person," that they proclaim her title in "our City of London and other places as to your wisdom shall seem good."

There was an uneasy silence in the council room as John Dudley finished reading Mary's letter. The councillors shuffled their papers or coughed, but the two duchesses, Frances Grey and Jane Dudley, present to hear Mary's words, began to sob. In a few moments, nearly hysterical, both left the room. The duke then grasped the opportunity, before any of his colleagues wavered in view of Mary's generous offer of a pardon, to discuss a reply. In short order, during which time both duchesses—calm now though with tear-stained faces—returned to the room, the councillors drafted an answer to Mary's letter. As the sound of Jane's barge could be heard on the sandy beach below, a mounted courier, urged to swiftness, carried the council's decision to the princess, now safe at Kenninghall Castle.

The council had spent most of the day at Syon House, and when Jane arrived with Lady Sidney, dusk had already enveloped the venerable old convent on the river. As they walked from the waterstairs, no one came to greet them. Entering the Great Hall, they found no one there and, peering outside what had been the nuns' cloisters, found they too were empty. Jane thought it unusual that none of the family, their servants—or even their pets—were about.

And then, suddenly, the Great Hall began to fill. William Parr, the Marquis of Northampton, entered and held the door for men Jane had often seen with her father—Arundel, Huntingdon and Pembroke. Behind them, Frances and Henry Grey walked with John and Jane Dudley, followed by the familiar faces of many of the Privy Council. It was not an unusual gathering—except for the presence of the ladies—and Jane was glad to see her mother.

Whatever Edward had "ordained," Frances Grey would be certain to explain it to her clearly. At the moment, what mattered most was that Guildford Dudley was not present.

Then, quickly, Will Herbert, the Earl of Pembroke, took her hand and kissed it and, as Jane was later to write, "began to make me complimentary speeches, bending the knee before me, their example being followed by several noble ladies, all of which ceremony made me blush." Jane was beginning to suspect what had happened, but what caught her attention most and held her almost speechless was the sight of her mother, Frances Grey, now *kneeling in front of her*. Never before had she seen her mother so submissive; it was frightening to see the one upon whom for years she'd depended—and been more than likely rewarded with blows, "nips and bobs"—suddenly so reverential. "My distress," Jane wrote, "was still further increased when . . . my mother-in-law entered and paid me the same homage. Then came the Duke of Northumberland himself who, as President of the Council, declared to me the death of the king and informed me that everyone had good reason to rejoice in the virtuous life he had led, and the good death he had." Dudley stressed that Edward had taken "great care of his kingdom, praying to our Lord God to defend it from all doctrine contrary to His, and to free it from the evil of his sisters." Dudley then explained Edward's aversion to Mary's Catholicism and her illegitimacy, as well as that of Elizabeth, which accounted for his consequent disinheritance of both. The duke then told Jane that she "was the heir nominated by His Majesty and that my sisters, the Lady Katherine and the Lady Mary Grey were to succeed me . . . at which words all the lords of the council knelt before me exclaiming 'that they rendered me that homage because it pertained to me, being of the right line' and they added that, in all particulars they would observe what they promised which was, by their souls they swore, to shed their blood and lose their lives to maintain the same."

Jane's face flushed as, again, everyone who had risen to listen to the duke's words now fell to the floor, their hands clasped in front, obviously waiting for her to speak.

Now that her worst fears had materialized—that Edward was indeed dead and had named her his heir—Jane could only observe the kneeling figures in stunned amazement. During those days at

Chelsea, she'd almost convinced herself that the king would live and never would she have to face the responsibility that—for all of Dudley's fine words—she felt was not rightfully hers. She hated Mary's Catholicism as much as anyone present, but how about Elizabeth? A stroke of the pen had previously rendered the girl illegitimate; certainly the council could find a way about that? A genuine sorrow for Edward, who'd been no older than she—and gone so soon—swept over her. His responsibilities were at an end, but they'd been left to *her*. How could she, sixteen years old in a few months, deal with such a burden?

It had been a long day. Jane had had no food since before noon, and the river journey, undertaken so hastily, had been warm, especially for one who did not tolerate sunlight easily. Now, as everyone still knelt, hands clasped before them, Jane felt her former nausea returning, and those nerves which had been so tormented at Durham House rebelled again. "On hearing all this, I remained stunned and out of myself," she was later to write, "and I call on those present to bear witness, who saw me fall to the ground weeping piteously and dolefully lamenting the death of the king. I swooned indeed, and lay as dead."

In moments, as the ladies comforted her, she recovered somewhat. But the brief respite from reality had not ended her terror and she cried that she had never sought and did not want the crown, "and it pleaseth me not."

"Your Grace doth wrong to yourself, and to your house!" John Dudley cried angrily, his face flushed, for he'd expected a quiet and quick submission from Jane. Recounting the terms of Edward's will, he was joined by Frances and Henry Grey, who loudly ordered their daughter to listen to what was being said and to obey. It was her duty to her dead king and to his realm, they said, and her reluctance and objection would in no way be tolerated.

Jane heard their words, especially *obey*, which instinctively she'd done all her life in order to avoid scenes or beatings. Lying there prone, she knew it was pointless to protest, and contemplating the councillors in their long robes, the duke and her father, swords at their sides, she lay crying on the floor, seeing their figures loom unnaturally tall. How could she fight them all? Jane would gratefully have accepted the beating of her life to have escaped the future she saw confronting her, but she realized there was no way out. These same men would take care of everything for her, just as they'd taken care of everything for Edward. She tried to find some assurance in the thought. If she *had* to be queen, at least she would not be alone, not any more alone than she'd always been. John Dudley, Henry Grey and the council would govern the realm to which Edward had devoted his life. And didn't she owe something to the memory of her dead cousin? The least she could do was to accept with gracious reverence the gift the king had given her and not behave like a mewling child—for which, for any other reason, she'd have received harsh punishment at home. If she was to be queen, she should act like one. She must make the best of the bargain that God, whose knowledge she must not question, had bestowed upon her.

With the thought of her Savior firmly in mind, Jane then raised herself to her knees and asked that all pray, that "if to succeed to the throne was indeed my duty and my right, that He would aid me to govern the realm to His glory." She saw satisfaction on her parents' faces and knew she'd done the correct thing; there would be no punishment that night.

The last thing she heard, as Lady Sidney came to show her to her room, was that the next day she would go to the Tower of London, where, as tradition demanded, she must remain until her coronation.

On Monday, July 10, four days after Edward's death, people crowded the banks of the Thames to watch the great cluster of barges as they sailed from Syon House to Westminster. The ornately carved, gilded and painted boats of the nobility shone in the sunlight and the music of the minstrels aboard wafted to the observers on the riverbanks as they attempted to distinguish Northumberland from Northampton or Arundel from Winchester. One particular barge—the royal barge—was easily recognizable. At one time or another, everyone had seen it carrying the old king and his queens; more recently they'd watched as it had taken their dying boy-king to Greenwich. Now it carried one young girl: Jane Grey, the Duke of Suffolk's daughter, and her family. Rumor had it she was to be their queen, although how that could be possible, none on the banks could say. And so until they knew more, they watched the exciting colorful panoply but, for the most part, remained silent.

It was a gloriously clear day and the debris that had cluttered the river shore after the great storm had been cleared from sight. For those inside the barges, at least, there was rejoicing and the boy still awaiting burial at Greenwich was forgotten. Now, as the great barges sliced through the clear water, as wherries and other small craft respectfully rowed to one side to let them pass and people fishing on the riverbank brought in their lines, the merriment aboard could be heard by all. The people gazed at the rich costumes, the flashing jewels on cap and sleeves, the gleaming swords, the vivid colors of flags, banners, even the bright clothing of the liveried retainers and rowers who manned the barges. Others came from little cottages or huts along the shore. In contrast to the cheering occupants of the barges, they too were silent.

At Westminster, Jane disembarked. Entering the Robing Chamber of the old palace of her Plantagenet and Tudor ancestors, she stood obediently as a heavily lustrous robe of crimson velvet appeared out of nowhere and was put about her thin shoulders. Clutching the unfamiliar weight of the splendid garment, Jane dutifully followed the palace officials and councillors as they led her to Westminster Hall. There, under the ceiling's flying angels, so old they defied belief, she sat with her family and the Dudleys at the long table on the dais, while other nobles and courtiers took their places at the banqueting tables along the great stone floor. Mindful it would be a long day, Jane forced herself to eat, to talk pleasantly with whosoever directed a remark her way, which thankfully was not often. She found it disturbing to be constantly bowed to, knelt before and to watch the servants avert their eyes as they served her.

Mercifully, the meal soon ended; ahead lay the river journey to the Tower. It was nearing three o'clock as the royal party, attended by all the court, emerged at old Westminster Hall's water-stairs, to wait patiently as barges lined up to take their noble occupants aboard once more. Jane entered the royal barge, seating herself on the single middle seat reserved for the monarch, and watched uncomfortably as her mother arranged the folds of the crimson robe about her. Suddenly, the Tower cannons—alerted by a signal from the opposite shore that the new queen was on her way—discharged their shot over the Tower gardens, the smoke coiling up along the river. There were shouts of approval from the barges as the minstrels began to play and the occupants waved to the great crowds lining the riverbank. Jane noticed that few waved back and there was no cheering, only the relentless noise of the guns, as salvo after salvo reverberated along the shore.

There were scattered groups at the Tower's broad stairs, which led directly into the great fortress's precincts. But, as on the river, there was no rejoicing, no cheers from the spectators, and Jane was acutely aware of their bold stares. She could not know how much of it was a simple curiosity to see the girl who'd dared call herself queen—and she the daughter-in-law of the most despised man in England! As she was helped from the barge, Jane saw Guildford Dudley, elegant in white and gold satin, his cap neatly placed beneath his arm, waiting. He made her a low bow as she approached. Then someone, a lady she'd never seen before, showed her a pair of *chopines*, clogs for her feet which would add three inches to her height, indicating Jane should let her strap them to her shoes.

In a moment the procession moved forward as Jane, clogs securely in place, clutched the robe which, away from the river breezes, felt heavily warm. The unfamiliar weight on her feet made walking awkward and she had to concentrate on each step so as not to stumble. But she realized what those extra added inches could do. Now she was almost at eye level with others, and that, of course, was the intention: Everyone must see her easily, for now she was queen.

Sir John Brydges, Lieutenant of the Tower, was waiting for her just inside the Water Tower gate. Old Will Paulet, the Marquis of Winchester, knelt reverentially and held out the keys to the Tower, symbol of royal authority over the ancient fortress. Quickly, John Dudley stepped forward and, taking the keys from the old man, presented them himself. The gesture was not lost on the observers or on Jane herself. She was now queen, but it was by milord Northumberland's leave that it was so. However, recognizing the symbolism of the gesture, she handed the keys back to Winchester and proceeded on toward the royal apartments in the White Tower. Everywhere people knelt and she hoped she was properly gracious. Glancing behind, she saw that Frances Grey had picked up the hem of her robe, which several onlookers viewed with either scorn or amusement. Embarrassed for her mother, who seemed unconcerned as she played trainbearer, Jane accepted that it was not to make her progress easier. As Dudley had felt compelled to hand her the Tower keys, her mother was determined to share in whatever glory the moment might hold.

One Genoese spectator, standing close by, later wrote:

> Today, I saw *Donna Jana Graia* walking in a grand procession to the Tower. She is now called queen, but is not popular for the hearts of the people are with Mary, the Spanish queen's daughter. . . . I stood so long near Her Grace that I noticed her color was good but freckled. When she smiled, she showed her teeth, which are white and sharp. In all a *graziosa persona* and *animata*. She wore a dress of green velvet stamped with gold, with large sleeves. Her headdress was a white coif with many jewels. She walked under a canopy . . . and her husband, *Guilfo* walking by her, dressed all in white and gold, a very tall strong boy with light hair, who paid her much attention.

After mentioning Jane's *chopines*, which she wore because she was "very small and short," the Italian noted, "This lady is very *heretica* and has never heard Mass and some people did not come into the procession for that reason."

By now, all the barges had disgorged their occupants, and the full Privy Council followed behind. The guns had ceased and the riverbank spectators had begun to disperse. The show was over, the pageant finished. They had seen a great throng of gilded barges with their rich and noble occupants. They had seen the powerful Northumberland and all his council, who somehow had maneuvered the crown to one of their own choosing. They had seen the clergy—obedient, respectful and apparently approving of their action. They had seen a little girl, with red-gold hair and freckled skin, so thin she seemed to disappear into a heavy crimson robe, so tiny she needed clogs to be observed, so subdued they argued she could *not* be the new queen. And if she was, she was not pleased at the honor.

Within the hour of Jane's arrival, "a proclamation was made with a trumpeter and two of the Heralds Kings at Arms and Mr. Garret, the Sheriff, riding with them." Reading from a parchment, the herald cried that "Jane, by the grace of God, Queen of England, France and Ireland, Defender of the Faith and of the Church of England and also of Ireland, under Christ on earth the Supreme Head . . ." was now proclaimed. The proclamation had been written by John Dudley with the help of Sir John Cheke, Edward's tutor, and Sir Nicholas Throckmorton, who was observed as "troubled therewith, misliking the matter." At Paul's Cross, Cheapside and Fleet Street, the little band of officials proclaimed, after loud blasts of the trumpet, that Jane Grey, greatniece of old Henry VIII, grandaughter of his sister Mary, "the French Queen," was now Queen of England. Again there was no cheering, no rejoicing, only curious stares and muffled murmurs. At Cheapside one young boy, Gilbert Potter, "a drawer at a tavern called St. John's Head within Ludgate," perhaps having imbibed more than his share of tavern ale, shouted, "The Lady Mary hath the better title!" Immediately he was apprehended and later nailed by his ears to a pillory in Cheapside; the ears had to be cut off to free him. In the streets surrounding Cheapside—as in all London—there was no celebratory feasting or bonfires and the bells had long ceased to ring.

But inside the White Tower, in the airily spacious apartments reserved for royal use, hung with costly tapestries and arras, with wheels of thick candles lowered from the high ceilings and soldiers with halberdiers at every door, Jane's entourage moved among the rooms with their impressively heavy carved chests and tables on the brightly colored Turkey carpets. The ancient custom of the monarch lodging in the Tower derived primarily from the protection it afforded from one's enemies during that period before the coronation. But the royal apartments were not fortresslike and Jane sat now under her cloth of state and received the kneeling Privy Council. Their submission made, John Dudley then announced that certain state responsibilities must be undertaken and Jane was led to a chair, given pen and ink and asked to sign the papers that the duke thrust in front of her.

Jane had hoped to go into the exquisite Chapel of St. John, built by William the Conqueror, where some fifty years ago her greatgrandmother Elizabeth of York had lain on her bier, dead of childbirth at thirty-seven. There'd been no opportunity all day for prayer and she yearned for the peace and quiet of the chapel, where she might free herself of her discomfort and the burdens she felt as heavily as the crimson robe she'd happily discarded hours ago. The papers were thick and, Dudley said, important. They were addressed to all the Lord-Lieutenants of England, proclaiming her queen, and they needed her signature at once.

The letters were too long to read and Jane felt it unseemly to question whether she need sign or not. Glancing through the pile, she noted one sentence asking her "trusty and well-beloved subject . . . to assist us . . . to disturb, repel and resist, the feigned and untrue claim of the Lady Mary, bastard daughter to our great uncle, Henry VIII of famous memory." Disturbed, she hesitated just long enough for Dudley to become impatient. Then, indicating that it was all part of her new and awesome responsibility, he showed her where to sign. Reluctantly, with a shaking hand, the girl picked up her pen and in the proper place signed,

Jane, the Quene

While Jane was leaving Chelsea, farther northwest Mary Tudor continued her flight into Norfolk. The exhausted princess soon arrived at Kenninghall Castle, and as news of King Edward's death reached the Border and her escape from Robert Dudley to seek refuge among them became known, many of the Catholic nobility and gentry came to her aid. Already, John Bourchier, the Earl of Bath, was on hand with a considerable force, and soon Mary was heartened by the arrival of such staunch friends as Sir Henry Bedingfield, Sir John Mordaunt and Sir Henry Jerningham. They were of the "old aristocracy," whose parents or even they themselves had defended her mother in those heartbreaking years of "the troubles." Safe in the Gog Magog hills, watching the burning of Master Huddlestone's Sawston Hall home, which had given her refuge, Mary realized how much she must depend on her friends.

"Let it blaze . . . !" she'd told Andrew Huddlestone as he watched, horrified, the violent destruction of his family home. "I will build Master Huddlestone a better Sawston . . . !" Mary's deep voice, so like her mother's, was commanding; Andrew Huddlestone never doubted but what, should God give her the opportunity, she'd do just that.

Huddlestone was there during the following hours when, at last, the king's death was officially proclaimed in the neighboring marketplace. Along with the proclamation, it became known that the Princess Mary, daughter of Henry VIII and Katherine of Aragon, was now at Kenninghall Castle, a refugee from John Dudley and the Privy Council's intention—and what *that* was, no one seemed to know. But it was implicit in the English character that their queen be protected, that she know of her subjects' loyalty. And so, within hours of Mary's arrival, the larger roads and tiny lanes of the Norfolk countryside were clogged with country squires and their tenants who left fields unharvested, with merchants who left businesses untended, with country lads and even some lasses, who joined the throng in a holiday mood, to take up in festive fashion and encamp on Kenninghall Castle grounds so the royal lady inside might know they were there should she have to fight for her crown. But they wondered—as did Mary—why should she have to fight? Hadn't old King Henry made her his heir?

The following morning, John Dudley's reply to her offer of pardon was received. As Jane rode in the royal barge toward the Tower, Mary and her advisers read Dudley's letter, which acknowledged her "supposed title," explaining that Edward, "a prince of most noble memory," had invested "our most Sovereign Lady, Jane" as Queen of England. Therefore their "most bound duty and allegiance assent unto her said grace and to none other" was obvious. The council noted that since the divorce of Mary's father and mother, she had been "justly made illegitimate and unheritable to the Crown Imperial of this realm. . . ." Therefore, since the nobles and great personages of the country had agreed, she, Mary Tudor, should "surcease by any pretence, to vex and molest any of our sovereign Lady, Queen Jane and her subjects, from their true faith and allegiance unto her grace." The letter finished on a condescending note, informing the princess that if she would be respectful and "show yourself quiet and obedient, as you ought, you shall find us all and several ready to do you any service that we with duty may." If she did not, said the council, "You may be otherwise grievous unto us, to yourself and to them [the realm]."

Mary glanced at the signatures. She knew every one, for many had served her father. Thomas Cranmer, William Paulet, John Russell—even Will Parr, brother of the woman who'd been her stepmother and dear friend! Henry Grey, Jane's father, and William Cecil, of whom she would have thought better. And there were those earls—Shrewsbury, Arundel, Pembroke and Huntingdon—all eager to ally themselves with power, even the ill-begotten power of such as the opportunistic Dudley, who'd helped them gain the riches and treasures they'd plundered from the church.

Mary had not anticipated such a reply. The most likely excuse for her treatment, she thought, was that Dudley or even another noble might, on religious reasons if no other, try to take her crown. But all along they'd intended it for another, and even now, reading the hateful words, Mary—who'd suffered exile and persecution in her earlier years and a subtle harassment for the last six since her father's death—hardly knew what to think of the treachery, the tremendous disloyalty that had put little Jane Grey, the daughter of one of her closest and most beloved friends, in a position to take her crown. Listening to her advisers' angry observations and threats of retaliation, Mary wondered how Jane had accepted the momentous change in her everyday life, even her destiny. The girl, she knew, was a ploy of the unconscionable Dudley. The very thought of a Dudley having the *power* to accomplish the setting aside of the rightful heir—herself—made Mary almost ill. But hot resentment would gain her little, she knew. What she needed now was support, and there was good evidence of it—growing daily—outside the castle walls.

And she must be safe, her advisers stressed. Now, more than ever, she must be protected from what obviously was to be a life-and-death struggle for the throne. Now, until they could muster adequate support for her, there must be no question of her security. The crowds on Kenninghall's grounds were only a small part of what she eventually might need, should Dudley decide to storm the castle.

Mary put the paper aside, her mind made up. Her plan might never work and she might be forced to flee for her life; therefore she should be near the coast where she might escape to Holland or Spain. Early on Tuesday, July 11, as Jane was awakening to face her first full day in the Tower of London, Mary and her faithful company of knights and ladies, of those nobles who insisted on

275

remaining with her, took horse and "never drew bridle" until she arrived at Framlingham Castle, the county seat of the Howards, the Dukes of Norfolk. Framlingham had three moats, and since dusk had fallen, torches were carried to light the way for the beleaguered princess and her exhausted train to enter. Mary's first order, once inside, was to proclaim herself Queen Regnant of England and Ireland and to order her standard to be flown. Within moments her flag was anchored over the ancient gatehouse, a challenge to the conspirators for her crown that courage, prudence and good intent might yet accomplish what was her right: the throne of England.

21

Queen Jane's first night in the Tower of London was a troubled one. Guildford had wished to stay with her, but in view of the long day's activities and the duties that awaited her on the morrow, she'd pleaded for a night alone. However, Jane knew she could not put him off forever. Queen or not, she would be expected to live with her husband as any other lady might and soon everyone would expect an heir. She realized that any return to Dorset Place, Sheen, Westhorpe or any of her father's other residences would probably be impossible. She would go as queen, not as Lady Jane Grey, eager to rejoin her tutor so she might resume her studies and the correspondence which had been so satisfying. In the future, she would go in state to Westminster, Greenwich, Windsor, Oatlands, Nonsuch and those regally beautiful castles and homes belonging to the monarch. Her freedom would be restricted, but then, she'd never possessed any real freedom of choice. She would be surrounded by ladies-in-waiting, whom she must select soon; she wondered if Mrs. Ellen would be allowed to stay. She suspected her parents would always be close by, and certainly Guildford's mother and father would be near, especially the duke, upon whom her father had told her she must rely. Then there would be

daily meetings of the Privy Council and she would have to listen
to their advice and do as they suggested, whether she liked it or
not. Already there was concern over the continuing absence of
William Cecil, "who would not be induced to meddle in the matter." She would have to meet those foreign ambassadors in the
outlandish dress the court laughed at almost as much as the envoys criticized the English garb. At least, Jane thought with some
satisfaction, she would be able to converse with them more fluently
than Edward had.

The thought of her dead cousin brought a pang, and all through
that first night alone in the cavernous Tower chamber, Jane listened dejectedly to the muted sounds of Tower life. As dampness
from moat and river seeped through window and doorway, making her sneeze, she heard the rustle of keys and the whispered
conversation of the guards making their rounds. There was the quiet
splash of oars as boats ground on the sandy Tower beach, the clang
of a portcullis as someone was admitted, the fragmented wisps of
conversation carried on the night air from other parts of the ancient buildings. As apprehension gave way to a restless relaxation,
Jane dozed at last, only to be soon awakened by the shrieking of
the Tower ravens as the guards flung them their food in the early
dawn. Now, wagons rumbled noisily by, bringing food and drink
to the Tower kitchens, and the carters shouted to each other. Horses
clattered in the courtyard near the Green, and a small procession
headed by the Tower chaplain walked toward the church for early
morning worship. Everywhere the old fortress came to life and soon,
outside the grim walls, the City bells began to toll.

Jane was relieved when Mrs. Ellen came to help her dress. She'd
just finished a light breakfast when William Paulet, Marquis of
Winchester, the Lord High Treasurer, was announced. Upon entering her chamber he bowed low, as an aide deposited several chests
at her feet. Puzzled, Jane wondered what the old marquis was about,
for already he was fumbling with lock and key. She waited patiently until the case was opened; inside she could barely see the
rich gleam of gems and gold.

As she'd breakfasted, Jane had told Mrs. Ellen how badly she'd
slept and that she suspected a recurrence of the illness she'd had
at Chelsea. Mrs. Ellen had touched her head and nodded. It was
the dews on the river from the day before, her companion said,

those pestilential and dampish dews which could give one a fever and account for her warm full head and cough. Now, as Winchester drew a heavy jeweled diadem from the velvet chest, Jane felt her whole body grow warmer—not with pestilential dews, but with anger. She put up a hand to ward him off, but the marquis interpreted the gesture as meaning she wished to hold the crown. When Jane again refused to touch it, he said, plainly puzzled, that he'd brought it to her "to see how it fitted." But even this logical explanation did not convince Jane. Again she refused to let him set the crown on her head, insisting she'd never asked to see any of the crown jewels, nor had she given anyone instructions to bring them to her.

The marquis, plainly regarding her reluctance as a bothersome feminine whim, held out the crown as one might a toy to a bashful child. "You may take it boldly," he said, "and soon I'll have another made to crown your husband with."

Astounded, Jane could only stare at the old gentleman as he stood there with the Crown of England in his hand, undoubtedly ready to hand her the Sceptre and Orb once he'd put it on her head. Why was it so difficult for him to understand she did not feel worthy of such a sacred symbol? How could he consider Guildford entitled to wear a crown? But she knew Winchester was serious. "Which thing," Jane would later write, "I for my part heard truly with a troubled mind and with ill will, even with infinite grief and displeasure of heart." When she again refused, angered at the man's insistence and disturbed by his intent for her husband, she wondered if Winchester's appearance might not make it look as though *she* had requested the regalia be brought to her. Winchester, his irritation at Jane's attitude now plainly evident, motioned to his servant to repack the chests. They were just leaving as Guildford Dudley entered.

Guildford had observed enough to guess what had happened, and as the chamber door closed, his good manners disappeared. What was the matter with her? he asked Jane bluntly. She was Queen of England and should have let old Winchester, who was only doing his duty, put the crown on her head! As he walked about the room, Guildford berated Jane, telling her she must learn to behave in a manner now befitting their position. If Winchester returned with the crown, then she should not anger the old man with her peculiar reluctance. When it came *his* turn to be fitted, he told Jane, he would not cause so much inconvenience!

Jane took a deep breath, well aware of the trouble she was about to cause. But she had to say it. Edward had left the crown to *her*, she explained patiently to her husband, and not to anyone else. She watched Guildford's expression change from one of irritated impatience to deep anger. She'd received Winchester sitting in the canopied chair of state, from which her feet could barely touch the floor. Now, Guildford's tall presence loomed in front of her and his eyes were cold, his expression petulant as she attempted to reason with him. It was not up to her, she said, to make him king. Only an Act of Parliament could do that. Hotly, Guildford argued that if his wife was a queen, then he was a king, and he could not conceive why she could not understand that. "I will be made king by *you* and by Act of Parliament!" he cried loudly, his voice shaking. Eventually, as Jane quietly persisted in stating there was nothing she could do, the boy burst into tears of frustration. At last, realizing he was not going to change his wife's mind, he consented to wait until Parliament acted. As he left, Jane's relief was tempered by the knowledge that undoubtedly he'd run immediately to tell his parents of her decision. No sooner had the door closed than Mrs. Ellen returned and suggested Jane go back to bed to gain the rest she'd lost the night before, to relieve what she thought might be a growing fever.

Lying there in the great canopied bed, unable to sleep, Jane pondered the thought of Guildford Dudley—who had not a drop of royal blood—as King of England. The incongruity of her own queenship was still strong; she was uncomfortable and apprehensive, even though Edward *had* bequeathed the crown to her, had made it *her* responsibility. Again, for the hundredth time, she wondered about Mary and Elizabeth. She guessed how deeply Mary's feelings would be wounded by the harsh language of the Proclamation, which John Dudley had already sent throughout the realm and abroad. Near tears, her head pounding with a hot, flushed feeling, Jane wished she knew how the two princesses had received the news of their brother's action, hoping they realized it had been none of her doing. She knew how proud both Mary and Elizabeth were, each in different ways, of their exalted heritage and their father. How would they feel when Guildford Dudley was anointed in the old abbey and Henry VIII's crown placed on his head?

Within hours Jane's mind was made up. She sent for Henry Fitzalan, the Earl of Arundel, and William Herbert, the Earl of Pembroke, long members of the Privy Council. In strong voice, with a confidence she was far from feeling, she said she was willing to make her husband a duke but not a king. To Jane's surprise there was little objection from either earl, and they nodded almost approvingly before they left. She could not know how much her own calm independent decision had impressed and surprised them, for they'd considered her a pliable tool of the Dudley-Grey faction. She could not know it had been to Arundel's sister that her own father, Henry Grey, had once been contracted before he married Frances Brandon, and that Arundel had sworn that someday he'd avenge his family's honor. She would have known that Pembroke's wife was the former Ann Parr, sister of her beloved Queen Katherine, and that while Will and Ann Herbert appeared to be close friends of John Dudley's, in reality both had collaborated with the duke more for the rewards in church lands and other plunder than for any approval of his politics, either religious or social. It was easy to be intimidated by someone as convincing and domineering as John Dudley when the danger was little and the profit great. But now, rich, powerful and secure—and uneasily aware of how it might all be lost—both earls were taking a second look at Dudley's insistence on placing Jane Grey on the throne. They did not need Guildford too, Arundel and Pembroke agreed. Already it would take much explaining to defend their actions to Princess Mary, should that ever be necessary, though privately neither earl thought the occasion would ever arise. Even though Jane was unaware of the reasons behind the earls' easy agreement regarding her husband, she was relieved.

But the relief was short-lived. Within hours the Dudley family had heard her decision, and, still white-lipped with anger, Guildford appeared in her chamber again. This time there were no niceties, and he upbraided the diminutive figure seated once more under her cloth of state, which Jane now regarded as much a refuge as the classroom had once been. Circling the chair, Guildford swore openly, chastising his wife for her decision. Then he flung his cap on a table before impatiently seating himself—aware, as was Jane, that to do so without the sovereign's express permission was considered a mark of disrespect. Jane was about to reprove her husband when his mother entered the chamber.

The duchess, learning of her daughter-in-law's decision from her son, Arundel and Pembroke, had lost little time in gaining Jane's Tower room. As Guildford shrugged his shoulders sulkily, putting cap to head, Jane Dudley, in hot indignation, shouted to Jane "in the coarsest terms," asking why her son was not good enough to share the crown? And how did Jane think she'd come to the crown anyway? Hadn't it been the Dudley family—Guildford's own father!—who'd helped her attain it? Then, aware she might be saying more than she should, the duchess changed her tactics and, with soft voice, pleaded with Jane that she think everything out clearly, that obviously if she was to be queen, her husband must be king. He could not be only a duke. The duchess's expression clearly revealed that when Jane came to her senses she'd regard the whole subject with more intelligence. But Jane's reply—that the crown was not a plaything for boys and girls—only infuriated her mother-in-law. Her temper clearly out of control, the duchess hurled accusations at Jane and threatened to make Guildford return to Syon and leave his wife alone. When Jane reiterated that she'd make her husband a duke but only the Parliament could make him a king, she thought Jane Dudley might strike her. So tense had the scene become that again Guildford began to cry and the duchess, her fury spent at last, grabbed him by the hand and pulled him from the room, slamming the door as she went.

Jane sat with hot, pounding head, her knees weak and painful from straining toward the floor, her skin flushed with what she suspected was fever as much as alarm over Guildford's and Jane Dudley's behavior. She'd been at court or listened to her parents' gossip often enough to know what others would make of her husband's and mother-in-law's actions. It would not be a good beginning for her queenship, and she had yet to face John Dudley when he learned of her decision. She wanted to talk to her own mother and father, to explain why she felt as she did, but they had not come to visit her since the river procession to the Tower.

At last, her voice trembling as much as her hands, she sent again for both Arundel and Pembroke, telling them they should ask Guildford to return to her "and behave in a friendly manner." Jane knew what she was asking for. She wanted her husband's under-standing and support and if she was to attain it, there must be harmony between them. The following days were going to be dif-ficult enough, and the sight of a man who wished to be king acting like a petulant child, with a mother shouting abuse at a girl who was supposed to be queen, would not present a pretty picture to the court. It would be better if she could get Guildford alone, and during the late afternoon he came. "Thus," Jane was later to write, "I was compelled to act as a woman who is obliged to live on good terms with her husband. Nevertheless, I was not only deluded by the duke and the council, but maltreated by my husband and his mother."

Jane's "delusion" was her complete trust in John Dudley's and the Privy Council's insistence that she was the rightful queen be-cause Edward on his deathbed had left the crown to her. Messen-gers had been sent abroad to the Low Countries, to Spain and France, announcing the accession of "Jane, the Quene." Even a Spanish envoy to the Low Countries, Don Diego Hurtado de Mendoza, saw nothing incongruous—since he was Guildford Dudley's godfather—in assuming that Guildford would share his wife's crown. "You are bound to obey and serve His Majesty and therefore it is reason we take him for your king," he told Sir Philip Hoby, the English minister at Brussels, who relayed the Span-iard's conversation to the Privy Council. De Mendoza might logi-cally have been expected to support Mary Tudor. Yet he said, "For my part of all others, I am bound to be glad that His Majesty is set in this office . . . and would as willingly spend my blood in his service as any subject he hath, as long as I shall see the Em-peror willing to embrace His Majesty's amity." So far, Charles V, the emperor and Mary's cousin, had not committed himself; in London, skeptical Simon Renard, his ambassador, was still aghast that the princess was even trying to claim her throne and had begged the Privy Council "to be good to the Lady Mary."

But the scene with Guildford made Jane realize she could not continue reluctant, and when the Marquis of Winchester again brought the crown jewels to the Tower, she "accepted the regalia with tears." This time, the old treasurer brought along boxes, cas-kets and chests from the Jewel Tower, containing baubles going back to the time of Jane's Plantagenet ancestors. Soon he was relieved to see that, once she'd put the regalia aside, there was a feminine, almost childlike pleasure in inspecting the contents of the various chests. Jane's parents had given her few jewels, and often what she wore was only loaned for the occasion. Now much of the contents of the royal treasury were spread before her, and intuitively she selected the small and exquisite pieces which would suit her diminutive size: "One dewberry of gold. A like pendant, having one great and three little pearls. A pair of beads of white porcelain, with eight gauds of gold and a tassel of Venice gold. Five small agates, with stars graven on them. A pair of bracelets of flaggon-chain pattern, connecting jacinths or orange-colored amethysts . . ."

Leaving the few pieces the new queen had selected—which she continued to turn wonderingly about in her tiny hands—Winchester packed up the treasure for its return to the Jewel Tower, convinced and relieved that, at last, royalty was acting as royalty should. The tears had disappeared and the new queen, despite her flushed face and warm hands, seemed pleased with her trinkets.

But Winchester was no more than in his barge before Jane put the beautiful jewelry aside, her pleasure vanishing in the presence of a hot congested head and dry throat. Wearily she crept into bed, glad to be alone, for Guildford was meeting with his father and the Privy Council, and undoubtedly they'd all discussed how he might be crowned with her. But even as the solace of sleep crept over her, she knew she'd remain as determined as she'd been all day. Her mother-in-law might storm and her father-in-law might rebuke her. Her own parents might even beat her. But never, never would she make her husband a king.

All the following day, Jane was ill and was beginning to suspect that John Dudley's real intent in persuading Edward to leave her the crown was so that his son might become king. Again her nerves were tormented and again she suspected poison. As her skin withered and peeled easily from her back, as hair fell easily from her head when Mrs. Ellen brushed it, Jane insisted that someone must be trying to kill her, but the older woman merely shook her head, telling her that many types of fever had the same effect. Exasperated, feeling almost abandoned, her stomach a tight knot, Jane passed from apprehensiveness to fright and then to terror. What could she do when even her own nurse didn't believe her? She ate and drank less than before and, despite Mrs. Ellen's pleas, at last convinced herself that she felt better.

In the meantime she noticed the unusual activity in the Tower precincts, as weapons of all sorts were deployed, as groups of soldiers carrying halberds, and archers with bows at the ready marched from the Tower. She had not seen John Dudley since the confrontation with his wife and son, and mercifully, neither had returned to her chamber. She'd spent her time in bed trying to stifle the pangs of terror even as she stifled the pangs of hunger. She did not know the martial preparations at the Tower were being duplicated throughout the City and nearby counties as a small army was assembled to march on Framlingham Castle and capture the stubborn Mary Tudor.

Ever since Jane's arrival at the Tower, John Dudley had been busy sending proclamations of her accession, attending Privy Council meetings and firming up, as well as he could, his daughter-in-law's queenship. Now he turned his attention to the indisputable fact that the thirty-seven-year-old Princess Mary meant to fight for her throne. Reports arriving daily from East Anglia emphasized that the English countryside had responded to her appeal for help and already it was rumored she had an army of more than thirty thousand. The longer he delayed, the stronger the princess would become. Dudley and the councillors knew she must be stopped, and soon. Everyone agreed that both Robert Dudley and his older brother John, the Earl of Warwick, were too young and inexperienced for such an important campaign, and on July 12, "It was decided that the Duke of Suffolk [Henry Grey] with certain other noblemen, should go towards the Lady Mary and fetch her up to London." Queen Jane need only to issue the proper commissions and her father and the small army already assembled could leave the following day.

In the late afternoon John Dudley, Henry Grey and the full Privy Council waited on Queen Jane in her chambers. She'd been told of their coming and had risen once more from her bed; Mrs. Ellen had brushed her hair and helped her dress. She was sitting in her chair of state, almost dwarfed by the canopied hangings, as John Dudley explained the impossible situation at Framlingham Castle, where more country squires, knights and nobles hurried to Mary's aid. It was the first indication Jane had had of Mary's resistance, and with a sinking heart she realized that the princess meant to fight back. When she asked Dudley what should be done, he said he intended to send Henry Grey, the Duke of Suffolk, into the field and bring the beleaguered princess back to the Tower. He himself would remain in the capital to see to the proper administration of the new government.

Jane listened. Her illness—nerves or poison, she knew not what— had taken its toll. She was weak and uncomfortable, feverish all over, especially her head, and nauseated a good part of the time. Her own nurse did not believe anyone was trying to poison her, but something was wrong. She had so little protection from anyone who might wish to harm her and she was not as popular as Mary. How could she be? A few days ago she'd been only Lady Jane Grey, older daughter of the Duke of Suffolk. Now she was queen. But no one was hurrying to *her* aid—John Dudley, her father and all the Privy Council had to *order* support for her! What would happen to her when Henry Grey left the Tower? How could she face the continued malice of Guildford's mother? What if her suspicion of poison was well-founded—would she be given more when her father had gone? And how would her mother feel with a sick daughter and an absent husband? There had been few occasions in her life when she'd pleased Frances and Henry Grey, but so far her deportment as queen had left them content. But now it appeared that her father, whom she knew would protect her from harm for every reason other than love, was to leave her.

Watching the council, Jane could not know that the two earls, Pembroke and Arundel, had already spoken with other councillors, advising them that while Henry Grey would be selected to capture Mary, their real intention was to force John Dudley to go. Already it had dawned upon both earls—and they knew their colleagues held similar thoughts—that Jane's accession had been a mistake, no matter that Dudley's influence with the dying Edward had given it some semblance of legality. Now their main intent was to remove the domineering and dangerous duke from London and from their presence. Only then could they act in concert to undo what they now saw as an incredible error of judgment. Already Mary's support had shown where the English people's hearts lay. Now the first move toward reinstating themselves into some semblance of credibility with Mary was forcibly to remove John Dudley from power. And that could only be accomplished when he was absent.

But the earls' motives were unknown to Jane Grey; all she'd heard was that her father was leaving London. She'd be alone in the Tower, completely at the mercy of the Dudleys. How could she fight these men who were making such important decisions? She knew she was no match for them, but she *was* queen and certainly it was her right to let them know what she thought, even though it might do little good. As she began to speak she felt her throat close over and tears come to her eyes. Before she knew what was happening, she was weeping unashamedly. Though she knew such an open emotional display was childish, there was little she could do about it. All the previous days' tensions, her worries about Guildford and what he and his parents might do to fight her, surfaced and she broke down. Even the stunned expression on the councillors' faces did not matter.

Sobbing, Jane begged the council "with weeping tears . . . that her father might tarry at home in her company." Henry Grey, standing to one side, showed open-mouthed astonishment, though he said nothing. Jane wondered if he would be angry at losing the opportunity to capture Mary Tudor. She watched the other councillors as they whispered among themselves and, for the first time, saw a tiny spark of what the royal authority might accomplish. They were *listening* to her; they had not laughed at her, argued or refused to consider her wishes. For Jane, whose parents had *never* listened to her, had laughed at her, argued and then strengthened their views with blows, "nips and bobs," the prospect that she might be obeyed was acutely startling. The thought that her father might not desert her after all, and she'd never be punished for her actions, was almost unbelievable. Jane was still struggling with fear of what her father might say when the councillors bowed, saying they would return to the Council Chamber and discuss her request. As they left, her tears subsided and the sobs became hiccups.

Back in the Council Chamber it was obvious that Queen Jane had been heard and was going to have her way. To a man, the Privy Council told John Dudley that the "voyage of the Duke of Suffolk was clean dissolved by the special means of the Lady Jane, his daughter," and they "persuaded with the Duke of Northumberland to take the voyage upon him, saying that no man was so fit therefor, because that he had achieved the victory in Norfolk once already."

The implication that he'd be as successful in suppressing Mary's rebellion as he had that of the unfortunate tanner, Robert Ket, was not lost on John Dudley. He knew the reputation he enjoyed in Norfolk. A strong soldier, eager to fight, the duke had no fear of what he might find at Framlingham or any place between it and London. He also knew Henry Grey to be a weak man, easily led, as he himself—and Thomas Seymour before him—had discovered. He'd wanted Henry Grey in command, since it was Grey's daughter who was queen, and having much to gain by keeping her in that position, he would be unlikely to desert their joint cause. In addition, Mary had always been fond of her Grey relatives. It was even possible that the princess—by now possibly seeking a safe way out of her troubles—might surrender to Henry Grey for that very reason! With Grey on the road and he, Dudley, in command of the council, there was no reason to expect anything but success. How could Mary continue to fight not only the entire English army but also those mercenaries he'd hired from abroad? How could she take London and the Tower, even with the impressive forces she'd gained?

What really bothered John Dudley deeply was what his absence from that very citadel of the monarchy—the City of London and its impregnable Tower—might entail. He knew how slim his hold on the Privy Council was. What would they do in his absence? As they encouraged him to undertake the commission because he was "so feared, that none durst once lift up their weapon against him," he remained doubtful. When they reiterated that "he was the best man of war in the realm, as well for the ordering of his camps and soldiers both in battle and in their tents, as also by experience, knowledge and wisdom, he could animate his army with witty persuasions and also pacify and allay his enemies' pride with his stout courage, or else to dissuade them if need were from their enterprise," he wanted to believe them.

But the councillors' arguments were convincing and eventually Dudley accepted that there was no way out. "Well," he said, "since you think it good, I and mine will go, not doubting of your fidelity to the Queen's Majesty which I leave in your custody." As the meeting ended with names of those "lords, knights and others [who] should go with him," the councillors again went to the White Tower. Jane had been told to await the end of their deliberations and though it was past her bedtime, she was there in her chair of state. As they told her of their decision, she "humbly thanked the duke for reserving her father at home, and beseeched him to use his diligence."

Wearily, John Dudley nodded. "I will do what in me lay . . ." he answered. Then, aware of the late hour, he and the councillors bowed and left. Again Mrs. Ellen came to help a relieved Jane Grey to her bed and this time the girl slept, exhausted by worry about her father, her health and the knowledge that Mary Tudor intended to fight for her crown.

The following morning, while Jane still slept, Durham House—the Dudley residence on the curve of the Thames—was alive with "carts laden with ammunition, and artillery and field pieces prepared for the purpose." John Dudley personally supervised the preparation and packing of his own harness and the additional gear he would need for a task he was undertaking with a doubting heart. Already the council was listing the troops that other nobles would raise and send to him at Newmarket. Already Princess Mary had been proclaimed at Norwich; there was not much time to waste. But Dudley felt he must apprise the council of his thoughts.

Accompanied by four of his sons, John, Ambrose, Henry and Robert, who would accompany him into Norfolk, he stood before his fellow councillors and told them that he was leaving "on behalf of you and yours as for the establishing of the Queen's Highness," that he was "adventuring our bodies and lives among the bloody strokes and cruel assaults of our adversaries in the open fields," and leaving the "conservation of ourselves, children and families at home here with you." Dudley was frank, saying that "if we thought you would through malice, conspiracy or dissension, leave us your friends in the briars and betray us, we could as well in sundry ways foresee and provide for our own safeguards." Instead, he was giving them his full trust, he emphasized, "which trust and promise if you shall violate . . . yet shall not God count you innocent of our bloods, neither acquit you of the sacred and holy oath of allegiance made freely by you to this virtuous lady, the Queen's Highness, *who by your and our enticement is rather of force placed therein than by her own seeking and request.*"

Dudley continued, impressive, while his fellow councillors listened intently. He reminded them of the "fear of Papistry's reentrance," telling them if they meant deceit, "God will revenge the same." At last he ended: "I can say no more. But in this troublesome time, wish you to use constant hearts, abandoning all malice, envy and private affections."

It had been an inspiring speech and the councillors entreated Dudley to depend on them. The duke replied that he did so; he was merely putting them "in remembrance thereof, what chance of variance whatsoever might grow amongst you in mine absence. And this I pray you, wish me no worse God speed in this journey than you would have to yourselves."

As everyone once more protested complete loyalty, a councillor approached Dudley. "My lord," he said, "if you mistrust any of us in this matter, your grace is far deceived. For which of us can wipe his hands clean thereof? And if we should shrink from you as one that were culpable, which of us can excuse himself as guiltless? Therefore, herein your doubt is too far cast. . . ."

"I pray God it be so," Dudley replied. "Let us go into dinner."

After dinner, the Earl of Arundel, passing through the Council Chamber, bade Dudley farewell, saying "he was very sorry it was not his chance to go with him and bear him company." Then he said good-bye to one of Dudley's companions, Tom Lovell, younger son of Lord Lovell. "Farewell, gentle Thomas, with all my heart." The old earl wrung the boy's hand and, bowing low, again wished the duke and his companion well.

Later that evening, the duke, his sons and several nobles went to the Tower for his commission from the queen. Returning to the Council Chamber, he said his farewell to the remaining lords, after which Will Parr, Henry Grey and several others accompanied Dudley to his Durham House home, "where that night they mustered their company in harness."

It was early morning on Friday, July 14, eight days after Edward's death and four days after Jane's accession, when "the Duke of Northumberland with other lords and knights with a great power of horsemen with artillery and munitions of war, departed from

London toward Norfolk to suppress the rebels." As an early morning fog rolled in from the river, John Dudley and more than six hundred men marched down the Strand and Fleet Street toward Shoreditch, intending to head northeast into East Anglia. Everywhere, early risers—the merchants and their apprentices, the shopkeepers and the wagons bringing produce into the City—were about. They watched, with cool intensity, the band of soldiers, the rumbling cannon and the cavalcade of horsemen bringing up the rear. Their silence bothered John Dudley, and turning to a companion, he said, "The people press to see us . . . but not one sayeth God speed us."

As the duke's forces left the City, a mile or so south, Jane was awakening in the Tower to learn that Lord Windsor, Sir Edmond Peckham, the royal cofferer, and a councillor, Sir Edward Hastings, had proclaimed Mary Tudor queen in Buckinghamshire. Later in the day, as the news reached the council, Sir John Gates, Captain of the Queen's Guard, was ordered to "send after the duke the carts with ammunition and the ordnance."

22

The weekend that John Dudley marched toward East Anglia was crucial to Mary Tudor. Safe in the vast fortress of Framlingham in the Suffolk countryside, she anxiously paced the rooms of the old castle, much of which dated from Saxon times, watching out the windows as new recruits to her cause arrived daily. Sir John Sulyard, a knight of Wetherden, was the first to reach her moated refuge; he was soon joined by Sir William Drury, a knight of Suffolk, and the county's High Sheriff, Sir Thomas Cornwallis. Soon Sir John Shelton and Sir John Tyrrell, representatives of strong Catholic families in what was an area deeply committed to the "new religion," brought their adherents and tenants to join the queen's muster. Soon, those encamped about the ancient buildings on the hill overlooking the River Orr jubilantly welcomed Mary as she walked out among them—a small, auburn-haired woman looking older than her thirty-eight years—and thanked them for their support before disappearing once more behind the moats' banks, rampant with golden iris.

Practical as ever, Mary did more than express her gratitude. She requisitioned church plate and money from Norwich, so "that if any soldier seemed in need of aught, his captain was to supply his wants as if by way of gift and charge the expense to her." She asked the bakers of Norwich to come to her aid with bread and requested three hundred quarters of malt ale to be brewed at Oxford. Ordnance, already mounted, soon arrived from Aldborough, and within days a proclamation of defiance was issued from Framlingham Castle, offering £1,000 in land to any noble, £50 to any gentleman and £100 to any yeoman who brought John Dudley, the Duke of Northumberland, to her as prisoner.

Framlingham offered more than safety to its royal guest. Though its former owner, Thomas Howard, the aged Duke of Norfolk, had languished in relative comfort in the Tower of London, cared for by servants since Henry VIII had imprisoned him there over six years previously, Framlingham had been kept in good repair. Each morning, Mary and her companions worshiped in the tiny jewellike chapel hung with a tapestry depicting the Life of Christ. The spacious rooms, stripped now of their costly treasures and furnishings, had survived not only the imprisonment of its aristocratic owner—the premier duke in England as well as its Earl Marshal—but also the rapacity of Edward Seymour, the Protector. When Norfolk, at his imprisonment for treason, learned that the Seymour family was determined to have Framlingham, he told Henry to bestow it instead on the royal children because, as he said, "It was stately gear"—intimating that the venerable old castle was not for the likes of the upstart Seymours, no matter that the king had married one of them. Henry had been pleased to accept the gift and Framlingham became a royal possession, to serve now as haven for a royal refugee.

Mary had chosen Framlingham not only because its three moats and forty-foot-high walls offered sanctuary, but because it was near the coast. At times, as if to convince herself flight was possible, she and a few of her advisers walked down the back of the castle hill, through a mile and a half of woodland to the sea. To the west, most forest roads surrounding Framlingham had been deliberately cluttered with tree limbs and debris which made them impassable. Should she have to flee, it would be by water, to either Spain or the Low Countries, where she'd convinced herself there would be a warm welcome.

Mary had appealed to the Spanish ambassadors in London and, through them, to her cousin Charles V, the Holy Roman Emperor. About that time, Lord Cobham and Sir John Mason, emissaries of the Privy Council which John Dudley had ordered to remain in the Tower until his return, approached Simon Renard and Jehan Scheyve, the emperor's ambassadors, to impress upon them the futility of any Spanish aid for Mary. The envoys revealed their fear that Mary's crown had, in reality, "been snatched for the Queen of Scotland [young Mary Stuart] under cover of conferring it upon the Duke of Suffolk's daughter," and since England apparently preferred a French alliance to one with Spain, they planned to leave the country soon. When the French ambassador, Antoine de Noailles, confirmed their hope that the French king would support Queen Jane, the council made its choice and the Spaniards wrote their home court that there was no way Mary could win her struggle. The princess herself had confirmed their worst doubts by saying "she saw destruction hanging over her unless she received help." When he received this information, the emperor—lacking any real sympathy for Mary's cause except religion—said he "rejoiced in the succession of Lady Jane and her husband." Everyone, Privy Council, foreign ambassadors, a French king and a Spanish emperor, now waited to see how successful John Dudley's coup would be. In the interim, Mary Tudor—like her mother before her—was virtually abandoned by all.

About five days after Mary's arrival at Framlingham, as John Dudley marched toward Bury St. Edmunds, six ships of war sent by the Privy Council sailed past the Suffolk coast. Their destination was Yarmouth, where the cannon and ammunition aboard would be distributed among the soldiers on land and at sea to use against the stout walls of Framlingham Castle, or else to intercept the flight by the princess abroad. Those supplies requisitioned by Mary had not as yet arrived in any great amount and everyone was fearful of the ships and their guns. Mary might hold out for days, for the castle was virtually unbreachable, but the small army encamped outside would be no match for cannon fire. Then siege would follow and, inevitably, submission in the face of starvation.

But stout old Sir Henry Jerningham had other ideas. In Yarmouth, the ships' captains were somewhere on shore and could not be found, so the old knight boarded a small boat to take him out to the ships, where he meant to test the sailors' loyalties. Word of his departure was given to the captains and they soon followed after him. As Jerningham reached the boats, the sailors, leaning over the rails, asked him "what he would have?" Sir Henry said he would have their captains, "who were rebels to their lawful Queen Mary." Noting the boats carrying the captains a short distance away, the sailors replied, "Ye shall have them or else we shall throw them to the bottom of the sea." In rapid consultation among themselves, the six captains, with mutinous crews on their hands, surrendered, and within hours the Yarmouth burgesses arrived to take possession of the ships. Sir Henry then rode back to Framlingham with the news, and "the Lady Mary and her company were wonderful joyous."

Mary celebrated by riding out from the castle on horseback to see those crowding about the castle grounds. They'd heard of the ships' surrender, and the sight of the princess, smiling and happier than they'd ever seen her, brought them to their feet and "they threw up their caps and fired their harquebuses." For the first time, Mary heard the cry "Long live our good Queen Mary!" For one as much deprived of affection and attention as her youthful usurper in the Tower, the crowd's warm display of love and loyalty was heartwarming; there were tears in Mary's eyes as she returned inside and went to her small oratory to pray.

Within hours, the news of the Yarmouth ships' desertion was relayed to the Privy Council, whom Dudley had ordered sequestered in the Tower until he returned with his royal captive. He did so for their own safety, the duke told them before his departure, and they must also be available to protect and advise Queen Jane. Dudley's real fear, however, was that once free, the everpresent cliques would form and his control would vanish, for inevitably, one faction always emerged the strongest. It had taken less than a day for the duke's worst fears to be realized.

Shut up in the Tower, hearing of the loss of the Yarmouth ships and that former councillor Sir Edward Hastings, who'd successfully decamped, had now mustered some four thousand men close to London, each noble became more fearful and suspicious of the other. Unknown to them, the Earl of Arundel—he who had so strongly proclaimed his loyalty to John Dudley—had already sent a secret message to Princess Mary that the duke was coming to take her. As the councillors busied themselves with state business and looked for funds for the London soldiers—who, with no pay, were deserting in large numbers—their main concern was how to deal with what they now viewed as approaching calamity. What would happen to their influence and the great wealth they'd accumulated under the Protector and Dudley since the old king's death? Suppose the duke did not win? Suppose Mary forgave him? Would her pardon extend to them, incarcerated now in her Tower of London along with the one who'd stolen her crown? Suppose Dudley, in view of all that was happening, went over to Mary and left them defenseless in Queen Jane's cause? And, should he possibly bring the fugitive princess to London, as he'd vowed to do, what would happen if the English people—and the London populace in particular—fought Mary's imprisonment?

With the nicety of mutual trust so completely absent, it was not long before the Privy Council—as Dudley had anticipated—separated into different groups, their previous declarations of loyalty and admissions of similar guilt forgotten. When Mary was proclaimed at Oxford, Devonshire and Cheshire, when a placard placed on a Queenhithe pump, in the very heart of London, stated "that the Princess Mary had been proclaimed queen in every town and city in England, London alone excepted," outright terror struck those who'd participated so readily in Dudley's mad gamble. Now all the Dudleys were absent except Guildford, who, as husband of the queen, had remained in safety at the Tower. Jane had recently made him Duke of Clarence, after which the boy who "of all of Dudley's brood had little of his father in him," had created a scene, insisting petulantly that because of his rank he should be served his meals in state and alone. The councillors, harassed by more important news, had complied. Regarding the make-believe king and queen playing their roles in the sumptuous royal apartments, each now looked for a way to save his own skin.

It was on that Sunday, July 16, the sixth day of Jane's reign, that Ridley, the Bishop of London, reviled Mary and her "popish creed" at Paul's Cross, calling her the "idolatrous rival" of Queen Jane, one who would bring foreign powers to England once she was queen. The princess was "so stiff and obstinate," Ridley shrieked, "that there was no hope of her to be conceived, but to disturb and overturn all that which with so great labors had been confirmed and planted by her brother."

As the people "who had not yet learned to associate the claims of inheritance with those of religious convictions" showed their displeasure by leaving, William Cecil now felt it safe to move the Privy Council toward some semblance of unity. It was difficult to discuss any plans in the Tower. But they could still, as the queen's Privy Councillors, hold meetings, even though they had to be in session when Henry Grey, Jane's father—whose loyalty to Dudley was still unquestioned—was conveniently absent.

Within hours, William Paget, previously scorned in what had become a happy exile at Drayton, was called back to the council table, where his experience, going back over thirty years, might be helpful. Many of Mary's supporters, numbering more than ten thousand, had assembled at his home and marched to Westminster, where they took possession of the ammunition and weapons stored in the crumbling old Palace of Westminster, "for the better furnishing of themselves in the defense of the Queen's Majesty's person and her title."

With ships defecting and congregations leaving, with commoners rising to Mary's defense and even the nobles' own servants afraid to serve them lest they be deemed traitors to Mary Tudor, the Earl of Arundel, at that first meeting, spoke for everyone when he said, "I like not the air. . . ." Earlier, the Earl of Pembroke had made a furtive attempt to leave the Tower but was respectfully turned back by a guard. It was frustrating for the recently widowed Herbert—wealthiest and most influential of all the councillors, with vast estates in the southwest and Wales, with thousands of tenants to constitute any army he might be willing to call—to be ordered back by a common guard. But he complied.

That evening as the Tower was locked up and the keys taken to the queen, Jane dutifully counted them, as her father had explained to her she must. One was lacking, and in a panic she informed the guard. It was then learned that old Winchester, the Lord High Treasurer, had actually managed to leave, obviously retaining a key to return sight-unseen when he chose. Foolishly, he'd gone to his own home in Broad Street, from which a guard of archers "did fetch him at twelve o'clock of the night . . . to the Tower."

When it was obvious Arundel spoke for everyone at that first meeting, William Cecil revealed that already he'd communicated with Princess Mary. It was the first step in the Privy Council's withdrawal of any further support for John Dudley. When they received a "sharply written" message from the duke asking for the promised reinforcements, which should have been at Newmarket, they sent a "slender answer" but no additional men or ammunition. Now each councillor began to "pluck in his horns," guard his tongue as well as his most private thoughts, and cast about among his presumed friends to see what might be salvaged. Following the example of the soldiers deserting for lack of pay and their own servants deserting for fear of reprisal, the English Privy Council now scrambled for any form of self-preservation which might retrieve their dubious honor, save their new titles and the impressive wealth plundered from church and estate confiscations over the past several years. The awesome scheme of altering the succession, which had seemed so feasible under John Dudley's dominating presence as he'd terrorized them into committing treason, at last crumbled. Within a day, the duke, waiting at Bury St. Edmunds, accepted that his worst fears had been realized, and high hopes, confidence and nerve failing, he fell back on Cambridge to await delivery of the troops and ammunition he'd need before going farther.

Cut off from any information about Dudley's campaign, Jane Grey could not know what her decision—to send the duke instead of her father to capture Mary—had wrought. Dudley's hold on the council was now a thing of the past. No longer could he terrify or threaten; now the councillors thought of little else but how they could justify their actions to Mary if that necessity arose. It was not only their own credibility and privileged positions, perhaps even their lives, that were at stake, but also those of their families. Pembroke's son, Lord Herbert, was married to Jane's sister Lady Katherine Grey. Lord Huntingdon's son was married to a Dudley daughter. Any decision Mary made affected not only the young girl they'd agreed should be queen, but many of their own children as well.

But Jane knew little or nothing of their dilemma or the drama taking place within the Tower walls. As Dudley marched toward Bury, there was another violent scene with her mother and mother-in-law, about Guildford's kingship. At the end of the argument, as the wrangling duchesses left, Jane was so drained of emotion that she let Mrs. Ellen lead her straight to bed. She signed another proclamation of her queenship which would be cried throughout London that day. At her father's order she wrote Thomas Howard, the imprisoned Duke of Norfolk, secure in his apartments a short distance from hers, asking his loyalty to her queenship, unaware that Mary at that moment was walking the grounds of Framlingham, Norfolk's castle, listening to the cry of "Long live good Queen Mary!" The aged Norfolk, wishing no involvement, was wise enough not to reply.

Jane's main contacts with the outside world were her parents, Guildford and his mother. The council did not inform her of any business unless her signature was required. If she wondered what was happening to John Dudley's campaign, she did not ask. It never occurred to Jane to inquire how the people of London viewed her queenship, or how they'd reacted to the probability that their beloved Mary might be brought a prisoner to the Tower. All her life, in most ways, Jane had been out of touch with reality and with those to whom she should have been closest. She'd lived out her young years aware of being unpopular with everyone but Mrs. Ellen, her tutor and those kind people like Queen Katherine and Kate Brandon with whom she'd felt wanted and secure.

Jane had about convinced herself that God Himself had ordained that her future lay as Edward Tudor had desired, and popularity as such had little or no meaning for her; she did not desire it nor would she have known how to use or seek it. Religion was the firm foundation of Jane Grey's existence, and in that first full weekend in the Tower, as she listened to the battling duchesses, signed what the council ordered and tolerated her husband's attentions, she often sought solace in the nearby chapel. Deprived as she'd been all her life of any normal love and affection, Jane would have been startled to learn how much she and Princess Mary had in common. While one had the crown, which the other desired as her natural possession, and both were using a religious fanaticism to replace, not enhance, any sense of reality, Mary, luckily, had intelligent advisers. Jane did not. The only competent, dependable one was the man she'd sent away in order to keep the weak and self-serving Henry Grey at her side. It was that decision, more than any other, which now served to bring her undesired queenship to an end.

* * *

On Tuesday, July 18, eight days after Jane Grey was proclaimed Queen of England, the Privy Council, frantic now in view of reports of uprisings, desertions and Mary's growing army, determined to leave the Tower. To do so, they needed Queen Jane's approval. Early that morning, after she'd signed an order to Sir John Brydges and Sir Nicholas Poyntz that they should raise forces "with the same to repair with all possible speed towards Buckinghamshire for the repression and subduing of certain tumults and rebellions," she and Henry Grey learned that the council—in view of the gravity of the situation—wished for an audience with the Spanish emperor's and the French king's ambassadors, but considered "that the Tower was not fit . . . to enter into at that season." They did not need the Duke of Suffolk, they said, suggesting he remain at his daughter's side while they dealt with the business of state. All of which "seemed reasonable to a . . . man of no great depth himself, and not like to penetrate to the bottom of a deep design, he gave way to their departure . . . little conceiving that they never meant to come back." Within moments of permission being granted, the full council rode out in state to their own homes, to see the families they'd left eight days before.

The following morning, Wednesday, July 19, they assembled at old Baynards Castle, now the possession of the Earl of Pembroke. Set out into the Thames, near Blackfriars and Paul's Wharf, the medieval castle—which had known the presence of Henry II and Richard III—was one of Will Herbert's favorite residences, large enough to hold the church spoils which had made the earl, who could neither read nor write, one of the wealthiest and most powerful men in England. It provided a sumptuous setting for the councillors—whose rooms at the Tower had held little luxury—as they now prepared to abandon John Dudley and the girl he'd chosen to become queen.

The Earl of Arundel took the initiative. He looked down the long table at his illustrious colleagues: his host, Pembroke; Winchester, the Lord High Treasurer; William Petre, the Lord Privy Seal; old Will Paget; Sir John Mason; Sir John Cheke, and several other nobles. Standing to one side, somewhat awed to be in the Privy Council's presence, were the Lord Mayor, several aldermen and other City dignitaries whom he'd asked to be present.

Addressing them all as "My lords and dear brethren," Arundel broke into a violent tirade against John Dudley. The man who only four days before had promised to "spend his blood" at the duke's feet now recounted his grievances of many years standing—how the duke had imprisoned him for almost a year during the time Dudley had schemed for the execution of the Protector but, "by the force of innocency and truth, I escaped the inextricable snares of my mortal enemy." Arundel did not say that, in indicting Dudley, he was also avenging a decades-long injustice against his sister, Lady Katherine Fitzalan, whom Henry Grey had jilted to marry Frances Brandon. "What shall we determine of him," Arundel cried, "who has designed to imbrue his hands, not in the blood of one or two, but utterly to destroy so many lives at one blow?" No longer was Dudley able to subdue and terrorize them, he said. "Now we may freely speak of our sentiments. The crown is due to Mary. . . ." Here, Arundel broke off to read parts of Henry VIII's will, which, since many of them had signed it, was hardly unfamiliar.

Laying the will aside, Arundel spoke of the foolish trap into which they'd all fallen: John Dudley's persistent belief in "the cause of religion . . . and the dangers of a foreign husband" which Mary Tudor might perpetrate upon the realm. Dudley had toyed with them there, Arundel said, for it was not ordained that Mary *had* to wed a foreign husband! It was enough that they'd risked their lives and those of their beloved families—the earl did not mention their material possessions—in the lure of Dudley's impossible gamble. Now they must think for themselves. "My lords and most worshipful brethren," he cried at the end, "I implore your prudence and equity. . . ."

It had been a notable performance and there was a respectful silence as Arundel sat down. Then, not to be outdone, the Earl of Pembroke leapt to his feet and, clapping his hand on his sword, shouted, "My lords, I am ready to fight with any man who should proclaim to the contrary. If the arguments of my Lord Arundel do not persuade you, this blade shall make Mary queen, or I will lose my life!"

For the next half hour the group discussed how their new loyalty might be enforced. Mary must be proclaimed in London at once, they said, and a proclamation was written to be cried immediately. Between five and six o'clock, the same time Jane Grey had been proclaimed queen some nine days earlier, the Privy Council and Lord Mayor, accompanied by four trumpeters and two heralds in scarlet and gold tabards, approached the Great Cross in Cheapside. The piercing sound of trumpets brought people from their homes in droves, and they listened, enrapt, as the proclamation of the Princess Mary to be their queen was read. Suddenly, the dissent and fear of the last nine days disappeared, and within moments the City erupted in an orgy of celebration, all the more pleasurable since none had foreseen it would ever occur. Everywhere people ran to tell late arrivals the news. Soon householders were dragging tables into the streets and apprentices began to lay the bonfires that soon blazed on every corner. Then, one by one, the bells of the City churches started to ring; they continued to ring throughout the night. An exultant spontaneity gripped everyone as the people shouted the good tidings that Mary, the old king's daughter, had been proclaimed. Someone filled the conduits with wine and soon the streets were thronged with those who feasted, danced, sang, laughed and cried until dawn. Several of the Privy Council filled their caps with gold coins, and as one observer wrote, "The number of caps that were thrown up at the proclamation were not to be told." Before marching off to St. Paul's, where a mighty *Te Deum* would be sung, the Earl of Pembroke filled and refilled his cap with coins to throw to the scrambling mob. The pandemonium continued noisily, leading another contemporary to write, "For my time, I never saw the like and by the reports of others the like was never seen. I saw myself money was thrown out of windows for joy, the bonfires were without number. And what with the shouting and crying of the people and ringing of bells, there could be no man hear what another said, besides banqueting and skipping the streets for joy."

Returning to Baynards Castle after Evensong, the councillors drafted a letter to John Dudley, demanding his submission and surrender, each agreeing as the meeting ended that if he did not obey, "We of the nobility . . . will . . . persecute him and his to their utter confusion." The Lord Mayor was agreeable to allowing milord Arundel to pursue Dudley, if he did not surrender of his own accord.

* * *

At the Tower, Jane heard the noise. Looking out the window she could see the great flaring bonfires, hear the cries and laughter, the sounds of a people exultant, released finally from the dread and worry that had held them captive for days. Had John Dudley returned so soon? Was Mary captured at last? Were they bringing her to the Tower now? Jane wished her father or Guildford were present so she might ask, but they were nowhere to be seen. She'd been ill all day and was worried about a promise to attend the christening of the child of a Tower official who had named his baby Guildford. In view of the activity outside, she now sent for Lady Throckmorton and asked her to stand in at the ceremony in her place. If her father returned, she wanted to be there in the royal apartments where he'd expect to find her.

At that moment, however, Henry Grey was not in the Tower. A message from the council at Baynards Castle had informed him what had happened. It instructed him to honor the proclamation of Mary Tudor and to order his daughter to relinquish the title of queen at once. The duke did as he was told and, climbing Tower Hill, shouted, "I am but one man, but I here proclaim the Lady Mary's Grace Queen of England!" Then he rode hastily to Baynards Castle, where, in the presence of his fellow councillors, he signed Mary's proclamation, a nicety his colleagues had forgotten the day before. Still unbelieving of what had happened, yet knowing he had no recourse other than to follow orders, the duke hurriedly returned to the Tower and climbed the turret stairs to Jane's apartments.

He found his daughter staring out the window with an anxious expression. In one corner was the chair of state, that richly hung, highly gilded chair with its deep-crimson cushioned seat and lavishly draped overhead canopy of the same color, all fringed with gold, which symbolized everything majestic. It enraged the man who for years—how long had it been since Thomas Seymour had said he'd make Jane Grey a queen?—had schemed for just such an honor and had, for nine days, seen it accomplished. The slim girl, pale and ill, silent as always, looked at him with wondering eyes; she really didn't matter. What she'd *represented* had mattered a good deal. But now it was gone, vanished as that chair and its beautiful hangings would vanish for another to sit on. . . .

At sight of her father, Jane went and sat in her chair as she'd been told to do whenever anyone entered the room. She and her father gazed at each other. From his distraught expression, she knew something had happened. She waited, frightened, wondering what had gone wrong.

"Come off the chair, my child, that is no place for you." The duke motioned for her to rise. As he briefly explained the Privy Council's revolt against John Dudley, the sounds of a city celebrating could plainly be heard, wafting over the Tower's grim old walls and moat to father and daughter as they listened to the celebration meant for another. The unusually gentle tone in her father's voice startled Jane. But it disappeared in a moment as the duke, in a few short strokes, ripped the crimson damask from the canopy and threw it in disgusted fashion onto the seat. He then told Jane she should dispense with her "royal robes" as well; she was no longer queen.

Obedient as always, Jane removed the long cloak and put it on top of the torn crimson hangings. "I much more willingly put them off than I put them on," she said, a slight testiness in her voice. "Out of obedience to you and my mother, I've grievously sinned. Now I willingly relinquish the crown. . . ." She waited a moment and then asked, "May I not go home?"

But already, without another word, her father was leaving. Jane went into her private chamber, where her mother, appearing more frightened than Jane had ever seen her, and Mrs. Ellen were in tears. Jane felt like crying herself as she tried to console them. She'd never wanted to be queen, she said, and, thankfully, now it was all over. Before long, Mary would come to take her place. Tomorrow she'd write a letter, telling the new queen all that had happened and asking forgiveness for herself and all her family. She didn't say whether or not she'd ask forgiveness for John Dudley. Maybe she should stay on in the Tower so she could tell Mary everything: of how she'd been made to play a part and had played it as best she could. Then perhaps she'd be allowed to leave for either Sheen or Syon; she cared little which one. She only wanted to go home.

As Ridley reviled and castigated Mary Tudor's "popish ways" in London, some seventy miles away in Cambridge, the Vice-Chancellor of the university, the very Protestant Edwin Sandys, delivered his sermon likening the dead King Edward to Moses and John Dudley to Joshua. Sandys, for all his aversion to Catholicism, did not relish the obligation. He did not consider Dudley a Joshua and was concerned over continued reports of Mary's growing support. But Dudley was there to order his compliance and Mary was not. The sermon was delivered, and early the next morning the duke left for Bury on his way to Framlingham Castle. Sandys was glad to see him go.

At the time the Privy Council was in session at Baynards Castle in London, John Dudley, with soldiers "whose feet marched forward, but their minds marched backwards," pushed forward to Bury St. Edmunds. To the rear, soldiers slipped behind hedgerows and disappeared into deep gulleys until Dudley was forced to admit his forces were insufficient to assault Framlingham's strong walls. Cursing the deserters, he returned to Cambridge "with more sad thoughts than valiant soldiers about him" and once again wrote to London for help. He'd begun to realize what had happened. The Privy Council, he now recognized, had delayed in order to allow Mary Tudor time to muster her forces and give *him* enough rope to hang himself. Even now, however, had he possessed a sufficient number of the men and weapons he knew he should have insisted upon before leaving London so hurriedly, it might be possible to win the contest at Framlingham. Yet, if he did so, what would he find in London? A rebellious council, bent on his blood, with confiscation of his estates and perhaps imprisonment or worse for all his family, especially Guildford, who'd so wanted to be king. All around him there were rumors of added support for Mary. Only recently the Earl of Oxford had declared for her. At last the report he dreaded arrived: Mary Tudor had been proclaimed in London. Dudley knew then there was no hope; the Privy Council had deserted him. The best he could do now was to follow their example and trust in the princess' mercy. He spent that evening in his lodgings, where he "sat moodily in his chair, lost in thought, then starting up, would pace the room, muttering."

The following morning, July 20, accompanied by Vice-Chancellor Sandys, John Dudley went to the Cambridge Market Cross, intent upon retrieving whatever he could from the shambles of his ambitious attempt to make his daughter-in-law queen. There was little concern for the young woman left in the Tower; now his main concern was for himself. Walking with Sandys, his mind whirling with those dreaded eventualities the next few days might bring, he was shaking with nervousness. Standing in full sight of those assembled in the busy marketplace, clutching his beard, the voice that had so terrorized and dominated a dozen grown men for two years ringing out over the square, Dudley identified himself. He said he'd acted under orders from the Privy Council, which he now understood had changed its mind. Therefore he, John Dudley, now changed his mind also. Filling his cap with coins, he threw it up in the air, shouting "God Save Queen Mary!" before bursting into tears. Ashamed at this show of emotion, he joked with the Vice-Chancellor, telling him Mary was a merciful woman and would certainly pardon him. Sandys was more practical. "Though the queen grant you a pardon," he said, "the lords never will. You can hope nothing from those who now rule."

Dudley returned to his lodgings, and within the hour a university sergeant-at-arms, one Slegge, entered his chambers and arrested him in the name of Queen Mary, ordering the dispersal of all his troops, except several who were to remain to guard their former commander. The morning's events had drained Dudley, but the thought of being a prisoner of his own men caused him to protest violently. "You do me wrong to withdraw my liberty!" he shouted at Slegge. "See you not the council's letters, without exception, that all men should go whither they would?" All were well aware that the council, in giving such orders, had commanded everyone to return to his own home in order to disperse Dudley's forces. But, overawed by the hot-tempered duke, Slegge complied and Dudley went to Great St. Mary's to hear the morning's service.

Later, he returned to his lodgings to learn that one son, Robert Dudley, had been captured outside of Bury St. Edmunds. The duke was with his other sons, John and Ambrose, talking of escape, when the door was flung open. Dudley had been in the act of pulling on his boots, heartened by his sons' affirmation that escape to France was indeed possible if they hurried. Certainly once Mary was on the throne, she'd not wreak vengeance on Jane Dudley, who was an old friend, nor on her cousin Jane Grey! In time they might even persuade the queen to forgiveness. Dudley had about convinced himself it was all possible, and he could scarcely believe the Earl of Arundel, silhouetted in the door, had arrived so quickly. He was glad it was Arundel, who'd sworn him deep loyalty. If he gave no trouble, perhaps things would go easier for him and his sons; it might still be possible to escape. Flinging his boot—and dignity—aside, he fell at the earl's feet.

"Be good to me, for the love of God!" he cried, aware of his sons' surprised dismay. "Consider I have done nothing but by the consent of you and the council."

"My lord," Arundel's voice held contempt. "I am sent hither by the Queen's Majesty and in her name, I do arrest you."

"I obey, my lord," the duke replied. "Yet show me mercy, knowing the cause as it is."

"My lord," Arundel replied coldly, "you should have sought for mercy sooner. I must do according to my commandment." He motioned to his soldiers, and the Dudley men were thrust out the door toward waiting horses.

Some distance away, as Dr. Sandys took his morning walk in a meadow by the river, he heard the bells ringing. Returning to his home, he was surrounded by "a rabble of papists" who called him traitor and threatened him with a dagger. Dragged outside, the bewildered Vice-Chancellor saw John Dudley and his sons being put on horses. Then he, too, protesting his innocence, was roughly ordered to mount and follow them to London.

23

When the bonfires died out and the bells ceased to ring, as the celebratory debris was removed from the streets and London resumed some degree of normality, its citizens awoke to the fact that they had a new queen, one who was not evident, while the former queen was in their midst at the Tower. Mary's triumph was not total. The Spanish ambassadors, unaware of the Privy Council's manipulations, were frankly dubious of her success. As Simon Renard had previously written to the emperor, the English "were so treacherous, inconstant, false, malicious and easily roused, that little trust is to be placed in them." He could not comprehend why the councillors had reverted so quickly to Mary. Only days before, he'd been about to leave England, convinced Dudley was more concerned with French cooperation, that Spain's influence was gone. When an old woman, seemingly honest, warned him that Mary should really *beware* of the Privy Council's intention, that their proclamation was meant only to deceive her, lure her to London and "induce my Lady to lay down her arms and then treacherously . . . encompass her death," he was appalled at such an ultimate duplicity, giving it more credence than the misguided woman deserved. He wrote Mary to keep her forces intact and not relinquish the position that God had given her. Reading the letter from one from whom she'd had every right to expect more, Mary could readily acknowledge God's assistance. But, exultant at the victory won with no battle or blood spilt in her defense, she could scarcely not recognize how much her own courage had assisted a Divine intervention. Mary considered her victory a sign from God that the time of the nonbeliever, the opportunist and troublemaker who'd plundered the Church of ritual, creed and treasure was at an end. Now its restoration would be her shining goal.

In the meantime, councillors came in person to beg her pardon. The first was her old friend Katherine Parr's brother, William, the Marquis of Northampton. Next Sir Robert Dudley, sent to take her prisoner at Master Huddlestone's house and now captive himself, arrived to ask the new queen's indulgence. Mary ordered their arrest and when Bishop Nicholas Ridley, who'd reviled her from Paul's Cross the previous Sunday, "was going unto the queen to beg his pardon, he was taken at Ipswich and there put in ward." Later he was "despoiled of his dignities and sent back on a lame, halting horse to the Tower." By the time Mary felt it safe to quit Framlingham for her own Essex residence, the prisoners were already in the Tower. Once safely at Beaulieu near Newhall, Mary heard that Jane Dudley was en route to beg for her husband's life. Within five miles of her destination, the distraught duchess was apprehended and ordered back to London; the queen had refused to see her.

In spite of such early success, however, it was still difficult for Mary to accept the swift turn of events and she remained patiently cautious. Simon Renard wrote the emperor, "The lords were all quarrelling among themselves and accusing one another. She [Mary] could not learn the truth on any point of the late conspiracy. She did not know who were guilty or who were innocent and, amidst the distracted advices . . . she could not tell whether she could safely venture to London or not." Mary was prudent. She could wait, she told her advisers, to enter the City of London, for her forces were growing daily. There was no need to hurry. Those followers who had accompanied her from Framlingham and were now encamped about Beaulieu openly told her they did not trust those "who had been the ministers of the usurpation" and she should take plenty of time before leaving their protection.

In the meantime, there was an abject letter from the Privy Council. Calling themselves "faithful and obedient subjects," they informed the woman whom only days ago they'd labeled "obstinate" and a "bastard," that they were now "your Highness' true and humble subjects in our hearts." They'd always been so, they affirmed, "and seeing hitherto no possibility to utter our determination herein without great destruction and bloodshed, both of ourself and others till this time . . ." they beseeched her Majesty "to pardon and remit our former infirmities and most graciously to accept our meaning which has been ever to serve your Highness truly."

One of Mary's first visitors at Beaulieu was Simon Renard himself, and it was soon obvious to the Privy Council that the Spanish ambassador's influence on the queen was going to exceed their own. Mary told the lords that "she would not recognize any of the laws which had been passed in the minority"—those years when, in her brother's name, Edward Seymour and John Dudley had despoiled the treasury, furthered the destruction of England's religious houses and forever changed the Church her father had left to the realm. She would act boldly, not vindictively, she said, for she would see justice done.

Then, hearing that her sister had been ill since their brother's death, Mary wrote Elizabeth a solicitous letter, ironically aware that now *no one* could prohibit any communication between them. She advised the younger girl to proceed to Somerset House in London to await her imminent entry. She then ordered the English ambassadors abroad, who'd so easily accepted Jane Grey's queenship, to be brought home. As for Jane herself, she was to remain in the Tower until Mary could see her. Most of all, the queen said, as she waited those few days until all the culprits had been apprehended, she wanted to arrange for the funeral of her brother, who still remained—some three weeks after his death—unburied at Greenwich.

At Beaulieu, as Mary received City officials from London who brought with them a "benevolence" of £500 in half-sovereigns of gold in a purse of crimson velvet, in the name of the Lord Mayor, aldermen and the Commons, "which gift she highly and thankfully accepted and caused the presenters to have great cheer in her house," the man most responsible for her victory arrived in London. Only eleven days after he'd left, John Dudley, his three sons and brother, Lord Ambrose Dudley, the Earl of Huntingdon, Sir Thomas Palmer, Sir John Gates, and Dr. Sandys rode in procession toward the capital Dudley had ruled since the Protector's execution. The Earl of Arundel, with four hundred "light horsemen, bows and spearmen," accompanied the forlorn group. As it had rained the night before, causing the whole party to seek refuge in a barn, the duke's scarlet cloak was bedraggled and damp. The throngs along the way were great and the soldiers kept close to the duke as cries of "Traitor! Traitor! Death to the traitor!" assailed him from all sides. Nearing the City gates, where merchants were opening their shops, he was openly jeered as he attempted to straighten his wrinkled clothing and—as the mob increased and pressed close—to regard them with some semblance of his former hauteur. Near Bishopsgate, Arundel told the duke to remove his hat, a submissive gesture at which Dudley scowled, but he complied, carrying it in his hand.

At Shoreditch the streets were crowded with people who came so close the guards had to strike with their pikes to keep them from assaulting the captive. Everywhere the pent-up hatred of years exploded, and the loud invective, threatening gestures and the possibility of violence so close made the frightened horses rear. Now, arrogance disappearing, Dudley stared straight ahead. But Arundel did not hurry the procession. There was ample time for hostile observors to pick up stones by the wayside. When there were none, they settled for the accumulated gutter filth or rotten eggs brought for the purpose. "Death! Death to the traitor! Long live the true queen!" they cried, throwing whatever they could. At Temple Bar, fearing someone would pull the duke from his horse by means of the shabby cloak, Arundel ordered Dudley to remove it. The duke sat there, haggard, unkempt, near tears, looking for all the world like the common criminal who so often passed through just such a mob on his way to execution. It was, Simon Renard wrote the Spanish emperor, "a dreadful sight." At last, mercifully, the Tower came into view. As they entered the Bulwark Gate, the bareheaded, muddied and besmirched Dudley alighted from his horse, bowed to those in attendance and prepared to enter. Behind him, his eldest son, John, the Earl of Warwick, still mounted, covered his face with shaking hands. Then, laying aside the reins, he put his head on his horse's mane and wept.

By July 29, everyone involved in the usurpation was in custody, including Henry Grey, Jane's father, as well as Edward's tutor John Cheke, who'd written the infamous proclamation. At last Mary felt safe; now no one would attempt to take the crown from her. The past tumultuous weeks had given her some taste of what that queenship she'd never expected to gain might give her in affection, loyalty and trust. For the woman who'd been either deprived, misguided or betrayed for much of her adult life, it was the most satisfying feeling possible, one she meant to spend her life in preserving, while doing what she might for the people from whom it came.

From her lodgings, Jane saw John Dudley's ignominious entrance into the Tower. On the morning after her father had departed for Sheen, her mother had fled also and Jane was left alone with Mrs. Ellen, Mrs. Tylney, Lady Throckmorton and a page. On that morning she was told to vacate the royal apartments and, clutching some books, had walked with her companions across the Green to the Gentleman-Gaoler's lodgings, a comfortable building adjoining the Lieutenant's house. Master Nathaniel Partridge, the Gentleman-Gaoler, greeted Jane at the door, his wife waiting respectfully behind. After deep bows, they escorted Jane to her chambers, saying they wished to make her as comfortable as possible. Jane had not slept well the night before, as the revelry in the City had continued until dawn and she was beset with worry: What would happen to her now, with mother and father gone and forbidden any communication with poor Guildford, who'd been removed to the Beauchamp Tower? There was some relief in the sight of her ladies scurrying about, unpacking the chests with her own simple clothing, putting her books, writing materials and other possessions in place, eager to make the rooms as pleasantly comfortable as possible.

Walking across the Green, someone had pointed out—perhaps hoping to make the best of an awkward moment—that Jane was not a prisoner. No one had arrested her. Though she understood and appreciated their thoughtfulness, Jane was startled, for she'd never considered herself a prisoner. She knew she'd mightily offended the rightful Queen's Majesty and therefore must remain in custody until that queen pardoned her. Since she'd never sought the crown but had been forced to accept it, Jane was not unduly alarmed for herself. She was more worried about her father, he being especially such a creature of Dudley's that he'd willingly committed treason. Would Mary pardon Henry Grey? Jane wondered. The new queen was a relative and devoted to Frances Grey. Certainly, years of close friendship counted for something? Implicit in all that had happened, Jane understood that her detention was a guarantee, a safeguard almost, that no one else would use her claim to—or Edward's gift of—the throne of England.

In those first few days in her new lodgings, Jane's main concern was how soon her parents would explain to Mary their part in the disastrous drama Dudley had created, and how soon she herself would be allowed to go home.

And then John Dudley was returned to the Tower. The Gentleman-Gaoler's lodgings faced onto the Green, and at midday, as the sun came out after an all-night storm, Jane and her companions watched the entry of the man who'd made her queen and captive. Dudley walked swiftly as ever, up the little hill toward the Green, which was lined with those members of the Privy Council who only days before had sworn him complete loyalty. Behind the duke, his eldest son, still weeping openly, followed his father as a prisoner. Jane was stunned at the scene. Never before had she seen the duke when he was not in complete command or control. But there was little of either now. Behind Dudley, a triumphant Arundel greeted those other councillors who'd waited all morning to see their former master's complete humiliation.

The sight angered Jane. Every one of them had signed Edward's "Device." Every one of them had agreed she should have the crown and had knelt in submission before her. But there they were now, deriding Dudley, awaiting a new queen, to pay the same fawning subservience they'd rendered to *her* for nine days. While she'd always hated John Dudley, Jane recognized his guilt as no worse than that of those who now gloated at his imprisonment. Sickened, her sense of justice outraged, she turned away from the window.

And, for the first time, Jane was frightened. She was comfortable now, more comfortable than she'd been across the gardens in that other apartment with its chair of state and the robe she must wear when anyone entered. But how long might her safety last, when someone as powerful as John Dudley could enter looking cowed and disgraced, an object of scorn to those who'd participated in his crime, eager for whatever might come their way in his further degradation? For the first time, Jane realized how very much alone she was. There was no one—despite Master Partridge's concern for her comfort—to whom she could turn for advice or an answer to the simple question of when she might be allowed to go home. The Privy Council had deserted her and were now eager to retrieve what they could from the shambles of their own making. Within an hour of Dudley's arrival, she heard that Mary had sent Jane Dudley, her mother-in-law, away without seeing her. Would that happen when her own parents asked for forgiveness? What would Mary say to *her* when she arrived in London? Would she even *see* her?

As night approached and Jane prepared to sleep in her unfamiliar chamber, she hoped Mary's arrival in London would not be delayed, that soon they might talk together and she could explain just what had happened. Until that time, she knew now, prisoner or not, she would never be allowed to go home.

On Thursday, August 3, "the Queen's Majesty came from Wanstead and about six of the clock at night, she lighted at Mr. Bramston's house at Whitechapel and there changed her apparel. And then, accompanied with gentlemen, squires, knights and lords, with a great number of strangers, all in velvet coats riding before her, which were about seven hundred and forty and, with all the King's trumpeters, heralds and Sergeants-at-Arms, she proceeded to pass through the City."

It was Mary Tudor's first evidence of the loving welcome her subjects had waited patiently for days to bestow. At the sight of the small woman, freshly garbed in a rich gown of purple velvet made in the "French fashion," her kirtle of purple satin "all thick set with goldsmith's work and a great pearl, with her foresleeves of the same set with rich stones," a loud roar rose from the waiting throng which was taken up by those on down the broad streets Mary had yet to enter. On her hood, was a "rich billement of stones and great pearl," and her palfrey was "trapped with gold embroi-

dered to the horse's feet." The large entourage that followed Mary
—the men of Oxfordshire, Buckinghamshire and Northamp-
tonshire—were as lavishly dressed, in uniforms of red-and-white,
green-and-white and blue-and-white, "the whole number of horsemen esteemed at ten thousand." The queen's love of color, jewels
and pageantry was evident in the pleasure that had transformed
her rather plain features with a becoming radiance.

At Aldgate she dismissed her colorful escorts, "trusting her person wholly to the care of the civic guard"—a gesture saluted by
the onlookers with loud cheers. Then, the Lord Mayor kissed the
Sceptre and handed it to Mary, who looked at it almost wonderingly. "My Lord Mayor"—her deep voice carried to those nearby—
"I heartily thank you and all your brethren, the aldermen, of your
gentleness showed unto me, which shall not be forgotten."

As the procession wound down Aldgate toward St. Botolph's
Church, the Princess Elizabeth and her own entourage followed.
The queen's younger half-sister had not been seen in months and
a tremendous roar greeted her appearance. Elizabeth's pale features flushed with excitement as the dark eyes of her Boleyn mother
swept over the crowd that pressed close. The princess was now
sixteen and her figure was slim and shapely, her fresh complexion
enhanced by her father's reddish-auburn hair. Her former preference for plain clothing had obviously been put aside, for she was
as magnificently dressed as her sister. Elated, holding up a hand
with its long tapering fingers in response to the people's welcoming roar, Elizabeth followed as Mary, just ahead, turned toward
Aldgate, "which was richly hanged with arras and set with
streamers." The loud acclaim of those she passed mingled now with
that of the citizens, as for the first time in years they caught sight
of Henry VIII's two daughters together.

From Leadenhall Street down Gracechurch, up Fenchurch and
down Mark Lane, the people of London shouted themselves hoarse.
Caps were thrown in the air as the citizens poured out their love
and affection for the queen and princess, and as the guns boomed
in a deafening salvo at the Tower, the procession wound its way
toward the Bulwark Gate. Sir John Brydges, the Lieutenant of the
Tower, waited at the entry. Bowing low, he received Queen Mary,
her face still glowing from the first outward acclaim and approval
she'd experienced in more than twenty years. There, waiting on

the Green, knelt the Duke of Norfolk, whose castle had just sheltered her. There was her "good Nann," Anne Stanhope Seymour, widow of the dead Protector, and, standing pale and withdrawn, twenty-five-year-old Edward Courtenay, one of the Plantagenet sprigs, imprisoned when he was ten because of his lineage and his father's attainder. Courtenay was a great-nephew of Mary's old governess, the Countess of Salisbury, beheaded after the plot that had resulted in her young kinsman's imprisonment. What would the old countess have made of such a sight? Two prelates, Cuthbert Tunstall, the Bishop of Durham, and Stephen Gardiner, the Bishop of Winchester, also waited. Prisoners for religious and political reasons—some for years, some for months—they knelt now in homage. Mary, who considered each as much a martyr as she'd been for the preservation of her own faith and convictions, went among them tearfully as she "gently saluted them, bidding them rise up." As they did so, she "kissed them and said, 'These be *my* prisoners!' " Laughing and crying at the same time, the men bowed and the women embraced, as Mary, color high and eyes alight with happiness, went up into the royal apartments.

She did not look to the Gentleman-Gaoler's lodgings, where the girl who'd vacated those chambers watched out the window at the emotional display taking place on the Green. Never once did the queen glance about to see where her other prisoner—the most important one—might be. As Jane looked on, hoping Mary Tudor might turn and at least acknowledge her presence, she could only have felt the first stirring of an abject despair mingling with the fright that had been her constant companion for the last two weeks.

Jane's fear remained the following morning. All night, the sounds of tramping feet of the soldiers leaving the Tower precincts, had frustrated her attempt to sleep. The sudden appearance of torchlight cleaving through the shadows of her room, only one floor above ground level, startled her; normally the Tower was a quiet place at night. Now, as the guards changed duty, they were noisier than usual, reporting that the queen and her sister had retired to their private apartments and the councillors had left for their homes.

Jane pictured Mary and Elizabeth in the rooms she'd just vacated, where no trace of her nine days' queenship remained. Surely they must wonder where she was? How long would it be before they sent for her? Had someone repaired the canopy her father had torn from the chair of state? Outside, the faint sounds of revelry continued until near dawn. It was an unusually hot night and Jane's rooms were not situated to receive the river breezes. Uncomfortably warm, aware her old fever might be returning, she tried to hold back her mounting terror and tears.

She wondered where John Dudley was in the great fortress. All the other Dudley sons and brothers, Guildford included, she knew to be in the Beauchamp Tower, only steps away. Her father must be nearby also. Mrs. Ellen had learned that Jane's mother had seen the queen while she was still at Beaulieu and, after flinging herself at Mary's feet, had begged a pardon for Henry Grey. Amid a flood of tears, Frances Grey pitifully lamented her dire state, saying her husband was not likely to live, for—like Edward—he'd been slowly poisoned by John Dudley. When Mary asked for proof, the duchess said the apothecary employed by Dudley had just committed suicide.

Whether Mary believed Frances Grey or not, the affectionate ties of years were powerful, and, perhaps glad to have had a somewhat reasonable explanation, she pardoned the duke. However, he was still too ill to leave the Tower and "in such case as no man judgeth he can live." Jane wondered if her mother had explained what had happened and had pleaded for her daughter's freedom as well as her husband's. What would happen to them all if her father died?

Already, Jane had had one unpleasant example of just how greatly her life had changed. She was happy to be queen no longer and wished only to return to her position as the Duke of Suffolk's daughter, renowned for her learning and her passionate religious convictions. On the morning she left the royal apartments, William Paulet, the Marquis of Winchester, had severely chastised Jane. The old Lord High Treasurer, who less than two weeks previously had thrust the crown at her, insisting she try it on, was brusque and unpleasant when he asked a bewildered Jane to return the crown and the crown jewels. After she'd asked Lady Throckmorton to have the chests and coffers assembled and given to Winchester, one parcel was found missing. Checking the inventory with a shaking hand, Jane said she knew nothing of the parcel, what it contained or what it was worth. Sternly, Winchester said she'd have to make good the deficiency.

Jane was puzzled. How, she wondered, could one reimburse the royal treasury for something of unknown value? But she said nothing, merely asking Mrs. Ellen to bring her a collection of coins she'd prized. Several of these, going back to the Plantagenet Edward IV and Henry VIII's reigns, were rare and valuable in comparison with the deteriorated worth of those of young King Edward's reign, which she'd used for alms and pocket money. Scooping them up, Winchester did not stay to count, but Jane knew she'd given the old man over £500, all the money she had in the world. How would she pay her servants, the guards and stewards who depended upon whatever coins she could give them as part of their subsistence? No one in the Tower starved except on order, but small luxuries in food and drink must be purchased with a coin or two given to those who brought them. Still, Jane said nothing, relieved to have the unpleasant episode behind her.

But Winchester was not appeased. Instead he looked at her own personal possessions, and eventually much of her clothing, caps, furs, even some old garters and clocks, as well as her cherished portrait of Kate Brandon, were included in the royal confiscation. She was relieved when the old marquis showed little interest in her books and writing materials. One possession from her days as a bride at Durham House was a black velvet-bound Prayer Book given by Guildford Dudley to her father, in which her husband had written: "Your loving and obedient son wisheth unto your grace long life in this world, with as much joy and comfort as ever I wish to myself, and in the world to come, joy everlasting, Your most humble son to his death, G.Duddeley [*sic*]." The book, which had replaced Jane's own, was her most treasured possession although the words, written in safer times, now troubled her.

It did more. Winchester's insulting behavior, her parents' obvious abandonment, Mary and Elizabeth's negligence—all combined to make Jane at last understand how completely *alone* she was. And now, as one by one those who might have come to her defense and did not—even John Dudley, responsible for all her troubles and likely to lose his head—her poise and confidence wavered. On that Friday morning in early August, as she rose from a sleepless night, the thought of freedom—so taken for granted when one had it and so cherished when one did not—sent Jane scurrying for her writing materials. There was still no thought in her mind of longer imprisonment or a more dire punishment, such as others faced. Mary was a forgiving woman, she knew. But Mary did not know the whole story, and early that morning, Jane took paper and pen in hand to tell the queen the truth.

24

In the following days, events moved swiftly. The former prisoners Thomas Howard, the Duke of Norfolk, and Stephen Gardiner, the Bishop of Winchester, re-joined the Privy Council and were restored to their sees and estates. On August 5, "at seven o'clock at night, Edmund Bonner came home from the Marshalsea [prison] like a bishop, and all the people by the wayside bade him welcome home, both man and woman, and as many of the women as might kissed him. And so he came to Paul's and knelt on the steps and said his prayers and the people rang the bells for joy." Mary made the mother of the long-time prisoner Edward Courtenay a Lady of her Bedchamber and ordered certain of the Protector's confiscated estates returned to his wife, three sons and daughters, most of whom had lived on relatives' charity since their father's execution. While Mary was at Beaulieu, the emperor had written Renard, "For God's sake, let her [Mary] moderate her lust of vengeance that probably burns in her supporters who have received injuries from the other party. These persons will be likely to exhort her to be very severe, which might give the people cause for unrest and discontent." Charles's comment shows just how little he knew of his aunt Katherine of Aragon's daughter.

Mary's natural leniency was evident in her surprising treatment of the Privy Council. On the morning after her entrance into the Tower, those councillors who, less than two weeks previously, had labeled her bastard arrived en masse. As the Princess Elizabeth looked on, they knelt in homage, explaining that though they'd signed Edward's "Device," they'd done so out of fear of what action John Dudley might take against them and their families if they did not. They begged her understanding of their unusual position and, with several in tears, asked her general pardon. Mary remembered those loyal lords such as Derby, Sussex, Bath and Oxford, who'd raised the country for her. Others such as Pembroke, Winchester, Arundel and Shrewsbury were powerful, with enough tenantry to make a small army, and she knew her one hold over them was continuation of their perquisites and privileges. If she punished them all, they asked, who would run her government? She'd have no council at all.

Mary, with no illusions regarding their loyalty, said she'd think on the matter. Few were guilty in the first degree, yet so many were guilty in the second degree, it was impossible to punish everyone. To make exceptions would be unjust and against her principles. Mary did not say, as well she might, that their attitude toward her for years preceding Edward's death had shown little consideration, less trust and certainly no loyalty. Although the reinstated Bishop of Winchester, Stephen Gardiner, urged that she be merciless with those who'd toyed with the crown, Mary could not find it in herself to make severe reprisals; she was not naturally inclined to harshness. When he chided her—and she, in turn, agreed that possibly she was wrong in exercising such tolerance—she at least had the consolation of knowing her own feelings mirrored those of the Spanish emperor.

Instead of the strong penalties Gardiner urged, Mary ultimately leveled severe fines with some loss of rank or title, a withholding of royal favor or some similar reproof. Within a week she'd pardoned the Privy Council. The Dudley sons and brother were pardoned, though kept in custody, with only John Dudley, along with those close confederates Sir John Gates and Sir Thomas Palmer, condemned to die. Henry Grey, Jane's father, had already been pardoned but still lay ill in his Tower chamber.

The council, relieved to be assuming some semblance of normality, busied itself with indictments concerning the prisoners as it began to take the measure of the new queen. One cause for concern, everyone agreed, was the growing influence of Simon Renard on Mary Tudor. The lords never understood that Mary, suffering betrayal and abandonment much of her life, disgusted and disillusioned now by their own behavior, trusted her Spanish cousin and his ambassador more than she did her own countrymen.

No one, however, questioned the new queen's industriousness. Early each morning, Mary rose to walk with her ladies-in-waiting in the Tower gardens for exercise. A Venetian visitor has left a record of Mary at this time: "She is of very spare diet and never eats until one or two o'clock, although she rises at daybreak when, after saying her prayers and hearing Mass in private, she transacts business incessantly until after midnight when she retires to rest. For she chooses to give audience, not only to all the members of her Privy Council, and to hear from them every detail of public business, but also to all other persons who ask it of her." He was impressed with Mary's jewels, for the new queen had no reluctance in accepting the same coffers and chests that had so dismayed Jane Grey. Already, too, the Wardrobe was preparing bolts of cloth and trim, selecting furs and gloves and other habiliments for the new queen's use.

Mary was eager to forget, as best she could, those years of deprivation—the poor clothing and food, the snide remarks on her birth, the assaults on her religious integrity. Emotionally overcome by the display of love and support at her entrance into London, she found that even her poor health—the constant headaches and toothaches, the stress which caused palpitations of the heart, and the bouts of melancholy that had plagued her for years—appeared momentarily improved. One who viewed her as "unlike in every respect to her father or mother . . . with eyes so piercing as to inspire not only reverence but fear," could hardly be expected, on short acquaintance, to guess that those qualities were intended to inspire neither emotion, but were merely the result of Mary's being extremely nearsighted. While visiting Mary at Beaulieu, Simon Renard had written to Perrenot de Granvelle, the Bishop of Arras, "I know the queen—so easy to get around, so simple, so little experienced in worldly matters, and such a novice in all things.

. . . To tell you between ourselves, what I think of her—I believe that if God does not preserve her, she will be lost." As he watched the council go unpunished and saw Mary's mercy extended to others, Renard was certain his first estimate had been sound.

But, with little assistance from the emperor or his ambassador, God *had* preserved Mary Tudor. Soon, Renard's constant presence at court and his private visits to the queen were greatly resented by the Privy Council. Already, Mary had told them she intended to disregard the laws made in Edward's minority, that she envisioned a general return to the religious, social and political policies of the England her father had left to his son. The emperor had advised her to "take very great care, at the outset, not to be led by her zeal to be too hasty in reforming matters that may not seem to be proceeding in a right manner, but to show herself accommodating. Let her conform with the decisions of Parliament, while abstaining personally from any action contrary to religion or to her conscience, and hear Mass apart in her chamber, without making any demonstration."

The emperor's advice, fortunately, coincided with Mary's own desires. That it might not agree with what her Privy Council— now greatly decimated by the imprisonment of so many members—wished, was something the queen was prepared to deal with when the time came. Mary lamented the Englishman's deep-seated hatred of the pope, of any foreign control over his worship. She would have preferred the reestablishment of the Roman Church, but was realistic. She was willing to compromise for that hybrid brand of Catholicism known as Henrician—the Church as her father had left it—minus papal loyalty but with much of the old ritual and creed. More than Simon Renard, and other foreigners who considered Protestantism a momentary aberration of the English which would eventually disappear with a strong monarch directing a return to the old Catholicism, Mary knew there must be compromise. She said, therefore, that she would force no one to accept the Mass, but insisted that those preferring the "old religion" should have the opportunity and the freedom to worship in that manner. And those who'd been misled into accepting the Protector's and Dudley's later tampering with ritual, and now wished to return to their old faith, should not be hampered. Mary believed that the majority of the English people would accept her wishes, which she considered generous. Hadn't they just won a bloodless victory for her? Hadn't that great outpouring of sympathy, support and love demonstrated their preference?

To show her intent, Mary issued two proclamations. The first promised liberty of conscience, which, ". . . albeit her Grace's conscience is stayed in matters of religion, yet she meaneth graciously not to compel or constrain other men's consciences, otherwise, then God shall put into their hearts a persuasion of the truth. . . ." The second promised that the cause of religion would be settled by "common consent," by an Act of Parliament. In the meantime, said the queen, epithets such as *idolater* and *heretic* should cease.

In her effort at reconciliation, Mary was lauded by the thoughtful, if not by her own bishops and Privy Council. They recognized and accepted, as she did not, the actual strength and popularity the "new religion" had gained in the years she'd remained cloistered, apart from the court and those opportunists who'd used the Church so viciously. It was a strength that many, "gorged with the spoils of the church, suspected of heresy and at best indifferent to religion," meant to preserve at all costs. Thus, try as conscience and a merciful nature led her, from the day Mary Tudor entered the Tower she was doomed—by those councillors, ambassadors and churchmen who acted in her name, but not always in her best interests. The proclamations remained pieces of paper "which the violent zeal of the Privy Council" often thwarted by applying very little authority to their intent or else destroying their meaning altogether by overofficious decisions.

Jane Grey's letter was given to Mary the morning after it was written. It held no surprises for the queen, but she was impressed by Jane's sincerity and the clarity with which she described what had happened. Jane did not excuse her own sin in acquiescing to Dudley's scheme, but hoped under the circumstances, the queen would be forgiving.

> Although my fault be such [Jane wrote] that but for the goodness and clemency of the queen, I can have no hope of finding pardon . . . having given ear to those who at that time

appeared, not only to myself, but also to a great part of this realm to be wise, and now have manifested themselves to the contrary, not only to my and their great detriment, but with common disgrace and blame of all, they having with shameful boldness made so blameable and dishonorable an attempt to give to others that which was not theirs. . . .

Jane lamented her "want of prudence" in accepting the crown, "for which I deserve heavy punishment," she wrote, stating she still hoped for Mary's understanding, "it being known that the error imputed to me has not been altogether caused by myself." Jane then described being taken from Chelsea to Syon and her reception by the Privy Council, "who with unwonted caresses and pleasantness, did me such reverence as was not at all suitable to my state. . . ." She did not spare Edward, either, telling the queen:

He [Dudley] then said that his Majesty had well weighed an Act of Parliament . . . that whoever should acknowledge the most serene Mary . . . or the Lady Elizabeth and receive them as the true heirs of the crown of England should be had all for traitors. . . . Wherefore, in no manner did he wish that they should be heirs of him and of that crown, he being able in every way to disinherit them. And therefore, before his death, he gave order to the council, that for the honor they owed to him . . . they should obey his last will.

Jane then described the homage paid by the councillors which had overcome her to the point where she'd fainted. She described her visit from old Winchester and her refusal to accept the crown, her reluctance to make her husband a king and the great displeasure this had caused her mother-in-law. Then she ended her letter:

As to the rest, for my part, I know not what the council had determined to do, but I know for certain that twice during this time, poison was given to me, first in the house of the Duchess of Northumberland and afterwards here in the Tower. . . . All these things I have wished to say for the witness of my innocence and the disburdening of my conscience.

Jane's letter confirmed everything Mary had suspected. Along with her refusal to take any stringent measures regarding religion, to exact any strong penalties against the majority of the plot offenders, she now insisted that Jane be left alone and unpunished, to remain in the Tower until those other prisoners were brought to trial. Mary recognized the pawn Jane had been, the part she'd been made to play. After a second reading of the poignant letter, the queen even convinced herself that her cousin would be safer in the Tower than in her own home with an absent, deathly-ill father and an emotionally overwrought mother. The council, relieved with their pardons and busy with indictments regarding their unfortunate imprisoned colleagues, did not press the matter of Jane Grey too closely. Under confinement as she was, she would be little problem.

But Simon Renard was appalled at Mary's easy acceptance of Jane's explanation. Even her continued imprisonment did not satisfy the Spaniard's desire to see the queen make an example of both Jane and Guildford. "An innocent girl should not suffer for someone else's crime," was the queen's response to all Renard's entreaties. "I will not consent that she should die." Mary said that "three days before they went to fetch her from Syon House to the Tower . . . she knew nothing of it, nor was she ever a party, nor did she ever give her consent to the duke's intrigues and plots. My conscience will not permit me to have her put to death." Subtly, Renard "set before her" the example of Maximus and his son Victor, both of whom had been executed by the Emperor Theodosius. Maximus died because he had usurped the crown; Victor because, "as the intended heir of his father," he would be dangerous if left alive. Mary was not impressed, saying Jane was not even legally wed to Guildford Dudley. Since Jane had been contracted to another—the Protector's son, Lord Hertford—and would likely have married him if his father had not been executed, her marriage to Guildford Dudley was not valid. "There could have been none," said the queen.

The religious toleration suggested by the emperor, and Mary's own eagerness to avoid any further dissension, were evident as she arranged for her brother's burial. While other matters might assume greater importance in the council's mind, Mary told Renard "she could not have her brother committed to the ground like a dog." She wanted a splendid funeral and felt it would be diplomatic and in keeping with her proclamations—and the Spanish emperor's advice of toleration—if Edward's own religious beliefs were respected. Thus, on August 8, the royal barge brought the king's body in its sealed coffin from Greenwich to Westminster Abbey. Those spectators who had not seen the boy alive in early spring, when he'd traveled to the old riverside palace, now lined the Thames to watch the barge, which proceeded slowly upriver so as many as possible might see. When the coffin was at last ashore and taking the long route to the abbey, with drums beating a dirge echoed by the horses' hooves and the slow shuffling feet of the black-clad mourners following in procession, a sobbing populace watched Edward Tudor's last journey toward a final rest. Headed by the Dean of Westminster, a choir sang psalms. Behind them, monks of the Greyfriars and heralds with their colorful banners of the king's Tudor, Seymour and Plantagenet ancestors followed. At last, behind Edward's Gentlemen-of-the-Household, rode a herald holding the young king's plumed helmet in one hand, his sword laid across his knees. Then, drawn by four black-caparisoned horses, came the coffin, borne in a wagon covered in cloth of gold. Atop was the effigy of the pale-skinned young monarch, lying in a rich cloak of white satin, with a crown placed atop the painted blond hair.

In the abbey, a "great number of children in surplices" gathered to attend the ceremony, which, as De Noailles said, was "a very shabby one, badly attended, without any lights burning, and no official invitations sent to the ambassadors." The French ambassador could not be expected to know that burning lights, being considered too "popish," were not part of a Protestant service. Since few foreign ambassadors were sympathetic to, or even knowledgeable of, the ritual of the reformed religion's burial service—for Edward was the first English king to be buried according to its rites—none had been invited. Thomas Cranmer, recently indicted by the queen for his part in Jane Grey's accession, had been left at liberty to conduct the dignified service, reading from his Book of Common Prayer. As the coffin was lowered into the end of the tomb of Edward's grandfather Henry VII, the standardbearers held their banners low and wands of office were broken by weeping officials and cast atop the coffin.

At the same time that the ceremonies of Edward's faith were being carried out in the old abbey, Queen Mary and four hundred mourners gathered in St. Peter's-ad-Vincula, the Tower church, to attend a solemn Requiem Mass for her dead brother, with Stephen Gardiner officiating. The service echoed Mary's desire to say farewell to Edward in her own way as well as praying for the repose of the soul she felt had been so misled by others. But at least one observer misunderstood, noting its futility by saying, "This was not in conformity with the laws of the Roman Church, since the prince died in schism and heresy. . . ."

Across the Green in the Gentleman-Gaoler's lodgings, Jane Grey, with Mrs. Ellen and Lady Throckmorton, watched from the windows as the mourners followed the retinue of priests resplendent in heavy embroidered copes, their golden miters gleaming in the sunlight. Everything she'd despised and excoriated for years was evident in the long, mournful procession, symbolized by the black-clad queen with the great golden cross at her waist.

Jane looked for Elizabeth, but the princess was absent. Had she attended the other ceremony for Edward at the abbey? Despite her illness and her confinement, Jane was flooded with resentment at the ceremony honoring a boy who had, with all the vigor and enthusiasm possible in one so young, cast aside, despised, even persecuted everything Mary represented. Had Elizabeth found the courage to confront Mary with her preference and evade the service?

The thought of her two cousins, each free within the confines of their rank, brought tears again. To the best of her ability Jane had tried to be brave. It was almost a month to the day since she'd entered the Tower, when many of those who now passed with doleful expressions to Edward's funeral service had knelt in homage to her. Mary had not replied to her letter nor sent any word of comfort. Jane wondered if the queen had even read those words she'd written so thoughtfully and carefully. Master Partridge had said her father, now recovered, had returned to Sheen and that most of the council and several of the Dudleys had been pardoned. But there'd been no pardon for the one who'd never wanted the crown. At times, it seemed to Jane as though everyone had forgotten her.

She remembered that summons from Chelsea to Syon, the pleasant ride on the river with Lady Sidney. What had happened to that other life? Did her tutor miss her as much as she missed him? What had happened to her sisters? And what had those treasured Swiss correspondents thought when they learned the girl they'd written to as tutor, fellow scholar and friend had become queen? And then, suddenly, was not a queen after all—just a prisoner awaiting judgment at the hands of a woman related by blood but practicing that religious faith they'd all scorned and stormed against for years. Often, in her younger years at Bradgate or Dorset Place, Jane had been terrified when cornered or persecuted by her parents' overwhelming and inexplicable criticism and physical violence. But then, through her own cleverness, tolerance and adaptability, she'd made a life for herself and survived.

But now, as the last of the procession entered the church and the beginning of the hateful service could be heard wafting over the Green through the warm August air, Jane recognized with tears and fear the irony of her predicament: that through a situation *not* of her making, she was now more of a prisoner than ever before. And in a situation—she was beginning to suspect—in which her very survival might be in question.

When John Dudley entered the Beauchamp Tower after his uncomfortably wet night in a barn and the fearful, sickening humiliation of being brought a prisoner to London, he'd collapsed, as ill in body as in spirit. During the next few days, the ruin of those plans for which he'd had such high and confident hopes, the memory of his power and the wealth he'd forfeited, plunged him into a grim despair compounded by fever and insomnia. There was no communication with his sons, and no councillor came to visit. The solitude, for one so used to tyrannizing a group of lords or an army of soldiers, was debilitating and there was plenty of time to ponder his position—how he had endangered not only his own life but those of his sons as well. Guildford, in particular, would be the most vulnerable. The thought of his sons' welfare dominated those days of bedridden discomfort, and at last, his fever and exhaustion abating somewhat, he set about to prepare a defense for which his practical nature told him there was little hope. But the effort was much in keeping with the indomitable nature and will of the man who'd almost stolen a crown.

There were many factors to consider. The queen, he knew, hated him, for he'd been no partisan of her mother in those days when the exiled Katherine of Aragon had needed all her friends. And only recently, in Jane's proclamation, he'd deemed Mary a "bastard." Ever since the Protector's death, he'd harassed the princess for celebrating the Mass, encouraging Edward to do the same instead of "winking" at the service, as the Protector had done. Aside from the queen, his chief judge at the trial would be the Duke of Norfolk. Despite the pleas of many to free the old noble, now ill and in his eighties, Dudley had kept him in prison since the death of Henry VIII. Yet in the end, he recognized his chief persecutors would be those lords—Arundel, Huntingdon, Shrewsbury and Pembroke—whom he'd oppressed for two years by the sheer bullying strength of his personality and ambition.

In the end, Dudley's ploy was to gain time. He did so by asking for spiritual counseling, a plea he felt would be well received by the queen, since he meant it to be in the Catholic faith of his youth, the same as the queen's own, and not in the "new religion" which he'd encouraged for years. The duke also formally requested that he be judged by his peers, in this case those very councillors whom he'd ruled so relentlessly. Dudley recognized the inherent danger, but hoped it might be somewhat balanced by sympathy for the man they'd aided and abetted in his crime.

But the Privy Council quickly recognized the maneuver. From the moment on August 18 when John Dudley—accompanied by his eldest son, the Earl of Warwick, and William Parr, the Marquis of Northampton—entered vast old Westminster Hall, hung with new banners and freshly carpeted for the occasion, the scene was reminiscent of the Protector's trial. And of another, some forty-four years to the day, when Dudley's father had been sentenced to die by the father of the present Duke of Norfolk, who, as Earl Marshal of England, now presided. As at Edward Seymour's trial, the same axe was carried before the accused, its edge facing outward, since no verdict had as yet been given. But at the Protector's trial, *he*, Dudley, had sat where old Norfolk now sat and Seymour had stood before *him*. Those same lords of the council

who'd judged Seymour were in their places, surrounded by lawyers in their scarlet and white hoods, by officials of the City of
London and the court.

Dudley bowed to his judges, listening carefully to the deposition which described his crime. Asked if he acknowledged its content, he bowed once more, saying he did. Then, "with great
reverence towards the judges [he] protested his faith and allegiance
to the queen, whom he confessed grievously to have offended."
Dudley said he had no defense of that fact but, before the trial
proceeded further, he would like to clarify two points: "First,
whether a man doing any act by authority of the prince's council
and by warrant of the Great Seal of England . . . might be charged
with treason . . . ? Secondly, whether any such persons as were
equally culpable in that crime, and those by whose letters and
commandments he was directed in all his doings, might be his
judges, or pass upon his trial as his peers?"

There was a moment of heavy silence in the Hall as the impact
of the duke's words echoed among the spectators. Dudley was implying, if not stating outright, that he'd acted with the authority
of the "prince's council," the very men sitting in judgment upon
him, and that they, being "equally culpable," were as guilty as he.

But old Norfolk would have none of it. Quickly he replied, saying the Great Seal the prisoner referred to "was not the seal of the
lawful queen of the realm, nor passed by authority, but the seal
of an usurper, and therefore, could be no warrant to him." Thus,
in a few words, the old duke deliberately misinterpreted the seal
Dudley claimed—that of Edward VI— implying it was the seal of
Jane Grey, "an usurper," and thus had no validity. As for the
prisoner's second question, asking if those equally guilty could sit
in judgment on him, Norfolk was firm, saying, "As long as no attainder were of record against them, they were nevertheless persons able in law to pass upon any trial and not to be challenged
therefore."

John Dudley had never been wont to fool himself and he did
not now; he knew he was beaten. As he listened to the verdict—
death by hanging, drawing and quartering—the axe was turned in
his direction.

In a firm voice he asked that the council be "humble suitors to
the queen's majesty" for three requests. First, that "I might have

that death [beheading] which noblemen have had in times past and not the other; secondly, that her Majesty will be gracious to my children, which may hereafter do her Grace good service, considering that they went by my commandment . . . and not of their own free wills and thirdly, that I may have appointed to me some learned man for the instruction and quieting of my conscience." Dudley then requested that the queen send two councillors "to whom I will declare such matters as shall be expedient for her and the commonwealth." As he was led from the Hall, he heard his son Warwick refusing to admit guilt, saying "he had followed his father and would share his father's fortunes." The Marquis of Northampton, not as brave, admitted his guilt and tearfully insisted he'd signed the "Device" at Dudley's strong insistence and therefore begged for mercy and the council's understanding.

The following day, the "learned man" requested by Dudley for his spiritual enlightenment visited him in the Beauchamp Tower. The council's selection, ironically deliberate or otherwise, was Stephen Gardiner, the Bishop of Winchester, imprisoned by Dudley and freed by Mary less than two weeks previously. Dudley was frank with the bishop, saying he "would do penance all the days of my life, if it were but in a mouse-hole . . . is there no hope of mercy?" If he could live a little longer, repentant for his crime, he said, he would die a more peaceful man.

Gardiner replied that Dudley's offense was so great, he must prepare for death. He advised the duke "especially to see that you stand well with God in matters of conscience and religion." Weeping now, all hope gone, Dudley replied, "I can be of no other faith but yours. I never was of any other, indeed." He said he'd furthered the cause of Protestantism "only out of ambition, for which I pray God to forgive me—and I promise I will declare that at my death."

The opportunity came the following day, when the duke made a public renunciation of the "new religion" in the Tower church, on which occasion the other prisoners, Northampton, Warwick, Sir John Gates and Sir Thomas Palmer, were also reconciled to the Roman faith. Kneeling during the Mass, they said the *Confiteor* with Stephen Gardiner. Then, embracing one another, they asked forgiveness, confessing "they were the same men in the faith . . . that they all would die in the Catholic faith."

Some forty spectators—councillors, citizens of London and court officials, including two sons of the dead Protector—had crowded into the Tower church to witness the scene. Exhibiting a touch of his old mastery, the duke addressed them. "My masters, I let you all to understand that I do most faithfully believe this is the very right and true way, out of the which true religion you and I have been seduced this sixteen years past, by the false and erroneous preaching of the new preachers, the which is the only cause of the great plague [Protestantism] and vengeance which hath lit upon the whole realm of England, and now likewise worthily fallen upon me and others here present for our unfaithfulness. And I do believe the Holy Sacrament here most assuredly to be our Saviour and Redeemer, Jesus Christ; and this I pray you all to testify and pray for me."

Later, after being conducted back to the Beauchamp Tower, Dudley told the elderly Sir Anthony Browne that "he certainly thought best of the old religion, but seeing a new one begun, run dog, run devil, he would go forward." In some way, Browne thought, the dictatorial duke appeared to have found a measure of peace.

When Jane was told of Dudley's conversion—which, so someone said, the French ambassador De Noailles had wryly described as a "miraculous recognition"—she waited again at the window, her one glimpse of the outside world, and watched her father-in-law return from the despised Mass. Between tears of anger mixed with laughter at the duke's change of heart, she called him "evil and false," using religion as a ploy for pardon. "I pray God," she said, "I nor no friend of mine die so."

But Dudley still had hope. When he heard he should prepare himself to receive "the deadly stroke" the following day, he wrote to the Earl of Arundel, "Alas, my good lord, is my crime so heinous as no redemption but my blood can wash away the spots thereof? An old proverb there is, and that most true, that a living dog is better than a dead lion." The duke said he would be pleased if the queen gave him only the life of a dog, for then "I might but live and kiss her feet and spend both life and all in her honorable services, as I have the best part already, under her worthy brother and most glorious father."

Arundel, with some semblance of mercy for his accused accomplice rising, spoke to Mary Tudor. The queen wavered in her implacable hatred for Dudley, especially when she heard from Gardiner's own lips that his conversion seemed sincere. But, relentlessly, Simon Renard hammered home to her that already she'd carried mercy beyond the point of reality. Was the prime mover of the whole plot that had almost stolen her crown now to be reprieved also? What would the emperor think? Mary's solution was to order a three-day stay of execution, with a priest to be sent to John Dudley so he might work for his soul's salvation.

Very close to the Beauchamp Tower, where her husband and father-in-law were prisoners, Lady Jane Grey still spent each day in the Gentleman-Gaoler's lodgings. The handsome two-story building faced the Green and the Tower entrance, and from its windows she could see the Lieutenant's residence as well as the visitors who entered and departed. Often, as she sat by the window, it became something of a game to guess—from who went in or came out—what was taking place within the Tower or even in the City itself. Soon after Edward's funeral Mary had gone to Richmond Palace, and many courtiers and Privy Councillors had gone with her. But there still remained visitors: Clergymen or officials, even a platoon of soldiers marching by, all provided some interest for the lonely Jane.

Within her quarters, there'd been little change. When it was known the queen intended to keep Jane confined for some time—for her own safety, it was said—Lady Throckmorton insisted she must return to her home. Master Partridge and his wife, Mrs. Ellen, Mrs. Tylney, and two servants did their best to keep Jane comfortable, providing companionship as well as service.

Each day began with prayers and a light meal. During Jane's detainment, the queen had allowed her custodian ninety-three shillings for food, candles and coal, with one pound for each of her servants. She was free to exercise in the Tower garden or along the Green, or down the little hill which sloped to the royal apartments. But Jane had never been as comfortable outdoors as inside. She had never enjoyed hunting and the sunlight, which freckled her fair skin and earned her more "nips and bobs" than she thought it worth. Walking filled her need for exercise, but she was always relieved to be back in her chamber, away from the guards' curious stares or the sight of a court official who, though he'd knelt before her once, now might bow only slightly, if at all, as he hurried on.

Before Lady Throckmorton left, Jane had sent her to the booksellers in Paul's Churchyard for new books and a fresh supply of writing materials; she had plenty of time for study. There were no visitors, which did not surprise her. Who would come to see a deposed and imprisoned queen? After a week with no response from Mary to her letter, Jane realized she was not likely to see her cousin until she was pardoned. There was no word from either parent. It would not be like them to pay attention to her in the Tower when they'd paid so little at home. By now, undoubtedly, they'd convinced themselves that she was the source of all their trouble.

Jane was saddened when she heard that John Aylmer, her beloved "Mr. Elmer"—aptly assessing he'd be unpopular and not at ease in the England of Mary Tudor's religion—had gone abroad, and so quickly there'd been no time for a proper farewell, not even a letter. But doubtless he was now with those Swiss friends who'd so brightened her younger days with their advice, lessons and compliments. Her reaction to another defection, however, was very different. Jane was appalled when she learned that Dr. Harding, the old Rector of Bradgate who'd been her teacher in those earlier years before John Aylmer and had later assisted in lessons with all three Grey girls, had converted to Catholicism.

At first she was unbelieving. It seemed impossible that the doughty old gentleman who'd thundered from the Bradgate chapel and—when he was present with Aylmer and Haddon—had scorned those Christmas revels at Dorset Place and at court as "pagan," could so dishonor his earlier belief. But it was so, and once proven, it provided Jane an outlet for all the emotion she'd repressed since she'd learned Edward had named her his heir. Almost sick with rage, she wrote Harding, "I cannot but marvel at thee and lament thy case, who seemed sometime to be the lively member of Christ, but now the deformed imp of the Devil; sometime the beautiful temple of God, but now the stinking and filthy kennel of Satan; sometime the unspotted spouse of Christ, but now the unshamefaced paramour of anti-Christ. . . . When I consider these things, I cannot but . . . cry out upon thee, thou white-livered milksop . . . sink of sin . . . child of perdition . . . seed of Satan." So intense was Jane's anger, she could not stop. Her words to Har-

ding contained all the disappointment and fear—an almost hysterical madness—which was the result as much of her own unjust
and difficult position as of the deep hurt she felt at the betrayal of
one upon whose integrity she'd have staked her life. Asking if he
would not tremble and quake contemplating St. Paul's predictions
of eternal punishment, Jane lamented, "Well, if these terrible and
thundering threatenings cannot stir thee to cleave unto Christ . . .
let the sweet consolation and promises of the Scriptures encourage
thee to take faster hold. . . ." She warned the old doctor, "Throw
yourself down with the fear of His threatened vengeance, for this
so great and heinous an offence. . . . Be not ashamed to turn again
. . . acknowledging that you have sinned against heaven and earth.
. . . Be not abashed to weep bitterly with Peter . . . to wash away,
out of the sight of God, the filth and mire of your offensive fall."
Her anger spent, Jane concluded with a simple rhyme:

> "Be constant, be constant: fear not any pain,
> Christ hath redeemed thee, and Heaven is thy gain."

The conversions of two men so close to her, tutor and father-in-
law, had stunned Jane more than she realized, for she could not
understand the reason for either. If Harding had felt Mary's accession presaged a return to the Roman Church, he could have gone
abroad, as had Aylmer. If Dudley had thought his recantation
would save his life, it had failed; there had been no reprieve from
Richmond Palace. It was well known that Simon Renard had insisted the duke and his two accomplices, Gates and Palmer, suffer
the full consequences. After that, Jane felt certain, she and Guildford would be set free. But in the meantime, one must guard one's
holy beliefs with one's life. What would it be worth if bought with
the lifeblood of one's own conscience?

John Dudley's plea to die the death of a nobleman—by beheading
instead of hanging, being cut down and disemboweled—had been
granted by the queen for him and his fellow prisoners, Sir John
Gates and Sir Thomas Palmer. The three met for the last time on
the morning of August 23 when they attended Mass at St. Peter's-
ad-Vincula before walking to the execution site on Tower Hill.
Previous to that, the duke had bade his sons an emotional fare-

well. The queen had respited the death sentence on the Earl of Warwick, the eldest, who'd returned to Catholicism along with his father. Dudley had maintained his dignity and control until he came to Guildford, his youngest. Then, composure gone, he'd taken the boy in his arms and "pressed him again and again to his breast, sighing and weeping . . . as he kissed him for the last time."

There had been less emotional farewells on the way from the Tower church, where the conspirators had heard their last Mass. Meeting Gates, Dudley said, "Sir John, God have mercy on us, for this day shall end both our lives, and I pray you forgive me whatsoever I have offended, and I forgive you with all my heart, although you and your counsel was a great occasion thereof. . . ."

Gates, as Captain of the King's Guard, had been one of Dudley's most avid supporters. But now, at this last moment, he refused to accept the duke's implied criticism and accusation. "Well, my lord," he replied, "I forgive you as I would be forgiven. Yet, it was you and your authority that was the only original cause of all. But the Lord pardon you and I pray you forgive me." Bowing to each other in one last gesture of courtesy, they walked with Sir Thomas Palmer out the Bulwark Gate and up Tower Hill, escorted by Sir John Brydges, the Tower's Lieutenant. On the way, they passed two of the Protector's sons who'd been told the previous day that Palmer's damaging testimony, crucial to their father's conviction, had been false.

It was near ten in the morning, and a crowd of more than ten thousand, including "the men of Hoxton, Shoreditch, Bow, Limehouse and St. Katherine's," jostled the eager spectators as they watched Brydges hand the three prisoners over to the Sheriffs of London and the guard. Word of Dudley's spectacular conversion had quickly spread throughout the City. Those who'd deeply hated the man responsible for the execution of "the good duke," the Protector, and for his arrogant control over Edward, viewed the surprising gesture with contempt. Dudley's support of the "new religion," his reputation, along with Grey's, as the "thunderbolt and terror of the Papists" had been in their eyes his one redeeming characteristic, and in his recantation he demeaned not only his falseness but their own strong loyalty as well.

Now, walking up the hill with Nicholas Heath, the Bishop of Worcester, who carried a crucifix in front of him, the three condemned men were assailed on all sides by the shouting throng. One angry woman broke through the guards' barricade. Thrusting a red-spotted handkerchief, a souvenir of the Protector's execution, at Dudley, she shouted, "Behold the blood which thou did cause to be unjustly shed now begins to revenge itself on thee!" Visibly shaken by the incident and the crowd's derisive jeers and shouts, Dudley and his companions kept on walking as the guards dragged the woman away.

At the scaffold site, Dudley agilely climbed the platform, which had been covered with sawdust. He turned to view the crowd which, as at the Protector's execution, stretched along the Tower ramparts and moat, beyond All Hallows' Church, out into the fields beyond Tower Hill. The sea of faces below the railings, some bearing satisfaction, some hatred, went unnoticed. Even the sight of court officials, the presence of the Protector's two sons and the constant angry cries for revenge did not disturb him; John Dudley was now clearly beyond caring.

Removing his surcoat, which he gave to the executioner—who was "lame of a leg and wore a white apron like a butcher"—Dudley, in a handsome gown of gray damask, walked to the railing and spoke. Confessing himself previously an "evil liver," he said now he was "worthy to die." He had been, he confessed, "a great helper" in that religion which was false, and therefore God had punished everyone, with the loss of Henry VIII and Edward VI, with rebellions, the sweating sickness, and "yet we would not turn." He required "all that were present to remember the old learnings, thanking God that he would vouchsafe him now to be called a Christian, for this past sixteen years he had been none." Dudley urged that everyone put aside covetousness, "for that was a great part of his destruction." He insisted his conversion was sincere and, turning to Bishop Heath, said, "I trust my lord, the bishop here, will bear me witness hereof," to which Heath replied, "Yea."

"I could, good people, rehearse much more," Dudley said, "but you know I have another thing to do, whereunto I must prepare me, for the time draweth away." He asked Mary's pardon, saying, "I have deserved a thousand deaths." As the lame executioner approached, as custom demanded, to ask forgiveness, Dudley said, "I forgive thee with all my heart. Do your part without fear. . . ."

He then knelt down, reciting the *De Profundis*, making the sign of the cross in sawdust.

As he prayed, the bandage which he'd tied about his eyes appeared to slip. Dudley now "rose again upon his knees and surely figured to himself the terrible dreadfulness of death." As the bandage was secured more tightly, he said nothing, but "in the act of laying himself out . . . he smote his hands together, as who would say, 'this must be,' and cast himself upon the beam [the block] where the executioner struck off his head at a blow."

Immediately, as at the Protector's execution, "you might see little children gathering up the blood which had fallen through the slits in the scaffold on which he had been beheaded," wrote a French priest later that night. "In this country, the head is put upon a pole and all goods confiscated to the queen."

But as the priest was doing so, John Cock, Lancaster Herald, a friend of John Dudley's, was on his way to Richmond, where he begged the queen if he might have Dudley's head.

"In God's name," Mary replied, "take the whole body and give your lord proper burial." Quickly, the herald returned to London to secure John Dudley's mutilated corpse. He buried it in the only remaining place in the Tower church of St. Peter's-ad-Vincula, just below the remains of Queen Anne Boleyn and Queen Katherine Howard and beside the body of his former enemy Edward Seymour, the Protector.

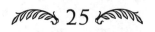

25

From her window in the Gentleman-Gaoler's lodgings, Jane had watched Dudley, Gates and Palmer say their farewells at the church after hearing their final Mass. She'd heard the shouting of the mob on Tower Hill as the men spoke their farewells and later seen the carts which carried the bodies and scaffolding back into the Tower precincts. The sight only increased her anxiety about Guildford. Though his older brothers—Robert had been the one delegated to take Mary Tudor prisoner—and one uncle had all been spared, there'd been no word on Guildford. While Jane had no doubt of her own eventual pardon—for the queen knew she'd never desired the crown for herself—would the same compassion be shown to Guildford, who'd been only too eager to follow his father's bidding, eager to share the crown with Mary's usurper? Would her own father, Henry Grey, plead for his son-in-law's life? Once Grey had recovered from his illness, he'd returned to Sheen. There'd been no word before he left, which had cost Jane tears of disappointment.

Jane wondered what Guildford and his brothers thought of the great tragedy their father's ambition had wrought. She knew how much her husband had loved his father and was frustrated in not being able to give some solace to the heartbroken boy. For herself, it would be the ultimate hypocrisy to offer any but the most perfunctory prayer for John Dudley's soul. Young and inexperienced as she was, Jane understood how great was the duke's sin, in using his genius for command, his undoubted courage and immense political skill in the ruthlessly ambitious manner which, instead of honoring his family, had doomed them all.

Jane's lonely hours of isolation had given her time to ponder her own position as well as Guildford's. No stranger to solitude, she nevertheless found the days long. In that previous life which now seemed so far away, she'd been free to seek whatever companionship or diversion she chose. Now, even that simple privilege was no longer hers. She could still study or read for pleasure from her handsome new books. She could play the lute, embroider or walk outside when she chose. But worry over how long Mary might keep her confined, as well as concern over what her future would be and whether her parents would blame her for all that had happened, revolved continually in her mind. Would Frances and Henry Grey, perhaps glad to be rid of the girl who'd caused so much trouble, send her to live with the Dudleys?

Master Nathaniel Partridge, into whose care Jane had been given, felt sorry for his young charge. He thought Jane, still almost a child, immensely exploited not only by John Dudley but by those influential men he saw in and about the Tower every day. There was little he could do to help except treat her with the respect due her rank and make certain she did not want for anything it was in his power to provide. Once she'd learned to trust him, Partridge found Jane pleasant, affable and easy to talk to. Though obviously much more intelligent than either he or his wife, the girl did not flaunt her scholarly ways to demean him as some might have done.

One way in which he'd tried to make the days brighter for Jane, as well as for his wife and himself, was to allow her to dine below in his quarters, a privilege Jane appreciated. On Tuesday, six days after John Dudley's execution, she appeared for the evening meal with Mrs. Jacob, her tiring woman. Master Partridge, unaware Jane was to be at table that evening, soon arrived with a guest. He apologized for the intrusion when he saw his charge at the table's end that was reserved for guests of quality. An observer, perhaps somewhat overawed at dining with someone who, a little over a month ago, had been Queen of England, has left a record of the conversation that commenced when Jane, eager to make her host and his guest feel at ease, "commanded Partridge and me to put on our caps," which they'd removed in deference to her sex and rank.

Jane then held out her glass and bade the guest "hearty welcome." She suggested a toast to Queen Mary, saying, "The queen's Majesty is a merciful princess. I beseech God she may long continue and send His bountiful grace upon her."

As the meal proceeded, the talk turned to the surprising conversion of John Dudley and the past week's controversy in the City. On August 12 all church sermons had been preached according to Protestant dogma and ritual. On August 19, to the consternation of many Londoners, the Mass was once more celebrated in St. Paul's. Though there was little doubt but what the larger part of England staunchly supported the "old religion," the citizens of a more sophisticated London were strongly Protestant. Already there'd been several scuffles and near-riots as the Mass was again introduced into their churches. When one aged priest, anxious to resume the beloved sacrament, ascended the altar in St. Bartholomew's Church, he was violently removed by the congregation. At Paul's Cross, Dr. Gilbert Bourne, the queen's own chaplain, had declaimed against the wrongful imprisonment of Bonner, the Bishop of London, by the Protestants, whereupon "certain lewd and ill-disposed persons made a hallowing and crying 'tho lyest!' that the audience was so disturbed, [and] the preacher was so afraid. . . ." When someone "drew a dagger and cast it at the preacher," the congregation—which included many of the court— "were so astonished to see the humor of the people and had as much ado by their means to see the said bishop conveyed in safety through the church, the people were so rude."

In her confinement, Jane had heard only scraps of information and rumors. "I pray you," she asked, somewhat startled, "they have the Mass in London?"

The visitor answered that the ritual had been celebrated "in some places."

Thoughtful for a moment, Jane replied, "It may be so, [but] it is not so strange as the sudden conversion of the late duke. For who would have thought he would have so done?"

The visitor answered, "Perchance he thereby hoped to have had his pardon."

As Partridge nodded in agreement, Jane looked at them both wonderingly. "Pardon?" she cried, more agitated than her host had ever seen her, "Woe worth him! He hath brought me and our stock in most miserable calamity and misery by his exceeding ambition. But for the answering that he hoped for life by his turning, though other men be of that opinion, I utterly am not!" Her face flushed with anger as she continued, "For what man is there living, I pray you, although he had been innocent, that would hope of life in that case—being in the field against the queen in person as general and, after his taking, so hated and evil spoken of by the Commons—and at his coming into prison so wondered at as the like was never heard by any man's time? Who was judge that he should hope for pardon, whose life was odious to all men?"

When the guest, warming to the discussion, offered some possible explanation of Dudley's behavior, Jane—increasingly angry and misunderstanding her companion's enjoyment of a good argument—replied, "But what will ye more? Like his life was wicked and full of dissimulation, so was his end hereafter! I pray God I, nor no friend of mine, die so. Should I, who am young and in my few years forsake my Father for the love of life? Nay, God forbid! But life was sweet, it appeared. So he might have lived, you will say, he did not care how." But, said Jane firmly, "He would have lived in chains to have had his life."

As the conversation ended and all made ready to leave, she said farewell. "But God be merciful to us, for He sayeth, 'Whoso denieth Him before men, he will not know Him in his Father's kingdom.'" As she left, she thanked Master Partridge for bringing a guest for dinner.

The conversation left little doubt in the visitor's mind that Dudley's execution had not mitigated Jane Grey's violent resentment against the duke—that her repulsion had only been increased by what she considered his false attempt to gain freedom by converting to the queen's faith. In addition to the memory of a pleasant evening with an unusual young woman, the visitor also had little doubt but that in similar circumstances, Jane would never do the same.

* * *

Seven weeks passed before Queen Mary returned to London from Richmond Palace. During that time, she'd formed her household, taking great pleasure in bestowing knighthoods and places of prominence about her on those friends who'd been faithful in adversity. Sawston Hall, Mr. Huddlestone's house burnt by Robert Dudley, was ordered rebuilt and its owner, along with faithful old Sir Henry Jerningham, joined a Privy Council becoming unwieldy in size, with differing factions. At Richmond she'd dealt with the executions and a wrangling council, the debts of Edward's reign—almost £200,000, which, though not her responsibility, Mary said she meant to honor, even as her council, aware of an empty treasury, wondered how. Like her brother, she was as concerned with her household expenses as with the garrison expenses in Ireland, on the Scottish Border and particularly in France, where the king, taking advantage of Mary's presumed political ignorance, was creating mischief in those proud English outposts of Calais and Guisnes. Bribery was another matter that concerned the queen, for it wore many faces: in the Parliament, among the justices and lawyers, in the dioceses and parish churches as well as in her own council. Mary wanted, above all, to be what her Spanish cousin the emperor had advised: "Not only must her chief care be for the kingdom's welfare, but she must manage to make all her people understand that this is her only object. Let her be in all things what she ought to be: a good Englishwoman."

But by far the most important matter facing her realm was the one of religion. Renard considered Mary too prudent and moderate in view of the behavior of her discordant, argumentative subjects. In London alone, there were more than fifteen thousand French, Flemish and German refugees, heady with enthusiasm for the "new religion," eager to fight for the belief for which they'd left their homelands, still intolerant of any attempt at compromise. Often the squabbling was carried into the queen's presence. Once, after she'd left Richmond, as she attended a service in the Tower chapel, Chaplain Walker approached Mary with a censer. Whereupon the officiating priest, Dr. Weston (who later, as Dean of Windsor, would be discharged for adultery) cried, "Shamest thou not to do this office, being a priest with a wife? I tell thee the queen will not be censed by such as thee!"

The religious agitation in her City of London—evident even in her own chapel—distressed Mary. While three quarters of the English people were Catholic, attached to the ritual and creed of the Roman Church, Mary recognized that they did not bear her devotion to the pope, resenting the interference of a foreign power, secular or spiritual, with English liberty. Accepting that there could be no return to Rome, the queen listened to Bishop Gardiner's advice that she, like her father and brother before her, must remain head of the English Church. Mary's reply, undoubtedly serious, bore a whimsical tone. "Women," she said, "I have read in Scripture, are forbidden to speak in the church. Is it, then, fitting that *your* church should have a dumb head?"

While she would "neither compel nor constrain other men's consciences," the queen did order the Lord Mayor not to suffer "open reading of the Scriptures in the churches or preaching by the curates, unless licensed by her." By August 23, the day Dudley and his conspirators died, there was mixed reaction among the populace to word that "the Mass at St. Nicholas Colabay, goodly sung in Latin, and tapers set on the altar and a cross in old Fish Street" and "the next day a goodly Mass was sung at St. Nicholas Williams, in Latin, in Bread Street." Murmurings led to arguments, arguments to physical violence, and in the London taverns, inns, homes and hovels, "the cause of religion" was again uppermost in everyone's mind. The council issued an order to each householder "to keep his children, apprentices and other servants in such order and awe, as they follow their work the weekdays and keep their parish churches the holy day." It had an effect, and soon the organ, that "instrument of the Devil," was heard again in St. Paul's as Bishop Bonner celebrated the Mass in the detested Latin. Tiny statues of saints, long hidden, appeared once more in many people's windows, and Sunday sermons, though crowded, were quiet.

One result created by the religious unrest was the detention of Thomas Cranmer, the Archbishop of Canterbury. After conducting the Protestant service for King Edward, his godson, the archbishop had remained in some diplomatic retirement at Lambeth Palace. On August 14 he paid his respects to the queen at Richmond—an innocent gesture which led to rumors that he had converted. When Mass was later celebrated at Canterbury Cathedral, it was further rumored that the archbishop had officiated. Hastily, Cranmer wrote an angry repudiation, a *Declaration*, which succinctly detailed his opinion of the Catholic creed and ritual and in which he requested the queen, "If her Grace will give me leave, I shall be ready to prove, against all that will say the contrary, that all which is contained in the Holy Communion . . . is conformable to that order which our Savior Christ did both serve . . . whereas the Mass, in many things, not only hath no foundation in Christ, His apostles, nor the primitive church, but is manifestly contrary to the same and containeth many horrible abuses. . . ." Stating that his own Protestantism was the "faith which hath been in the church these fifteen hundred years . . . we shall prove that the order of the church set out at this present, in this Church of England by Act of Parliament, is the same that was used in the church fifteen hundred years past . . . and so shall they [the Catholics] never be able to prove theirs." The document was widely copied, posted in Cheapside and Paul's Cross, lending heart to the dispirited Protestants.

Later, commanded to appear before the Privy Council, Cranmer repented his hasty action. Not in the letter's content, he stressed. "But I am sorry that the said bill went from me in such sort as it did." Shortly thereafter, the archbishop was ordered to the Tower.

But not before there was time for him to flee. When urged, indeed encouraged, to do so, he replied it would not be fitting, considering the post he held, ". . . and to show that he was not afraid to own all the changes that were by his means made in religion in the last reign." Others, confronted by the government's purposeful tolerance, eagerly took advantage to leave England. Already the bishops of Wells, Chichester, Exeter, Ossory, the deans of Christ Church in Oxford and Westminster in London, as well as Durham and Canterbury, had fled to the Continent. Flemish weavers, encamped in the glorious ruins of Glastonbury Abbey by the Protector, soon departed. When the hot-tempered Bishop Hooper was summoned to appear before the council, his appointment left plenty of time for flight. When Hugh Latimer, the Bishop of Worcester—noted for his persecution of "heretics" of the Catholic variety, and who had excoriated Thomas Seymour at his funeral service—was summoned, the man delivering the order was frank to say he'd been told "not to tarry for him." Failing to take advantage of the opportunity, Latimer, too, joined Cranmer in the Tower. Bishop Gardiner told Renard that when Protestant foreigners failed to take advantage of the council's purposeful laxness, they were informed their own king or emperor might extradite them, to their great peril. Usually, said Gardiner, that worked.

Next to religion, the gravest issue facing the queen was her marriage. Even during her younger years, when Henry VIII had considered a match for his daughter, Mary had frankly told him—as she now told her council—that she preferred to remain single. The matter of her marriage, especially to a foreigner, had been one of Dudley's strongest arguments for setting aside the succession. But now the Privy Council and Renard insisted she must consider a husband, for how could a woman be expected to rule alone? She must wed and bear an heir.

There were several candidates: the King of Denmark, the Prince of Piedmont, the King of the Romans, and Don Luiz of Portugal. But everyone—Privy Council, foreign ambassadors, even Mary—knew there were only three serious contenders for her unwilling hand. One was the emperor himself; the second, his son Philip; the third, her own countryman Edward Courtenay. Repeatedly Renard stressed the importance of a Spanish marriage, and the queen's ladies-in-waiting spoke of little else. Mary recognized Courtenay's appeal and eligibility. A grandson of Edward IV, he'd been compensated for his long imprisonment by her gift of the earldom of Devon and her reception of him with much honor at court, where his mother, the Marchioness of Exeter, was her dearest friend. But Mary also recognized that even though Courtenay, as Renard wrote the emperor, had "much civility in him which must be deemed natural" rather than acquired, the boy was also weak, vain, easily led and, as if to make up for those years of deprivation, had become dissolute, a steady patron of the "stews," the notorious brothels on Bankside. His debauched life aside, Mary did not like Courtenay personally. That she was sincerely reluctant to wed, that the suggested bridegrooms, with the exception of the emperor, were years younger than she, were factors considered unimportant by both the English council and Renard.

Those closer to and fond of Mary Tudor were more frank. Reginald Pole, the son of her martyred governess, the Countess of

Salisbury, and now a cardinal in Rome, told Mary to remain single. Other than Courtenay, he advised, there was no one of sufficient rank in her own country whom she could marry. To wed in Spain or France would be to incur enmity, jealousy and, inevitably, war. Better that she work for the restoration of the English Church with the Holy See and, above all, see that those stolen ecclesiastical lands were returned to the Church; the succession would take care of itself.

Pole's sensible advice was seconded by Friar Peyto, who'd been at the Tudor court long enough to have boldly criticized Mary's father during the days of his marital marathon. Peyto wrote the queen, "Do not marry or you will be the slave of a young husband. Besides, at your age, the chance of bringing heirs to the crown is doubtful and, moreover, would be dangerous to your life." Ignoring the frank presumption of one she'd known since childhood, Mary found the advice sensible. Only her council and Renard thought otherwise.

But in the end, Renard had his way. When Giovanni Commendone, the pope's chamberlain, brought the queen a papal blessing, Mary said that in spite of her own personal desire to remain unwed, she now considered marriage a duty of State and conscience. Soon Renard was able to write the emperor, "She felt confident you would remember that she was thirty-seven years of age, and would not urge her to come to a decision before having seen the person and heard him speak, for as she was marrying against her private inclination, she trusted your Majesty would give her a suitable husband." Though aware of Mary's natural reluctance to wed, as well as the aversion of the English people and council to marriage with a foreigner, Renard still considered he and his emperor knew best.

Renard also continued to pursue the matter of "Jane of Suffolk." While the Spanish emperor had recommended mercy, he'd been startled by Mary's clemency in executing only three of the conspirators. Through his ambassador, he now continually emphasized that "she [Mary] could never reign in security while that lady [Jane] lived, for the first faction, when strong enough, would set up her claim again." Again, Mary told Renard she "could not find it in her heart or conscience to put her unfortunate kinswoman to death." When Renard extolled the dangers of pardoning Jane, Mary replied that "it was but imaginary, and every requisite precaution should be taken before she was set at liberty."

Mary had been impressed with Jane's letter, which, Renard emphasized, was a strong indictment of everyone but herself. While the Privy Council worked on the formality of a trial for the remaining prisoners—in which their official pardons were almost certain—the Dudley survivors were all allowed liberty to walk in the Tower gardens and receive visits from their families. Within days, Robert and Ambrose Dudley's wives were permitted to remain in the Beauchamp Tower chambers with their husbands; only Guildford and Jane were kept apart. Guildford, whose confinement was the most solitary, occupied his time in carving an elaborate memorial to the Dudley family in the heavy oaken wall of his chamber. Complete with the Northumberland ragged bear and staff, there were lions, roses and thistles, as well as some verse which, as it became difficult, he soon abandoned. As a final touch he carved JANE, a small, perhaps affectionate reminder of the wife he'd not seen in so long, although they were but a short distance apart.

But the council, prodded by Renard, also requested that Mary sign the death warrant for Jane and Guildford Dudley. The lords were anxious to show their zeal for the new queen, and what better way than to urge the death of the two from whom they were so anxious to disassociate themselves? All the councillors, fervid Protestants but weeks ago, now piously attended the queen's Masses. Recognizing how fortunate they'd been to escape with fines they could well afford or reproofs that time would erase, they agreed examples must be made of the conspirators who so far—thanks to Mary's compassion—had escaped the death penalty. They knew the queen was anxious that no more bloodshed mar the beginning of her reign. But, eventually, she'd have to deal with the prisoners. In order to give her time to absorb her responsibilities, Renard and the councillors put aside for the moment the affairs of state, church and prisoners, so that Mary and they could effectively plan her coronation.

Jane Grey celebrated her sixteenth birthday still in the Gentleman-Gaoler's lodgings. It was a day like any other day, beginning with prayers, a walk in the Tower gardens where the air was now more brisk, even piercingly cool with an autumn breeze off the Thames. She'd begun to know the different sounds of river life, from the cries of the oarsmen, the boatmen, the sailors on the great ships sailing on toward Greenwich and the open sea, as they called to those visible on the Tower leads or on the beach. Jane could not see the river from her quarters; sometimes, at the topmost part of the hill near the Wardrobe, she could catch a small glimpse of blue water alive with activity. But the sound and smell were there.

She had much to think about. Even one confined in the Tower could listen, and Jane had always been a good listener. Master Partridge and others brought news of the outside world to her in many ways—in open conversation or in things she heard as they spoke with others. Some she could observe herself, as when—during the last week of that sultry September, on a day free from the summer storms that had plagued London for weeks—she watched the coronation procession leave the Tower. Three days previously there had been a great flurry as Mary arrived by water, her barge filled with her ladies-in-waiting and the Princess Elizabeth, to wait the requisite time in the Tower before her coronation. As her two cousins walked amid much gaiety, chattering with those whom Jane recognized—Susan Clarencieux, Mary's beloved confidante; old Mary Baynham, the "mother of the maids"; and Sir Thomas More's granddaughter, young Katherine Bassett—she felt a lump in her throat. Now, on this happy occasion, how could the queen continue to ignore her? Certainly after Mary was crowned there would be little point in keeping her confined. Would the queen send for her then? Might she not even make her cousin part of that happy, laughing, feminine world that suddenly Jane longed for with a desire almost physical?

Three days later she watched the queen's departure. Elegant in a gown of blue velvet furred with ermine, Mary walked down the little hill, mounted her horse and rode out the Bulwark Gate to the cheers of those five hundred gentlemen and nobles who'd been assembling since dawn to lead her to Whitehall. There someone had brought the old Gog and Magog statue from the Guildhall and "Gog's head nearly wobbled off his gigantic shoulders" as he nodded to the smiling queen. For hours the sound of the procession, as it wound through the City, could be heard back in Jane's quarters, disappearing finally in a great pealing of bells with deafening gunfire from the Tower beach. Later, Jane learned from Master Partridge that the crown on Mary's head had been so heavy that she'd had to steady it with her hand. All through the streets, their triumphal arches hung with arras and bunting, platforms crowded with "charity children"—who weeks ago had sung Calvinstic hymns but now dutifully invoked the saints' blessing on their new sovereign—the procession of singing choirs, orators and trumpeters continued. Princess Elizabeth followed the queen in a chariot covered in cloth of gold which she shared with Anne of Cleves. Through the City streets the caparisoned horses and splendidly garbed riders moved slowly in a spectacle some might see only once in a lifetime. It was nearly dusk when the queen reached Whitehall Palace, for she'd stopped long enough to admire the antics of Peter the Dutchman on the weathercock of old St. Paul's. At Temple Bar, Mary remembered to thank the Lord Mayor for the £20,000 the City had contributed for the celebration.

On the following day, the sounds of festivity wafted downriver from Westminster as Queen Mary, accompanied by Princess Elizabeth, walked on the blue cloth laid from Westminster Hall to the old abbey across the road. Then, as the choir sang, trumpeters blared forth the news of the queen's coming, and Mary went down the great nave hung with rich arras and strewn with fresh rushes. Bishop Gardiner, officiating in the absence of the imprisoned Thomas Cranmer, asked those assembled if they accepted Mary as their queen. With a tremendous roar the people answered, "Yea, yea, yea! God Save Queen Mary!" Then those lords who weeks before had knelt before Jane Grey now knelt before Mary and swore to be "faithful and true, and faith and truth bear to you, our sovereign queen and lady." Later, at a banquet in old Westminster Hall, Dymoke, the hereditary champion of England, rode into the Hall on his horse and flung his gauntlet to the floor, a challenge to anyone who might question the queen's right. When no one responded, the Hall again erupted and Queen Mary rose to drink her champion a toast. All day the feasting and celebrations continued. As Jane Grey went to bed that evening she could hear the revelry of the Tower guards and sentries; by midnight, the illumination of a large bonfire built on Tower Hill flickered throughout her chamber.

A Tower sentry told Mrs. Ellen that some prisoners' doors had been left open that day to allow their escape and many had fled to freedom up the hill and into the lanes north of the Tower. But Cranmer, Ridley and Latimer had chosen to remain. Jane was desolate at the thought of Cranmer's apprehension and the seeming ease with which the hated Catholicism was being so easily restored; she was enraged at the duplicity of those councillors who'd previously been committed to Protestantism. Walking in the Tower grounds, where she now knew each pathway and tree; in the garden, where each bush and bloom was familiar; acknowledging the sentries' easy smile or deferential nod; or in the coolness of the church, where the rawness of the stone near the altar revealed her father-in-law's last resting place, Jane fought an ever-growing sense of futility. Mary Tudor had won her crown, the love of the English people, the support of the Privy Council and the English nobility. Yet in her comfortable confinement, Jane knew herself to be more of a prisoner than those whose doors had been left open on coronation day. Was she, her Majesty's cousin, less important than they? What was the point of keeping her, her Dudley husband and brothers-in-law confined any longer?

The same question was one Simon Renard relentlessy asked Queen Mary. The wily ambassador had bided his time. First the queen's attention had been taken by her coronation and the question of her marriage. Now, one more matter especially close to her heart must be accomplished. On October 4, nearly three months after Edward's death, the queen opened the Parliament, its main purpose being to annul all previous acts passed in Henry VIII's reign which related to Katherine of Aragon's divorce. By that annulment, the stain of illegitimacy which had clung to Mary Tudor for almost twenty years now passed to Elizabeth, for if one queen's marriage was legal, that of the one who'd followed her was not. Next, the religious laws of Edward VI's reign were repealed and England officially returned to the Catholic fold—Henrician Catholicism to be sure, with the complete abrogation of papal authority, but with a celibate clergy and the Mass restored. In only one instance did the nobility deny their queen. When Mary asked for the return of church lands, the lords remembered old Lord Russell, who "hearing Mary might very likely order his share of the church lands to be handed back to the monks [of Woburn Abbey], he cast, with a fierce oath," his large golden rosary beads into the fire. Now, the lords "immediately showed her that whatever might be her own hopes or wishes, their minds on that point were irrevocably fixed." But the queen's disappointment was tinged with triumph, for she had her legitimacy and her faith now established by law. The lords were equally pleased; their plundered lands, the basis of most of their wealth, were now as legally theirs as the queen's title.

Disappointed that she'd had no word from the queen after the coronation, Jane had hoped Parliament would take some action that would result in her going home. Now, certainly, Mary would have time to consider what must be done with the survivors of the Dudley plot. But as her sixteenth birthday passed unnoticed by everyone except Mrs. Ellen and Mrs. Tylney, as the last days of October waned and there was no word from the queen or her council, the physical confinement, incessant worry, the lack of any intellectual challenge or pleasure took its toll. Once more Jane went to her bed, feverish, unable to eat, weeping for no reason at all, uninterested in her books or music. Her lodgings, comfortable and clean, the kindly Partridges and her own ladies were simply not enough. Never before had Jane appreciated what freedom really meant. Restrained as she'd been all her life by her family's harsh words and physical violence, nevertheless she'd never felt confined, except possibly by her own fear of them—a fear, she now recognized, which was nothing compared to the fear she felt for . . . what? Continued imprisonment? Death?

As she lay, weak and uninterested in anything but the hope to get through each day, Jane's one release was when, on her knees, she prayed to God that He in His wisdom would send her home. One of her greatest fears was that if He had sent this trial to test her, she might somehow fail.

Jane was just beginning to feel better when she learned from Master Partridge that the queen had finally agreed to wed. Several councillors, leaving the church, had been discussing it, Partridge said, although from their words he did not think the news would be public soon. While he did not say so, his tone indicated that once Mary's marriage was settled, then she'd deal with the conspirators' fate. Quickly Jane grasped at the news, eager to learn of anything that might urge the queen to action. It was to be Philip of Spain, Partridge said, the twenty-seven-year-old son of the Holy Roman Emperor who would be the husband of England's queen. And from the tone of the councillors' conversation and their grave expressions, he said, he did not think they approved of Mary's choice.

26

The news of Queen Mary's choice of Philip of Spain for her husband was met with mixed feelings throughout the realm. With the Englishman's centuries-old hatred of foreigners, few favored the union. As rumor succeeded rumor, the queen's desire to wed with Spain only increased the English dislike of "foreigners who would sit in high places," and in the country's more remote areas, hatred of "the coming of the Spaniard" increased daily. Despite the fact that Mary's grandmother had been the great Isabella of Spain, the insular Englishmen, fearful and proud, considered their queen would be subject politically as well as personally to the arrogant Philip. Then England would suffer the establishment of the Inquisition, their national heritage would be sacrificed as they became an appendage of the Holy Roman Empire, and worst of all, there would be a return to the papacy. The French ambassador, De Noailles, vigorously preyed on every native fear that "foreigners would rule in their country," sparing no one his opinion that England had sealed its own fate. Privately, he urged the French king to further the marriage plans of the Dauphin to little Mary Stuart, heir to the Scottish crown through her grandmother Margaret Tudor, Henry VIII's sister.

While Jane Grey was unaware of such public reaction, her feelings were as fearfully personal. Politics had never interested her, except when they concerned the "cause of religion." She was not surprised that the half-Spanish and very Catholic Mary had chosen Philip. But what caused the slight improvement in her health to decline immediately was the knowledge that now there was *another* reason to delay her return home. Heretofore, Jane had excused or rationalized Mary's reluctance to pardon her. The queen could do nothing, she'd told herself, until the Privy Council had consolidated her accession. Later, there'd been the coronation festivities and the event itself, which had taken much time. Jane had about convinced herself that once Mary's throne was secure—when there were no more diversions or responsibilities—she'd be released.

But now the queen had chosen a husband, and even more time would be spent negotiating the marriage contract. Once that was completed, Jane realized, she might even have to wait until Philip's arrival and the wedding, which was already scheduled for the summer, had taken place. The thought of eight or nine more months of confinement sent her into deep despair.

She could not know that such despair—for different reasons— was being reflected throughout the nation. She could not know how much Mary had been constantly pressured by Simon Renard, who stressed what "a menace to her liberties" the forthcoming union of Mary Stuart and the French Dauphin would be. Mary, whose reluctance to wed was sincere, had exhibited modesty and an honest doubt that she, a maid of nearly thirty-eight summers, should become a wife. Yet, privately, there'd been a sudden and inexplicable yearning to join that coterie of married women about her and perhaps even to experience motherhood. Once, as Renard extolled Philip's eligibility, Mary clutched his arm in a strong grip. "Oh," she asked, "do you speak as a subject whose duty is to praise his sovereign, or do you speak as a man?"

Scenting victory, the startled Renard said the queen might take his life if she found Philip different from his description. Quickly he advised Mary of Hungary, Philip's aunt, to send the Titian portrait of Philip so the queen might judge for herself. With it came a letter advising Mary that it would "serve to tell her what he is like—but that she must remember to put it in a proper light and look at it from a distance, as all Titian's paintings have to be looked at."

As Mary first gazed at the portrait, she hardly heard Renard's words that Philip had since "filled out and grown more beard." She saw only a handsome young man in elegant dress, with kindly blue eyes, the son of her mother's nephew and from her mother's country, whom she might trust as much as she trusted the emperor. The neat, fine figure pleased Mary Tudor. This man could be her husband—the husband she'd never expected to have. Overcome at the thought, she whispered her thanks and quickly left the room. The following day, in great agitation, she told Renard that "she'd wept over two hours that very day, praying God to inspire her in her decision." Writing the emperor, the ambassador reported, "She believed she would agree to the proposal made to her by your Majesty of a marriage with my Lord, our Prince. . . . She felt she could not do otherwise than follow your Majesty's good and trusty advice. . . . She could not say any more without bursting into tears."

At last, on October 31, almost a month after the coronation, in a poignant scene in her chamber Mary told Renard that "As the Holy Sacrament had been in her room, she had invoked it as her protector, guide and counsellor and still prayed with all her heart that it would come to her help. She then knelt and said the *Veni Creator Spiritus* . . ." with Susan Clarencieux, her companion, and the ambassador joining in. "When the queen got up . . . she felt herself inspired by God," Renard later wrote the emperor, and tearfully gave him "her promise to marry His Highness there, before the Holy Sacrament, and her mind, once made up, would never change, but that she would love him [Philip] perfectly and never give him cause to be jealous."

Her decision made, Mary remained edgy and unsure, putting off a meeting with Bishop Gardiner and a deputation from the House of Commons who wished to discuss her marriage, not knowing her heart had already made that decision. The queen occupied herself in asking the advice of trusted household officers. Gardiner, she said, had already told her that "England would never abide a foreigner, that Courtenay was the only possible marriage for her in England, and that, as for Prince Philip, the country would not accept him willingly." Unhappily, her household officers and several of her ladies agreed, one even telling her that if she married Philip, it would mean war with France.

Their advice confirmed Renard's belief that Mary had four enemies "who would never rest till they had destroyed her or were themselves destroyed—the heretics, the friends of the late Duke of Northumberland [John Dudley], the courts of France and Scotland, and lastly, her sister, Elizabeth." From the day he'd met Mary Tudor, Renard had relentlessly stressed the danger of Elizabeth, the favorite of the Protestants and next in line for the crown, even writing the emperor, "The Lady Elizabeth is greatly to be feared, for she has a power of enchantment and I hear that she already has her eye on Courtenay as a possible husband." He had little but contempt for the English, saying Mary's subjects were restless, turbulent, as changeable as the ocean of which they were so fond, and Mary, above everything, needed "the aura of a powerful prince." Already, during the queen's first Parliamentary session, Renard had seen how Catholic and Protestant, nobleman or gentleman, had found themselves in a rare unity against any foreign marriage for their queen. All of which Mary was uncomfortably aware, but certain that, with Renard's help, she could win over her council and people.

During that first week of November, Simon Renard told Mary the trial of the conspirators must be held. Already they'd been in prison for more than three months and Parliament had attainted them well over five weeks ago. Already the queen had delayed too long; some decision must be made about whether they were to remain imprisoned, be pardoned or suffer the ultimate penalty. On this issue, the vacillating Mary must decide.

And this time the queen agreed. Irritated by the ambassador's suggestion of royal indecisiveness, and aware the trials would divert the council's attention away from the subject of her marriage, the queen appointed the competent Sir Richard Morgan, Chief Justice of the Court of Common Pleas, as judge. Morgan was a Catholic who'd suffered imprisonment in the Fleet during Edward's reign for attending the forbidden Mass at Mary's house. Once released, he'd fled to Mary at Kenninghall and later received a knighthood from the new queen.

Mary was firm in her commission, directing Morgan "to administer the law impartially . . . notwithstanding the old error amongst you, which did not admit any witness to speak, or anything else to be in favor of the adversary, [the prisoner]. . . . It is my pleasure that whatever can be produced in favor of the subject shall be heard. . . ." The "old error" the queen spoke of so disparagingly was the practice—common to most trials—of assuming the prisoner's guilt beforehand, of forbidding any evidence that might prove otherwise, of refusing to hear any petitions or testimonies on the prisoner's behalf. It is evidence of her desire to give the conspirators every advantage. Even if they were convicted, there was no intention on Mary's part to proceed to the extremity of the law.

But public opinion ran high on Monday morning, November 13, as an unusual procession left the Tower. Word had gone abroad that John Gage, the Constable of the Tower, had received orders from Thomas White, Mayor of London, and Thomas Howard, the old Duke of Norfolk, "to bring up . . . the accused, to wit, Thomas, Archbishop of Canterbury, Jane Dudley, Guildford, Ambrose and Henry Dudley," to be tried for treason. The punishment, as everyone knew, was death by hanging, drawing and quartering, which might by royal mercy be changed to beheading.

Jane had been informed of the trial only the evening before, and instinctively, her fear was tempered with relief. *At last* something was being done. Sir John Brydges, the Lieutenant of the Tower, had not appeared overly concerned when he, with Master Partridge, arrived with the summons. Afterward, as she discussed the news with Mrs. Ellen and Mrs. Tylney, Jane tried to be objective. Her ladies, hoping to hide their dismay, agreed the hearing was only a formality which the Parliament had ordered. And although Jane must stand trial with the others, she should not be overly worried. Hadn't the queen pardoned her own father, who'd been more deeply embroiled in the plot than his daughter? they asked. No one mentioned what might happen to the other Dudleys—especially Guildford.

Mrs. Ellen's mention of her father, meant to be comforting, sent Jane to her desk, for she felt a strong need to communicate with her family, a deep desire to let them know of *her* feelings, since they had not seen fit to inform her of theirs. While she fully expected Mary's mercy, she wanted those responsible for her situation to be aware of her predicament.

Jane wrote hastily, addressing the letter to her father. After the traditional greetings, she described what had happened, how she must appear on trial the following day. She ended with her most personal thought:

> If I may without offence rejoice in my own mishap, meseems in this I may account myself blessed, that washing mine hands with the innocency of my face, my guiltless blood may cry before the Lord, mercy, mercy to the innocent! And yet I must acknowledge that being constrained, and, as you wot [know] well enough, continually assailed, in taking upon me I seemed to consent, and therein offended the queen and her laws, yet do I assuredly trust that this mine offence towards God is much the less, in that being in so royal an estate as I was, mine enforced honor never agreed with mine innocent heart.

She did not reread the letter, but asked Master Partridge to send it to Sheen at once. She felt some relief, since, as best she could, she'd acknowledged her only guilt: that of accepting the crown.

Having unburdened herself, Jane was in as much control as she could muster upon leaving her familiar chambers the following morning. If the need to proclaim her innocence had roused any stab of remorse or pity in her father's heart, she would never know. Although the messenger had returned to the Tower, there'd been no reply from Sheen. Ever since daybreak, soldiers and officials had been arriving inside the Tower precincts. But as she stepped outside her lodgings, Jane was jolted at the sight of so many waiting to escort only five prisoners.

Mrs. Ellen had chosen Jane's gown of long black velvet with a small Bible hung by a golden chain at her waist. A black hood edged in jet beading and velvet covered her hair, and she carried a small prayer book beneath the long black cloak. Jane took her place in the procession of prisoners who, surprisingly, had been ordered to *walk* to the Guildhall, a goodly distance away. Mrs. Ellen and Mrs. Tylney had asked, in view of Jane's extreme youth and the absence of any family, if they might walk with her, and permission had been granted. They, too, were garbed in black and stood close to Jane as all waited silently to be told what they must do.

It was a frosty morning and Jane was grateful Mrs. Ellen had insisted upon the cloak. Ahead, she saw that Thomas Cranmer was the first prisoner in line. Before him was the Gentleman-Chief Warder, who bore the axe, now turned away from them. Following Cranmer were the Dudley men: Lords Henry, Ambrose and Guildford. For the first time in months, Jane saw her husband, handsome in a black velvet suit slashed with white satin. Quickly, the boy left the guards and came to stand near her. They exchanged no greeting. It was obvious to Jane that Guildford was very frightened.

In a moment the procession moved out the Bulwark Tower Gate, up the hill past the execution site. Jane watched as Guildford averted his eyes from the place where his father had died almost three months ago. As they moved on through Eastcheap, Gracechurch Street, past the Cornhill and on into the Poultry, four hundred halberdiers were spaced along the way to keep the peace. But there was no trouble. From roadway or window, the spectators gazed at the prisoners in silence—some with pity, some with contempt. At first Jane found great release just in being out in the open. It felt good to walk through the familiar streets with the bracing, icy air off the river, at which she'd gazed so appreciatively before they'd turned up Tower Hill. But soon the onlookers' silence, the steady tramp of the guards accompanying the procession in which no one spoke, so startled and discomfited Jane that she opened her small prayer book and kept her eyes on its pages as she walked along.

The old Duke of Norfolk, as High Steward and Earl Marshal of England, presided at the trial. Norfolk was no stranger to such proceedings, having witnessed—and passed sentence at—the trials of his nieces Anne Boleyn and Katherine Howard. Recognizing Jane Grey's rank, he motioned her to a chair draped with scarlet cloth with a matching footstool; Mrs. Ellen and Mrs. Tylney came to stand behind her as she seated herself. Thomas Cranmer was ordered to a boxlike pew separated only a short distance from Guildford, Ambrose and Henry Dudley. Robert Dudley had already received an official pardon, having had, in the queen's and council's opinion, the least responsibility in the plot. Gazing at the prisoners, Jane found it difficult to accept that she and Guildford could be accused—perhaps even found guilty—with all those others. *All* the Dudleys had been deeply implicated, while Archbishop Cranmer was charged with treason for spreading abroad seditious libels with his *Declaration*. And so many of the councillors who sat now a short distance away to watch this spectacle were equally responsible. *She'd* never wanted the crown nor conspired to attain it. Guildford, however, *had* wanted it, but only after the Privy Council—with Edward's "Device" as guide—had consented to both his and Jane's having it.

As she waited for Justice Morgan to commence the proceedings, Jane looked about the ancient Guildhall, with its massive Gog and Magog statue now back in place after being part of the queen's coronation festivities. The Lord Mayor and Sheriffs were instantly recognizable in their scarlet satins and sables, with glistening gold chains of office around their befurred necks. Everyone who could squeeze into the venerable old building was there, and Jane saw many who'd been in and out of her parents' homes or been at court in the year when she'd lived there with King Henry and Queen Katherine Parr. The thought of that happy time almost brought tears. What would Kate Parr and her other dear friend Kate Brandon, the Dowager Duchess of Suffolk, think of these proceedings, ordered by their other equally dear friend and stepchild, Mary Tudor?

Hoping to quell any tears, Jane concentrated on the outward religious changes in the old Guildhall. Instead of the plain table of Edward's Protestantism, there was now an altar with six golden candles and a crucifix. As the Lord Mayor's chaplain opened the proceedings, everyone knelt to say the *Veni Sancte Spiritus*, followed by yet more prayers in Latin. The formalities out of the way, the prisoners' indictments were read out and each was asked to answer. No one had coached Jane or advised her what her behavior should be. When it came her turn, she replied as had the others: "Not guilty." No effort was made to cross-examine the prisoners; no one spoke in their defense or offered any explanation of the charges. After a delay of twenty minutes, a jury of Middlesex citizens dutifully returned a verdict of "Guilty."

Jane was grateful for her chair, the footstool and Mrs. Ellen's reassuring hand on her shoulder. To hear the hated word made the whole proceeding unreal. And when the charges were again read and each prisoner was asked to reply and this time to *agree* with the verdict and answer "Guilty!," she wanted to scream it was not so. Yet she, too, answered as the others, since it was obviously expected she do so. Again, she felt the concern and apprehension that had been her constant companions during those months she'd waited for Mary's mercy. Only now it was a deep, roiling fear.

And the words of Chief Justice Morgan, shocking in their finality, were almost unendurable. As he passed sentence, condemning Jane Grey to be burnt alive or beheaded "as the queen shall please," his voice trembled and his eyes appeared caught by the young girl's shocked stare, as though she could not believe his words. Quickly he proceeded on. Thomas Cranmer and Guildford Dudley were to be hanged at Tyburn, but a pardon was extended to both Lord Ambrose and Lord Henry Dudley. Again, Jane could scarce believe what she was hearing. All the other Dudley men were *free;* only she, Guildford and Cranmer were to suffer. The merciless sentence pounded in her ears, and anger—unfamiliar because of its long repression—rose in her at the injustice, and she fought back the tears as she clutched at Mrs. Ellen's hand. But already the court was reciting the *De Profundis* and ahead lay the long walk back to the Tower. This time the axe would be pointed at her, a sign of condemnation.

And this time there was not much silence. The axe told the whole story, and the onlookers were moved to pity for the two luckless young people—still no more than a boy and a girl—who even they, no strangers to political realities and inequities, knew had been pawns of John Dudley and the Privy Council. They'd wanted their Queen Mary, to be sure, but not at the price of an innocent girl's head, even if she was the daughter of the hated Duke of Suffolk. And he'd gone free! There were mutterings and angry exclamations, even some outright calls of solicitude and prayer from the throng, which had increased as word of the Guildhall trial had spread throughout the City. They were directed especially at the thin, childish figure dressed in black and the boy who, head down, followed some distance away.

But all Jane could hear was Justice Morgan's shocking words: *to be burnt alive or beheaded as the queen shall please . . .* Which way would please Mary? Would the queen have let her endure this punishing ordeal if she truly meant to pardon her? Trembling, Jane again clutched at Mrs. Ellen's arm. Her old nurse was weeping openly now, looking as frightened as Jane felt. Hoping to calm her forlorn companion as well as herself, to shut out the indignant cries from the growing multitude—which she did not as yet comprehend showed their concern—Jane opened her prayer book. Perhaps the inspiring words would help put the crowd, the soldiers and her fellow prisoners from her mind on the long dreary walk back to the Tower. There would be time enough for her own tears then.

Christmas passed as just another day. The Yule log burned in Master Partridge's quarters and Jane and her ladies were invited to sip warm wine there in celebration. The New Year went unnoticed, the pleasant traditional exchange of gifts forgotten in the depression that permeated the Gentleman-Gaoler's lodgings. Little had changed since that day at the Guildhall. Jane's liberties had not been curtailed, but on days when the weather was pleasant and she walked in the gardens, she did so more to please Mrs. Ellen than because she desired the exercise. She could have gone out the gate and walked up Tower Hill, she was told—with a proper escort, of course. But that would bring her to the execution site where John Dudley had recently died and where Thomas Seymour had died almost five years ago. Where she might die if the queen did not show mercy. Often she passed Thomas Cranmer; they nodded, nothing more. Master Partridge told her that Guildford was allowed to walk on the Beauchamp Tower leads, and Jane knew that would please her husband, for from that height he could see the busy river traffic and London Bridge. But as she passed the Beauchamp entry, she did not look upward.

For herself, the only rewarding time of day was that spent in her chamber in prayer. The Tower church, little St. Peter's-ad-Vincula, now contained Catholic emblems; its mitered priest swung the hated censer and later intoned in Latin. She no longer went inside. Her studies had come to a halt, as concentration seemed impossible. Though she'd not been forbidden any communication with the outside world, she wrote no letters. She'd written the queen and her father—two who might have helped her—and received no reply. The pleasant rooms of her lodgings were now a true prison, not a temporary haven for one uncondemned and awaiting pardon. She cherished the warm companionship of her ladies, but after they'd served her, dressed her, and accompanied her on her walks, there was little else they could do; she knew the confinement was as difficult for them as for her.

Jane had been pleased to learn the queen had taken her sisters, Lady Katherine and Lady Mary Grey, into her service, giving them generous allowances. If nothing else, it showed that Mary's animosity or displeasure did not extend to her entire family; they were not suffering because of her. She'd miss Katherine and Mary if and when she returned home. There'd never be any place at court for the girl so presumptuous as to have worn England's crown.

But, Jane wondered, when would the queen reprieve that dreadful sentence? *To be burnt alive or beheaded, as the queen shall please*—the words still haunted her anguished dreams. As the New Year arrived, Jane counted the days—forty-eight days—which had passed since the trial. Forty-eight opportunities for the queen to have pardoned her, and Guildford as well. Had Mary changed her mind, waiting only for the holidays to end to see the sentence carried out? As the first weeks of the new year, 1554, passed and she walked the grounds for the exercise and fresh air Mrs. Ellen said she must have, Jane wondered and waited.

And then, suddenly, her liberties were curtailed. Master Partridge was almost apologetic, explaining she must not leave her lodgings again. From her window Jane watched as cannons were placed on each tower top. Mrs. Ellen, who still walked outside, said the beach and towers facing the river were bristling with additional guards. Sounds from the City seemed muted, as though not as many people were in the streets, and Mrs. Ellen said even the river traffic appeared less. *Something* was happening, and perversely, Jane experienced the first little stab of interest in weeks. Whatever it was, it would add some diversion to the boring, predictable, depressing days of imprisonment.

At last, when it seemed as though as many soldiers as possible had crowded into the Tower, when carts bringing ammunition and supplies rumbled day and night, when even the Privy Council, usually at Westminster or Richmond with the queen, could be seen entering the royal apartments, Jane could contain herself no longer.

She summoned Master Partridge, whom she'd not seen for almost two weeks, and asked him what was happening. At first she'd feared that possibly it might be a prelude to the queen's carrying out the Guildhall sentences. But guns, soldiers and cannon would not be needed for that; all that was required was a scaffold and an executioner—or a stake.

Master Partridge told Jane all she wished to know. The country was up, he said, against the queen's marriage. Sir Peter Carew and Sir Gawain Carew in Devonshire and Cornwall, and Sir Thomas Wyatt in Kent were marching on London. They meant no harm to the queen's person, Partridge stressed, but only wished to impress upon her the extent of England's hatred for a marriage with Spain. Already, Mary's popularity had waned considerably in view of her insistence on marrying Philip, in her disregard of her people's feelings. If she did not consent, Partridge said, she would be deposed in favor of Elizabeth, who would then be married to Edward Courtenay, an eventuality the Protestants looked on with much favor.

There were even sympathizers on the Privy Council, Partridge said. The Earl of Huntingdon, for one, was known to favor the rebels. Jane remembered Huntingdon well. Katherine Dudley had been married to his son on the day she'd married Guildford; the earl had been one of Dudley's major supporters. Jane remembered how astonished she'd been that his only punishment had been a royal reprimand and a fine.

And then, suddenly, she forgot the earl and asked Partridge to repeat his words. Stunned, Jane could scarcely believe what he was saying. While the Carews in the West Country and the thirty-three-year-old Wyatt in Kent were the prime leaders in the rebellion, the man who was to raise the Midlands—and had already fled to Bradgate, his home in Leicester—was Henry Grey, the Duke of Suffolk, her father.

Horrified, Jane thanked Master Partridge, who emphasized again that no one meant any harm to the queen's person. It was just that she was being so obstinate, he said, insisting on the Spanish marriage, which no one wanted. Once the rebels had convinced her that the country would not stand for it, surely she'd understand? If Mary was deposed, the emperor would hardly send his son to marry a woman who was no longer a queen, would he? Either way, the rebels would win. Then, thinking perhaps he was saying too much, Partridge bowed and left.

Once the door closed, Jane, ignoring the comforting words of Mrs. Ellen and Mrs. Tylney, fled to her room. She was too frightened, and at the same time too full of anger to pray; even that release was now denied her. How could her father be so foolish? *He'd* been in prison only months ago—had he forgotten what it was like? Had he forgotten he still had a daughter incarcerated and under sentence of death? Whether the plot was successful or not, had he forgotten that the woman against whom he was rebelling held that daughter's life in her hands? With a stroke of the pen she could free her or send her to be burnt alive or beheaded. Why had he done such a thing?

The question had no more than crossed Jane's mind than she knew the answer. Henry Grey, in crossing the royal will and allying himself with the rebels, however distinguished they might be, however noble their motives, had never considered his daughter. Ambition was the reason for his misguided action, just as it always had been. She as a person meant nothing to him, nor to her mother, who she was certain had encouraged him to join the rebels. Their daughter was expendable and might be sacrificed for the greater gain. If the rebels won and Mary agreed to give Philip up in order to keep her crown, would any sensible person think she'd spare the daughter of one who'd helped prevent that marriage? And if the rebels lost, the result would be the same. There was no way Henry Grey's action could be defended or explained.

In any event, Jane knew her father's behavior had settled her fate. She would not be going home again.

The
Stage

27

The betrothal of Queen Mary and Philip of Spain was officially
announced in the Presence Chamber at Westminster on January
14, 1554, by Stephen Gardiner, the Bishop of Winchester. Gardiner had wangled excellent terms in the marriage contract with
Spain. Mary's jointure would be 30,000 ducats to be paid an-
nually, with the crowns of Burgundy and the Low Countries,
Spanish possessions, for any child the couple might have. Philip
was to be king only during Mary's lifetime; presumably, when she
died he would return to Spain. Neither he nor any other Spaniard
could sit on the Privy Council, hold any office at court, in the army
or navy, or "have custody of any forts or castles." Gardiner was
proud of the restrictive terms which, maddeningly, the English did
not seem to understand or appreciate, and he ended his announce-
ment with a declaration "that we were much bounded to thank
God that so noble, worthy and famous a prince would vouch-
schafe to so humble himself, as in this marriage, to take upon him
rather as a subject than otherwise. . . ." Gardiner stressed that
the "queen should rule all things as she doth now. . . ." The
bishop's words, however, did not quiet the people's fear, and "this
news . . . very much misliked . . . also heavily taken of sundry

men . . . and thereat almost each man was abashed, looking daily for worse matters to grow shortly after."

And from Thames-side wharves to Paul's Cross and Churchyard, from the Temple to the Tower, Londoners continued to show their distaste for the Spanish marriage, which they were certain would be accompanied by invasion and confiscation of English land and rights, making them subjects of Philip's countrymen. On New Year's Day the Imperial embassy, which would so generously grant Gardiner's demands, had arrived in England "for the knitting up of the marriage of the queen to the King of Spain." As they rode through London, schoolboys pelted them with snowballs, "so hateful was the sight of their coming." On the following day, the official reception took place when the Spaniards, headed by Count Egmont, the Prince de Gavre; the Sieur de Courrieres, Jean de Montmorency; and de Nigry, Chancellor of the Order of the Golden Fleece, landed at Tower Wharf to a great peal of guns from the Tower. Awaiting them "in very gorgeous apparel" were old Sir Anthony Browne and, at Tower Hill, Edward Courtenay, the young Earl of Devon. After greeting them "in most honorable and familiar ways," Courtenay, his hand on Egmont's, led them through Cheapside and on to Durham House in the Strand. Along the way the people of London, "nothing rejoicing, held down their heads sorrowfully." Ten days later, the rebellion of which Master Partridge told Jane had begun.

Originally, the uprising had been scheduled for Palm Sunday, March 18. But, as Mary entertained the Spanish envoys at Hampton Court—where "they had great cheer as could be had and hunted and killed, rag and tag"—the plot was prematurely revealed by none other than Edward Courtenay, who, though apprised of the conspiracy, had been given little responsibility. His many years in the Tower had not equipped him for even the simplest participation in fighting; the young man could barely handle firearms or a bow and arrow. But he'd been told that, should Mary be deposed and Elizabeth become queen, then *he* would be her husband, that a Plantagenet would again sit on the throne of England. The earl, his superb ego generously laced with unbridled ambition, had agreed with the French ambassador, De Noailles, that such a union could only strengthen his own claim to the English crown. Thus Courtenay—the least equipped for intrigue—was the chief figurehead and beneficiary in the plot to prevent the queen's Spanish marriage. Perfectly timed, the uprisings would occur in Devon, Leicestershire, Kent and Wales, and the queen, caught unawares and with little resources of men or money, would be forced to submit or be deposed. Already, of the major conspirators, Sir James Crofts, a former Deputy of Ireland, had left the court to raise an army from his vast holdings in Wales and along the Severn border; the Duke of Suffolk, Henry Grey, would muster his forces in Leicester; the Carews, Peter and Gawain, would raise the West Country; while Sir Thomas Wyatt, the thirty-three-year-old son of Anne Boleyn's poet-lover, would lead the Kentish rebels.

In London, Courtenay, "so timorous that he would suffer himself to be taken before he would act," according to De Noailles, had delayed leaving for Devon. When the horses were ready, he was not; when the weather was poor, he would wait until it had improved. When he ordered an armorer to trim a coat of mail, boasting of how he would wear it, the words were carried to Stephen Gardiner, who'd shared the young man's imprisonment in the Tower. Suspecting Courtenay might be involved in an insurrection, rumors of which, by mid-January, had begun to reach London, the bishop summoned the earl, for whom he'd developed a close affection during their long incarceration. Sternly he "reproached him for offending against the queen's goodness."

Criticism from one who'd assumed the role of a father in Courtenay's eyes was too much for the weak young man, and under the bishop's adroit questioning he confessed everything. Immediately summonses went out to bring in the treasonous nobles. By that time, however, Peter Carew had escaped to France aboard a vessel secured by a young "Master Walter Raleigh," Crofts remained in Wales, and the brunt—and the blame—of the heretofore well-organized rebellion now fell on Thomas Wyatt.

The rebel uprising caught Mary Tudor unaware. She'd fallen in love with a portrait and now the most important thing in her life was her marriage. The queen anticipated Philip's arrival with all the frustrated longing of more than twenty deprived and embittered years. Half-Spaniard, trusting the emperor more than her own councillors, Mary wanted a husband who would be not only her comfort but a support, a buffer between her and those courtiers whose loyalty she questioned as much as she did their advice. "Let the prince come," she told Renard, "and all will be well." Mary had convinced herself that her subjects' distaste for her marriage was a momentary aversion which would somehow disappear in the reality of Philip's splendid presence. Renard was not so certain, writing the emperor that several councillors had advised him that "Your Majesty would do as well to see to it that the Spaniards who are to come be as modest in demeanour as the pride and insolence of the English would have them, for otherwise these people will not be held back from inflicting upon them some irreparable outrage."

As details of the conspiracy were made known to the Privy Council, several privately wondered if the queen could hold out against such forces. Sensing their attitude, Mary ordered each to sign a document approving her marriage. She then asked for additional troops, which the council—divided, as usual—appeared reluctant to approve. When word came that the yeomen, farmers, laborers and squires of Kent were clearly intent upon rebellion, the queen herself asked the Lord Mayor and Sheriffs of London and "diverse of the best commoners" for help. Soon—as Jane had observed in the Tower—"the City began to be kept with harnessed men." The queen then summoned those nobles absent from court. All her past experience had shown Mary how fickle the loyalty of any courtier, councillor or noble might be, and her own guard was only two hundred soldiers. Her best defense lay in having everyone present, naked to examination by herself as well as each other. Thus, any defection or formation of a powerful clique would be immediately apparent. When it was noted that Henry Grey, Jane's father, had not signed the document approving her marriage, the queen sent a messenger to Sheen for his signature and summoned him to London.

It was on the twenty-fifth of January, the same day the Privy Council learned the full extent of the conspiracy, that the messenger arrived at Sheen, the old Carthusian priory on the river near Richmond, with an order for Henry Grey to return to court. Two days previously, Thomas Wyatt had visited Grey to conclude plans for the uprising, which both still assumed was a secret. Wyatt, who'd traveled much in Spain where "he'd imbibed an utter detestation of its inhabitants and their ways," solicited Grey's help in preventing the queen's marriage. And, spoken or unspoken, there was the implication that the duke's daughter Jane Grey might once again be put forward as a claimant to the throne, should the queen be deposed. Wyatt appeared confident of victory. Weren't their troops, the simple Englishmen and gentry and the nobles' retainers, greater than any the queen could muster? And were there not councillors—the powerful Earl of Huntingdon for one—willing to help by raising his tenantry at Ashby-de-la-Zouch if for no other reason than the opportunity "to remove certain councillors from about the queen" whom he considered troublesome?

Reading the royal summons, Henry Grey smiled. "Marry," he told the messenger, "I was just coming to her Grace." Holding out a handsomely shod foot, he said, "You may see I am booted and spurred and ready to ride. I will but break my fast and go." He gave the man some small coins, ordering a servant to see that he had food and drink. Then, forgetting the generosity of the queen who had spared his life, forgiven his duplicity, returned his £20,000 fine and restored his property, Grey took fifty followers and fled northward. Before he left he sent a servant, John Bowyer, to London to obtain 100 marks from the duke's City residence and advise his confederate the Earl of Huntingdon to bring his troops to Leicester.

Some four days later, united with his brothers, Lords Thomas and John, Henry Grey arrived in Leicester. Along the way from London, in each city or small village he had proclaimed against the queen's marriage. But the Mayor of Leicester, one Master Thomas Davenport, was disturbed when his distinguished visitor explained his intent. "My lord," the mayor said, "I trust your Grace meaneth no hurt to the queen's Majesty?" Laying his hand on his sword, Henry Grey replied, "No, Master Mayor. He that would her any hurt, I would this sword were through his heart; for she is the mercifullest prince, as I have truly found her, that ever reigned, in whose defense I am, and will be, ready to die at her foot." He rebelled, he said, against the Spanish marriage only.

When the royal messenger returned to court from Sheen with the news of Grey's defection, and as the council learned of Wyatt's activities, Jane's liberties at the Tower had been abruptly curtailed. Again Mary asked for additional troops, and again the council, "unwilling to check too soon a demonstration which, kept within bounds, might prove the justice of their own objections" to the marriage, refused to sanction any additional musters. Angrily, on her own, the queen appealed to officials of the City Corporation; they rewarded her initiative with five hundred men. These troops, combined with her own two hundred guard, Mary placed under the command of one of the few nobles she trusted, the aged Duke of Norfolk, with the faithful Sir Henry Jerningham as Captain of the Guard. Realizing the queen meant to fight, the Earl of Huntingdon—whose presence and troops Henry Grey was awaiting in Leicester—flung himself at Mary's feet, imploring that he be the one commissioned to pursue and capture the treasonous duke.

As Huntingdon rode northward to take Jane's unsuspecting father, Thomas Wyatt's men held the bridge over the Medway at Rochester. Previously, Norfolk had sent a herald into the town with the queen's proclamation "that all such as would desist their purpose should have a frank and free pardon." But it had had no effect. "Each man," said an observer, "cried they had done nothing wherefore they should need any pardon. And that quarrel which they took, they would die and live in it."

Later, as Norfolk's troops prepared to besiege the bridge, the captain of the queen's forces, Alexander Brett, drew out his sword, crying, "We go about to fight against our native countrymen . . . and our friends in a quarrel unrightful and wicked." The rebels, he shouted, were loyal Englishmen all, resisting the proud Spaniards who, when they ruled, would make the English "slaves and villains, spoil us of our goods and lands, ravish our wives before our faces and deflower our daughters in our presence." The captain said he and his men were fighting for the "avoiding of the great mischiefs and inconveniences" likely to afflict the realm with Philip's coming. "Wherefore, I will . . . spend our blood in the quarrel of this worthy captain, Master Wyatt," Brett concluded, raising his sword. Watching his captain's emotional change of heart, the Duke of Norfolk looked on dumbfounded.

Within moments, five hundred of the queen's soldiers with eightfield pieces of ordnance—Mary's complete artillery and forces—were streaming across the bridge toward the rebels, shouting, "A Wyatt! A Wyatt!" as Norfolk, still stunned at the loss of his troops and "somewhat abashed," fled with Sir Henry Jerningham not far behind.

Elated, Wyatt cried, "As many as will tarry with us shall be welcome; as many as will depart, let them go." Now, with fifteen hundred soldiers, including the queen's own, the rebel leader gave the order to march to London.

In the Tower, Jane waited eagerly and fearfully for each day's news. Master Partridge and Sir John Brydges did not deny her any information, and what they did not tell her, Mrs. Ellen learned from the Tower sentries or on her solitary walks in the streets outside the moated fortress. Guildford, she heard, had been transferred to the Bell Tower but was still allowed to walk on the leads. But Jane no longer went outside. It mattered little. She still could not understand her father's defection and feared its consequences. What made him think he could win against the queen? Yet, when she learned that the rebel Wyatt was nearing London—that Mary's own soldiers had gone over to his cause—hope flared up. Possibly, just possibly, the uprising might succeed! The queen's marriage might be prevented or she might be deposed. But how would either eventuality help her, Jane Grey? Would Mary forgive Henry Grey his defection and carry out that unspeakable sentence against his daughter? If she lost and Elizabeth became queen, would she pardon Mary's prisoner as Mary had pardoned Edward's? On her knees, Jane prayed for hope and courage in the forthcoming days of uncertainty.

And then, suddenly, an eerie calm settled over the City. There was great activity in the Tower as detachments of soldiers arrived and left, as councillors emerged from the Lieutenant's house to watch the cannon rumbling past them toward the gates. From her window, Jane watched it all with Mrs. Ellen and Mrs. Tylney. Thomas Wyatt was nearing Southwark, they heard; already the Tower guns were being pointed to the opposite river shore. After Londoners had barricaded their doors, dismantled their shops, taken down their signs—some even fleeing to the wooded parts of Islington or Hackney for safety—the queen decided to act. Mary had ignored her Privy Council's advice that she seek refuge in the Tower, though Gardiner had gone on his knees and begged her to do so. With few exceptions, she knew her councillors would side with the victor and she refused to cloister herself in a fortress where she might eventually find herself prisoner. Instead, she told her dismayed advisers, she would speak to her people directly.

On Wednesday, January 26, Candlemas Day, as Thomas Wyatt skirmished on the approach to the City's boundaries, "the Queen's Majesty, with her lords and ladies, riding from Westminster . . . at three o'clock in the afternoon," arrived at the ancient Guildhall, where Jane had recently been sentenced. After being received by the Lord Mayor and aldermen of London, Mary "came down into the Great Hall . . . where was hanged a rich cloth of estate, she standing under it" upon a dais with Lord Chancellor Gardiner and her Privy Council standing behind her. If any Londoner wondered what was in the queen's heart, he had not long to wait. In her deep man's voice, contrasting so vividly with her tiny stature, Mary spoke. "I am come to you in mine own person to tell you that which already you see and know," she said. "That is, how traitorously and rebelliously, a number of Kentish men have assembled themselves against us and you. Their pretense . . . was for a marriage determined for us; to the which ye have been made privy." He, Wyatt, the queen continued, was using her marriage "as a Spanish cloak to cover their pretended purpose against our religion. . . ." Warming to her task, Mary said Wyatt had even "demanded to have the governance of our person, the keeping of the Tower and the placing of our councillors." As the people began to murmur among themselves, Mary impressed upon her "loving subjects" that she was "wedded to the realm and the laws of the same"; that they had promised her their allegiance and obedience. *She* was the true inheritor of the crown, she told her awed listeners, possessing the same regal state of her father, Henry VIII, and *he* had always known his people to be faithful and loving subjects. Now, the queen cried, she asked only the same for herself. "And I say to you on the word of a prince . . . assure yourselves that I, being your lady and mistress, do as earnestly and tenderly love and favor you. And I, thus loving you, cannot but think that you as heartily and faithfully love me. And then, I doubt not but that we shall give these rebels a short and speedy overthrow."

Mary then acknowledged the contention about and misunderstanding of her future marriage. Before making her decision, she said, she'd listened to the advice of the Privy Council. She reiterated that her marriage would hurt no one, for if so, "I would never consent thereunto, neither would I ever marry while I lived!" She promised, on the word of a queen, that "if this marriage shall [not] be for the high benefit and commodity of the whole realm, then I will abstain from marriage while I live."

A taut silence had gripped everyone in the vast old Guildhall as the queen spoke. No one wished to miss a word. Now, nearing the end of her speech, Mary, looking relieved, said, "And now, good subjects, pluck up your hearts and like true men, stand fast against these rebels, both our enemies and yours, and fear them not for—I assure you—I fear them nothing!" As she prepared to leave, Mary told her listeners that Lord Howard would be a noble defender of the City "from spoil and sack, which is the only aim of this rebellious crew."

Stepping down from the dais, exhilarated with her effort, Mary saw many people in tears. Then, suddenly, the respectful silence that had attended her speech was broken as a deafening roar split the air, and, laughing and crying at the same time, the crowd surged toward their monarch, now trying to make her way to the Council Chamber. "God Save Queen Mary! God Save the Queen!"—the cheers resounded to those waiting outside, only to be taken up by others in the crowded nearby streets.

At the Tower, Jane heard the shouts of the throng accompanying the queen to the Three Cranes in the Vintry, where her barge waited to return her to Whitehall. Later, Master Partridge told Jane that as the royal craft pulled away from the Vintry waterstairs, Mary had whispered to the bargeman. Then, as those lining the riverbank watched in amazement, instead of heading westward, back to the palace, the craft had set out in the direction of London Bridge and the Southwark side of the river where Wyatt and his rebels were expected at any moment. The royal challenge was implicit in the gesture and the crowd broke into loud cheering. After lingering for a short time near the end of the bridge, the barge then turned and proceeded slowly homeward.

When the rebels at last arrived in Southwark, they learned that the queen's pardon still held for the soldiers. But a reward was offered for their leader, and "Master Wyatt, upon the proclamation that whosoever will take him should have £500 in money, did cause his name to be fair written . . . and set upon his cap," so all would know who he was. Quickly, the gates of London Bridge had been slammed shut and the drawbridge taken up. Every boat on the river was ordered "brought over to the London side and commanded there to stay." As the Tower's Lieutenant, Sir John Brydges, watched the quiet river and the rebels' standards, which could be clearly seen moving through the Southwark woods, he impatiently told a sentry, "I much muse that they are not fought withall. By God's mother! I fear there is some traitor aboard that they be suffered all this while!" Brydges could not understand why the queen would not fight. "For surely, and if it had been about my sentry, I would have fought with them myself, by God's grace!" All the City gates were closed and "the streets were full of harnessed men" as orders went forth to break up all the bridges within fifteen miles of London. If Wyatt could not cross London Bridge— nor anywhere else—he was marooned on the river's other side.

And so it continued for three uneasy days. After the Tower guns had been shot off six or seven times, Mary ordered them silenced; too many innocent people in Southwark might be killed. At last, realizing he could not take the bridge, Wyatt moved on toward Kingston, and Londoners breathed easier.

At Kingston the rebel leader found the bridge broken, but "then caused he three or four of his soldiers to leap into the water and swim to the other side, who loosed the western boats, which there lay tied, and so brought them over to the other side." Soon these lumbering craft, loaded with artillery, with horses swimming behind, crossed to the Middlesex shore. By eleven o'clock the following morning, Ash Wednesday, February 7, the dauntless rebel leader with his hungry and half-frozen comrades had conquered the pelting rain and miry roads and had reached Knightsbridge.

Again Londoners barricaded doors, shut down their shops, removed their signs and "there was much running up and down in every place . . . aged men were astonished, many women wept for fear, children and maids ran into their houses . . . much noise and tumult was everywhere." At dawn, men beating drums "went through London at four of the clock, warning all soldiers to . . . repair to Charing Cross." By nine o'clock Wyatt was at Hyde Park Corner, where, turning down the lane toward St. James's palace, the forces of the Earl of Pembroke cut off the rebel leader and four hundred of his soldiers from the remainder of his army. Sighting Wyatt at Charing Cross, Edward Courtenay, his former companion in rebellion, turned tail and fled toward Whitehall, crying, "All is lost! All is lost!" His followers, believing the earl, took up his cry as another, Lord Cornwallis, shouted scornfully, "Fie, my lord, this is the action of a gentleman?"

In the palace, "the queen's ladies made the greatest lamentation . . . they wept and wrung their hands . . . saying they would all be destroyed this night!" When Courtenay arrived within Whitehall's gates, "then should ye have seen running and crying of ladies and gentlewomen, shutting of doors and such a shrieking and noise as it was wonderful to hear." But Mary remained calm, rebuking Courtenay scathingly, "It is *your* fond opinion, that durst not come near to see the trial!" Mary wanted to "enter the field to try the truth of her quarrel and to die with them that would serve her." When the queen learned Wyatt had been cut off from his main body of troops, she said, "Well then, fall to prayer and I warrant you we shall hear better news anon. For my lord [Pembroke] will not deceive me, I know well." Then, remembering Pembroke's previous deceptions, she said, almost to herself, "If he would, God will not, in Whom my chief trust is." Mary then stepped out onto the palace balcony and spoke to the distracted and terrified Londoners who'd crowded inside Whitehall's gates for some protection from what they viewed as a rebel triumph. A shower of arrows from one of Wyatt's captains into the palace windows only increased the chaos.

But the loss of those many men cut off by the Earl of Pembroke had severely damaged Wyatt's chances. With his small band of troops, he reached Temple Bar and marched along Fleet Street to Ludgate, "his men not going in any good order or array." A terrified few, he saw, were deserting.

At Ludgate, Wyatt, still wearing the cap with his name on it, pounded on the City gate and demanded to be let in. Already, marching along Fleet Street, he'd seen how Londoners had fled, slamming their doors in his face as much from fear that they'd be thought rebels themselves as for their lives. He'd hoped the majority of citizens, and those City officials who feared for Mary's Spanish alliance as much as he, would come to his aid. How wrong he'd been was evident in the response from behind Ludgate wall when Lord William Howard cried, "Avaunt, traitor! Thou shall not come in here!" Despondent, Wyatt turned and, with his weary, mud-spattered and hungry troops, marched to the Bell Savage Inn courtyard, where everyone rested for a short while. At last, pushing on toward the Temple, "certain horsemen . . . met and then began the flight again to wax hot 'til a herald rode to Wyatt and said, 'Sir, you were best by my council to yield. You see this day is gone against you and in resisting you can get no good, but be the death of all these, your soldiers.' The messenger, William Harvey, Clarencieux Herald, said perhaps the queen would be merciful, "if you stint so great a bloodshed as is like here to be."

Wyatt, accepting now that there was as little chance of his entering the City as there'd been of crossing London Bridge, wearily agreed. "Well," he said, "if I shall needs yield, I will yield me to a gentleman." Sir Morris Berkeley rode forward and "bade him leap up behind him," which Wyatt did, "and so carried them behind upon their horses to the court," where they passed by the window from which Queen Mary and her ladies watched. On the way, they saw bodies of the slain—rebel Kentishman, royal soldier or citizen—lying in the streets, or kicked into the gutter for the easier passage of mounted troops. Others, hurt and nursing their wounds, sat dazed in doorways or by the bodies of the dead, and "the noise . . . was so great and shrill, that it was heard to the top of the White Tower" at the Tower of London. When Wyatt, on his way to the riverside fortress, was perceived as prisoner, "the many hollow hearts rejoiced in London at the same." By five o'clock that night, Wyatt and his confederates—including Alexander Brett, who'd joined the rebels at Rochester Bridge—were taken by Sir Henry Jerningham and turned over to Sir John Brydges at the Tower.

As the news of Wyatt's surrender traveled throughout London, a messenger from the Midlands brought news to the queen that two days before, Henry Grey, the Duke of Suffolk, and his brother Lord John had been taken prisoner at Coventry by the Earl of Huntingdon and, a few hours before the Wyatt rebellion had ended, had arrived at the Tower.

Henry Grey had had little success in Leicester. The Midlands people had not rallied to him in the large forces he'd expected; even bribery was not enough to persuade them to take up arms against the queen. During the next few days several of his men, seeing the duke's cause as lost, deserted. At Newark "he saw all the gates fastened," and informing city officials that the Earl of Huntingdon "would take his part," he sent word to the earl to hasten northward. Grey, anticipating Huntingdon's arrival with fresh troops, rode "in full armor" on to Coventry, intending then to take Kenilworth and Warwick castles. Several loyal to the duke in Coventry had prevailed upon town officials to keep the gates open for him, even ordering one to ride to Grey, urging him to hurry lest others, less committed to his cause, learned of his coming and closed the gates because "he had not forty pounds . . . that may be discouraging to men that peradventure shall look for money at his hands." But the messenger would not budge. It was late, he wanted his sleep and would leave on the morrow, he said. During the next hours, as the duke's followers pleasantly pondered the "undoubted spoil and peradventure destruction of many rich men" which would result from any battle, the Coventry officials received news from London to be on their guard and replaced those at the gates, forcing the conspirators to withdraw. Thus, when the duke arrived late that afternoon and confidently demanded entrance to the city, the gates remained shut.

Stunned at his reception, Grey was conferring with his companions when a message arrived that the Earl of Huntingdon had taken possession of Warwick Castle. Then Henry Grey knew his cause was lost. Without Coventry, Kenilworth and Warwick, he had no base for any Midland uprising. Obviously, with memories of the hated John Dudley still in mind, the people had no wish to aid his old confederate. Grey realized then how sorely he'd mistaken his Northern neighbors' loyalty, for many were even now riding to Huntingdon's support. Wryly, the duke watched them go; he, better than most, knew the great benefit of allying oneself as soon as possible with the victor.

In moments he, his brothers and a few remaining soldiers rode hard to one of the many Suffolk estates, Astley Park, five miles outside Coventry. There, Grey distributed what money he had left among his soldiers and bade them flee. Lord Thomas Grey, in a servant's uniform, rode for Wales, presumably to join Sir James Crofts, while the duke, with his remaining brother, Lord John, "put himself under the trust of one Underwood, a gameskeeper of his park at Astley."

In the morning, they learned the Earl of Huntingdon had issued a proclamation for their capture. Nerve failing, Henry and John Grey left the cottage just as Huntingdon's soldiers appeared on the outskirts of Astley Park. Quickly, John Grey fled to a nearby barn, while the duke hid himself in the trunk of an old decaying tree "two bow shots south of Astley Church." There the duke, ill now from the effects of the previous day's appalling weather, remained while Huntingdon's men prowled the grounds. Two days later, the gameskeeper, frightened at what might happen should Huntingdon learn he'd sheltered Grey, went to Warwick Castle and revealed where Henry Grey was hiding. Soldiers and dogs were quickly dispatched to the park. They soon found Henry Grey's hiding place, later discovering John Grey, miserably cold, huddling under a bale of hay. The two, half-starved and ill from exposure, were taken to the Mayor of Coventry and, three days later, handed over to the Earl of Huntingdon. Within an hour they were bundled off to London, reaching the City gates just as the Wyatt rebellion was coming to an end. After being led through the streets, still littered with the debris of fighting, Henry Grey, "pale as a ghost and shivering," his demeanor more dead than alive, arrived at the Tower a few hours before Wyatt himself was brought in.

A short distance away, at Temple Bar, Simon Renard, the Spanish ambassador, enjoyed the fruits of his own victory. Mary had gone to the Temple to congratulate her troops and there she signed the death warrant for "Guildford Dudley and his wife," naming February 9, two days later, as the day of execution. Henry and John Grey, Thomas Wyatt and other rebel confederates, Mary had earlier proclaimed, "had threatened her destruction and to advance the Lady Jane Grey and her husband." By her words, or Renard's, Mary revealed her honest though mistaken belief that the uprising had supported Jane's cause rather than opposed her Spanish marriage. For Renard, it mattered little which charge the queen needed to justify her action. As he wrote Philip, "Your Majesty need have no fear for your crown, as Jane of Suffolk and Guildford are to be beheaded and the whole house of Suffolk obliterated by the execution of the three brothers whose death, as heretics, will contribute to the firm reestablishment of religion."

Later, at Whitehall Palace, the queen—who'd never doubted her victory—had an emotional scene with her councillors, especially

Huntingdon, for whom she had lavish praise. To Will Herbert, the Earl of Pembroke, who'd cut off Wyatt's advance, she gave a more tangible reward—a diamond ring—at which the earl burst into tears. Within moments the other councillors, relieved that victory was again theirs, were also weeping. Nearby, Simon Renard observed the scene with satisfaction. Later that night he would write the emperor, "Jane of Suffolk and her husband are to lose their heads."

But still Mary appeared reluctant. Flushed with the victory she'd never doubted God had given her, she was also mindful that His mercy might be extended to several of the prisoners who'd been led by false beliefs and false promises. Renard was appalled that once again Mary might pardon some of the conspirators. "Let the queen's clemency be accompanied by a little severity," the emperor caustically wrote his ambassador. But Henry Grey laid all the blame for the insurrection on the departed Peter Carew and Thomas Wyatt, the queen told Renard. He replied that throughout London, daily executions were taking place and naked corpses hung from more than thirty gibbets from Cheapside to the Thames and Southwark, from Tyburn Tree to Tower Hill. In Kent the executions were already under way. With stoic courage many submitted to hanging, drawing and quartering; others were dragged screaming to their fate. While Mary recognized the severity of the main conspirators' crime, she found it difficult to be merciless to all. When four hundred prisoners, "with halters about their necks," were led from prison, they lined up and marched to the palace where Mary—to Renard's open disgust—watched from a gallery gatehouse window as the bedraggled prisoners all went down on their knees in the cold February mud and begged her pardon. With a gracious gesture, she freed them all.

So when the queen again mentioned mercy, Renard emphasized the hundreds of torn, mutilated, burnt or hanging bodies of those who had challenged her—and Spain. Mary's lack of desire for revenge mystified the ambassador. How could she countenance pardoning Jane Grey, her husband and father, while so many others had suffered the ultimate penalty? Severely the ambassador lectured the queen, telling her she'd been too negligent in the aftermath of the Dudley conspiracy. Had she treated *all* the rebels harshly then, there'd have been no second traitorous outbreak. Not only should Jane Grey and her family suffer, said Renard, but so should Elizabeth, who was surely embroiled with young Courtenay, whom the rebels had meant to put on the throne if they had won.

At last, recognizing Mary's stubbornness, the ambassador asked the Earls of Arundel, Winchester and Pembroke to speak to the queen, for he knew their advice would be the same. Once John Dudley had revealed his aim to put Jane Grey on the throne, all three earls had supported him. Winchester had given Jane her crown; all had signed the proclamation labeling Mary Tudor a bastard, unworthy of the throne. Now that Mary was truly queen and all her opposition was in prison, those embarrassing living reminders of their fall from grace must go. Soon the son of the powerful Holy Roman Emperor would arrive in England; there must be no lingering trace of their treasonous behavior about to remind the queen and her husband of their past indiscretions.

So now those same "lords of the council who had been the most instrumental, at the death of Edward VI, in thrusting royalty upon poor Lady Jane, and proclaiming Mary illegitimate . . . became earnest councillors for that innocent lady's death." To do anything less, they emphasized earnestly, would be regarded as a weakness by her subjects and the emperor, who might never send his son to be the husband of a woman who could not govern her "loving people." At last, Mary, fatigued and torn and recognizing her advisers' sensible counsel, signed the death warrants for all.

 28

Jane Grey was not surprised when, as the rebellion ended, she was told to prepare for execution the following morning. All night the Tower grounds had been bright as day, with torches flaring everywhere as soldiers came and went, as cannon rumbled in through the gates, and prisoners—including Wyatt and his captains—were brought in. She'd had little rest, for her rooms overlooked the Green which was the noisiest. Even so, the knowledge that she would now die held little shock. During those few days when it seemed Wyatt might be successful, she'd allowed herself to hope that—once the fighting and any resulting political upheaval had ended—her innocence might be recognized, that she might even be saved. Then her inherent common sense prevailed and she knew there was no escape. Jane had watched from her window as her father and uncle, ill and forlorn-looking, arrived as prisoners at the very place where Henry Grey had brought her as queen. She knew then for a certainty there was no hope.

But she'd not expected retribution to be so quick. Of course there'd be no trial, for she'd already been sentenced. But she, like any criminal, could petition the queen. Then Jane remembered she'd already done so in that letter in which she'd told Mary what had happened in the Dudley conspiracy. There'd never been a reply, although intuitively Jane felt that the queen understood. Other than that, why hadn't she been executed along with John Dudley? Or had her youth saved her? Jane had almost convinced herself the queen was only waiting for the proper time to release her—perhaps into honorable custody at her own or a Dudley home—until remembrance of that unhappy time when she'd had to fight for her crown had passed.

And then her father had committed a further treason and the chance was lost.

Yet when a pleasant-faced Doctor Feckenham, the queen's chaplain, came to her lodging on that morning of February 8 and told her she must prepare for execution the next day, Jane's first reaction was almost one of relief. *Now she knew.* She listened dry-eyed as, behind her, Mrs. Ellen and Mrs. Tylney began to weep. "I am ready to receive death patiently," she told her black-robed visitor, "and in whatsoever manner it may please the queen to appoint." Jane said that while she was young enough to be frightened "at what I have to go through . . . I fervently hope the spirit will spring rejoicingly into the presence of the Eternal God." It helped to know that she would not be burned. Beheading, she'd heard, was quick and painless if the executioner was skillful. She asked after Guildford. "He is innocent," she told Feckenham, "and only obeyed his father in all things." The priest nodded but said Guildford, too, must die on the morrow. And when he offered his spiritual services, Jane said politely that she wanted a minister of the reformed religion sent to her, not one of the Roman Catholic faith. "I have no time for that controversy," she told the priest impatiently, as she said good-bye and turned to her distraught companions.

But, Jane found, accepting the inevitable was not easy. She was not yet seventeen, and until a few months ago, a whole life had lain ahead of her. What would her fate have been had Mary pardoned her? Life in an obscure country manor with Guildford Dudley, undoubtedly, exiled from the court for their treasonous behavior. With the exception of Guildford's presence, that would not have been wholly unendurable, for most of her life at Bradgate had been solitary. But she'd always had her studies, with exciting and limitless sanctuaries to which her mind might travel. In normal circumstances her scholarship might even have taken her abroad to meet those brilliant, sophisticated, inquiring minds she'd corresponded with. She remembered the generous advice that had so inspired her, opening up a world she'd never envisioned in the quiet classroom with John Aylmer. They had, in truth, opened another world for her soul.

It was of that soul which now, particularly, Jane knew she must be careful if it was to travel to God when her head was cut off. Every day of her life, when she'd been in no danger at all, she'd prayed for her soul's welfare. In the past months, she'd prayed to be strong, to be shown the way to freedom or accept what her fate must be. Now, with the news the priest had just given her, she must pray not only to endure the brutality of the next day, but must also petition God that her soul be protected and salvaged, for it was the only part of her that would live on. Leaving her companions to their tears, Jane went dry-eyed to her room to kneel beside her bed and pray.

Then, as was her custom, she went to her desk. There was much she had to do, and very little time in which to do it. Books, paper and pen had always been her friends, and now, more than ever, they would solace her in the hours ahead. She wondered what her family thought of the queen's order. Did they even know? Her mother would lose not only the daughter who'd been such a disappointment, but also the husband whom, less than six months before, she'd persuaded the queen to pardon. Jane Dudley, Guildford's mother, had lost her husband, seen her sons as prisoners and now would lose the youngest one, the boy nearest her heart whom she could deny nothing. Jane thought of her sisters, Katherine and Mary, How, she wondered, would they fare at the court of a queen who'd had their older sister's head cut off?

Then, realizing such thoughts were wasteful—she had so little time left!—Jane wrote to her incarcerated father, putting her thoughts on paper in a letter remarkable for its forgiveness.

Father—Although it hath pleased God to hasten my death by you, by whom my life should rather have been lengthened, yet can I patiently take it, that I yield God more hearty thanks for shortening my woeful days, than if all the world had been given into my possession, with life lengthened at my own will.

And albeit I am well assured of your impatient dolours, re-doubled many ways, both in bewailing your own woe, and especially, as I am informed, my woeful estate; yet, my dear father, if I may without offence rejoice in my own mishap, herein I may account myself blessed, that washing my hands with the innocence of my face, my guiltless blood may cry before the Lord, "Mercy, to the innocent!"

And yet, though I must needs acknowledge that being con-strained, and, as you know well enough, continually assayed; yet, in taking [the crown] upon me, I seemed to consent, and therein grievously offended the queen and her laws, yet do I assuredly trust, that this my offence towards God is so much the less, in that being in so royal estate as I was, my enforced honor never mixed with mine innocent heart.

And thus, good father, I have opened unto you the state in which I presently stand, my death at hand, although to you it may seem woeful, *yet to me there is nothing more welcome than from this vale of misery to aspire to that heavenly throne of all joy and pleasure*, with Christ our Savior, in whose steadfast faith (if it be lawful for the daughter so to write to the father) the Lord that Hitherto hath strengthened you, so continue to keep you, that at last we may meet in heaven with the Father, Son and Holy Ghost. Amen. I am,

Your Obedient Daughter 'til Death,
Jane Duddeley [*sic*]

Having written the letter and seen it sent to Henry Grey, whose cell was across the Green, Jane felt better. Perhaps it might be some comfort to her father; to write it had been a comfort to her. Tomorrow she would write her sister Katherine. There would be time before the execution, but now, having bared her thoughts to her father, she was too tired. She would not write to her sister Mary, who was too young to understand. Nor would she write to her mother. Frances Grey would not expect any communication and Jane realized she herself would not know what to say. It would be better—after the letters had been written and her prayers had been said—to try and comfort Mrs. Ellen and Mrs. Tylney, who were so devastated they could scarce serve her.

When Jane arose the next morning, thanking God in her prayer for the composure she hoped would carry her through the day, she was stunned when Dr. Feckenham arrived to say that the queen—hoping some spiritual enlightenment might come to Jane through the priest's ministrations—had sanctioned a reprieve of three days for both her and Guildford. Feckenham explained that Jane's remark that "she had no time" for proper religious observance before her execution had sent him flying to the queen to beg for those extra days in which the girl might receive religious comfort, even instruction. Implicit in his words, Jane saw, was the conviction that during those days he might rescue her from religious heresy.

"Alas, sir! I did not intend what I said to be reported to the queen, nor would I have you think me covetous of a moment's longer life." Jane was almost in tears. "I am only solicitous for a better life in Eternity and will gladly suffer death since it is her Majesty's pleasure." Dismayed, Jane told the priest he'd misunderstood her meaning. Already, emotionally, she'd accepted that she would die that morning and now her courage was strong. To wait three more days would try that courage and be even more difficult for Mrs. Ellen and Mrs. Tylney. If Feckenham truly harbored any optimism of converting her, it meant her last hours were to be spent in the very controversy she'd hoped to avoid.

Dr. Feckenham was no stranger to tragedy, religious or otherwise. The thirty-nine-year-old priest had spent time in the Tower in Edward's reign for preaching an anti-Protestant sermon and had not been freed until Mary won her crown. Already he'd used his considerable influence with the queen to obtain release or mitigate the punishment of some of the lesser prisoners. Even so, the queen "could not go about the city without beholding the ugly sight of dangling corpses at every turn of the street." The magnificent *Te Deum* which had been sung at St. Paul's the day before had been marred by processions of prisoners being taken for sentencing at Westminster Hall; parishioners had had to wait to enter the church until they passed. Feckenham was strongly drawn to the slight young girl, the freckles on her skin so prominent against the pallor of confinement. He knew her story well and admired her calm demeanor in the face of a death she did not deserve; he deplored the sad fate of one so innocent, so blatantly the object of other's ungodly ambition.

And despite their differing faiths, he marveled at Jane's stoic courage, that admirable serenity with which she'd accepted her appalling sentence. It hurt, however, that she would die with all the wrong beliefs. Feckenham, already noted for his conversion skill, was not unaware of the luster that would enhance his calling if he could convince Lady Jane Grey of the error of her ways. It would impress not only the queen but also those many misguided others who clung so staunchly to Edward's Protestantism. It would be a spectacular coup, not only personally, but for the Church. Therefore, he suggested they "dispute" on the different theological points of view that separated their faiths.

"This disputation," Jane replied wearily, "may be fit for the living, but not for the dying. Leave me to make my peace with God. You are much disappointed if you think I have any desire of a longer life. . . ."

But Feckenham insisted. He'd been sent, he told a troubled Jane, "from the queen and her council to instruct you in the true doctrine of the right faith. . . ." He hoped, he said, there would be "little need to travail with you much herein."

"I heartily thank the Queen's Highness, which is not unmindful of her humble subject," Jane said ruefully. "And I hope, likewise, that you no less will do your duty therein both truly and faithfully, according to that you were sent for." The good doctor, she could see, felt he had a job to do; she should not hinder him.

Jane had been sentenced to die on Friday, February 9. On the following day, the dedicated Feckenham continued intent upon converting one he regarded as a hapless and misinformed young woman. Jane Grey, he knew, had lived in the country much of her life and, like her father, was staunchly Protestant, having undoubtedly received religious instruction from a less than learned country priest. Feckenham, buttressed by his own deeply held faith, was confident of his power of persuasion. And so, with these two brilliant and unusual contenders, a remarkable dialogue ensued as each fought for the integrity of a soul.

There was quiet in the room of Jane's lodgings as Dr. Feckenham began. When he asked Jane what was required of a Christian man, she replied, "That he should believe in God the Father, the Son and the Holy Ghost, three persons and one God. . . ." When she answered, in reply to a question as to how one should love one's neighbor, "that it was best shown by feeding the hungry, clothing the naked and giving drink to the thirsty," Feckenham, pretending ignorance, asked why it was "necessary unto salvation to do good works also, and it is not sufficient only to believe?" To which Jane's answer was that certainly while "faith only saveth," it was also proper that a Christian "followeth his Master, Christ" and do good works as Christ had done when He was on earth.

Impressed in spite of himself, Feckenham then concentrated on those divisive tenets of Scripture that set him and Jane Grey apart. "How many Sacraments are there?" he asked. Quickly, Jane replied, "Two: the one the Sacrament of Baptism, and the other the Sacrament of the Lord's Supper."

No, Feckenham shook his head confidently, denying her answer. "No, there are seven. . . ."

"And by what Scripture find you that?" Jane asked sharply, so flustering the priest, he answered, "Well, we will talk of that hereafter." Then he asked Jane to explain her two Sacraments. Choosing her words carefully, she said that the baptism water "is a token to me that I am a child of God." As for the other Sacrament—her words came slowly, so there would be no mistaking her meaning—when "offered unto me [it] is a sure seal of testimony that I am by the blood of Christ . . ."

Feckenham disagreed. "Why? What do you receive in that Sacrament? Do you not receive the very blood and body of Christ?" Heatedly, Jane shook her head. "No, surely, I do not so believe!" She received neither flesh nor blood, she cried, but only bread and wine which, when eaten and drunk, would "put me in remembrance how that for my sins the body of Christ was broken. . . ." Then why, asked Feckenham triumphantly, "Did Christ speak these words—'Take, eat, this is my body?' Require you any plainer words? Doth he not say it is his body?"

But Jane would not have it. "I grant, he saith so," she replied curtly, "and so he saith, 'I am the vine, I am the door'—but he is never the more for that, the vine or the door. . . ." When Christ said that, Jane emphasized, *he was alive*, sitting at the table with his apostles. He was in the flesh and broke the bread and drank the wine. But he meant his words to be symbolic only.

After a few hours, sensing defeat, Feckenham told Jane she did not give the Church much credit, "grounding your faith upon such authors as say and unsay both in a breath. . . ." To which Jane replied, "No, I ground my faith on God's word, not the church. . . ."

"Well, I am sorry for you," Feckenham said, honestly grieved, "for I am sure we two shall never meet [in the next world]. . . ." Vigorously, Jane nodded, saying such was true, "except God turn your heart, for I am assured, unless you repent and turn to God, you are in evil case." Disappointed and moved in spite of himself, the priest prepared to leave, recognizing that Jane Grey's faith was as unbreachable, as powerful as his own. Yet, impressed with her dignity and piousness, he nevertheless wished to do Jane one last service and asked if he might accompany her during those last hours on Monday.

Knowing the queen would send no other spiritual adviser, Jane consented. Now she and Feckenham knew each other well; she was confident he'd do everything possible to make those last moments bearable. And there was something else. During those hours she and the priest had debated, there'd come the startling awareness that not all Catholic priests were instruments of the devil with false doctrines, corrupt practices and stern punishment for those who believed differently. It was an awakening moment for Jane. She'd been satisfied with her own staunch defense against the hated Roman Church and yet it came as something of a shock to accept that one as honestly devout and sincere as Feckenham could believe in a creed and ritual which she considered foolishly senseless at best, evil and misleading at worst.

But she was also grateful that once Feckenham had realized she would never capitulate, that he'd never change her, he had not abandoned her. He'd see her to the scaffold as a friend, even a Roman Catholic one.

Queen Mary had ordered that, because of her royal rank, Jane Grey's execution should take place inside the tower, on the Green. Guildford, however, would die as his father had done, at the execution site outside on Tower Hill. All the following day, Guildford, "in a flood of tears," bewailed his fate, especially when he heard that Jane would not be with him on that last walk. Quickly, he sent word to the queen that he would like one final opportunity to see his wife before they died. Mary replied that "if it would be any consolation to them, they should be allowed to see each other." But when the message was delivered to Jane, who was struggling to maintain the calm composure of the previous day, she declined, replying to Mary that "it would only disturb the holy tranquillity with which they had prepared themselves for death." To Guildford she sent a message that she feared her presence "would rather weaken than strengthen him—that he ought to take courage from his reason, and derive constancy from his own heart—that if his soul were not firm and settled, she could not settle it by her eyes, nor confirm it by her words." He would do well, she ended, "to remit this interview till they met in a better world, where friendships were happy and unions indissoluble, and theirs, she hoped, would be eternal." Jane hoped her words would comfort her husband, but she did not need Guildford's tears; her own were too near the surface. Already, outside on the Green, she could hear the sound of men talking or laughing together as they hammered the scaffold into place. Jane kept away from the window and stayed in her room. It also kept her apart from Mrs. Ellen and Mrs. Tylney, who were wan and tired and burst into tears at the slightest provocation. Much as she loved them, their despair did her little good.

On Sunday, February 11, Stephen Gardiner, the Bishop of Winchester, preached before the queen in her chapel and "asked a boon of the queen's Highness that like as she had before time extended her mercy, particularly and privately, so through her leniency and gentleness much conspiracy and open rebellion was grown," he hoped that "she would now be merciful to the body of the commonwealth and conservation thereof, which could not be unless the rotten and hurtful members thereof were cut off and consumed." By the import of Gardiner's words, "the audience did gather there should shortly follow sharp and cruel execution." The service ended as the very Catholic Gardiner "prayed for King Edward the VI in his sermon and for the souls departed."

At the Tower of London, one of those whom Gardiner had described as "rotten and hurtful" was spending her last full day on earth writing. Again pen and paper were a comfort to Jane Grey and her mind was filled with what she had to say. When she discovered a few empty pages at the end of her Greek Testament, she filled them with a message to her fourteen-year-old sister, Katherine:

> I have sent you, good sister Katherine, a book, which although it be not outwardly rimmed with gold, yet inwardly it is more worth than precious stones. It is the book, dear sister, of the laws of the Lord; it is His Testament and Last Will, which he bequeathed unto us wretches, which shall lead you to the path of eternal joy, and if you, with a good mind, read it, and with an earnest desire follow, it shall bring you to an immortal and everlasting life. It will teach you to live and learn you to die. . . .

By her death, Jane had realized, Katherine Grey would become her father's heir. However, she told Katherine, the knowledge in her last gift, the Testament, "shall win you more than you should have gained by the possession of your woeful father's lands, for as if God had prospered him, you should have inherited his lands." It made Jane wonder just how much of her family's wealth would be left when whatever was to happen to Henry Grey was over. Traitors' lands and possessions were usually confiscated. Would the queen keep Katherine and Mary Grey about her with their £80 a year? What would become of her mother? Would the queen leave the family any Suffolk possessions at all?

More than once in her confinement Jane had thought of Katherine Brandon, the Dowager Duchess of Suffolk, that dear friend of Queen Katherine Parr, with whom she'd enjoyed those enchanted summer days at the little manor house at Chelsea in what now seemed another lifetime. The untimely death of Kate Brandon's sons had given Henry Grey the Suffolk dukedom, after which the duchess had married again. But Stephen Gardiner had been a merciless opponent of the outspoken Kate Brandon's Protestantism. When she'd become the mother of a new daughter, Susan, Kate realized there was no place for her in Mary Tudor's England and, on the past New Year's Day, had fled from her mother's home in the Barbican to join her husband in exile on the Continent. What, Jane wondered, would her old friend think of the manner in which the Suffolk wealth—those homes and treasures of Charles Brandon's—had been treated? How it would now all be confiscated by the Crown and lost forever to the family?

Bringing her thoughts back to her sister's message, Jane wrote to Katherine Grey that the contents of her little Greek Testament were "such riches as neither the covetous shall withdraw from you, neither the thief shall steal, neither yet the moth corrupt. . . ." Then, realizing how little space she had left, she ended:

> And as touching my death, rejoice as I do and consider that I shall be delivered of this corruption, and put on incorruption, for I am assured that I shall for losing of a mortal life find an immortal felicity. Pray God grant you and send you of His grace to live in His fear, and then to die in the love. . . .

Then Jane's self-control dwindled and sudden tears blotted the last few sentences. Quickly, she wrote: "Farewell, good sister, put your only trust in God, who only must uphold you," and signed herself "Your loving sister, Jane Duddeley."

Later that day, Sir John Gage, the Constable of the Tower, brought to Jane's rooms her father's Prayer Book, explaining that the duke had left it when he'd previously been imprisoned during the Dudley conspiracy. It was the same book, Jane recognized, that Guildford had given her father months before. When Gage offered to return it to her father and asked if she wished any message to accompany it, Jane wrote, beneath Guildford's original dedication:

> The Lord comfort your Grace and that in His word wherein all creatures only are to be comforted. And though it hath pleased God to take two of your children, yet think not, I most humbly beseech your Grace, that you have lost them. But trust that we, by leaving this mortal life, have won an immortal life. And I, as for my part, as I have honored your Grace in this life, will pray for you in another life.
> Your Grace's humble daughter,
Jane Duddeley

Throughout those last communications, even though some of the lines to Katherine Grey were smudged with tears, Jane's steely strength had been evidence of that strong faith to which she'd committed her mind and soul, and which she expected to see her through those final hours. So, putting her farewell messages aside, she went to her room to pray. Perhaps the depth of her emotion would shut out the sounds of hammering at the scaffold. After that, she must persuade Mrs. Ellen and Mrs. Tylney to accompany her the next day so they could decently dispose of her body afterward, for there was no one else.

The following morning Jane arose early and asked Mrs. Ellen and Mrs. Tylney to join her in prayer in her room. She hoped by her own quiet manner to comfort the women, whose grief still consumed them. Several times during the night, as she'd snatched at sleep for brief bits of time, she'd heard them whispering and weeping in the room nearby. But when they came to kneel with her, Jane was relieved to see that though their eyes were swollen and red-rimmed, they were dry; they'd accepted at last that their sorrow would do their beloved charge little good. Their strong determination to control their emotions and not unnerve her made Jane yearn to embrace them, as she'd done so often in the years of growing up, using Mrs. Ellen's warm and comfortable shoulder to cry upon whenever she needed it. But such behavior would serve no purpose; her companions knew how much she loved them. Now, Jane hoped only to maintain a composed and dignified demeanor for that last grim moment on the scaffold. She wondered if Guildford had anyone—servant, friend or brother—to share a last solacing moment with him. She'd meant her message to be consoling, but he might not have accepted it that way. Master Partridge had told her of Guildford's disappointment in not seeing her one last time. But Jane knew she had done the right thing, preserving their emotional strength for the bitter time ahead.

She'd been told Guildford was to go first, and by ten o'clock she heard the sounds of the crowd gathered at the execution site on Tower Hill. She knew how difficult that would be for Guildford, whose courage had never been tested in even the simplest trials, who'd been catered to and pampered by a doting family all his life. She told Mrs. Ellen and Mrs. Tylney she would watch his departure from her window, though she doubted he would be able to see her, even if he knew where to look.

Shortly before ten, Sir Anthony Browne, Henry VIII's old Master of the Horse, met Guildford, dressed in a suit of somber black velvet "slashed with a dark-colored cloth," at the Beauchamp Tower. The boy had refused Dr. Feckenham's services and, not being allowed a Protestant minister, had no "ghostly father" to accompany him on his last walk. In sympathy, Browne, accompanied by Master John Throckmorton "and many other gentlemen," came to escort Guildford, and it was Browne, a friend of John Dudley's, who kindly took the young boy "by the hand" to deliver him to Sir Thomas Offeley, the Sheriff of Middlesex, at the Bulwark Gate. Then, as soldiers cleared a path, the small group walked slowly through the crowd toward Tower Hill.

All those attending Guildford knew how unpopular were the executions of Lady Jane Grey and her husband. Already the City was filled with corpses dangling from gibbets, tree limbs or even the doorways of their own houses. Mutilated bodies of those hanged, drawn and quartered were displayed at London Bridge, along Cheapside and by the Temple; the sickening odor of death filled the air as the rotting corpses were removed to be replaced by a fresh batch. The sheriff saw at once that his soldiers would not be needed to quell any disturbance, for the youth and lack of any real guilt of the prisoners had seemingly inspired a strong compassion from the crowd and it was shown now in their respectful silence. Many of the women were in tears, while others offered soft cries of encouragement as Guildford, weeping openly now, looking neither right nor left and still clutching Browne's hand, walked steadily up the hill until he reached the scaffold. There, with the mien of one impatient to have done before his courage disappeared, he took off his doublet, unfastened his collar and then "kneeled down and said his prayers." Then, "holding up his eyes and hands to God many times . . . at last, after he had desired the people to pray for him, he laid himself along, and his head upon the block, which was at one stroke of the axe taken from him." This time there was no cheering as there had been at John Dudley's death, and quickly and silently the crowd dispersed as the executioner, having hastily flung Guildford's body and head into a waiting cart, walked back to the Tower, the sheriff and others following behind.

In Jane's room, Mrs. Ellen and Mrs. Tylney finished dressing her in the same severe black dress she'd worn to her sentencing in the Guildhall. Earlier, she'd watched Guildford as he left, surrounded by Browne and his companions; he had not turned to look for her. Now Jane forced herself back to the window to look at the scaffold below on the Green. She wanted to absorb completely the place where she was to die so it would not be strange when she stepped upon it. It was small, newly made and strewn with fresh hay. After a moment she saw Sir John Brydges leaving his lodging to come for her. It was time.

As she watched, with Mrs. Ellen standing beside her, a cart rumbled by. With a gasp, Mrs. Ellen attempted to pull Jane from the window. But it was too late for both had seen Guildford's body. He lay, plain for all to see, sprawled ignominiously in death, the severed head wrapped in a bloodstained cloth at his feet. Both watched, horrified, yet unable to turn away. "Oh! Guildford! Guildford!" Jane cried, hand to her mouth. "The ante-repast is not so bitter that you have tasted, and that I shall soon taste, as to make my flesh tremble." Then, as if to give herself and Mrs. Ellen comfort, she whispered, "But that is nothing compared to the feast you and I shall this day partake of in Paradise." She forced herself to watch as "his dead carcass [was] taken out of the cart. . . ." And then, as Sir John Brydges, accompanied by his brother Sir Thomas, the Deputy-Lieutenant of the Tower, entered the room, Jane gave way to tears.

In the next hour she knelt alone, praying for the return of that steely self-control which had been her ally the past few days. As everyone waited patiently—for the officials refused to hurry her— Jane's composure returned. At last, at about eleven o'clock, the drums outside began to beat and the bells of All Hallows' Barking and the Tower church began to toll. Slowly, a small procession from the Gentleman-Gaoler's lodgings began to form. Jane Grey was of royal blood and her status in death was to be observed as reverently and distinctly as it had been in life.

As she emerged on the arm of Sir John Brydges, Jane appeared startled by the company of two hundred Yeomen of the Guard waiting to escort her the small distance to the scaffold. The executioner, clad in tight-fitting scarlet worsted, a giant with swelling muscles, his features hidden in a hooded mask of scarlet, stood next in line. The black-robed priest, Dr. Feckenham, crucifix in hand, waited with several Tower chaplains. Now that her poise had returned, Jane looked almost serene. As the fresh, icy air off the river blew the folds of her long black dress about her, she swiftly took her place in the procession. This time she wore no *chopines*. No longer was she a queen whom everyone must see. Many of those crowding about the White Tower were surprised at the diminutive size of the prisoner, who looked little more than a child.

Holding her Prayer Book—a refuge, as it had been on that long walk to the Guildhall—Jane repeated the words she knew by heart. Her calm contrasted with the demeanor of Mrs. Ellen and Mrs. Tylney, who, facing that bitter last moment, wept openly. But Jane seemed not to hear.

Just before leaving her room, Sir John Brydges, saddened at the fate of the young girl to whom he'd become warmly attached during her seven months in the Tower, had asked for some memento that he might have for his comfort. Calmly, Jane had sat one last time at her desk and, in her little book of prayers, had written:

Forasmuch as you have desired so simple a woman to write in so worthy a book, good Master Lieutenant, therefore I shall as a friend desire you, and as a Christian require you, to call upon God to incline your heart to his laws, to quicken you in his ways, and not to take the word of truth utterly out of your mouth. Live still to die, that by death you may purchase eternal life; and remember how the end of Methusael [sic], who we read in Scripture was the longest liver that was of a man, died at the last: for, as the preacher says, that there is a time to be born and a time to die; and the day of death is better than the day of our birth.

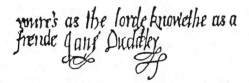

your's as the lorde knowethe as a frende Jane Duddley

The words may have comforted Jane, for as she made ready to climb the scaffold, she turned confidently to Feckenham and said, "Go now. God grant you all your desires and accept my own warm thanks for your attentions to me. Although indeed"—she gave the priest a semblance of a smile—"those attentions have tried me more than death can now terrify me." Swiftly she climbed the steps, "nothing at all abashed, neither with the fear of her own death . . . neither her eyes moistened with tears, although her two gentlewomen . . . wonderfully wept," an observer would later write. As she stood, patient and tiny in the middle of the scaffold, a murmur swept through the crowd, visibly touched by her youth and courage.

Ignoring the sight of the scarlet-clad executioner, Jane asked Brydges if she might say a few words. The Lieutenant nodded. Standing at the scaffold rail, she gazed at the clustered throng below and, in a clear, calm voice, spoke:

"Good people, I am come hither to die and by a law I am condemned to the same. The fact, indeed, against the queen's Highness was unlawful and the consenting thereto by me, but touching the procurement and desire thereof by me or on my behalf, I do wash my hands thereof in innocence, before God and the face of you, good Christian people, this day. . . ." As if to impress her blamelessness upon everyone, Jane "wrung her hands" almost as if washing them clean of sin. Then she continued, "I pray you all, good Christian people, to bear me witness that I die a true Christian woman, and that I look to be saved by none other means, but only by the mercy of God, in the merits of the blood of his only son, Jesus Christ."

And then, though the words she spoke hardly applied, Jane, humble and penitent to the end, made her peace with God, saying, "And I confess, when I did know the word of God, I neglected the same, loved myself and the world, and therefore this plague or punishment is happily and worthily happened unto me for my sins. And yet I thank God of his goodness that he hath thus given me a time and respite to repent." She waited a moment, silent, and then concluded. "And now, good people, while I am alive, I pray you to assist me with your prayers." Below, on the Green, many knelt in prayer on the cold earth.

Seeing Feckenham had, despite her remark, accompanied her to the scaffold, Jane asked him, "Shall I say the *Miserere* psalm?" Immeasurably moved by the girl's calm strength, the priest found it difficult to say more than "Yea." Together, "in a most devout manner to the end," Jane then said the *Miserere mei, Deus* in English while, behind her, Feckenham intoned it in Latin. Rising, Jane saw the distress in the priest's face and, softening, whispered, "God, I beseech Him abundantly reward you for your kindness to me. . . ." Then, seeing the man still could not speak, she leaned over and kissed him on the cheek, perhaps—even in that solemn moment—wondering how as little as several days ago, such a gesture would have been unthinkable.

Then Jane gave Mrs. Tylney her gloves and handkerchief, which the woman accepted wordlessly. She handed her Prayer Book to Sir John Brydges, saying, "You asked me for a parting memory of me. . . ." Seeing Mrs. Tylney and Mrs. Ellen so overcome, she began to untie her gown herself. The executioner went to her, thinking to help, but she brushed him away curtly, saying, "Let me alone." The sight of Jane seemingly helpless caused the two women to stop weeping, and they came forward to assist her with her headdress and neckerchief, removing her outer dress so that she stood in the cold air in an undergarment with close-fitting sleeves. Mrs. Ellen's last gesture was to give her a handkerchief to "knit about her eyes"; she was so agitated she could scarcely hand Jane the cloth.

Then the executioner knelt before Jane and asked her forgiveness, "which she gave most willingly." And then what Jane had dreaded most—that traditional five minutes when everyone must wait for any reprieve from the monarch—had to be endured. No one present expected any such mercy, yet everyone waited—Jane beginning to shiver or tremble in her thin cloth garment—until the time was up. When the executioner showed her where to stand upon the straw, Jane saw the block, which heretofore had been out of sight. She gazed at it for only a moment, saying to the executioner, "I pray you dispatch me quickly." As he nodded, she started to kneel but, still uncertain, asked, "Will you take it off before I lay me down?"

"No, madame," the man replied, and Jane, with steady hands, tied the handkerchief about her eyes, shutting out her last glimpse of the world. But in so doing, she'd also shut out the sight of the block. Behind her, Feckenham had begun to pray, and sobbing, Mrs. Ellen and Mrs. Tylney embraced each other so they might not see the actual deed. As they waited, a heart-wrenching cry could be heard from Jane. "Where is it? What shall I do?" And then, her voice shaking, *"Where is it?"*

Frozen with horror, all watched, seemingly unable to respond as Jane groped in the air for the block, imploring help from anyone. At last, since all on the scaffold seemed incapable of action, "one of the standers-by," taking merciful pity upon the victim, climbed the scaffold steps and guided Jane's hands to the block. Holding it firmly, she laid her body on the straw, her head upon the block, and stretched forth her hands in signal to the executioner that she was ready. "Lord, into thy hands I commend my spirit" were her last words.

And so, as a chronicler living in the Tower and witnessing the event would later write, "she ended. . . ."

But not quite. Later, after her grief-stricken ladies had taken Jane's body for burial to the Tower church, after those belongings that had survived the Earl of Winchester's depredations had been gathered together and her lodgings cleaned, Sir John Brydges read another inscription on the last page of the Prayer Book Jane Grey had given him. It obviously had been written within the last few hours of her death—eight months short of her seventeenth birthday—and indicated once more her desire to be forgiven for breaking the law, for having committed the sin of accepting the Crown. The three small verses speak of Jane's strong belief in her vindication:

IN LATIN: If Justice is done with my body,
my soul will find mercy with God.

IN GREEK: Death will give pain to my body for
its sins, but the soul will be justified before God.

IN ENGLISH: If my faults deserve punishment, my
youth at least and my imprudence were
worthy of excuse. God and posterity
will show me favor.

Afterwards

Mrs. Ellen and Mrs. Tylney

According to Jane's biographer Richard Davey, Jane's two servingwomen were not allowed to attend to her body immediately. Apparently no one had determined that since the Tower church, St. Peter's-ad-Vincula, had been returned to the Catholic form of worship, a "heretic" like Jane Grey could not be buried within its hallowed walls without an ecclesiastical license. Dr. Feckenham, therefore, rushed to either the queen or the Archbishop of York, Nicholas Heath (Cranmer, the Archbishop of Canterbury, being still in prison), to gain the needed permission. In the meantime, Jane's body lay exposed for at least four hours and was seen by Francois, the brother of Antoine de Noailles, the French ambassador, as he entered the Tower upon his return that day from France. De Noailles saw Jane's body upon the scaffold and was "amazed at the immense quantity of blood that had poured out of so small a corpse."

At last, Mrs. Ellen and Mrs. Tylney were allowed to place the remains in a plain deal coffin, and Jane Grey was buried without any religious ceremony whatever, near two dead queens, the Protector and Guildford Dudley. Centuries later, when Queen Victoria ordered the church to be cleansed and repaired, a coffin "containing the remains of a female of diminutive stature, with the head severed from the body" was opened. The skeleton crumbled when exposed to air, and the ashes were then enclosed in an urn and placed under the oval inscription in the chancel which records Jane's execution. There has always been a legend at Bradgate that her body was taken back to her old home and buried there, at which time the servants pollarded the trees in her memory. At the turn of the century, some of these trees were still in existence.

What happened to Mrs. Ellen is unknown; she is mentioned no more in the lives of Frances Grey or her two daughters, Mary and Katherine. Mrs. Tylney, who was a relative of the Duchess of Norfolk, undoubtedly retired to live in a Norfolk home.

Henry Grey

Jane's father was brought to trial for treason five days after her death. The Earl of Arundel sentenced Henry Grey, thus avenging a decades-long grudge against the man who'd rejected his sister to marry Frances Brandon. The duke was beheaded on Tower Hill on February 23, 1554, and his body buried in the Tower church. His head, however, was sent to a Grey residence in the Minories, which had been a former convent. It was kept in an airtight box of oakwood and placed in the chapel. The box, acting as a preservative, kept the head intact. Much later, it was given to nearby St. Botolph's Church near Aldgate where it still remains and is sometimes shown.

Frances Grey

While her daughter and husband lay in prison under sentence of death, Frances Grey remained at Sheen, enjoying the attentions of Adrian Stokes, "a ginger-headed lad" of twenty-one, one of the Suffolk grooms and fifteen years her junior. On March 9, two weeks after her husband's execution and one month from the time of Jane's original execution date, Frances Grey married Adrian Stokes. Historians have ever after wondered why the great duchess, of the blood royal, would so demean herself, but since she gave birth to a daughter the following November, it is more than possible she was pregnant at the time of her marriage. The daughter died soon after birth.

There was always a warm welcome at Queen Mary's court for Frances Grey, despite the fact that the queen had ordered the execution of her cousin's husband and daughter. The friendship continued, with Frances often taking precedence over the Princess Elizabeth. When Elizabeth eventually came to the throne, their relationship was not as intimate nor was she as generous to Frances as Mary had been. What with no financial help from the monarch and many of the Suffolk estates confiscated, Frances Grey lived the next few years in considerably reduced circumstances. She died in 1559, five years after Jane, at the age of forty-three. Queen Elizabeth gave her cousin an impressive funeral and her ornate tomb may still be seen in St. Edmund's Chapel in Westminster Abbey. Its inscription notes her two husbands, but there is no mention of her daughters.

Katherine Grey

Katherine was fourteen when Jane died. When Elizabeth became queen four years later, she kept Katherine and Mary Grey at court, as much for surveillance as from any real fondness, since both were in line for the throne. Katherine was pretty but light-headed and both girls lacked any real common sense. Soon after Jane's death, Katherine's marriage to Lord Herbert—a formality only—was dissolved. In 1560, six years later, Katherine married Edward Seymour, young Lord Hertford, the Protector's eldest son, in a secret ceremony which, had the queen known of it, she would certainly have prevented because of Katherine's nearness to the throne. Within months the girl was pregnant, and a furious Elizabeth had both bride and groom arrested and sent to the Tower, where Katherine bore a healthy son. The new Lieutenant of the Tower was an understanding man and he often let the two prisoners meet. Inevitably, Katherine was again pregnant and had yet another boy. Two healthy males in the succession for a Virgin Queen who'd decided against marriage was too much for Elizabeth and she banished both young Seymour with one child and Katherine Grey with the younger son to perpetual exile in private homes away from court for the remainder of their lives. Both wrote many long, imploring letters to the queen, William Cecil and the council, but won no forgiveness. Katherine died from tuberculosis in January 1568 at the age of twenty-seven. Seymour was then released and married again twice. He spent much time and money during the rest of his life attempting to prove the validity of his marriage to Katherine Grey, not only for his sons' legitimacy but to ensure their inheritances. He did not obtain it until 1608, five years after Elizabeth's death.

Edward Seymour lived to be eighty-three. At his death in 1621, an ornate tomb was erected in Salisbury Cathedral, and the effigy placed beside his image was that of his first wife, Katherine Grey. Some part of her body was brought, fifty-three years after her death, from its final resting place in Yoxford Church and interred with that of her husband.

Mary Grey

The youngest Grey girl, dwarfish—she was only four feet tall—and unattractive, also incurred Elizabeth's strong displeasure when, in 1565, at the age of nineteen, she, too, married without permission and below her station. Her groom was Thomas Keyes, "the biggest gentleman in this court," according to Sir William Cecil. Keyes, a Sergeant-Porter, or gatekeeper, was "over forty" and a widower with seven children. His unusual height contrasted so strongly with his wife's unnatural size that the two presented an incongruous sight, affronting many. Yet they seemed genuinely fond of each other. Mary said all she wanted, in view of her two sisters' dire fates, was to live as normal a life as possible. But Elizabeth, angry at the way the Grey girls had treated what she considered her generosity, said she "wanted no little bastard Keyes," and less than two weeks after her marriage, Mary was sent into house arrest in a succession of homes, while Thomas Keyes went to the Fleet Prison. There he suffered from the confinement of his huge frame in a small cell. After more than a year in prison, with his health jeopardized, Keyes was sent to his home village of Lewisham and later to Sandgate Castle on the Kentish coast, where he still sought permission to live with his wife. It was never granted and he died in September 1571, six years after his marriage to Mary Grey.

Mary Grey continued to be kept at the queen's charge in several private homes, a burden to her keepers, although she continually implored the queen to release her that she might care for her husband's children. She was living with her step-grandmother, Katherine Brandon Bertie, the Dowager Duchess of Suffolk, at Grimsthorpe in Lincolnshire, at the time her sister Katherine died. Six months after her husband's death, Mary Grey was released from private custody and, virtually penniless, went to live with her stepfather, Adrian Stokes, in the Charterhouse.

During the next several years, Elizabeth allowed Mary's return to court, which, diplomatically, Mary visited on several occasions. But she always preferred a quiet life. Mary Grey died April 20, 1578, seven years after her husband, at the age of thirty-three.

Queen Mary

Mary wed her Prince Philip in the July following Jane's execution and embarked upon three years of misery, hoping to gain her husband's love and return an unwilling English nation to Catholicism. But Philip cared little for Mary Tudor and returned to Spain as soon as possible, especially when he realized the queen would never bear an heir. Inevitably, the bishops who'd suffered imprisonment and degradation at the hands of the Protestants during Edward's reign gained control, for as her marriage and subsequently her health faded, so did Mary's interest in government. Soon the religious martyrs—willing to endure the agony of the stake and the gallows—appeared, all victims of the Church's lust for a revenge that has labeled Mary Tudor "Bloody Mary" for all time.

Sick, heartbroken and alone, hated by her people and ignored by her churchmen and ministers, Mary Tudor died in 1558 at the age of forty-two, only four years after her courageous fight for the throne. She is buried with Elizabeth— "Partners in the war and in the kingdom of the dead, we, Elizabeth and Mary, sisters in the hope of Resurrection, sleep here"—in Westminster Abbey, not far from their brother, Edward Tudor, and their grandparents Henry VII and Elizabeth of York.

Jane Dudley, the Duchess of Northumberland

The mother of thirteen children—several of whom died at birth—the duchess was devastated by the death of her husband and youngest son. Hoping to regain some part of the Suffolk property, she went to live with her daughter Lady Mary Sidney, until Queen Mary gave her permission to live in the little manor house at Chelsea where Jane Grey had stayed with Katherine Parr and Princess Elizabeth. The duchess did not live long enough to see one of her middle sons, Robert Dudley, become the great Earl of Leicester, a favorite of Queen Elizabeth. Jane Dudley died at Chelsea in 1555, eleven months after Jane Grey's execution, at the age of forty-six. She is buried in Chelsea Old Church.

Katherine Brandon Bertie, the Dowager Duchess of Suffolk

When Elizabeth became queen in 1558, Katherine and Richard Bertie returned to England from exile. They lived at Katherine's manor of Grimsthorpe in Lincolnshire, since many of their estates had been confiscated. Elizabeth returned some of them, but the duchess never again lived the life of grandeur she'd known as Charles Brandon's wife. In her new marriage, Katherine had two children, Susan and Peregrine, and much of her life after her return from exile was spent with them in the North. Peregrine later became a well-known Elizabethan commander, one highly thought of by the queen.

Much like her old and dearest friend, Katherine Parr, who'd devoted so much time to the furthering of the "new religion," Katherine Brandon Bertie continued in such work until her death. Those who lived on her Northern estate and in nearby churches heard services in English, and it was due to the duchess's influence that an English Bible was placed in every area church.

Katherine died September 19, 1580, at the age of sixty and is buried at Spilsby Church near Grimsthorpe. Her husband died a year later.

Sir Thomas Wyatt

The rebel leader was condemned to death and was beheaded on April 11, 1554.

Sir John Cheke

Edward's famous tutor was arrested in 1553, at the same time as John Dudley, and spent a year in the Tower. He was released in 1554, after which he obtained a license from Queen Mary to go abroad. He had traveled in Switzerland and Italy for two years when, suddenly, he was kidnapped on the road between Brussels and Antwerp. Blindfolded and a prisoner, he was returned to England and the Tower on the pretext that "he had overstayed his leave of absence." In the Tower he recanted his Protestant beliefs. He was then freed, but died a few months later in 1557 and was buried in St. Alban's Church in Wood Street in London which was destroyed in the London Blitz in the 1940s.

Abbot Feckenham

Noted for his kindness to political prisoners and for his skill in religious conversion—it was Feckenham who was responsible for John Cheke's recantation—the good doctor was made Abbot of Westminster in 1556. There he was responsible for much of the repair and restoration of the decaying old abbey church, which had been neglected for decades.

Two years after Elizabeth became queen, however, his fortunes changed. The "last Abbot of Westminster" was offered a bishopric if he would renounce his papal allegiance, but he refused, even taking his case to Parliament. In 1559, Feckenham and all other monks of the Benedictine Order were expelled from Westminster, some with pensions. Still protesting the "new doctrines," Feckenham was sent to the Tower, where he remained for three years before suffering a longer imprisonment in the infamous Marshalsea. In 1574, now nearing sixty years of age, he was released on bail and sent to live in the Fen district with the Bishop of Ely. He died in 1584, thirty years after Jane Grey's death, at Wisbech Castle, still a prisoner of the queen.

John Aylmer

When Mary Tudor became queen, Jane's beloved "Mr. Elmer" fled to the Continent, to the company of those controversial religious zealots at Zurich, Geneva and Strasbourg with whom she had corresponded. When Elizabeth ascended the throne, he returned to England and was made archdeacon of Lincoln, where he had the opportunity to dispute theologically with Abbot Feckenham. In 1566 he was consecrated Bishop of London, where, forgetting his own religious persecution, he "strained his authority" in persecuting the new breed of Protestants, the Puritans. He became so unpopular that Elizabeth, ever a disciplinarian herself, was obliged to remove him to another see. Before that could be accomplished, he died in 1594, forty years after Jane Grey's death. He was buried in Old St. Paul's.

Elizabeth

Elizabeth was highly suspected, along with Edward Courtenay, of being a prime mover in the Wyatt Rebellion. She was sent off, in virtual exile, to Woodstock Castle, where she remained until long after Mary's wedding, when finally Philip had her brought back to court. There she walked a tightrope politically and in religious matters until that day in November 1558 when William Cecil brought her the news at Hatfield Palace that her sister, Mary Tudor, had died. "It is the Lord's doing; it is marvelous in our eyes . . . !" was her emotional response.

That day commenced the forty-five-year reign of a woman who, remembering the mistakes of her sister, Mary and her brother, Edward, the fate of her mother, Anne Boleyn, and those other queens who'd been her stepmothers, never married. She was married to England, she always said, and she worked until the day she died, March 24, 1603, at the age of seventy—the longest-lived of all the Tudors—for what she considered to be her country's best interests.

Additional Notes of Interest on Personalities, Sites and Incidents

Suffolk House

Suffolk House was located on what today is Borough High Street in Southwark, directly across London Bridge. It was a large mansion, with four turrets, within walking distance of the Church of St. Saviour, earlier known as the Church of St. Mary Overie (over the water) and today as Southwark Cathedral. The church, where Jane Grey's parents were married, is a precious part of Tudor London which escaped the Great Fire of 1666 and the bombs of World War II. Both it and Suffolk House may be seen in Anthony van den Wyngaerde's "Long View of London," drawn in 1544, when Charles Brandon lived there with his duchess, the former Katherine Willoughby. Today the spot where Suffolk House stood is occupied by an apartment building known as Brandon House.

Margaret Beaufort

Margaret Beaufort's great-grandmother Catherine Swynford had been the governess of John of Gaunt's children by his duchess, Blanche of Lancaster. As his mistress, she had four illegitimate children by John, later becoming his third wife about 1396. After the marriage the pope issued a Bull legitimizing her children, and a year later the English Parliament confirmed their legal status. However, their original birth status, plus the clandestine marriage of Owen Tudor and his queen, Catherine of Valois, Margaret's husband's parents—a marriage that many believed had never taken place—always rendered Margaret Beaufort's claim to the throne for her son Henry questionable, at least by his enemies.

411

Catherine of Valois

Catherine of Valois, the widow of Henry V, bore Owen Tudor four children. The eldest, Edmund, married Margaret Beaufort and died a year later before his son, Henry, was born. The second son was Jasper Tudor. Jasper, born at Hatfield, was later the Earl of Pembroke, and he, along with Margaret Beaufort, fought for young Henry's rights. He never wed but had an illegitimate daughter who married a Londoner, William Gardiner. Stephen Gardiner, destined to play such a formidable part in the lives of Henry VIII and his daughter when she was Queen Mary I, was reputedly their son. Because of their height and other resemblances, many contemporaries thought Gardiner was an illegitimate brother of the king. Owen, the third Tudor child, became a monk and lived a quiet life at the abbey of Westminster in London. He was still alive—a very old man—when his nephew Henry VIII sat on the throne. The last child, a daughter named Tacina, married Lord Grey of Wilton, one of Henry Grey's ancestors.

Lord Thomas Stanley

Lord Thomas Stanley was a trusted minister of Edward IV, brother of Richard III. He bore no such loyalty to Richard, who upon his accession sent him to the Tower for a short time. Whether because of his new wife's ambitions—he married Margaret Beaufort two years before Bosworth—or because he suspected Richard had disposed of Edward's two sons, the little princes in the Tower, he turned traitor with little conscience. He died in 1504.

Jane Grey's birth

No historian has ever been able to find the exact date of Lady Jane Grey's birth. But several have stated that "legend has it" that she was born the same day as Prince Edward, Friday, October 12, 1537. Jane's father, then Marquis of Dorset, went to Edward's christening on the 15th, and—as Richard Davey states in his comprehensive biography, *The Nine Days' Queen*—"He would scarcely have done so if his own wife, a member of the royal family, had not been safely delivered." As Jane Grey's grandmother the Dowager Marchioness of Dorset was at Edward's christening and not at Jane's, it seems safe to assume they were taking place at roughly the same time.

The King's Divorce

Henry VIII's request to Pope Clement VII to have his marriage annulled was not unusual, and he most certainly expected there would be few complications. Kings, queens and emperors had been accommodated by the pope before, when for reasons varying from lack of an heir to disenchantment with one's mate, divorces or annulments had been granted. But in Henry's case, the pope could not allow him to divorce Katherine of Aragon. Her nephew was Charles V, the Holy Roman Emperor, who for political, religious and dynastic reasons did not want the divorce to occur. It was during the time of the divorce proceedings, in 1527, that the emperor's forces invaded Italy, forcing the pope to flee when the brutal sack of Rome occurred.

ADDITIONAL NOTES

Bradgate

Parts of Jane Grey's ancestral home—the chapel, kitchen and walls—still remain in Bradgate Park. In 1928, 828 acres were presented to the City and County of Leicester, "that for all time it might be preserved in its natural state for the quiet enjoyment of the people of Leicestershire." Tame deer, red and fallow, approach the visitor—for hunting, the passion of Jane Grey's parents, is now prohibited over land that has never been farmed since before the Norman Conquest. In the nearby village of Newton Linford there is a church with a stained-glass window, a memorial to Lady Jane Grey.

Whitehall

Today's Whitehall follows exactly the route of Tudor Whitehall. The route, a wide dirt road, commenced at Millbank with its slaughterhouse and the site where the ferry took horses across the Thames to Lambeth Palace (marked by today's Horseferry Road) and ended at Charing Cross. It was commonly referred to as "the streete." It passed through two gates, the King Street Gate and the Holbein Gate, and continued on past the Tiltyard—today's Horse Guards Parade—to end near the Eleanor Cross at Charing. Along the way one passed the orchards and gardens belonging to Westminster Abbey and the little Church of St. Margaret. The dilapidated ruins of the Palace of Westminster occupied the site of today's Houses of Parliament; nearby were the Jewel Tower and venerable old Westminster Hall which still remain. Old names such as "Sanctuary" and "Old Palace Yard" mark the sites where such buildings or areas were. The Cenotaph and the Banqueting Hall occupy the approximate site of the Holbein Gate. The buildings of Cardinal Wolsey's York House with its famed White Hall—which Henry VIII took as his residence and which was used by all successive Tudor monarchs—were later destroyed by fire, but their locations are not difficult to ascertain. Hidden in the parklike area of the Embankment between Villiers and Buckingham Street are the waterstairs to Wolsey's old York House. They were the entrance from the river to the complex of buildings that became the royal palace of Whitehall, which gave its name to "the streete." Its location—now almost a modern city block inland—shows how much of the wide Thames was sacrificed to build the Embankment.

Katherine Willoughby Brandon, the Duchess of Suffolk

Katherine Willoughby was the daughter of Maria de Salinas and Lord William Willoughby d'Eresby. She was born about 1518 or 1519, and named after Queen Katherine of Aragon. Her mother, Maria, was a companion of the Spanish queen, who as a fifteen-year-old princess had come to England in 1501 to marry Prince Arthur, the oldest son of Henry VII. Maria was faithful to the queen in her exile and Katherine died in her dearest friend's arms in January 1536. Young Katherine was educated with the Princess Mary and, when her father died and her mother remained away from the court with the Spanish queen, she became a ward of the king's sister Mary Tudor and her husband, Charles Brandon, the Duke of Suffolk. Katherine Willoughby was about fourteen when the duchess

413

died, and several months later she married her benefactor, the duke, thus becoming Jane Grey's stepgrandmother.

Chelsea Manor House

The Manor House at Chelsea was a smaller version of St. James's Palace, which still stands at the foot of St. James's Street in London. It was built by Henry VIII so his children would have a place away from court in the cleaner air of Chelsea. It was situated not far from the large estate of the executed Thomas More and near to Chelsea Church. In Tudor times, the river was not embanked and visitors arrived either by boat, to step directly onto the beach, or came down the winding lane later called "the King's Road." The entrance to the small Manor House was on today's Cheyne Walk, and the site is designated by a historical plaque. In many of the backyards of the adjoining streets—particularly the Carlyle House on Cheyne Row—remnants of some of the garden walls of Chelsea Manor House still remain.

John Aylmer

The exact date of the arrival of Jane Grey's first tutor is unknown. Elizabeth Jenkins, in her *Elizabeth, the Great*, says Jane was four years old. Other biographers, such as Richard Davey in his *The Nine Days' Queen*, conjecture that an early teacher might have been the Reverend Haddon, Rector of the church at Bradgate, who instructed Jane in Scripture. All authorities agree that Jane's education commenced—as did that of many privileged English children of the time—when she was very young.

Margaret Plantagenet Pole, the Countess of Salisbury

Margaret Pole was a daughter of Edward IV's brother Clarence, who died in a butt of malmsey wine in the Tower of London. She was one of Katherine of Aragon's closest friends. When Katherine's young daughter, Princess Mary, was made Princess of Wales and sent from court to live in Ludlow Castle near the Welsh Marches when she was only nine years old, the queen appointed Margaret Pole to be her governess. Throughout all of Mary's ordeal of her parents' divorce and her mistreatment by Anne Boleyn, Margaret Pole remained loyal to Mary and her mother, both of whom hoped that Mary might one day wed Margaret's son, Reginald Pole. Eventually, when Reginald became an exiled cardinal in Rome and the intrigues of her Plantagenet family proved troublesome to Henry and his ministers, the countess was removed from Mary's house and later imprisoned. She was found guilty of a dubious treason—more for the behavior of her sons and other family members than for any fault of her own—and sentenced to die. Upon ascending the scaffold on Tower Green and ordered to lay her head on the block, she refused, telling the executioner "if he would have it he must get it as he could. . . ." While others held her, her head was hacked from her shoulders.

Sir William Sherington

Sir William Sherington, or Sharington, was one of the most unscrupulous frauds of his era. A Norfolk man of good birth, he was created a Knight of the Bath at

ADDITIONAL NOTES

Edward's coronation and, at the time of his association with Thomas Seymour, was Treasurer of the Bristol Mint and owner of several prosperous estates including Lacock Abbey in Wiltshire, which still exists. After Seymour's arrest, Sherington turned traitor, giving all evidence needed to convict Seymour, and then threw himself on the Protector's and the Privy Council's mercy. He was pardoned, bought back his confiscated estates and—undoubtedly to remove him from court—was appointed Sheriff of Wiltshire. He died two years later, in 1551.

The Dudley Family

John and Jane Dudley had eight sons and five daughters in all. Of these, three boys and one girl died as infants or before they were ten. The most famous were Robert, who became the great Earl of Leicester and, allegedly, the only man Queen Elizabeth ever loved, and Mary, wife of the Sir Henry Sidney who was at Edward's bedside when he died. They were parents of the famous poet Sir Philip Sidney, who died in battle in the Netherlands during the latter part of Elizabeth's reign.

Edward's burial

The Zurich Letters contain a letter to Bullinger from an English correspondent, John Burcher, in which, a month after Edward's death, Burcher blames John Dudley for "committing a horrible and portentous crime." He enumerates Edward's symptoms, then states, "the perpetrators of the murder were ashamed of allowing the body of the deceased king to lie in state, and be seen by the public . . . wherefore they buried him privately in the paddock adjoining the palace and substituted in his place a youth not unlike him."

Since John Dudley had more to gain by Edward's continuing to live than by his death, it is doubtful he deliberately had the king poisoned, and his permitting the female quack to attend Edward during his last days might easily have been one wild last attempt to succeed where the physicians had failed. But if a boy so similar to the king in appearance was so "providentially" found at just the right time, it would certainly indicate that the bogus body must have been that of a boy murdered for the purpose.

Baynards Castle

Baynards Castle, built by Baynard, the Norman, was situated about three-quarters of a mile above London Bridge toward Westminster. Once the residence of Richard III, it had fallen into ruins by the end of the fifteenth century and was rebuilt by Henry VII. The property, with its courtyards, gardens and orchards, stretched to where the Bank of England is today. Much of it was destroyed in the Great Fire of 1666; some of it was still standing in 1809. The Mermaid Theatre and Restaurant now occupy the site, part of which has been excavated in the past decade.

William Paulet, the Marquis of Winchester

Paulet is a good example of how a Tudor noble survived during the changing times of his era. Henry VIII gave Paulet the home of Sir Thomas More after More's execution. He was Great Master of the Household for Edward VI, later for Mary I, and also for Elizabeth when she came to the throne. During Edward's reign he was also Lord High Treasurer. His religious beliefs were as the government dictated. Thus, under Edward he was Protestant, under Mary a Catholic and, later, a staunch supporter of Elizabeth's Church of England. When asked how he'd managed to survive during so many religious changes, he answered, "By being a willow and not an oak!" He died in 1572 at the age of ninety-seven and is buried in Chelsea Old Church.

An Inventory of Jane Grey's Belongings

The State Papers at Hatfield include a lengthy description of Jane Grey's belongings brought to her at the Tower of London. The complete inventory is so ridden with useless items she'd have little need of—and so lacks items she undoubtedly hoped to have included—it points to its having been very hurriedly compiled. A sampling of the list shows several mufflers of sable, velvet and other furs, hardly needed in July. Thirty-six buttons and many clocks of copper and silver, as well as "three pairs of garters having buckles and pendants of gold," were included, along with more useful ornately jeweled hats, caps and shirts. Gowns and cloaks seem to be lacking. There was "one dog collar wrought with gold bells," probably retained by Jane as a sentimental memory of an old pet and, more poignantly, "two little images of wood, one of Edward VI and the other of Henry VIII." Also "a picture of the Lady of Suffolk in a gold box" and "a picture of Queen Katherine Parr that is lately deceased." The picture of "the Lady of Suffolk" was most certainly not Jane's mother, but of Katherine Brandon, the Duchess of Suffolk until her two sons died. Kate Brandon was one of Katherine Parr's best friends and as devoted to Jane as the queen had been.

John Dudley's Plea

J. G. Gough, the editor of *A Chronicle of Queen Jane and Two Years of Queen Mary*, from which many details of Jane's incarceration and execution have been taken, states that when John Dudley, during his trial, referred to the Great Seal of England as giving him authority—and presumably protection—for his actions, he was actually referring to the seal given "by authority of Queen Jane, to his commission of Lieutenancy of the Army, which had also been signed by the Privy Councillors."

This is extremely doubtful, since the whole basis of Dudley's assumption of authority was that given under the Great Seal by Edward VI to Jane Grey. Dudley, faced with charges of treason, would hardly have appealed for clemency or understanding using the Great Seal of the usurper, but the valid one of the king.

Sir Richard Morgan

Morgan retired from the bench in 1555, twenty months after Jane's execution. Foxe, in his *Acts and Monuments*, says that "Judge Morgan, that gave the sentence against her, shortly after fell mad, and in his raving, cried continually to have the Lady Jane taken away from him, and so ended his life." He was buried in St. Magnus Church at the City side of London Bridge.

Bibliography

Besant, Walter. *London in the Time of the Tudors*. London: 1904.

Bindoff, S. T. *Tudor England*. New York: Penguin, 1950.

Burnet, Gilbert. *The History of the Reformation of the Church of England*. Oxford: 1865.

Burton, Elizabeth. *The Pageant of Early Tudor England*. New York: Charles Scribner & Sons, 1977.

Byrne, Muriel St. Claire. *Elizabeth Life in Town & Country*. London: Methuen & Co., 1961.

Calendar State Papers—Venetian, ed. R. Brown. London: Longman & Co., 1864.

Domestic Series (Edward VI & Mary I), ed. R. Lemon. London: Longman, Green, 1861.

Foreign (Edward VI & Mary I), ed. W. B. Turnbull. London: Longman, Green, 1861.

Spanish, Vols 5, 6 and 11. London: Longman, Green, 1867.

Chapman, Hester. *Lady Jane Grey*. London: Jonathan Cape, 1962.

———. *The Last Tudor King (Edward VI)*. London: Jonathan Cape, 1958.

Constant, G. L. *The Reformation in England*. New York: 1966.

Davey, Richard. *The Nine Days' Queen*. London: Methuen & Co., 1909.

———. *The Sisters of Lady Jane Grey*. New York: E. P. Dutton, 1912.

Dickens, A. G. *The English Reformation*. New York: Schochen, 1968.

Dutton, Ralph. *English Court Life*. London: B. T. Batsford, Ltd., 1963.

Ellis, Henry, ed. *Original Letters Illustrative of English History*. London: 1824.

Elton, G. R. *England Under the Tudors*. London: Methuen & Co., 1962.

———. *Reform and Reformation, England 1509–88*. London: Edward Arnold, 1977.

Emmison, F. G. *Tudor Food and Pastimes*. London: Ernest Benn, 1964.

Erickson, Carolly. *Bloody Mary*. Garden City, N.Y.: Doubleday & Co., 1978.

———. *Great Harry*. New York: Summit Books, 1980.

Fisher, H.A.L. *A Political History of England from the Accession of Henry VII to the Death of Henry VIII*. London: 1906.

Foxe, J. *Acts and Monuments*, ed. G. Townsend. London: 1843.

Froude, J. A. *A History of England from the Fall of Wolsey to the Death of Elizabeth*, Vols V, VI. London: Scribner, Armstrong & Co., 1872.

Gairdner, James. *A History of the English Church . . . From the Accession of Henry VIII to the Death of Mary*. London: 1902.

Grafton, Richard. *A Chronicle*, ed. Henry Ellis. London, 1809.

Green, Mary Evelyn Wood. *Lives of the Princesses of England*. 1849.

Hall, Edward. *A Chronicle*, ed. Henry Ellis. London, 1809.

Harbison, E. H. *Rival Ambassadors at the Court of Queen Mary*. Oxford: 1940.

Holgrefe, Pearl. *Women of Action in Tudor England*. Iowa State University Press: 1977.

Holinshed, Raphael. *Chronicles of England*. London: 1807.

Jenkins, Elizabeth. *Elizabeth, the Great*. New York: Coward McCann, 1959.

Innes, Arthur D. *England Under the Tudors*. London: Methuen & Co., Ltd., 1905.

Luke, Mary. *Catherine, the Queen*. New York: Coward McCann, 1967.

———. *A Crown for Elizabeth*. New York: Coward McCann, 1970.

———. *The Ivy Crown, A Biographical Novel of Queen Katherine Parr*. Garden City, N.Y.: Doubleday & Co., 1984.

Mackie, J. D. *The Earlier Tudors, 1485–1558*. Oxford: The Clarendon Press, 1952.

Madden, Frederick. *The Privy Purse Expenses of Princess Mary*. London: William Pickering, 1831.

Martienssen, Anthony. *Queen Katherine Parr*. London: Martin, Secker & Warburg, 1973.

Mattingly, Garrett. *Catherine of Aragon*. Boston: Little Brown & Co., 1941.

Morris, Christopher. *The Tudors*. New York: John Wiley & Sons, 1967.

Newman, Bernard. *The Shires*. London: Robert Hale, Ltd., 1968.

Nichols, J. G., ed. *The Diary of Henry Machyn* (1550–63). London: Camden Society, 1848.

BIBLIOGRAPHY

————. *Chronicle of the Greyfriars*. London: Camden Society, 1852.

————. *Literary Remains of Edward VI*, 2 vols. London: Roxburghe Club, 1857.

————. *The Chronicle of Queen Jane and Two Years of Queen Mary* (possibly by Rowland Lea, a resident in the Tower and an official of the Royal Mint). London: Camden Society, 1850.

————. *Narratives of the Days of the Reformation*. London: Camden Society, 1859.

Nicolas, N. H. *The Literary Remains of Lady Jane Grey with a Memoir*. London: 1825.

Paul, John E. *Catherine of Aragon and Her Friends*. New York: Fordham University Press, 1966.

Plowden, Alison. *Tudor Women, Queens and Commoners*. New York: Atheneum, 1979.

Pollard, A. F. *England Under Protector Somerset*. London: 1900.

————. *The Political History of England*, Vols V–VI. London: 1913.

Prescott, H.F.M. *Mary Tudor*. New York: The Macmillan Co., 1953.

Read, Conyers, ed. *Bibliography of British History—Tudor Period*. Oxford University Press: 1933, revised 1959.

————. *The Tudors*. New York: W. W. Norton & Co., 1936.

Read, Evelyn. *My Lady of Suffolk: A Portrait of Lady Catherine Willoughby*. New York: Random House, 1963.

Robinson, H., ed. *Zurich Letters*. London: Parker Society, 1846.

Salzmann, L. F. *England in Tudor Times*. London: Russell & Russell, 1969.

Seymour, William. *Ordeal by Ambition*. New York: St. Martin's, 1972.

Sidney, Philip. *Jane, the Quene*. London: Swan Sonnenschein & Co., Ltd., 1900.

Smith, Lacey Baldwin. *Henry VIII, the Mask of Royalty*. Boston: Houghton Mifflin Co., 1971.

————. *The Last Will & Testament of Henry VIII*. Hartford, Conn.: Trinity College, 1962.

Stone, J. M. *History of Mary I, Queen of England*. London: Sands & Co., Ltd., 1901.

Strickland, Agnes. *Lives of the Tudor and Stuart Princesses*. London: 1868.

————. *Lives of the Bachelor Kings of England*. London: 1902.

————. *Lives of the Queens of England*, Vols V, VI. London: 1902.

Strype, John. *Ecclesiastical Memorials*. Oxford: 1822.

————. *Life of Sir John Cheke*. Oxford: 1821.

Taylor, I. A. *Lady Jane Grey and Her Times*. London: D. Appleton & Co., 1908.

Thompson, Craig R. *The English Church in the Sixteenth Century*. Folger Shakespeare Library, University of Virginia Press, 1958.

Tytler, P. F. *England Under the Reigns of Edward VI, and Mary.* 1839.

White, Beatrice. *Mary Tudor.* New York: Macmillan & Co., 1944.

Williams, Penry. *Life in Tudor England.* New York: G. P. Putnam & Sons, 1964.

Wriothesely, Charles, ed. *A Chronicle of England During the Reign of the Tudors*, ed. W. D. Hamilton. London: Camden Society, 1875.

⚜ INDEX ⚜